AFRICAN HISTORICAL DICTIONARIES
Edited by Jon Woronoff

Historical Dictionary of
SOUTH AFRICA

by Christopher Saunders

African Historical Dictionaries No. 37

The Scarecrow Press, Inc.
Metuchen, N.J., and London
1983

Library of Congress Cataloging in Publication Data

Saunders, Christopher C.
    Historical dictionary of South Africa.

    (African historical dictionaries ; no. 37)
    Bibliography: p.
    Includes index.
    1. South Africa--History--Dictionaries. I. Title.
II. Series.
DT766.S23 1983   968'.003'21   83-8614
ISBN 0-8108-1629-6

PREFACE

Dr. Christopher Saunders has produced an invaluable tool for anyone who is concerned with South African history and the present state of that country. The core of the book--the Dictionary--provides succinct, accurate information on all aspects of South Africa's complex society. It is very strong on social, economic and political history; it explains with admirable clarity the nuances of the country's bizarre legal history; and it shows how developments in South African historiography have been connected with developments in the history of the country and of the world beyond it.

The admirable Chronology and Bibliography are fine supplements to the Dictionary. There are many reference books on South Africa, but none covers the subject as this book by Dr. Saunders.

Leonard Thompson
Charles J. Stillé Professor
of History
Yale University

Dedicated to the hope that within the near future APARTHEID will be merely a subject for historians to study.

TABLE OF CONTENTS

EDITOR'S FOREWORD

Although but one of fifty countries on the African continent, South Africa has aroused the most interest in the international public. Articles and editorials are written regularly about events both within the country and regarding its relations with the rest of the world. In some cases this flow of information sheds light; more often than not it just kindles heat.

It is not surprising that a country with serious racial problems, one in which it is the minority which still has the greater say while the other races play a secondary role, will not be popular in African or world bodies. The relations with South West Africa (Namibia) and some independent countries, to say nothing of the existence of Bantustans, run against present-day trends. But even this springs from a long and painful history and the interactions of its peoples.

Therefore, whatever one's views, it certainly does not hurt to have a deeper understanding of just what South Africa is, how it became that way, who the people are who shaped its destiny thus far, what the hopes and aspirations of all segments of the population may be. It is also useful, regarding a subject where things are often reduced to their simplest expression, to see just how complex a country this is.

Speaking of minorities and majorities is fine. But it is still better to realize that these races are further divided into various groups, each with its own tendencies. There are, among the whites, people of very different ancestry and persuasions, including some who reject the present status. Among the others are not only blacks but people of different tribal origins, contrasting lifestyles, varying political allegiances, and also differing approaches to the same problems. And this does not even include the broader range of alternatives when the "Coloured" and Asian population are considered.

Thus, the situation in South Africa is anything but simple and straightforward and one purpose of this Historical Dictionary is to show how terribly variegated it is. This is done through entries on many of the participants in the great debates, and the repeated wars, whose names are well known in South Africa if sometimes less so abroad. It also covers crucial events and interesting aspects of everyday life. Even for South Africans, it is wise to be reminded occasionally of the broader dimensions so as not to get lost in specific details, no matter how important.

This is obviously not an easy task. It is not simple to take a neutral view of many persons and events. Even subjects like economics, education, and religion are hard to approach objectively. We are therefore extremely fortunate that the author of this book, Christopher Saunders, has done such a fine job of drafting these entries so clearly and precisely. Rather than ignore the controversy surrounding certain issues, he introduces it as well while leaving the reader to decide.

Dr. Saunders is Senior Lecturer in History at the University of Cape Town. His doctorate from Oxford University dealt with the history of the Transkei. Since then, he has written widely on various aspects of Cape and South African history and has recently been preparing a major work on the history of Cape Town. With such background, he has proved to be a very knowledgeable and reliable author for this guide to South Africa.

Jon Woronoff
Series Editor

AUTHOR'S NOTE

Compiling a dictionary of this kind on a country as large and complex as South Africa is a daunting undertaking. Decisions on what to include and what to omit were taken partly on the basis of my own interests, knowledge, and judgment of significance, but also with a view to what readers of the book would be likely to find most useful. More attention is given to recent South African history than to the more distant past. The availability of the volumes of the <u>Dictionary of South African Biography</u> led me to curtail biographical entries drastically. I tried to avoid duplicating material in the other volumes in this series on southern African countries, some of whose history is part of the history of South Africa itself. Reference should be made to them where appropriate.

I would like to thank Mr. Woronoff, General Editor of this series, for asking me to write this volume. I am indebted to the relief lectureship scheme of the University of Cape Town, which gave me two months off teaching at the beginning of 1982, and allowed me to spend much of it on this project. I have inevitably drawn heavily on the work of others, and acknowledge my deep debt to them. Thanks to those friends in Cape Town who helped, and especially to Pam.

NOTES ON USE OF THE DICTIONARY

1. Both in the chronology and in the dictionary itself words in capitals indicate relevant entries, but such reference to other entries is made only the first time a word or term appears in any particular entry. To avoid too many capitals, entry headings that appear very frequently have not always been capitalized the first time they appear in other entries. Such frequently-used headings include the names of places such as Cape Town, Johannesburg, Durban, and Port Elizabeth; regions such as the Cape, Natal, Orange Free State, Transvaal, and Zululand; and peoples, whether Africans, Afrikaners, "Coloureds," English-speaking whites or Indians.

2. What to call people has long been a particularly vexed matter in South Africa, with its obsession with racial categorization. In this book "white" is generally used in preference to "European," and "black" does not mean Africans only, but Africans, "Coloureds" and Indians. For further clarification see the entries under these group names.

3. Headings are always given in full, never in abbreviated form. Reference should be made to the list of abbreviations on p. xi where appropriate.

ABBREVIATIONS AND ACRONYMS

AAC	All-African Convention
AMEC	African Methodist Episcopal Church
ANC	African National Congress
APO	African People's Organisation
ASP	Afrikaanse Studentebond
BPC	Black People's Convention
cf.	compare
CP	Communist Party of South Africa
CI	Christian Institute
DEIC	Dutch East India Company
DRC	Dutch Reformed Church
FOSATU	Federation of South African Trade Unions
HNP	Herstigte Nasionale Party
ICU	Industrial and Commercial Workers Union
LMS	London Missionary Society
NGK	Nederduitse Gereformeerde Kerk (Dutch Reformed Church)
NP	National Party
NRC	Natives Representative Council
NUSAS	National Union of South African Students
OB	Ossewabrandwag
PAC	Pan-Africanist Congress
PFP	Progressive Federal Party
R	Rand (in 1982 worth approximately U.S. $1)
SACTU	South African Congress of Trade Unions

SADF	South African Defence Force
SANNC	South African Native National Congress
SAP	South African Party
SASO	South African Students Organisation
SWA	South West Africa (Namibia)
SWAPO	South West African People's Organisation
TUCSA	Trade Union Congress of South Africa
UN	United Nations
UNTAG	United Nations Transitional Assistance Group
UP	United Party

CHRONOLOGY

All capitals indicate a relevant dictionary entry

Date, A. D.	Event
c. 3rd century to 10th century	Early IRON AGE
c. 500	LYDENBURG HEADS
c. 600	Earliest IRON AGE site in the TRANSKEI (Mpame)
c. 1000	Beginnings of the Later IRON AGE
c. 1300	Date by which oral tradition suggests that NGUNI people were living in the foothills of the DRAKENSBERG
1488	PORTUGUESE ships under Bartolomeu Dias round Cape; Europe informed of South Africa's existence
1497	PORTUGUESE squadron under Vasco da Gama sails along South African coast on its way to India; members of the expedition provide the first detailed information on the indigenous inhabitants
1590s	Dutch and English ships begin to put in regularly in Table Bay and trade with the KHOIKHOI
1652 (6 April)	Van Riebeeck arrives in Table Bay to found a settlement; beginnings of KHOIKHOI dispossession
1657	First FREEBURGHERS granted farms inland of Table Bay
1658	Birth of CAPE SLAVERY
1659	First European-KHOIKHOI war
1673-77	Second European-KHOIKHOI war

xiii

1685	District of Stellenbosch established
1688	Arrival of French Huguenot settlers
1702	Whites travelling east from the Cape first meet BANTU-SPEAKING Africans near Somerset East
1713	Smallpox epidemic
1745	District of Swellendam established
1779	Cape-XHOSA conflict begins in the ZUURVELD
1795	First BRITISH occupation of the Cape
1799-1802	Cape-XHOSA war; Great KHOIKHOI rebellion
1803	Cape handed over to the Batavian Republic
1806 (Jan.)	Second BRITISH occupation of the Cape
c. 1806	Madlathule famine in Natal/Zululand area
1807	BRITISH abolition of the slave-trade
1811-12	Africans expelled from the ZUURVELD
1816	Registration of Cape slaves enforced
1818	Battle of Amalinde
c. 1818	Dingiswayo defeated by Zwide; see MFECANE
1819	Battle of Grahamstown; see FRONTIER WARS
c. 1819	ZULU under Shaka defeat Zwide at Gqokoli Hill
1820	Arrival of 5000 BRITISH settlers
c. 1821-c. 1831	Wars of the MFECANE
1823	Slave conditions at the Cape ameliorated
1823 (June)	Battle of Dithakong
1825	Slave revolt in Worcester district
1827	Cape Charter of Justice
1828	ORDINANCE 50; death of Shaka
1829	Establishment of the KAT RIVER SETTLEMENT

1834 (Dec.)	First Legislative Council at the Cape End of CAPE SLAVERY
1834-35	Cape-XHOSA WAR
1836	Beginning of the GREAT TREK
1837	VOORTREKKERS enter Natal
1838	VOORTREKKERS begin Transvaal settlement; battle of BLOOD RIVER; Republic of Natalia founded
1843	BRITISH annexation of Natal
1846-47	War of the Axe on Cape eastern frontier
1847	BRITISH KAFFRARIA annexed; ORANGE RIVER SOVEREIGNTY proclaimed
1850-53	Mlanjeni Cape-XHOSA war; KAT RIVER SETTLEMENT rebellion
1852	Sand River Convention: independence of the Transvaal recognized by Britain
1854	Bloemfontein Convention: independence of the Orange Free State recognized by Britain; first Cape parliament
1856	ZULU civil war
1856-57	XHOSA CATTLE-KILLING
1858	Free State-Basotho war
1860	First INDIAN indentured labor to Natal
1865-66	Free State-Basotho war
1867	Discovery of DIAMONDS
1868	BRITISH annexation of BASUTOLAND
1869	Treaty of Aliwal North arranges BASUTOLAND's boundaries; DIAMOND digging begins at Kimberley
1871	BRITISH annexation of the DIAMOND fields
1872	PASS law introduced on the DIAMOND fields; Cape Colony granted responsible government

1875   Lord CARNARVON proposes CONFEDERATION

1877   SHEPSTONE proclaims BRITISH annexation of
                TRANSVAAL

1877-78   Cape-XHOSA war

1879   BRITISH-ZULU war; BRITISH-PEDI war

1880   TRANSVAAL WAR OF INDEPENDENCE; Cape-
                Basotho war; TRANSKEI rebellion; Griqualand
                West annexed to Cape Colony; formation of the
                AFRIKANER BOND

1881   BRITISH defeat at Majuba; Pretoria Convention
                grants Transvaal limited self-rule

1882   IMBUMBA YAMA NYAMA formed

1883   KRUGER elected State President of the Trans-
                vaal

1884   First Publication of Imvo Zabantsundu, JABA-
                VU'S newspaper

1885   Annexation of BECHUANALAND
     (Dec.)   Discovery of main GOLD reef on the WIT-
                WATERSRAND

1886   Beginnings of exploitation of main GOLD reef;
                founding of JOHANNESBURG

1887   Telegraph completed from CAPE TOWN to
                JOHANNESBURG; BRITISH annexation of ZULU
                land; Cape Parliamentary Voters Registration
                Act

1888   BRAND succeeded by Reitz as President of the
                ORANGE FREE STATE

1889   Establishment of DE BEERS monopoly at Kim-
                berley

1890   RHODES becomes Prime Minister of the Cape

1892   RAILROAD reaches JOHANNESBURG from
                CAPE TOWN; Cape Franchise and Ballot Act;
                ETHIOPIAN Church founded

1893   Natal gets responsible government; Gandhi ar-
                rives in Natal (see INDIANS)

1894   Cape GLEN GREY ACT; Cape annexation of
                Pondoland; Natal INDIAN Congress founded

1895 (29 Dec.)   JAMESON RAID

1896   Steyn elected President of the Free State;
                  ETHIOPIAN Church joins African Methodist
                  Episcopal Church; deep-level GOLD mining
                  begins on the WITWATERSRAND

1897   Rinderpest epidemic among cattle; MILNER
                  appointed HIGH COMMISSIONER for South Africa

1899 (Oct.)   Outbreak of the SOUTH AFRICAN WAR

1900   MAFEKING relieved; BRITISH occupation of
                  Bloemfontein, Johannesburg, and Pretoria;
                  KRUGER leaves for exile; MILNER becomes
                  Administrator of the ORANGE RIVER COLONY
                  and the Transvaal

1902 (31 May)   TREATY OF VEREENIGING ends SOUTH AF-
                  RICAN WAR: African Political Organisation
                  founded

1904 (May)   First CHINESE laborers arrive to work on
                  GOLD mines; Transvaal Ordinance reserves
                  44 jobs for whites

1905   Report of the LAGDEN (South African Native
                  Affairs) COMMISSION
         (March) STRIKE of CHINESE LABOR at the North
                  Randfontein mine

1906   BAMBATHA REBELLION in Natal; passive re-
                  sistance in Transvaal by INDIANS

1907   Repatriation of CHINESE LABORERS from the
                  Transvaal begins; Transvaal and ORANGE
                  RIVER COLONY granted responsible govern-
                  ment; white miners' STRIKE on WITWATERS-
                  RAND

1908 (Oct.)   NATIONAL CONVENTION meets to consider
                  UNIFICATION

1909   South Africa Act passed by British Parliament;
                  INDIAN passive resistance in Transvaal; LA-
                  BOUR PARTY founded

1910 (31 May)   UNION; Louis BOTHA becomes first Union
                  Prime Minister

1911   Mines and Works Act (COLOR BAR regulations
                  made under it); Native Labour Regulation Act
                  makes it a crime for Africans to leave their
                  jobs

1912 (Jan.)   South African Native National Congress formed
                   in Bloemfontein; DUBE elected President
     (April)   South African Races Congress formed under
                   JABAVU
     (Dec.)   HERTZOG leaves BOTHA's cabinet

1913 (June)   NATIVES LAND ACT
     (July)   White miners' STRIKE on the WITWATERSRAND
     (Nov.)   INDIAN passive resistance against Immigration
                   Act; African women demonstrate against PASS-
                   ES in Free State

1913-14   White labor unrest

1914 (Jan.)   NATIONAL PARTY formed under HERTZOG;
                   SANNC delegation goes to England to protest
                   NATIVES LAND ACT
     (Aug.)   WORLD WAR I begins
     (Sept.)   AFRIKANER REBELLION

1915   Capture of German South West Africa
                   (NAMIBIA)

1916   Report of the Native Lands (Beaumont) Com-
                   mission

1917   Industrial Workers of Africa founded; Birth of
                   ANGLO-AMERICAN CORPORATION

1918 (June)   STRIKE by African sanitation workers in
                   JOHANNESBURG
     (Oct.)   Spanish INFLUENZA EPIDEMIC

1919 (Jan.)   INDUSTRIAL AND COMMERCIAL WORKERS
                   UNION formed; SANNC delegation attends Ver-
                   sailles Peace Conference
     (Aug.)   Death of BOTHA; SMUTS becomes Prime Min-
                   ister
     (Aug.)   Union Parliament accepts mandate for South
                   West Africa

1920 (Feb.)   African mineworkers' STRIKE
     (March)   SMUTS forms new government
     (Oct.)   African demonstrators shot in Port Elizabeth

1921 (Feb.)   General election: SMUTS increases his parlia-
                   mentary majority
     (May)   Israelites shot at BULHOEK
     (July)   COMMUNIST PARTY OF SOUTH AFRICA
                   formed

1922 (Jan.)   White miners' STRIKE
     (March)   RAND REVOLT

1923	Natives Urban Areas Act
(April)	NATIONAL PARTY and LABOUR PARTY form electoral PACT
(May)	SANNC renamed AFRICAN NATIONAL CON-GRESS
1924	INDUSTRIAL CONCILIATION ACT
(June)	Victory of NATIONAL PARTY-LABOUR PARTY PACT; HERTZOG Prime Minister
1925	Wage Act; South Africa reverts to the GOLD standard; AFRIKAANS becomes official language
(Nov.)	HERTZOG's Smithfield speech
1926	Mines and Works Amendment (COLOR BAR) Act; Balfour Declaration defines relations with Britain; HERTZOG's "Native BILLS" published; Communists expelled from the ICU
1927	Nationality and FLAG Act; Immorality Act (see MISCEGENATION); Native Administration Act
1928	Iron and Steel industry established by Act of Parliament
1929 (June)	General election: NATIONAL PARTY wins 81 seats
1930	Native (Urban Areas) Amendment Act; FRAN-CHISE given to white women; SEME elected President of ANC
1931	FRANCHISE Laws Amendment Act removes property and literacy qualifications for white voters; Statute of Westminster passed by Imperial Parliament
(Dec.)	PASS-burning campaign culminates in violence in DURBAN
1932	Report of the Carnegie Commission on "POOR WHITES"; Report of the Native Economic Commission
(Dec.)	South Africa goes off the GOLD standard
1933 (March)	HERTZOG invites SMUTS to form a coalition
(May)	Coalition parties win overwhelming victory in general election. SMUTS Deputy Prime Minister
1934 (July)	Purified NATIONAL PARTY formed under MALAN
(Dec.)	FUSION: formation of the UNITED PARTY
1935 (Dec.)	National Liberation League established;

HERTZOG BILLS published; first meeting of
the ALL AFRICAN CONVENTION in Bloemfontein

1936 (April)   Representation of Natives Bill (removing Afri-
                      can FRANCHISE) passed by 169 votes to 11
     (May)   Natives Trust and Land Act

1937   Natives (Urban Areas) Amendment Act; Native
                      LAWS Amendment Act enforces INFLUX CON-
                      TROL; NATIVES REPRESENTATIVE COUNCIL
                      begins work

1938 (May)   General election: UP wins 111 seats, NP 27
     (Dec.)   Centenary of GREAT TREK celebrated

1939   Asiatics (Transvaal Land and Trading Act)
     (4 Sept.)   House of Assembly votes 80-67 against neutral-
                      ity in WORLD WAR II
     (5 Sept.)   HERTZOG resigns after the Governor-General
                      refuses his request to call a general election
     (6 Sept.)   SMUTS becomes Prime Minister; war declared

1940 (Jan.)   HERTZOG's followers merge with MALAN's in
                      Reunited NATIONAL PARTY
     (Dec.)   Xuma elected ANC President

1941 (Jan.)   AFRIKANER PARTY formed
     (April)   South African troops enter Addis Ababa,
                      Ethiopia

1942   Draft constitution for South African REPUBLIC
                      published; plans for OSSEWABRANDWAG coup
                      uncovered; many interned
     (June)   South African division captured at Tobruk,
                      North Africa
     (Dec.)   17 killed in Pretoria riot

1943 (Feb.)   Formation of Anti-CAD (see "COLOURED"
                      POLITICS)
     (July)   General Election: UP 71, NP 43
     (Dec.)   Formation of ANC Youth League authorized;
                      formation of NON-EUROPEAN UNITY MOVE-
                      MENT

1944 (March)   Mpanza and followers SQUAT on vacant ground
                      in Orlando location

1945   Natives (Urban Areas) Consolidation Act; End
                      of WORLD WAR II

1946   Asiatic Land Tenure and INDIAN Representation
                      Act

(June)	INDIAN passive resistance campaign begins
(Aug.)	African Mineworkers' STRIKE
(Nov.)	Adjournment of the NATIVES REPRESENTA-TIVE COUNCIL

1946-47   SQUATTER movement in Johannesburg

1948   Report of the Native Laws (FAGAN) COMMIS-SION

(May)   General Election: NP wins 70 seats, AFRI-KANER PARTY 9, giving them a majority of 5 over the UP and LABOUR

(Aug.)   Suburban railroad APARTHEID in the Cape Peninsula

(Dec.)   Death of Jan Hofmeyr

1949   Prohibition of Mixed Marriages Act

(Jan.)   ZULU-INDIAN riots in Durban

(Dec.)   Program of Action adopted by the ANC

1950   GROUP AREAS ACT; POPULATION Registra-tion Act; Immorality Amendment Act; Suppres-sion of Communism Act; COMMUNIST PARTY dissolves itself

(May)   STAY-AWAY in Transvaal; 18 killed by police

(26 June)   National day of protest and mourning

1951   Bantu Authorities Act; Separate Representation of Voters Act to remove "COLOUREDS" from common voters' roll; TORCH COMMANDO ac-tive in protest

1952 (March) Separate Representation of Voters Act ruled invalid

(6 Apr.)   Van Riebeeck tercentenary festival and protests

(26 June)   DEFIANCE CAMPAIGN begins

(Aug.-Sept.)   Arrests of DEFIANCE CAMPAIGN leaders

(Oct.-Nov.)   Riots in various cities

(Dec.)   DUNCAN and others arrested for DEFIANCE

1953   Criminal Law Amendment Act; Public Safety Act; BANTU EDUCATION ACT; Native Labour Act; STRIKES by African workers illegal

(April)   General election: NATIONAL PARTY wins 94 of 156 seats

(May)   LIBERAL PARTY formed

(Oct.)   Congress of Democrats formed

1954 (April) FEDERATION OF SOUTH AFRICAN WOMEN established

(Oct.)   Tomlinson Commission reports

(Nov.-Dec.)   MALAN retires; STRIJDOM becomes Prime Minister

1955 (March)   Formation of SOUTH AFRICAN CONGRESS OF
                TRADE UNIONS
     (June)   Congress of the People at Kliptown; the FREE-
                DOM CHARTER adopted
     (Nov.)   Enlarged Senate elected

1956 (Feb.)   Joint sitting of both Houses of parliament
                validates removal of "COLOURED" voters
                from the common roll
     (Mar.-Apr.) ANC accepts FREEDOM CHARTER
     (9 Aug.)   Mass anti-PASS demonstration by women at
                Union Buildings, Pretoria
     (Dec.)   Countrywide arrests for TREASON

1957   Native Laws Amendment Act grants government
                power to forbid African-white contact; Alexandra
                Bus Boycott
     (26 June) STAY-AWAY protest
                Resistance in Sekhukhuniland and Zeerust in
                Transvaal

1958 (April)   General election: NP wins 103 of 163 seats in
                Assembly
     (Aug.)   STRIJDOM dies; VERWOERD succeeds as Prime
                Minister
     (Nov.)   "Africanists" break away from ANC

1959   Promotion of BANTU Self-Government Act; Ex-
                tension of UNIVERSITY EDUCATION Act intro-
                duces APARTHEID to all higher education
     (April)   Formation of the PAN-AFRICANIST CONGRESS
     (Nov.)   Eleven UP members resign, form PROGRES-
                SIVE PARTY
     (Dec.)   ANC decides on anti-PASS campaign

1960   Representation for Africans in parliament
                abolished; Riots at Cato Manor, Durban
     (Feb.)   "Winds of Change" speech by British Prime
                Minister Macmillan to South African Parliament
     (21 Mar.) Police open fire on crowd at SHARPEVILLE:
                69 killed
     (26 Mar.) Police announce PASS LAWS suspended
     (28 Mar.) ANC week-long general strike of mourning for
                dead begins
     (30 Mar.) State of Emergency proclaimed. Peaceful
                march of 30,000 Africans into central Cape
                Town
     (8 April) ANC and PAC banned
     (April)   20,000 people detained; random assaults of
                blacks in streets of Cape Town; STRIKE broken;
                PASS LAWS again enforced
     (April)   Attempted assassination of VERWOERD

(June)	Pondoland revolt; eleven Africans killed by police at Ngquza Hill (see RURAL RESISTANCE)
(31 Aug.)	End of State of Emergency
(5 Oct.)	REPUBLIC referendum: 52.3 percent of white voters vote in favor; Government indemnified for acts during the unrest
1961 (March)	VERWOERD withdraws South Africa's application to remain in the COMMONWEALTH
(March)	TREASON TRIAL ends with acquittal
(31 May)	Birth of the REPUBLIC; South Africa leaves the COMMONWEALTH; state of emergency; 10,000 detained; STAY-AWAY meets poor response
(Aug.)	VERWOERD appoints VORSTER Minister of Justice and Police; VORSTER appoints General van den Bergh head of the Special Branch
(Oct.)	SABOTAGE by National Liberation Committee (later African Resistance Movement); General Election: NP 105, UP 49, PROGRESSIVES 1; LUTHULI wins Nobel Peace Prize
(16 Dec.)	SABOTAGE campaign by UMKHONTO WE SIZWE begins
1962	SABOTAGE and repression
(June)	Sabotage Act makes SABOTAGE a capital offence; house-arrest introduced and BANNING powers extended
(Nov.)	Paarl riot: 2 whites killed; UNITED NATIONS General Assembly votes for economic and diplomatic SANCTIONS against South Africa
1963 (May)	Ninety-day DETENTION WITHOUT TRIAL introduced; Mass arrests and detentions
(July)	Arrest of UMKHONTO leaders at Rivonia, Johannesburg; four of them escape
(Nov.)	First election for TRANSKEI Legislative Assembly
(Dec.)	TRANSKEI self-government
1964	Numerous SABOTAGE trials Eight Rivonia accused sentenced to life imprisonment; first TRANSKEI Legislative Assembly inaugurated with local government powers; African Resistance Movement members jailed
1965	Members of underground COMMUNIST PARTY jailed; DETENTION WITHOUT TRIAL for 180 day periods introduced; Bram FISCHER goes underground, is recaptured after 10 months; harsh repression used in attempt to liquidate

	underground ANC in eastern Cape
(11 Nov.)	Rhodesian U. D. I.
1966 (May)	General election: NP wins 126 seats, UP 39, PROGRESSIVES 1
(Sept.)	VERWOERD assassinated; VORSTER becomes Prime Minister
(Oct.)	LESOTHO becomes independent
1967	Terrorism Act provides (section 6) for indefinite DETENTION WITHOUT TRIAL; Physical Planning Act tightens INFLUX CONTROL; diplomatic relations established with Malawi
1968	Prohibition of Political Interference Act; PROGRESSIVE PARTY drops black members and becomes an all-white party; LIBERAL PARTY dissolves itself; "COLOUREDS" ' Representatives in parliament abolished
(August)	Dr. Hertzog dropped from the cabinet
1969	Bureau of State SECURITY established; SOUTH AFRICAN STUDENTS ORGANISATION formed
(Sept.)	VERKRAMPTES expelled from NP; HERSTIGTE NASIONALE PARTY formed
1970	Bantu Homelands Citizenship Act
(April)	General election: NP loses 9 seats to UP; no HNP candidates returned
1971 (May)	Ten years of the REPUBLIC celebrated; protests under the slogan "What is there to celebrate?"
1972	BLACK People's Convention formed; Africans in "white areas" brought under Bantu Affairs Administration Boards
1973 (Jan.)	Durban STRIKES begin; GOLD price begins to rise
1974 (April)	Coup in Lisbon, Portugal; General election: NP maintains its position
1975 (July)	South African troops cross into ANGOLA
(Aug. /Sept.)	More South African troops enter ANGOLA
(Oct.)	South African troops drive up ANGOLAN coast, taking port towns
(Nov.)	South African troops take Benguela; independence of ANGOLA; Cuban troops arrive; BREYTEN-BACH sentenced to 9 years for "terrorism."
(Dec.)	South African troops take losses from Cubans

1976 (Jan.)   South Africa withdraws troops to near
                         NAMIBIAN border
       (March)   South Africa withdraws troops from ANGOLA
       (16 June)   SOWETO REVOLT begins
       (Aug.)   Uprising in suburbs of CAPE TOWN
       (Oct.)   TRANSKEI "independence"
       (Dec.)   Violence in CAPE TOWN's African townships

1976-77   Continuous unrest; over 700 deaths, many de-
                         tentions, stay-aways; boycotts of schools

1977   Proposals for new CONSTITUTION announced
       (June)   Guerilla shoot-out in Johannesburg; two whites
                         killed
       (12 Sept.)   BIKO killed in detention
       (Oct.)   CHRISTIAN INSTITUTE, SASO, BPC, WORLD
                         newspaper and other organizations BANNED;
                         mandatory arms embargo imposed by UN Secur-
                         ity Council
       (Nov.)   General Election: NP 145 seats; PROGRESSIVE
                         PARTY 16
       (Dec.)   "Independence" of BOPHUTHATSWANA

1978 (April)   South Africa accepts western plan for NAMIBIA
       (May)   MULDERGATE revelations begin
       (Sept.)   CROSSROADS SQUATTERS attacked by police
       (Sept./Oct.)   VORSTER retires as Prime Minister and is
                         succeeded by Pieter BOTHA; Vorster becomes
                         State President
       (Oct./Nov.)   Further MULDERGATE revelations; Mulder re-
                         signs; TREURNICHT elected Leader of the NP
                         in the Transvaal

1979 (Jan.)   Skirmish at Zeerust in western Transvaal be-
                         tween S.A. police and guerillas
       (April)   Reprieve for CROSSROADS community; South
                         Africa raises objections to ceasefire proposals
                         for NAMIBIA
       (June)   MULDERGATE revelations implicate VORSTER,
                         who resigns as State President
       (Sept.)   Van Zyl Slabbert (PROGRESSIVE PARTY) be-
                         comes Leader of the Opposition; VENDA be-
                         comes "independent"; Government announcement
                         that African TRADE UNIONS are to be recog-
                         nised
       (Nov.)   ANC and BUTHELEZI meet in London

1980 (Jan.)   GOLD price reaches peak of $850 an ounce
       (April)   ZIMBABWE independence
       (Feb.-Dec.)   55,000 black high school pupils boycott classes,
                         especially in the Cape Peninsula; 45 shot by
                         police in CAPE TOWN area in June violence
       (June)   SABOTAGE attack on Sasol oil from coal plant

1981 (Jan.)   High school pupils suspend boycott and return to classes; abortive Geneva conference on NAMIBIA; South African forces raid ANC headquarters in Matola, MOZAMBIQUE; 122 dead in flood at Laingsburg, Cape

(April)   NP suffers loss of support to both right and left in general election, while retaining its large majority; revival of Western initiative on NAMIBIA, under leadership of Chester Crocker, American Assistant Secretary of State for African Affairs

(May)   Campaign against REPUBLIC day celebrations
(Aug.)   Operation Protea raid against SWAPO in ANGOLA
(Oct.)   Government agrees in principle to end COLOR BAR in mining; Western contact group present new proposals for a NAMIBIAN settlement

(Nov.)   Operation Daisy against SWAPO; South African forces advance 150 miles into ANGOLA; 45 mercenaires return to South Africa on a hijacked Air India jet after their abortive coup attempt in the Seychelles

(Dec.)   CISKEI granted its "independence"

1982 (Jan.)   South Africa hesitantly accepts first phase proposals of Western contact group on NAMIBIA

(Feb.)   Commission of inquiry into the mass media makes recommendations that would subordinate the press to state control; white trade unionist dies in detention; GOLD price drops back sharply; 22 right-wing NP members of parliament vote against the Prime Minister

(March)   16 rebel members of parliament, led by TREURNICHT, are ousted from NP and form the CONSERVATIVE PARTY

(April)   BOTHA meets President Kaunda of Zambia
(May)   President's Council makes recommendations on CONSTITUTIONAL CHANGE involving "COLOURED" and INDIAN participation in central and local government

(June)   South Africa accepts second phase proposals of the Western contact group on NAMIBIA; South African government announces that KANGWANE and part of KWAZULU are to be transferred to SWAZILAND

(July)   NATIONAL PARTY federal congress approves the government's proposals for CONSTITUTIONAL CHANGE: a strong executive president and the election, on separate voters' rolls, of "COLOUREDS" and INDIANS to separate chambers in the central parliament

(Aug.)   The World Alliance of Reformed Churches declares APARTHEID a theological heresy and suspends membership of the two main white DUTCH REFORMED CHURCHES

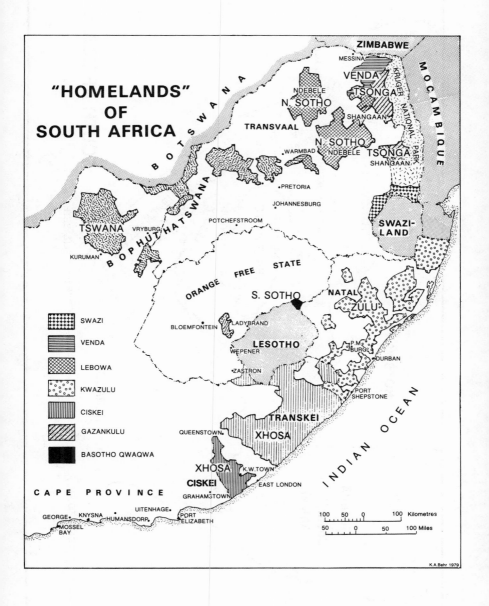

"HOMELANDS" OF SOUTH AFRICA

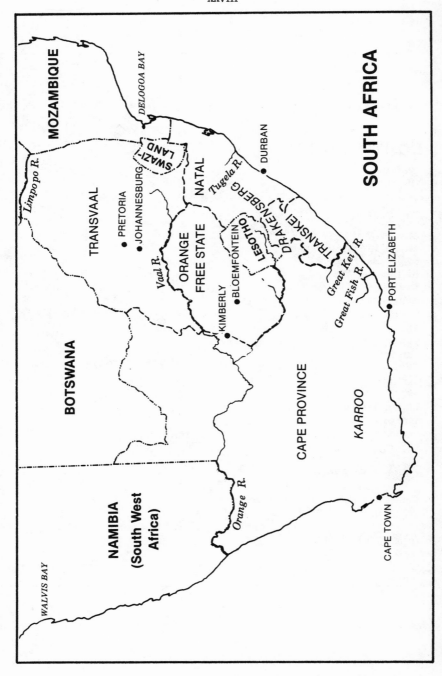

INTRODUCTION

Geography has fashioned much of South Africa's history.
Though the country is roughly one sixth the size of the United
States, and reaches from the Limpopo River in the north to
the southernmost tip of the African continent, much of it is
dominated by the great African plateau that occupies so much
of East, Central, and Southern Africa. Tilted up on its eastern side, the plateau falls sharply to the coastal lands, most
spectacularly in the Drakensberg mountains. Climate influenced the distribution of human settlement in the region even
more than relief. In the eastern half, the sweetveld pasture
of the coastal belt and the flat highveld savannah were both
well suited for cattle grazing. In the west the land becomes
progressively dryer, until in the northwest it is desert. Only
a small pocket in the extreme southwest has winter rainfall
and a Mediterranean climate. There, at the northern end of
a narrow peninsula on the southwestern extremity of the continent, the first permanent European settlement was made in
1652.

Historians today recognize that South Africa's history
began long before that date. For a very long time the only
inhabitants of the southern part of the continent were hunting
and gathering peoples, whose most noticeable legacies were
the mounds of shellfish remains they left along the coasts and
the pictures they painted on the walls of the caves they occupied. Just under 2000 years ago, it is thought, some
hunter-gatherers who had learnt to domesticate cattle and
sheep entered what is now South Africa, perhaps north of the
junction of the Orange and Vaal rivers, and moved with
their animals westward along the Orange and south to the
Indian Ocean, and then to the Cape Peninsula. Though Europeans later disparagingly called them Hottentots, they knew
themselves as Khoikhoi. People of a Negroid physical type,
who probably entered South Africa not much later than the
Khoikhoi, and who unlike them used iron and grew crops as
well as kept cattle, settled both down the fertile coastal belt

1

and on the highveld. They spoke a dialect of a language
which much later would be called Bantu. And then at the
end of the fifteenth century voyagers from Europe set foot
on South African soil for the first time. Within a few years
of the start of a permanent European settlement on the shores
of Table Bay, slaves were introduced, the first from Africa
but the greater number, over a period of one hundred and
fifty years, from Asia.

The history of South Africa from the mid-seventeenth
century is in the main the story of the interaction of these
peoples. The hunter-gatherers were mostly exterminated,
by disease more than warfare, or they withdrew to the des-
erts of the north. The Khoikhoi lost their grazing lands to
other pastoralists or to agriculturalists, and became a landless proletariat. Many were assimilated, as were the slaves,
into those today classified "Coloured" in the South African
government's racialist terminology, a category chiefly com-
prising people of mixed descent. The societies of the far
more numerous Bantu-speakers, on the other hand, were
much better able to resist the white intruders than were the
Khoikhoi. Though Africans lost much of the land they occupied when the whites arrived, they did not lose all of it.
Even those communities with continued access to land were,
however, forced in the long run to send men out to work on
white-owned farms, in the gold mines, or more recently, in
secondary industry.

South Africa's recent history has been viewed from
several perspectives. To some it is primarily the story of
remarkable growth. Though not otherwise well endowed by
nature, South Africa happened to be rich in minerals, and
above all, gold, which made possible major secondary industrialization. From another perspective, economic progress
was made possible by a unique system of labor coercion based
on race, and the creation of its particular system of racial
capitalism is therefore the main theme of its recent past.
Yet others see that past as the story of the rise of Afrikaner
power, or of the attempts to overthrow the system of racial
domination that made South Africa by the 1980s perhaps the
most universally despised country on earth. South Africa's
history, in short, is infinitely complex. This dictionary
must inevitably be superficial and highly selective. It is
nevertheless hoped that within the constraints imposed by the
size and form of the volume, the entries constitute a reasonably comprehensive, as well as reliable body of information

on South Africa's history, and the bibliography a useful guide to the best of the wealth of scholarly writing that has been devoted to that history.

THE DICTIONARY

ABDURAHMAN, Abdullah (1872-1940). The most influential figure
in "COLOURED" POLITICS this century. The grandson of slaves
who bought their freedom, he was the first Cape Muslim (see
ISLAM) to attend the South African College in Cape Town. He
then went to Glasgow University, where he trained as a medical
doctor. Elected to the Cape Town City Council in 1904 and to
the Cape Provincial Council in 1914, he remained on both bodies
until his death. He was also, from 1905 until his death, President of the African Political (later Peoples') Organisation (APO)
and editor of its newspaper from 1909 until it folded in the early
1920s. Between 1927 and 1934 with D. D. T. Jabavu (for whom
see ALL-AFRICAN CONVENTION, J. T. JABAVU) he convened
a series of conferences to bring "Coloureds," Indians and Africans together, but little of significance was achieved. By the
1930s the APO had declined and was little more than a mutual
benefit, burial and building society. Abdurahman came under
increasing attack from younger, more radical "Coloureds," including his daughter Cissie Gool (1897-1963), a fiery democrat
who, like her father, was a long-time member of the Cape
Town City Council.

AFRICAN NATIONAL CONGRESS (ANC). The South African Native
National Congress (SANNC), founded at Bloemfontein in January
1912, the first permanent South Africa-wide African political
organization, survived as the preeminent voice of African nationalism, changing its name in 1923 to African National Congress. Pixley SEME, the moving spirit behind its founding,
and the other leading figures in the early ANC were drawn from
the small elite of highly educated Africans, whose Christian mission backgrounds underpinned their essentially liberal, bourgeois
aspirations. Their main goal was the maintenance of the Cape
African FRANCHISE and its extension to the other provinces.
When they realized that Britain would not intervene in South
African affairs, they continued to hope that white liberals would
be able to persuade the all-white parliament to reduce discrimination against people of color.
   From 1912 to 1949 the ANC's basic strategy was peaceful
petition, aimed at winning moderate concessions through negoti-
ation. It sent a delegation to Britain to protest the NATIVES
LAND ACT in 1914 and another to Europe in 1919 at the time
of the Versailles Peace conference. The militancy of African
workers on the Witwatersrand in the post-World War I years

5

only briefly pushed the Transvaal branch into a more radical
posture. During the 1920s the ANC was eclipsed by the INDUS-
TRIAL AND COMMERCIAL WORKERS UNION, which, unlike the
ANC, could claim a mass membership. When Josiah Gumede
(c. 1875-1947), elected president in 1927, began working closely
with communists, conservatives within the ANC rallied and replaced him by the cautious Seme (1930). In the early 1930s the
ANC remained disorganized and minuscule, and when the threat
to the Cape African franchise came to a head in 1935, it was
not the ANC but a new umbrella body, the ALL-AFRICAN CON-
VENTION (AAC), which took the lead in protest. When the
AAC took steps to become a permanent body, however, Seme
and other ANC members rejected it, insisting that the ANC remain the mouthpiece of African nationalism. Though attitudes
to participating in HERTZOG's new NATIVES REPRESENTATIVE
COUNCIL varied, most ANC leaders did serve on it at one time
or another.
      A new generation, disillusioned with the NRC and stimulated
by the eclipse of the colonial powers during World War II, began from 1943 to press for a more militant stance, based on
mass support. The ANC Youth League, founded in 1944, rejected the old "language of supplication." The removal of the
Cape African franchise had freed the ANC from a concern with
individual participation in the political system and facilitated the
development of a new ideological stance. This was provided
above all by Anton Lembede (1914-1947), first President of the
Youth League. A Catholic intellectual, he expounded an ideology
of Africanism: Africans were oppressed as a people. He looked
forward, not to a return to the past of the old Cape tradition,
but to liberation won by Africans themselves. Hostile to the
left wing in the ANC, which included members of the COMMUN-
IST PARTY who pressed for closer links with the CP, he nevertheless wanted the ANC to adopt more militant tactics.
      Lembede died young, but in 1949, the year after the NA-
TIONAL PARTY came to power on its APARTHEID platform, the
Youth League got its way, and the ANC adopted a Program of
Action committing it to strikes, boycotts and civil disobedience.
Together with the South African INDIAN Congress, with which
closer ties were forged in 1947 and renewed after the DURBAN
RIOTS of 1949, it staged protests against unjust laws and then
in 1952 launched the DEFIANCE CAMPAIGN. ANC membership
suddenly shot up from a few thousand to 100,000. Support was
greatest in the eastern Cape, which had been the seedbed of
African nationalism.
      After the collapse of the Defiance campaign, the ANC played
a central role in the CONGRESS ALLIANCE. It was Z.K. Matthews (1901-1968), a Professor at FORT HARE and leading intellectual within the ANC, who suggested that a Congress of the
People be held. The ANC's involvement in the campaigns to
oppose MASS REMOVALS from the western areas of Johannesburg and to boycott the new BANTU EDUCATION schools (1955)
was, however, half-hearted, and the dispute within the ANC over
its adoption of the FREEDOM CHARTER in 1956 reflected discontent

with the leadership as well as unhappiness with the multiracialism of the Congress Alliance and the mild socialism of the Charter. In 1958 the "Africanists," claiming they were in the Lembede tradition, withdrew from the Transvaal conference of the ANC, and the next year formed the rival PAN-AFRICANIST CONGRESS (PAC).

When the activist PAC spoke of organizing a boycott campaign and one against PASSES, the ANC decided to hold massive antipass demonstrations beginning on 31 March 1960. These plans were preempted by the PAC, the SHARPEVILLE shootings occurred, and on 8 April 1960 the ANC found itself a banned organization (see BANNING). The following year the Nobel Peace Prize was awarded to its banned leader, Albert LUTHULI, for his long commitment to non-violence. In that year, ironically, its underground leaders decided to embark upon SABOTAGE and guerilla war (see UMKHONTO WE SIZWE). An external mission was set up under Oliver Tambo (1917-), who had left the country after Sharpeville, to mobilize world opinion and train military cadres. Within the country the sabotage of the early 1960s provoked harsh repression. Nelson MANDELA and his Umkhonto colleagues were given life sentences, while thousands of ANC members, especially in the eastern Cape, were arrested and convicted for ANC-related activities. A decade of demoralization followed, with the exile leadership taking a long time to organize effective action. An attempt to send a party of ANC guerillas through Rhodesia (now ZIMBABWE) to South Africa in 1967 failed when they were attacked by Rhodesian forces at Wankie.

The decision by the exile party at Morogoro, its Tanzanian headquarters, in 1969 to admit non-Africans to membership helped produce considerable ideological dissent within the leadership in the early 1970s. As in the 1950s, those of an "Africanist" persuasion complained that non-Africans, and especially members of the Communist Party, were exerting too great an influence. A group of eight prominent anti-communist dissidents broke with the ANC in 1975. In 1979 four white intellectuals, critical of the ANC for failing to focus its activities on the organization of the South African proletariat, were suspended (see LEGASSICK).

The late 1970s was a period of resurgence for the ANC. Though the BLACK CONSCIOUSNESS movement had arisen in part out of disillusionment with the ANC, and though the ANC played little or no part in the SOWETO REVOLT, it benefitted from the new militancy. Many of the perhaps 4,000 blacks who fled Soweto and elsewhere entered ANC military training camps in ANGOLA, MOZAMBIQUE, and Tanzania, from which some returned to South Africa with their Soviet-made weapons. By 1978 the revitalized ANC was showing its strength through numerous acts of sabotage. Diplomacy was not neglected, however, and in 1979 the exile leadership met Gatsha BUTHELEZI and other INKATHA leaders in London. This "honeymoon" was brief, with the ANC soon resuming its attacks on Buthelezi as a government stooge. The ANC had had links with Nkomo

rather than Mugabe, but soon after the transfer of power in
ZIMBABWE it opened an office in Salisbury (now Harare).
    As it entered the 1980s, the ANC sought to win for itself
acknowledgment as the sole legitimate representative of the
African people. A more socialist program adopted at the 1969
Tanzania conference was downplayed, and the Freedom Charter
proclaimed as its manifesto for the future South Africa.

AFRICAN NATIONALISM see AFRICAN NATIONAL CONGRESS;
    BLACK CONSCIOUSNESS MOVEMENT; PAN-AFRICANIST CON-
    GRESS; and follow references under those headings.

AFRICAN POLITICAL (later PEOPLES') ORGANISATION see
    ABDURAHMAN; "COLOURED" POLITICS.

AFRICANS. This book follows usual practice in scholarly writing
    in English on South Africa and uses "Africans" for BANTU-
    SPEAKING peoples. In the late 19th century, "KAFFIR," the
    most common term used for such people up to that time, began
    to acquire increasingly pejorative connotations, and it was grad-
    ually replaced by "Native" in general usage. By the 1950s,
    however, whites began to realize that "Natives" implied that
    Bantu-speaking people were indigenous to the country and whites
    were not. The government first adopted "Bantu" and then
    BLACK. But if "black" was used for Bantu-speaking people,
    there was no satisfactory general term for those not classified
    white in South Africa's racial terminology. So "black" is used
    here for Africans, "COLOUREDS" and INDIANS.
    Use of "Africans" to mean Bantu-speakers is nevertheless
    unsatisfactory from several points of view. It may suggest
    that non-Bantu-speaking KHOISAN were not Africans, whereas
    they lived in many parts of the country before the arrival of
    Bantu-speakers. It implies that "Coloureds," Indians and
    whites are not Africans and have no claim to that term. By
    the 1960s many whites had come to see themselves as Africans.
    After the establishment of the REPUBLIC (1961) in particular,
    government spokesmen referred to whites as people of Africa,
    with no other home, an interpretation accepted by leaders of
    African countries to the north in the Lusaka Manifesto of 1969.

AFRIKAANS. In the late 17th and early 18th centuries the form of
    DUTCH spoken at the Cape developed differences in pronuncia-
    tion and accidence, and to a lesser extent in syntax and vocabu-
    lary, from that of Holland. The role of KHOIKHOI, slaves and
    people of mixed descent, in promoting this process, and the in-
    fluence of the Malay-Portuguese lingua franca spoken at the
    Cape, both remain controversial. While the Dutch of Holland
    remained the language of officialdom and of culture, the new
    creolized form, often called Cape Dutch or belittled as "kitchen
    Dutch," eventually developed into a separate language, though
    one which was long regarded as unsuitable for literary use.
    The first book published in Afrikaans appeared in 1856, but it
    was not until the mid-1870s that S.J. du Toit (1847-1911), a

DUTCH REFORMED CHURCH (DRC) clergyman, and others at
Paarl, twenty miles inland from Cape Town, began using it as
a vehicle for cultural expression.   In quick succession they produced a journal, Die Afrikaanse Patriot (1876), a concise gram-
mar (1876), and a history (1877).
   A second phase in the Afrikaans language movement began
after the SOUTH AFRICAN WAR, and was in part a response to
MILNER's attempts to anglicize the Afrikaner people of the
Transvaal.   One of the central figures was J. D. du Toit (1877-
1953), son of S. J., who wrote poetry under the nom-de-plume
"Totius."   D. F. MALAN was one of the young DRC clergymen
who came out strongly in support of Afrikaans at this time.   An
Akademie (Academy) was founded in 1909 to promote the language
and its scientific study.   In the early 1920s the influential Cape
Town newspaper De Burger and the DRC journal, De Kerkbode,
both switched to Afrikaans.   In 1925 parliament declared that
"Dutch" included Afrikaans, and from then Afrikaans in effect
replaced Dutch as the other official language.   It was not until
the early 1930s, however, that a translation of the Bible into
Afrikaans was completed, and it was only afterwards that the
work of the poet N. P. van Wyk Louw (1906-1970) and others gave
Afrikaans standing as a literary medium.
   In the late 1870s Afrikaans had been closely associated with
the struggle against British imperialism.   A century later,
though the tongue of Breyten BREYTENBACH and Beyers NAUDE,
and of most "COLOUREDS," it was closely associated, especially in the minds of Africans, with Afrikaner domination and
APARTHEID.   After 1948 Afrikaans became the language of
government: bilingualism became obligatory in the civil service,
and as relatively few English-speakers could or would speak
Afrikaans, the civil service became Afrikaner-dominated (some
English-speakers in top posts were replaced on ideological
grounds).   The government's insistence that Afrikaans be used
as the medium of instruction in African high schools in the
southern Transvaal was the spark that set off the SOWETO
REVOLT.   In the aftermath of the revolt this requirement was
dropped.   Among "Coloureds" there was increasing use of English rather than Afrikaans.   But in 1976 a huge Taal (language)
monument was completed high on a hill above Paarl.   At its
base was inscribed "Dit is ons erns" ("This is our passion").
(See also AFRIKANERS.)

AFRIKANER BOND (1880-1911).   The first, and until the late 1890s
   the only organized political party at the Cape.   Its origins lie
   in the cultural and political revival among Cape Afrikaners in
   the 1870s (see AFRIKAANS).   Its founder, S. J. du Toit (1847-
   1911), sought to establish it as a pan-Afrikaner movement, and
   branches were formed in the Orange Free State and Transvaal.
   But under Jan Hendrik Hofmeyr (1845-1909), its leader in the
   Cape parliament, it focussed on Cape politics, and by throwing
   Bond support behind various English-speaking politicians, Hofmeyr made and unmade Cape Prime Ministers.   From 1890 the
   Bond, representing Afrikaner agrarian interests, formed a firm

alliance with the mining magnate Cecil RHODES. Hofmeyr's
nationalism was inclusive rather than exclusive, and he accepted as an Afrikaner anyone whom he believed sought to promote the interests of South Africa. Though in favor of raising
the FRANCHISE qualifications in 1892, he backed the non-racial
franchise and believed that all voters should be free of discriminatory laws. There was no color bar in the Bond's constitution, but it had no black members and did not want any. It
nevertheless received JABAVU's support in 1898.

After the JAMESON RAID fiasco, Hofmeyr and the Bond
broke with Rhodes. When the Bond emerged from the bitterly
fought election of 1898 with a small majority, Hofmeyr gave his
support to the government formed by W. P. Schreiner (1857-
1919). Disorganized by the SOUTH AFRICAN WAR, the Bond
failed to defeat the PROGRESSIVE PARTY in 1904, but its fortunes revived in 1908, when it became in effect the governing
party. It then worked closely with the Afrikaner parties in the
two ex-republics to achieve UNION. After that, the various
Afrikaner parties themselves united to form the SOUTH AFRI-
CAN PARTY, the members of which agreed to differ on the
divisive issue of "native policy."

AFRIKANER BROEDERBOND (Afrikaans: "band of brothers"). Influential secret organization to promote Afrikaner interests.
Founded in 1918, it had only 512 members by 1930, but after a
full-time secretary was appointed in 1931 its membership grew
to 1,396 in 1935. By the late 1970s it had 12,000 members.
All male, they included most key figures in all sections of the
Afrikaner elite.

The Bond's first major achievement was the establishment in
1929 of an umbrella organization, the Federasie van Afrikaanse
Kultuurverenigings (Federation of Afrikaner Cultural Organizations) which soon dominated Afrikaner cultural life. In 1934 the
majority of Broeders opposed FUSION as a sell-out to British
imperialism and gave their support to MALAN'S NATIONAL
PARTY (NP). General HERTZOG, who was not a member,
clashed openly with the Broederbond, as did his successor
SMUTS, who in 1944 forbade teachers and civil servants to belong to it. But the Bond, working to improve the economic
position of the Afrikaner and to identify the NP with the cause
of Afrikaner nationalism, played an important role in Malan's
victory in 1948. Since then every Prime Minister has been a
member. Perhaps most influential under VERWOERD, when it
retained a measure of independence of the NP, it became a
mere arm of the party under VORSTER. When it censored
those who broke away from the NP to join the HERSTIGTE
NASIONALE PARTY, dissidents began releasing information
about its activities to the press. By 1982 it had recovered a
measure of independence, and again opened its membership to
Afrikaners who were not members of the NP.

AFRIKANER NATIONALISM. In the 1930s and after, Afrikaner
nationalists propagated the myth of a monolithic nationalism

which had welded the volk (people) together from the time of
the GREAT TREK. In fact, Afrikaner nationalism was born in
the late 1870s as a response to the challenge of British imperialism, particularly at the time of the TRANSVAAL WAR OF
INDEPENDENCE (1880-81). But the feeling of common consciousness among Afrikaners throughout South Africa soon
waned after the end of that war and the recovery of Transvaal
independence. It revived with the JAMESON RAID, which was
seen as an imperialist plot against Transvaal Afrikaners and it
reached a new peak of intensity during the SOUTH AFRICAN
WAR and its aftermath, when Afrikaners struggled to resist
MILNER's anglicization policy.

The South African war also divided Afrikaners, for the
bittereinders ("bitter-enders") had fought on, while the hensoppers ("hands-uppers") and the "joiners" had collaborated with
the British. Many of the collaborators were BYWONERS, who
suffered severely in the war and in the aftermath were forced
to move to the towns. They found ENGLISH-SPEAKING WHITES
dominated commerce and industry, and that Africans--who unlike the Afrikaners were not fully proletarianized, but who often
left families in the rural areas--were prepared to work for very
low wages. The nascent group consciousness the Afrikaners had
formed in earlier clashes with these two groups was now reinforced in the urban setting. Mobilized on ethnic lines by such
institutions as the DUTCH REFORMED CHURCH, the AFRIKANER
BROEDERBOND and the NATIONAL PARTY, Afrikaners saw
themselves as a group apart. This brought economic rewards.
One Afrikaans insurance company, founded in 1919, had as its
motto: "Born out of the Afrikaner people to serve the Afrikaner
people."

Both HERTZOG and MALAN believed that only if Afrikaners
could remain distinct, would they be able to resist absorption by
the dominant English culture. They rejected the broad "South
Africanism" of BOTHA and SMUTS, the fusing of Afrikaners and
English in "one stream," in favor of a "two stream" approach.
But then in the mid 1930s Hertzog himself joined "the enemy"
(see FUSION) and it was left to Malan to seek to rally Afrikaners behind his purified NATIONAL PARTY (NP) as the vehicle
of an exclusive Afrikaner nationalism. Great emphasis was now
laid on the Afrikaner's "civil religion," the notion of a divine
calling and a sacred history. Smuts' entry into WORLD WAR II
was seen as another betrayal to British imperialism. Afrikaner
workers were detached from non-Afrikaner dominated TRADE
UNIONS and swung behind the NP. Fearing African competition
for their jobs, Afrikaner workers were attracted to its anti-
black stance. Thanks to the numerical preponderance of Afrikaners in the white community, the greater weight given to the
rural vote and the ethnic mobilization achieved by 1948, sufficient unity was obtained for political power to be seized in the
election of that year, since when it has remained in Afrikaner
hands.

AFRIKANER PARTY (1941-1951). After SMUTS had taken South

Africa into WORLD WAR II, HERTZOG and his followers joined
Malan in a Herenigde (Afrikaans: "Reunited") NATIONAL PAR-
TY.   But old suspicions soon flared up and by the end of 1940
the Hertzogites had broken with Malan.   Early in 1941 they
formed the Afrikaner Party.   After all its candidates had met
defeat in the 1943 general election, its leader--N. C. Havenga
(1881-1957)--made overtures to the UNITED PARTY, but SMUTS
rejected them.   In 1947 Malan and Havenga agreed that their
parties would not compete against each other in the next election.   The Afrikaner Party then gained 9 seats in 1948, enabling
the NP to form a government.   After South West Africa
(NAMIBIA) was given 6 seats in the House of Assembly in Cape
Town, and Nationalists had been returned for all of them, the
Afrikaner Party was no longer needed for Malan's majority, and
it was soon absorbed by the NP (1951).

AFRIKANER REBELLION (1914).   Armed protest led by some of
the BOER heroes of the SOUTH AFRICAN WAR against South
Africa's decision to invade German South West Africa (see
NAMIBIA).   Of the 7, 000 Free Staters and 3, 000 Transvalers
involved, many were poor Afrikaners, who hankered after a
return to republican independence.   Using Afrikaner COMMAN-
DOS, BOTHA and SMUTS put down the rebellion without much
difficulty, and the rebels were treated leniently, except for
Jopie Fourie (1878-1914), who had not resigned from the Defence Force and who was executed for shooting at government
forces under a flag of truce.   HERTZOG, who opposed the invasion of South West Africa, was careful not to give overt support to the rebels, but he benefitted from the rebellion, for
Botha and Smuts became branded as betrayers of Afrikaners,
and Fourie was paraded as a martyr.

AFRIKANERS.   Term applied in the late 20th century to whites
whose home language was AFRIKAANS.   Less than 7. 5 percent
of the total population, they were the dominant minority.   In
previous centuries, "Afrikaner" was sometimes used to mean
"native of Africa," i. e. one who identified with--and was usually
born in--South Africa rather than Europe.   "Afrikaners" (variant form Afrikander) could, then, be English-speaking or black.
The ancestors of the present Afrikaners were often called
BOERS, or Cape Dutch.   Descendants of immigrants of largely
Dutch, but also French and German extraction, they had by
1800 been welded into a volk (people) with a distinct patois
(which would come to be called AFRIKAANS), a Calvinist morality, strong family ties and a sense of common destiny as people of Africa who had a special status because of their origins,
culture, and color.   With BRITISH rule, some prominent
Afrikaner families, especially in Cape Town, became anglicized.
Others sought to maintain their identity through the DUTCH RE-
FORMED CHURCH and their language.   Some fled British rule
in the GREAT TREK.   Among the latter there developed a sense
of being God's chosen people, and an identification with the people of Israel.   It was not until the late 19th century that

AFRIKANER NATIONALISM can be said to have emerged. In
that century, as subsequently, Afrikaners have often been bitterly divided, not infrequently over the very issue of how best
to preserve Afrikaner identity.
   Throughout the 20th century they have formed between 54 and
58 percent of the white population. In 1970 they numbered 2.1
million. Whereas in 1880 less than 1 percent lived in towns,
by 1970 over 80 percent lived in small country towns or the
large urban centers.

AGRICULTURE. Knowledge of farming is thought to have entered
   South Africa along with iron technology and the kind of pottery
   characteristic of the early IRON AGE. There is evidence for
   both cereal cultivation and livestock keeping in the Transvaal
   from the 3rd century A.D. Until recently it was assumed that
   these IRON AGE farmers were BANTU-SPEAKERS; archaeologists are now less certain. The Later Iron Age farmers, from
   about A.D. 1000, who were definitely Bantu-speaking, engaged
   in more sophisticated farming and began to exchange agricultural produce. In African societies tillage was usually en-
   trusted to women; men cleared the ground while the women
   sowed, weeded, gathered, and threshed the crop. The main
   grain crop was sorghum (often called KAFFIR corn), which
   from the 18th century was gradually supplanted by the newly
   introduced maize (corn; mealies).
      In the late 17th century white settlers at the Cape began the
   intensive production of both wheat and wine. In the 18th century wine became the staple export of the southwestern Cape.
   The BRITISH 1820 settlers pioneered scientific farming in the
   ZUURVELD or Albany district. With the introduction of the
   merino sheep, wool became the major item of export from the
   eastern Cape in the 1830s.
      The introduction of the ox-drawn plough by missionaries in
   the 19th century encouraged Bantu-speaking Africans to give
   more attention to cultivation, increased areas open to such
   cultivation, and meant men became more active in tillage. A
   relatively prosperous African peasantry emerged in response
   to new market opportunities. The growth of population consequent on the discovery of first DIAMONDS and then GOLD created large internal markets for food. For a time African
   farmers in BASUTOLAND and elsewhere supplied the new demand, but in the last years of the 19th century it was cheaper
   to import wheat from America to the WITWATERSRAND than
   obtain it locally. Roughly from the time of the SOUTH AFRI-
   CAN WAR, white farming gradually began to become much more
   commercialized and productive. White farmers, whose votes
   were weighted more than urban ones, received massive state
   aid, and the competition from the independent African peasantry
   was eliminated (see BUNDY THESIS). The gold mines were
   relatively heavily taxed and part of the revenue transferred to
   agriculture. A subsidy system introduced after 1924 ensured
   that farmers received higher than world prices for their products. This process culminated in the Marketing Act of 1937, in

terms of which central marketing boards were established. The rate structure on the railways subsidized the movement of agricultural products, especially for export, and farmers were allowed special income tax concessions.

By the late 1970s South Africa was exporting 20 percent of its agricultural output. Maize, grown mainly in a triangle of land in the northern Orange Free State and southern Transvaal, was by far the largest crop (over 14 million tons in 1981), followed by sugar, grown mainly on Natal's north coast, and then fruit, most of which was produced in the southwestern Cape and exported through Cape Town. The country was also the world's fourth largest exporter of wool. (See also ECONOMIC CHANGE.)

ALL-AFRICAN CONVENTION (AAC). An umbrella organization set up to co-ordinate and lead African protest against the HERTZOG BILLS, and in particular the removal of Cape Africans from the common voters' roll. Over 400 delegates attended the inaugural meeting in Bloemfontein in December 1935. Though SEME of the AFRICAN NATIONAL CONGRESS (ANC) had been one of the convenors, the leading figure in the AAC--elected its president at the inaugural meeting--was D.D.T. Jabavu (1885-1959), son of J.T. JABAVU. Like his father, D.D.T. Jabavu had not participated in the ANC. The AAC was prepared to accept a qualified FRANCHISE, but took a firm stand on the retention of the Cape African franchise, which the younger Jabavu called "the noblest monument of the white man's rule." It also pointed to the gross inadequacy of the additional land promised to Africans. An AAC delegation sent to Cape Town held a series of meetings with the Prime Minister, to no avail.

After the Hertzog Bills became law, the AAC lost cohesion. Many leading members decided to contest seats on the new NATIVES REPRESENTATIVE COUNCIL. SEME and others withdrew when the AAC became a permanent body in 1937. The ANC now entered a period of resurgence, and its leadership did not approve of the way the AAC moved after 1937 towards the formation of a joint front with "Coloureds" and Indians. In 1943 Jabavu took it into the NON-EUROPEAN UNITY MOVEMENT as an affiliated organization (see also "COLOURED" POLITICS). In the 1940s the AAC built links with certain rural areas-- especially the TRANSKEI--and began to acquire a mass following, but this new thrust was not consolidated and in the 1950s it was the ANC rather than the AAC that gained peasant support. (See also RURAL RESISTANCE.)

AMABUTHO (plural; singular ibutho) (Zulu: "those gathered together"). Groups of men or women of roughly the same age. The transition of male amabutho from circumcision sets into military units stationed at royal barracks (amakhanda) has usually been seen as crucial to the process leading to the formation of the ZULU kingdom. In that state, women as well as men were brought together in age-sets. Recent work has stressed that the amabutho had important non-military functions: besides colonizing new land or acting as a garrison among a

newly conquered people, they provided labor for the king. The
restrictions the king placed on the marriage of members of an
ibutho--typically they were forbidden to marry for fifteen to
twenty years after recruitment--gave him control over their
labor power during that period.
   It is believed that systematic and large-scale buthaing began
in the northern NGUNI area in the late 18th century, at a time
of increasing competition both for scarce resources and for a
share in the benefits of trade with DELAGOA BAY. Rulers began to replace circumcision with extended service, military and
non-military. This innovation remained fundamental to the organization of the Zulu kingdom throughout its independent existence. (For context see also MFECANE.)

AMANDLA (Zulu: amandla ngawethu: "power is ours"). Shouted
   slogan, accompanied by clenched-fist salute, much used in the
   1950s and again in the 1970s, by AFRICAN NATIONAL CON-
   GRESS and then BLACK CONSCIOUSNESS and INKATHA supporters. (Cf. MAYIBUYE I AFRIKA.)

ANGLICAN CHURCH see Robert GRAY.

ANGLO-AMERICAN CORPORATION. Conglomerate launched in 1917
   by Ernest Oppenheimer (1880-1957), a key figure in the DIA-
   MOND industry, who rose to become chairman of DE BEERS
   CONSOLIDATED MINES in 1929. Though legally and adminis-
   tratively independent, De Beers became part of the Anglo empire. Oppenheimer's disposal of diamond stocks financed its
   GOLD-mining ventures on the far west WITWATERSRAND and
   then in the new Orange Free State gold field, which it opened
   up after World War II. By 1980 it was responsible for 37 percent of South Africa's gold production. In the 1950s it began to
   diversify into other minerals on a large scale, including uranium
   and platinum, and into other forms of industry. In 1960 its
   non-mining industrial interests were worth £30 million, by 1969,
   £143 million. The process continued: it went into property in
   the 1970s, life insurance in 1982, and it acquired extensive investments round the world. With subsidiaries in Zambia and
   other African countries, it backed the government's OUTWARD
   POLICY. A number of its leading officials worked for the
   PROGRESSIVE PARTY.

ANGLO-BOER WAR see TRANSVAAL WAR OF INDEPENDENCE
   (1880-1881) or SOUTH AFRICAN WAR (1899-1902).

ANGLO-ZULU WAR see ZULU; FRERE; CONFEDERATION;
   NATAL; TRANSVAAL.

ANGOLA. A group of Afrikaner settlers--the "Thirstland trekkers"
   from the Transvaal--entered southern Angola in 1881, where
   they lived mostly as hunters, mercenaries for the PORTUGUESE
   in campaigns against local people, or as transport riders. As
   Angolan independence approached in 1975, many of their descen-

dants returned to South Africa.   In that year the South African
government was pressed for aid by UNITA (Union for the Total
Independence of Angola), a pro-Western nationalist movement
which sought to prevent the MPLA (People's Movement for the
Liberation of Angola) taking over the country as the Portuguese
withdrew.   With encouragement from the United States Central
Intelligence Agency, the South Africans sent an armored column
of 2000 men north from NAMIBIA.   This moved quickly up the
Angolan coast, capturing the port towns.   By November 1975,
when the Portuguese left, large numbers of Cubans had arrived
in support of the MPLA, and after a few clashes with them the
South African force withdrew to the south.   There the South Africans protected the hydro-electric scheme built as a joint
Portuguese-South African project on the Cunene river, until in
March 1976, under strong international pressure, they pulled
out of Angola altogether.

This intervention ensured that the new MPLA government
would be hostile to South Africa, helped introduce a large Cuban
presence into Angola, and drew upon South Africa intense criticism from the international community.   The OUTWARD POLICY
was brought to a sudden stop.   The triumph of the MPLA contributed to the assertive mood among South Africa's blacks seen
in the SOWETO REVOLT.

The month after having agreed to the Western plan for
NAMIBIA, South African forces launched a massive raid on a
SWAPO refugee base at Cassinga well into Angola (May 1978).
Thereafter South African forces repeatedly raided into southern
Angola, attacking SWAPO's bases and destroying its logistical
support.   There were occasional clashes with the Angolan army.
By late 1981 South African forces were in virtual occupation of
the southern-most Cunene province.   A massive raid in August
of that year took South African forces over 100 miles inside
Angolan territory.   Throughout this period South Africa was
giving military and other aid to UNITA, enabling it successfully to continue its guerilla war against the MPLA government.
(See also PORTUGUESE.)

ANTHEM.   The question of a national anthem became a heated one
in white politics in 1938, when HERTZOG claimed that, because "God Save the King," which had been sung on state occasions, was the British anthem, South Africa had no official
anthem of its own.   He then ordered that both "God Save the
King" and "Die Stem van Suid-Afrika," written in Afrikaans in
1918 and long an unofficial anthem, should be played on state
occasions.   When "Die Stem" became the only official anthem
in May 1957, English-speakers saw this as another sign of the
Afrikanerization of the country; few of them bothered to learn
the words of the English version ("The Call, " 1952).

Africans had their own anthem: see NKOSI SIKELEL'I-
AFRIKA.

ANTI-COLONIAL REBELLIONS.   After blacks had, by a variety of
means, including conquest in FRONTIER WARS, been subjected

to white control, they on a number of occasions rebelled in attempts to throw off that control.   Between 1799 and 1802 many
of the KHOIKHOI of the eastern Cape joined still-independent
XHOSA in an abortive attempt to recover their lost freedom.
Half the settlers of the KAT RIVER SETTLEMENT rose in revolt against the colony during a Cape-Xhosa war in 1851.   The
LANGALIBALELE affair (1873), petty episode though it was,
shocked the Natal colonists just because it was the first rebellion of any significance in their colony.   Yet another Cape-
Xhosa war (1877-78) provided the context for revolts by portions of the GRIQUA both east and west of the DRAKENSBERG
and of the Tlhaping (see TSWANA) (1878).   Less than three
years after that last Cape-Xhosa war, much of the TRANSKEI
that had been brought under white rule without force rose in
revolt, at the same time as the SOTHO north of the Drakensberg went into rebellion against Cape rule (1880).   The
Cape was able to subdue the rebellion in the Transkei without
calling on the aid of British troops.   North of the mountains,
it was unable to reassert its authority, and had decided by
1883 to hand BASUTOLAND back to Britain to rule.   The last
major revolt of this kind in the Cape took place among the
Tswana of the Langeberg mountains in 1897, the last in South
Africa occurred in Natal in 1906.   Like all the others except
the Sotho one, BAMBATHA's REBELLION was soon suppressed,
with much loss of life on the rebel side.   After that, African
resistance took non-violent forms (even the Israelites of BUL-
HOEK used violence only when surrounded) and it was not until
the 1960s that first SABOTAGE and then armed struggle (see
UMKONTO WE SIZWE) took resistance into a new phase.
    For anti-colonial rebellions by whites see, e.g., BLACK
FLAG REVOLT; GREAT TREK; and under FREEBURGHERS;
SEPARATISM.

APARTHEID (Afrikaans: "apartness"; pronounced, ironically,
    "apart-hate").   First used in the Cape NATIONAL PARTY (NP)
    newspaper Die Burger in 1943, "apartheid" was adopted as a
    slogan by the NP in the 1948 election.   It meant an intensifica-
    tion of RACIAL SEGREGATION, a doctrinaire commitment to
    separation in all spheres.   To the outside world, the word came
    to sum up South Africa's abhorrent race policies, its institu-
    tionalized and legalized racial segregation.
        The relationship between post-1948 apartheid and earlier
    forms of racial segregation is a matter of controversy.   Some
    emphasize the continuities, and point to the fact that segrega-
    tion was accepted by most whites as the customary way of life
    before 1948.   Clearly many of South Africa's race laws--see,
    e.g., NATIVES LAND ACT; URBAN SEGREGATION--were en-
    acted long before 1948.   But whereas there had been a prag-
    matic, ad hoc quality to much pre-1948 segregation, apartheid
    was a revolutionary, totalitarian doctrine, which trumpeted
    separation as the ideal to be applied as consistently and rigor-
    ously as possible.   And after 1948 there was a massive exten-
    sion of segregation: see, e.g., "COLOUREDS"; GROUP AREAS;

MISCEGENATION; PETTY APARTHEID.
    Because of international criticism of "apartheid" the South
African government began to drop the use of the term from the
late 1950s, and speak instead of SEPARATE DEVELOPMENT,
which suggested more positive connotations. Some called the
latter "grand apartheid," the idea that Africans should govern
themselves in their own "HOMELANDS" (see also BANTUSTANS).
"Grand apartheid" was distinguished from "PETTY APARTHEID,"
Jim Crow-style segregation where people mixed together.
    After the death of VERWOERD, the chief ideologue of "grand
apartheid," the ruling Afrikaner elite gradually and very tortu-
ously freed itself from a dogmatic commitment to separation in
every sphere. It came to realize that continued adherence to
blatant racial discrimination was counter-productive to continued
Afrikaner survival. So there was some removal of "petty
apartheid" and this was held up to the outside world as evidence that "apartheid was dead."   The far more important
"grand apartheid" remained very much alive.

APPRENTICESHIP (or "inboekseling": Dutch: "those booked in").
    In the 18th century young KHOISAN boys and girls, seized in
raids or military campaigns, were brought up in the households
of TREKBOERS as "apprentices." Children were bound to their
masters until they were adults, and their children were then in
turn bound. A British proclamation of 1812 sought to regularize
such indentured servitude by enforcing "apprenticeship" from 8
to 18 years only. Though "apprentices" were often, in terms
of their indentures, to be given some form of instruction, this
was very rarely done. The 39,000 slaves "apprenticed" for
four years after emancipation in 1834, received little or no instruction. Nor did those freed from slave ships captured by
the British navy after 1808--over 4,000 of these "Prize Negroes" were indentured in the colony between 1808 and 1844 for
fourteen year periods. The VOORTREKKERS knew that it
would be a condition of British acceptance of republican independence that there be no revival of slavery in the interior, so
they too used "apprenticeship": African children were seized
and forced to work, and there was some buying and selling of
such "apprentices."

ASIANS see INDIANS.

AZANIA. A Greek form of the Persian word zanj-bar (Zanzibar)
    meaning "land of the blacks," it was used for the east African
    coast from the 1st century A.D. In the 1970s it was increas-
    ingly taken over by black South Africans as a more authentic
    "African" name for their country. After the BANNING of the
    BLACK CONSCIOUSNESS organizations in 1977, an Azanian
    People's Organisation (Azapo) was founded (April 1978) with
    similar objectives.

BAASSKAP (Afrikaans: literally, "boss-ship," i.e., blatant racial domination). When Prime Minister in the 1950s, STRIJDOM admitted that the NATIONAL PARTY policy of APARTHEID was one of baasskap. His successor VERWOERD realized that baasskap was morally indefensible and hoped to deflect international criticism by reformulating the policy as SEPARATE DEVELOPMENT.

BAKER, Herbert (1862-1946). The most significant figure in South African architecture. Went to South Africa from England in 1892, became a close friend of RHODES, and designed everything from modest houses to the Union Buildings, Pretoria. He left South Africa in 1912.

BALLINGER, Margaret (1894-1980). An immigrant to South Africa from Scotland in 1904, and educated at Rhodes and Oxford universities, she was from 1920 a lecturer in History at the University of the Witwatersrand. She was forced to give up that post when she married William Ballinger (see INDUSTRIAL AND COMMERCIAL WORKERS UNION) in 1934. Three years later she entered parliament as Natives' Representative (see FRANCHISE) for the Cape Division, having been asked to stand by the AFRICAN NATIONAL CONGRESS. A forceful critic of government policy and strong champion of African interests, she retained her seat until African representation was abolished in 1960. A founder of the LIBERAL PARTY, she was its first president from 1953 to 1955, but disliked its swing to the left in the late 1950s. In retirement she wrote From Union to Apartheid (1969), which described the assault on LIBERALISM.

BAMBATHA REBELLION (1906-07). The last armed revolt in South Africa organized on a pre-colonial basis. The main precipitant was the poll tax imposed on all adult African males in Natal at the end of 1905. In February 1906 two white police officers were killed by armed Africans in the Richmond district, south of Pietermaritzburg. Martial law was then proclaimed and the militia sent in. Bambatha, a Zulu sub-ruler, who lived north of Pietermaritzburg in the Umvoti district, became the focus of resistance. He and his followers retreated to the Nkandla forests, where they engaged the Natal forces in guerilla struggle. In June 1906 this resistance was crushed at the Mome gorge, but further outbreaks continued in northern Natal into the following year. Between 3,500 and 4,000 Africans were killed, and some two dozen whites. Whites mainly blamed "ETHIOPIANISM" but though some KHOLWA, mostly members of African independent churches, did take part, the majority remained neutral and were regarded as traitors by the rebels. Though the Zulu paramount gave no open support to the rebels, he was put on trial for alleged involvement (see further under ZULU).
The uprising promoted ideas of political co-operation both among whites and among Africans. In showing up the Natal government's weakness, it provided a reason for UNION. The British government believed that small weak states would inevitably be prone to brutality and panic in their treatment of Africans, while many in the Cape were highly critical of Natal

mismanagement in African affairs.   See also ANTI-COLONIAL
REBELLIONS.

BANNING.   Persons, meetings, organizations and publications were
all banned under South African law.   An amendment to the
Riotous Assemblies Act of 1929, which gave the Minister of
Justice the power to order any individual to leave a magisterial
district, was used to restrict the movement of union leaders and
political opponents.   Very much wider powers were given the
government by the Suppression of Communism Act of 1950 and
used extensively thereafter.   The typical "banning order" issued
under that Act, as amended, restricted an individual to a magisterial district, required him or her to report regularly to the
police, prevented anything said by the person from being quoted,
excluded him or her from visiting such places as educational
institutions, factories, and harbors, and prevented him or her
from meeting socially with more than one person at a time.   A
banned person was usually the subject of constant police sur-
veillance to see whether the banning order was strictly adhered
to; if the police suspected it was not, the person was brought to
court.   There was no appeal to the courts against a banning order, which was usually for five years, often renewed thereafter.
From 1962 banning orders sometimes meant total or partial
house arrest, the banned person being prevented from leaving
his or her home.   From 1956 banning was extended to banish-
ment: hundreds of Africans were forced to move to remote
areas, where they were then restricted.   (They included the
wife of Nelson MANDELA.)   Major political prisoners were usually banned or banished, or both, on completion of their prison
sentences.   In all, almost 2, 000 people were banned in the
1950s, 60s and 70s.
   The Suppression of Communism Act also provided for persons
to be "named" for promoting the aims of communism, which
was extremely broadly defined.   Such "named" persons were
then "listed" and forbidden to attend gatherings or belong to
certain organizations, while nothing they said could be quoted
and nothing they wrote published.   The Act also outlawed the
COMMUNIST PARTY.   Under other legislation the major African political organizations were banned: the ANC and PAC in
1960, BPC and SASO in 1977.   The CHRISTIAN INSTITUTE too
was banned in 1977.   Various left-wing and African newspapers
were forced to close down.   Between 1950 and 1980 some
20, 000 publications were banned under various laws (see CEN-
SORSHIP).

BANTU EDUCATION.   An educational system for Africans designed
to fit them for their role in APARTHEID society, as VERWOERD,
architect of the Bantu Education Act (1953), conceived it: "There
is no place for [the African] in the European community above
the level of certain forms of labour. ...   It is of no avail for
him to receive a training which has as its aim absorption in
the European community. "   In 1953 90 percent of African
schools were state-aided mission schools; the 1953 Act removed

control of African education from the churches and provincial
authorities and placed it under a separate central government
department.   Only the ROMAN CATHOLIC CHURCH attempted
to keep its schools going without state aid.   The 1953 Act also
separated the financing of education for Africans from general
state expenditure and linked it to direct tax paid by Africans
themselves.   Though Bantu Education was designed to isolate
Africans and prevent them receiving "subversive" ideas--
Verwoerd also closed down adult night school programs for
Africans--black indignation at being given inferior education
became a major focus for resistance (see, e.g., SOWETO
REVOLT).

BANTU-SPEAKERS.   Bantu ("people," from the plural prefix "aba"
and "-ntu," the stem for person in NGUNI languages) was the
name the Cape Town-based philologist Wilhelm Bleek (1827-
1875) used as a classificatory term for the group of languages
distinct from SAN and KHOI languages.   It is not known when
and how Bantu languages spread into South Africa.   It is commonly assumed that Bantu-speaking people, of Negroid physical
type, were the first to use iron technology and the first mixed
farmers in the region (see IRON AGE, AGRICULTURE), and
therefore that the Bantu language entered from the north early
in the Christian era.   But this remains highly speculative, and
some archaeologists now believe that it was only with the advent
of the Later Iron Age (c. A.D. 1000) that Bantu-speakers settled south of the LIMPOPO RIVER.   Continuities in pottery
styles at Phalaborwa in the eastern Transvaal lowveld strongly
suggest that the present-day Bantu-speaking people of the region
are the direct descendants of those who lived in the area almost
a millenium ago.
      From the modern Transvaal and Natal, Bantu languages
spread south into the Orange Free State and the Transkei in
two broad streams.   Those who were to be called NGUNI-
speakers settled down the eastern seaboard, between the
DRAKENSBERG mountains and the Indian Ocean, while SOTHO-
speakers established themselves on the interior plateau south
to the ORANGE RIVER and westward as far as there was summer rainfall.   They did not penetrate beyond the 20-inch rainfall line, which runs north through South Africa from the coast
near present Port Elizabeth.
      By the mid-17th century, Bantu-speaking mixed pastoral and
vegecultural farmers occupied most of the well-watered areas
of the country, except only for the extreme south-western portion.   All lived in relatively small, but well-ordered polities,
much stronger and more complex than those of the semi-
nomadic KHOIKHOI pastoralists, some of whom were gradually
absorbed into Bantu-speaking groups.   While one estimate puts
the number of Khoikhoi at that time at 200,000, the number of
Bantu-speakers was many times that figure, and may have been
anywhere between one and two million.
      In all Bantu-speaking societies cattle played an important
ritual and prestige role.   They could be exchanged for women,

who were both producers and bearers of children (see LOBOLO).
Lent out to clients, cattle could attract followers (see SISA).
They served as a medium of exchange, and were a source of
products for clothing and household manufacture, such as cloaks
and skins, shields and gourds. Eaten only on ceremonial occasions, their milk was a major item of diet. Even more significant in NGUNI than in SOTHO society, they seem to have out-
numbered the human population at least from the Later IRON
AGE. During the FRONTIER WARS vast herds of cattle were
seized by whites from African peoples. In 1856-1857 Africans
on the Cape frontier slaughtered their own cattle in vast numbers (see CATTLE-KILLING) The rinderpest epidemic of
1896-1898 reduced herds by up to 80 percent in some parts of
the TRANSKEI and had almost as disastrous effects in the
Ciskei, forcing many Africans onto the labor market. Just
when the herds were beginning to recover, East Coast fever
spread through Natal and the Transkei in 1912-1913, again killing up to 80 percent of the cattle in some districts. When the
administration subsequently insisted on the regular dipping of
cattle, to kill the ticks that transmitted the fever, there was
considerable resistance by African peasants, especially in the
northern Transkei. (For crop cultivation see under AGRICUL-
TURE; ECONOMIC CHANGE.)
     From the early 1960s the South African government began to
replace "Native" (which no longer seemed appropriate, for
whites did not see themselves as aliens, non-natives) with
"Bantu" as the official term for AFRICANS. "Bantu" was disliked by Africans themselves because of its associations with
apartheid and inferior treatment, and "a Bantu" and "Bantus,"
forms often used, were grammatical nonsense. After 1977 the
government replaced "Bantu" with "BLACK" (see under that
heading for the way "black" is used in this book).

BANTUSTANS. VERWOERD and Dr. W.M. Eiselen, his Secretary
of Native Administration, were the architects of the policy of
transforming the African RESERVES into self-governing states,
the Bantustans. Verwoerd ruled out the possibility of full independence for these states in 1951, but in 1959 that became
the goal of policy. Formulated in part as a response to increasing international pressure on South Africa to give some
political rights to Africans, it was a policy designed to maintain and strengthen white supremacy in the greater part of the
country.
     As the Bantustans were given their "independence" from
1976, large numbers of Africans, whether they lived in the
Bantustans or not, were deprived of their South African citizenship and made citizens of the new states. Were all Bantustans
to be led to independence (or absorbed by other states; KANG-
WANE, the Bantustan for Swazis, by SWAZILAND; QWA QWA,
the Bantustan for southern SOTHO, by LESOTHO), then ultimately there would be no Africans with South African citizenship, or
any claim to rights within South Africa.
     There were three main phases in the evolution of the Bantus-

tan policy.   The Bantu Authorities Act (1951) created a hierarchical system of authority in the reserves in which appointed
chiefs and headmen played a key role.   Territorial authorities
were set up for each so-called ethnic group (except the XHOSA,
who, for historical reasons, were given separate authorities
either side of the Kei river).   Chiefs who did not co-operate in
the new system were deposed and replaced, while those who co-
operated became more clearly identified as instruments of the
State.   There was considerable resistance at the popular level
to the implementation of Bantu Authorities, especially in Pondoland in the TRANSKEI and in Sekhukhuneland in the eastern
TRANSVAAL (see PEDI; RURAL RESISTANCE).

The Promotion of Bantu Self-Government Act (1959) recognized eight "national units" on ethnic grounds, and provided the
machinery for these territories to be led to self-government.
The units (also called HOMELANDS, black states, or national
states) created from the former reserves, were TRANSKEI and
CISKEI, both for the Xhosa; KWAZULU for the ZULU;
BOPHUTHATSWANA for the TSWANA; LEBOWA for the North
SOTHO; VENDA; GAZANKULU for the THONGA; Kangwane for
the Swazi; and Qwa Qwa for the southern Sotho.   A separate
unit was later created in the Transvaal for the Ndebele
(KWANDEBELE).   The Transkei, which had the largest single
block of land under African occupation, was the first to be
given limited self-government in 1963.

The third phase took the Bantustans from self-government
to full "independence."   Again the Transkei led the way, being
given its "independence" in 1976, followed by Bophuthatswana,
Venda, and the Ciskei.   The Africans who rose to power in the
other Bantustans, and in particular Gatsha BUTHELEZI in
Kwazulu and Cedric Phatudi in Lebowa, refused to consider
"independence" for their territories.   Because the whole Bantustan policy was an integral part of APARTHEID, none of the
"independent" Bantustans received international recognition.
Each was recognized only by South Africa and the other independent Bantustans (though the Transkei did not recognize
Ciskei, because it wanted all Xhosa in one political unit).   For
the new ruling elites "independence" meant a certain power and
status, considerable investment by Pretoria, and the opportunity
to rid their countries of the racial indignities of apartheid.
They were quick to use authoritarian methods against their opponents, and--with the exception of Bophuthatswana--their regimes were soon notorious for corruption.   The possession of
a casino--forbidden in South Africa--was often the best-known
token of "independence."

The reality was that the Bantustans were rural slums, totally dependent on South Africa.   In 1979 only one--the minute
Qwa Qwa--consisted of a single block of land.   Though up to
January 1982 the South African government had spent R592
million buying land for "homeland consolidation," the Bantustans remained highly fragmented.   Whereas in 1960 about a
third of the African population of South Africa lived within
these territories, because of some adjustments of borders, a

fierce INFLUX CONTROL policy and forced MASS REMOVALS,
over 40 percent lived in them in 1980.   In 1955 a government
report found that the maximum number of people they could
support was 2.3 million; by 1981 there were three times that
number in the Bantustans.   In that year they contributed only
3 percent to the country's total output.   Well over half their
economically active men were away working as MIGRANTS at
any one time.

BARRY COMMISSION.   Cape government commission on Native
Laws and Customs which sat under the chairmanship of J.D.
Barry (1832-1905), a judge of the Cape's Eastern Districts
Court.   Appointed as the last armed resistance to Cape rule
east of the Kei took place, it collected a mass of valuable
evidence from SHEPSTONE and many others, and its report
helped direct Cape African policy away from "identity"--one
law for all--towards differential administration for the large
population of the TRANSKEI.

BASTARDS (Basters).   In the 18th century this term was used for,
and accepted by, the offspring of mixed unions of whites with
people of color, most commonly KHOIKHOI but also, less frequently, slaves.   The offspring of African-Khoikhoi or slave-
Khoikhoi unions were sometimes known as Bastard-Hottentots.
Children produced of extramarital liaisons between whites and people of color were not usually regarded as white (see also MISCEGE-
NATION), and Bastards were not usually accepted as FREEBURGH-
ERS.   Only in a few rare cases were children born out of wedlock of
white fathers and Khoikhoi mothers baptized and accorded burgher
status.   Most offspring of white-Khoi unions were regarded by
whites as "free persons of color," "free" because they were not
slaves (cf. CAPE SLAVERY; FREE BLACKS).   Rejected by
white society, Bastards often formed separate communities on
or beyond the Cape's northern borders.   There they lived a
precarious existence, between the advancing TREKBOERS and
the indigenous peoples.   Most Bastards used the name with
pride, viewing themselves as far superior to Khoikhoi without
"white blood."   There is some evidence that "Bastard" acquired a cultural meaning and was extended to poor whites or
Khoikhoi who spoke some DUTCH and possessed firearms.
One group of Bastards living north of the ORANGE RIVER in
the early 19th century was persuaded by a London Missionary
Society MISSIONARY to change its name--because of the stig-
ma attached to illegitimacy--to GRIQUA.

BASUTOLAND.   The name given by whites to the country of the
BaSOTHO, or southern Sotho.   For its early history see under
MOSHWESHWE.   Annexed by the British HIGH COMMISSIONER
in 1868, it was taken over by the Cape two years later.   The
magisterial system that colony imposed provoked Sotho resistance: a revolt in the southwest of the country in 1878 was
followed by general resistance in 1880 when the Cape attempted
to disarm the Sotho.   The war of the guns (1880-81) ended

without a Cape victory, and, unable to re-assert its authority,
the colony asked Britain to take over direct responsibility for
the territory.   From 1884, Basutoland once again fell under the
High Commissioner and was no longer part of the Cape.   In the
1870s Basutoland supplied large quantities of grain to the DIA-
MOND fields, but by the early 20th century it was importing
food and exporting only MIGRANT LABORERS.   By the time
Britain led the country to independence in 1966, it was suffering dire poverty.   (See also HIGH COMMISSION TERRITORIES;
LESOTHO.)

BECHUANALAND (land of the TSWANA).   Believing that the
TRANSVAAL's westward expansion was threatening the strate-
gically and economically important ROAD TO THE NORTH, and
fearing that the Transvaal might eventually link up with German
South West Africa (see NAMIBIA) and cut the Road completely,
Britain annexed what it called Bechuanaland in 1885.   A large
area north of the Molopo river became the Bechuanaland Protectorate, ruled from London through the HIGH COMMISSIONER
until 1966, when it acquired independence as Botswana.   The
territory south of the Molopo, the Crown Colony of British
Bechuanaland, was incorporated into the Cape in 1895.   Much
of the latter was eventually to form part of BOPHUTHATSWANA.

BIKO, Steve (1947-1977).   The leading figure in, and the martyr of,
the BLACK CONSCIOUSNESS MOVEMENT.   Born in Kingwil-
liamstown, he attended a Roman Catholic school in Natal, then
the University of Natal Medical School.   A delegate to congresses of the NATIONAL UNION OF SOUTH AFRICAN STU-
DENTS, he led those African students who founded the separate
SOUTH AFRICAN STUDENTS ORGANISATION in 1969.   Dropping
his medical studies, he emerged as an outstanding organizer and
theoretician.
     Biko hoped through Black Consciousness to awaken Africans
to a new sensitivity to their oppression.   He defined it as the
antithesis to WHITE RACISM, a way of ridding the colonized of
their slave mentality.   Its cry was "Black man, you are on
your own"; slogans and ideas were freely borrowed from the
American Black Power movement.   "Black" meant oppressed,
and the movement gained some support among the Coloured and
Indian intelligentsia.   But if its rhetoric was radical, its program was essentially liberal and its supporters came from the
black universities and the church seminaries, not from the urban proletariat.
     From 1973 Biko endured BANNING and other harassment.
In September 1977 he died while in the custody of the SECUR-
ITY POLICE.   The Minister of Justice issued statements suggesting he had died of a hunger strike, and referred to his
death in callous terms.   The subsequent inquest revealed that
he had died of brain damage and other injuries, had been kept
naked and chained while injured, and then transported in the
back of a landrover from Port Elizabeth to Pretoria, where he
died.   The magistrate who presided at the inquest failed to find

any person responsible for his death.   Biko's family sued the
state for damages and in 1979 settled for an out-of-court payment of R65, 000.   In that year a law was passed requiring
newspapers to clear any story containing allegations of police
misconduct with the police themselves.   The policeman in
charge of Biko in Port Elizabeth, Colonel Goosen, received
promotion in 1981.

Biko's murder provoked an outraged reaction both in South
Africa and abroad.   The government responded by BANNING
various individuals and organizations in October 1977, including the BLACK CONSCIOUSNESS organizations Biko had been
involved with.   His death and the government clamp-down led
to the imposition of a mandatory arms embargo by the UNITED
NATIONS Security Council (see MILITARY).

BLACK.   The BLACK CONSCIOUSNESS MOVEMENT of the late
1960s and early 1970s defined as blacks all those discriminated
against on the grounds of race.   The older inclusive terms for
Indians, Coloureds, and Africans, "non-white" and "non-
European," were vehemently rejected because they were negative and did not promote the new aggressive image sought by
the leaders of Black Consciousness.   (Some blacks began to
call whites "non-blacks.")   But the alternative use of "blacks,"
to refer only to Africans, remained widespread, and was taken
over by the government itself from 1977.   Though the government accepted that "Bantu" was disliked by those of whom it
had been used, "African" could not be translated into Afrikaans,
except as Afrikaner or Afrikaan, which would be confusing,
while "black," with its stress on color, fitted in with government policy.   Whether Indians or Coloureds called themselves
"blacks" depended on whether or not they saw it to be in their
interests to identify with Africans.   Whether Africans spoke of
"blacks" in the wider sense depended on their preparedness to
work with these other groups.

In this book "black" is used in the more inclusive sense, to
refer to Africans, "Coloureds," and Indians (but cf. FREE
BLACKS).

BLACK CONSCIOUSNESS MOVEMENT.   In reaction to both WHITE
RACISM and white liberal paternalism, blacks decided in the
late 1960s that they must act on their own.   The all-black
SOUTH AFRICAN STUDENTS ORGANISATION (SASO) took the
lead in forming the Black People's Convention (BPC), an umbrella political movement, in 1972.   The BPC's aim was "to
unite and solidify the Black people of South Africa with a view
to liberating and emancipating them from both psychological and
physical oppression."   Seeing the struggle in color, not class
terms, it remained chiefly the vehicle of young black intellectuals and urban dwellers, and never won wide worker support.
Various black self-help, legal aid, and community programs
were started.   But in 1973 the government, which to begin with
had allowed the movement freedom because it seemed to fit in
with SEPARATE DEVELOPMENT ideology, began to clamp down

on it.   Virtually the whole leadership of SASO and BCP was
BANNED.   In 1974 pro-Frelimo (see MOZAMBIQUE) rallies
were broken up by the police.   In 1975 twelve BPC and SASO
leaders were charged under the Terrorism Act, and nine convicted.   Black Consciousness contributed significantly to the
ferment behind the SOWETO REVOLT, and BPC and SASO remained active despite the attacks on them.   But in September
1977 Steve BIKO, honorary president of BPC, died in detention
and the following month these and other Black Consciousness
organizations were BANNED.

The Black Consciousness leadership was bitterly hostile to
the BANTUSTAN policy and those prepared to work within it
were seen as collaborators, weakening black resistance.   Black
Consciousness, in turn, was much criticized by the AFRICAN
NATIONAL CONGRESS for placing too much emphasis on race,
for being elitist and out of touch with the masses, and for not
accepting the FREEDOM CHARTER.   The PAC was more sympathetic, even claiming, without justification, that it was responsible for the introduction of Black Consciousness into South
Africa.   Several former members of the PAC were, however,
among the leading figures in the Black Consciousness Movement.

BLACK FLAG REVOLT (1875).   When white DIAMOND diggers at
Kimberley barred the entrance to the local jail to prevent one of
their number being imprisoned, they raised a black flag as a
symbol of rebellion.   In June 1875 BRITISH troops arrived from
the Cape, and the rebellion was suppressed.   The rebels were
acquitted in the trials that followed, and the governor of Griqualand West dismissed for his handling of the affair.   The rebellion has recently been seen to mark the transition from the
dominance of merchant capital and the small independent digger
to that of industrial monopoly capital on the diamond fields.

BLACK SASH.   An organization of white women, originally the
Women's Defence of the Constitution League, founded in 1955
to propagate respect for the constitution at the time of the
"COLOURED" VOTE ISSUE.   Its members stood in silence in
public places, carrying placards and wearing white dresses
crossed by broad diagonal black sashes, a symbol of mourning
for the government's treatment of the constitution.   While such
picketing has continued, mainly on civil rights issues, the
Sash's most significant work in the 1970s was carried out in
its "advice offices" in urban centers.   These tried to help
Africans with such problems as INFLUX CONTROL, unemploy-
ment, contracts, housing, and pensions.

BLOOD RIVER, Battle of (16 December 1838).   To avenge the ZULU
attacks on the VOORTREKKERS in Natal, a trekker force of 470
men under Andries Pretorius (1798-1853) set out to encounter
the Zulu army.   Their laager at Blood river--their ox wagons
were formed into a tight circle and lashed together--was attacked by 10,000 Zulu.   Over 3,000 died from trekker bullets;
casualties on the trekker side were three men wounded.   After

this disaster, the Zulu had to recognize trekker claims to Natal. The trekker force had made a vow to celebrate the day if they were victorious, and in the 20th century 16 December (also the day the TRANSVAAL WAR OF INDEPENDENCE was begun, and KRUGER buried) became a day of great emotional significance for AFRIKANERS, on which speeches were made stressing their divine mission and proclaiming their faith that God would stand with them against their enemies.   Oddly, the day was known as "Dingaan's day," after the ZULU ruler, until renamed, more appropriately, Day of the Covenant in 1952 (Day of the Vow in 1980).

BOER (Dutch/Afrikaans: "farmer").   In the 18th century it meant a white farmer (a semi-nomadic pastoral farmer was a TREK-BOER).   In the 19th century the term came to be used for AFRIKANERS in general (e.g. in Boer-British relations), or for the white inhabitants of the VOORTREKKER republics, or for those who fought on the republican side in the SOUTH AFRICAN WAR.   When used by English-speakers, it often had derogatory connotations, suggesting backwardness and lack of culture.

BOPHUTHATSWANA.   BANTUSTAN for the TSWANA.   Given its "independence" in 1977, it then comprised seven non-contiguous pieces of land in the central and western Transvaal and the northwestern Cape, as well as Thaba Nchu in the Orange Free State.   In theory it was the political home for some 2.5 million Tswana, but only 1 million of these lived within Bophuthatswana.   In the early 1980s hundreds of thousands of people, many not Tswana, lived in the sprawling rural slum of Winterveld some twenty miles north of Pretoria, but just within Bophuthatswana's border.   Though it enshrined in its independence constitution a Declaration of Fundamental Rights enforceable by the courts, it inherited South African laws, including the Terrorism Act (see DETENTION WITHOUT TRIAL) and the Mines and Works Act (see JOB COLOR BAR), which prevented Africans from obtaining certain jobs on the mines.   Its economic potential was greater than that of the other Bantustans; platinum, chromite, copper, asbestos, and manganese were all mined within Bophuthatswana.

BOTHA, Louis (1862-1919).   Son of VOORTREKKER parents, he spent his early life in the northeastern Free State.   Having aided Dinuzulu in the ZULU civil war in 1884, he settled in the New Republic (see ZULU).   During the SOUTH AFRICAN WAR, in which he became a general, he showed himself an outstanding tactician.   One of those involved in the founding of HET VOLK, he emerged as Prime Minister of the Transvaal (1907) after the first elections under responsible government.   Forging a close bond with SMUTS, he preached conciliation between AFRIKANERS and ENGLISH-SPEAKING WHITES and the need for UNION.   With the achievement of Union, he became first Prime Minister.   When he could tolerate HERTZOG no longer,

he ousted him from his cabinet. He lost much Afrikaner support through his decision to put down the AFRIKANER REBEL-
LION with force in 1914. The following year, however, the
occupation by South African forces of German South West
Africa (NAMIBIA) was regarded as a triumph. Despite ill-
health, he attended the Paris Peace Conference, only to die
shortly after his return to South Africa. (See also SOUTH
AFRICAN PARTY.)

BOTHA, Pieter Willem (1916-). Son of a wealthy Free State
farmer, he abandoned his university sutidies in the Free
State to become a full-time organizer for the NATIONAL PAR-
TY (NP) in 1936. Entering parliament after the 1948 election,
he became Cape leader and Minister of Defence in 1966. That
he was elected Prime Minister by the NP caucus (the parliamentary members meeting together) in 1978 owed much to the
MULDERGATE scandal which divided the Transvaal members of
the caucus and gave Botha the support of the Free State bloc.
An authoritarian leader, Botha's "adapt or die" rhetoric in the
first eighteen months of his premiership suggested he might
wish to move his party in a reformist direction. With right
wing opposition to reform within the party, and increased support for the HERSTIGTE NASIONALE PARTY, talk of reform
ceased in 1981. But when Botha conceded that the NP accepted the idea of power-sharing with "Coloureds" and Indians
(see CONSTITUTIONAL CHANGE), TREURNICHT and other
right-wingers left the party (February-March 1982; see CON-
SERVATIVE PARTY).

BOTSWANA see BECHUANALAND.

BRAND, Johannes Henricus (1823-1888). Cape lawyer and parliamentarian who was summoned from Cape Town to be President
of the ORANGE FREE STATE in 1864, an office he held until
his death. Under his leadership, the Free State seized the
land west of the Caledon River from the SOTHO and would have
taken more had not Britain annexed BASUTOLAND in 1868.
Brand was then able to say that the Free State had "solved"
its "native [African] problem." Unable to obtain the DIAMOND
fields for the Free State he did persuade the British to pay
£90,000 compensation for them in 1876. An able administrator
--the Free State became known as the "model republic"--Brand
acted as conciliator between the Transvaal and Britain in 1881
(see TRANSVAAL WAR OF INDEPENDENCE). He continued to
prefer closer co-operation with the Cape than with the Transvaal, though he became more favorably disposed towards the
latter in his last years, after the discovery of GOLD there.

BREYTENBACH, Breyten (1940-). Educated at the University of
Cape Town, he left South Africa in 1959 and lived as a painter
and poet in Paris. He became known as an opponent of
APARTHEID when the South African government refused his
Vietnamese wife a visa to accompany her husband to Johannes-

burg to receive a major literary prize.   In 1972 he and his
wife did return, a visit described in his A Season in Paradise.
In 1975 he returned again, alone and in disguise, travelling under an assumed identity.   Arrested as he was leaving, he was
tried and found guilty of being a member of a white wing of the
AFRICAN NATIONAL CONGRESS called Okhela and given a nine
year sentence.   In 1977 he was tried again on new terrorism
charges, but found guilty only of having smuggled letters and
poems from jail.   In the late 1970s, as his works were translated from AFRIKAANS into English, his poetry began to acquire international recognition.

BRITISH KAFFRARIA (from KAFFIR).   The land of the XHOSA between the Keiskamma and Kei rivers annexed by Sir Harry
Smith (1787-1860), Cape governor and HIGH COMMISSIONER,
in terms of his high commission in 1847 at the end of a major
FRONTIER WAR.   Because an African-inhabited territory, it
was ruled directly by the high commissioner until 1860, when
the legality of the annexation was ensured by constituting it a
separate Crown colony.   By the mid 1860s the imperial government insisted that the larger colony take over its responsibilities
in the area, and from the first day of 1866 it became an integral part of the Cape.   After the CATTLE-KILLING, Sir George
GREY had been able to settle white settlers, mostly Germans,
in British Kaffraria.   The result today is a "white corridor"
which separates the CISKEI from the TRANSKEI.

BRITISH RULE.   Britain took over the Cape from the DUTCH in
1795 during the French revolutionary wars because of its strategic significance on the sea-route to India.   It was returned to
the Dutch (the Batavian regime in the Netherlands) in 1803, but
three years later another British expeditionary force reconquered
it.   From the naval base of SIMONSTOWN British naval patrols
went out after 1808 to intercept ships involved in the then-
outlawed slave trade.   In the peace negotiations at the end of
the Napoleonic wars, Britain retained the Cape (1815).   Again
this was chiefly for strategic reasons--to prevent the sea-route
between Europe and the countries of the Indian Ocean being controlled by a hostile power.
    Nevertheless, the Cape increasingly became important for
what it was as well as where it was.   The British acquired,
not merely the Cape peninsula, but a large colony.   The volume of maritime traffic--most of it British--calling at Cape
Town increased by 800 percent between the 1790s and the mid
1830s; by then the colony's exports were worth almost half a
million pounds.   With the development of the export trade in
wool from the eastern Cape (see ECONOMIC CHANGE), the
commercial significance of the Cape was greatly enhanced; by
1870 colonial exports were worth over £37 million.
    When they first arrived, the British made few changes:
DUTCH remained the official language and Roman-Dutch law was
retained.   But the British established a much stronger and more
efficient colonial state.   In 1811-1812 the British army helped

the colonists expel some 20,000 Africans from the ZUURVELD, the most easterly portion of the colony. A large group of British immigrants was settled there in 1820, ensuring both that the eastern districts would take on a British character (see ENGLISH-SPEAKING WHITES) and that the army would continue to play a vital role on that frontier until the power of the XHOSA was crushed, which was not until 1878, after a number of costly wars had been fought.

Though the British were concerned to establish the conditions for commercial expansion at the Cape, they also wished to devolve the responsibility of ruling the colony onto local whites. A legislative council was created in 1834, but for two decades the imperial government resisted settler demands for an elected assembly, fearing it would be used against the black population, and when representative government was granted it was on condition that the FRANCHISE was non-racial. A bi-cameral Cape parliament was established in 1854. In 1872 came responsible government, when the parliament gained control over the executive, leaving Britain with little more than the power to reserve certain kinds of legislation for imperial approval.

After the abolition of the slave trade, British humanitarians continued to work for the amelioration of the lot of slaves, then for emancipation itself. Humanitarian influences from London helped reshape Cape society (see CAPE SLAVERY; ORDINANCE 50) and provoke the GREAT TREK. For a time British officials were unsure whether to follow the trekkers and extend British rule, or recognize their independence. In the end, NATAL was annexed, the TRANSVAAL's independence was recognized in 1852, as was that of the ORANGE FREE STATE, after the four-year interlude of the ORANGE RIVER SOVEREIGNTY, in 1854. The interests of economy dictated that Britain withdraw from direct rule of the interior. But other interests--humanitarian, strategic--led to the annexation of BASUTOLAND in 1868. The opening of the DIAMOND fields then led Britain not only to annex the territory in which they lay, but also to attempt to reorder the entire country. CONFEDERATION, which would allow Britain to withdraw from direct responsibilities in the region, seemed to require, as interim measures, both the conquest of the major independent African states, and direct British rule of the TRANSVAAL. So Britain was led into major wars with the ZULU and the PEDI, as well as the TRANSVAAL WAR OF INDEPENDENCE. British power was able to achieve what the white colonists were not: the tipping of the balance of power in the white man's favor, a decisive contribution to the establishment of white supremacy in South Africa as a whole. In the early 1880s Britain entered another period of withdrawal, but it did not last long. With the Cape having proved incapable of ruling BASUTOLAND, Britain took it over. German involvement in the region (see NAMIBIA) then helped speed up a "scramble" which brought Britain BECHUANALAND in 1885 and Zululand in 1887.

It was the new economic power of the Transvaal (see GOLD) which led to Britain's most costly involvement in South African

affairs. Some have argued that fear that its new power might
threaten the sea-route to the east led British officials to push
the Transvaal into war; others assert that the war was fought
to enable a new South African state, more attuned to the interests of mining capital, to be forged. In the event it was the
SOUTH AFRICAN WAR that made it possible for Britain, within
less than a decade of the end of the war, to hand over power to
representatives of the white minorities in four self-governing
British colonies, and the achievement of UNION finally enabled
her to withdraw her troops from a South Africa safely within
the empire. For another half century strong links were retained (see, e.g., SMUTS). Even after South Africa established its REPUBLIC and withdrew from the COMMONWEALTH
as a result, Britain was its chief--and then a major--trading
partner, and remained the source of by far the largest amount
of foreign capital invested in the country. Besides that, the
large ENGLISH-SPEAKING WHITE community in South Africa,
most members of which were of British origin, ensured that
ties would remain. (See also HIGH COMMISSIONER; HIGH
COMMISSION TERRITORIES.)

BROEDERBOND see AFRIKANER BROEDERBOND.

BULHOEK. Enoch Mgijima (1868-1928), leader of an ETHIOPIAN
sect known as the Israelites, preached a millenial message
which claimed the Israelites as the chosen people. The sect
built a village for itself at Bulhoek, near Queenstown in the
eastern Cape, and in 1921 the SMUTS government demanded
they move off the land they occupied, where they were waiting
for the end of the world. When they charged the police and the
soliders surrounding them, 163 were shot and killed (24 May
1921), in what was called, by Smuts' critics, the Bulhoek massacre. After serving a brief sentence, Mgijima continued the
work of his church, which survives in the area today.

BUNDY THESIS. In a seminal article in African Affairs (1972) and
then in The Rise and Fall of the South African Peasantry (1979),
Colin Bundy, a South African based at Oxford University, argued that African agriculturalists responded positively and successfully to new market opportunities in the 19th century. The
growth of such a peasantry producing for the market was encouraged by both merchants and MISSIONARIES in the eastern
Cape in the middle decades of the century. With the development of the DIAMOND fields a vast new market for foodstuffs
opened up, and again Africans met many of the new demands.
But after 1886 mining and farming interests sought to force
Africans into wage labor. Pressures on land, the imposition
of taxes, the competition from those white farmers who now
began to commercialize, all helped force the African peasantry
out of business. Rinderpest (1896-97) and then East Coast fever
(1912-1913) both decimated the cattle herds of the Africans of
the coastal belt, and aided this process. But the decline of
African agriculture was essentially brought about, Bundy argued,

by a state-aided assault on the peasantry. The poverty of
African agriculture in the 20th century, therefore, was not
caused by any unresponsiveness to market opportunities, as
had previously been suggested, but was a direct result of
massive state intervention on behalf of white mining and commercial farming interests.

Bundy exaggerated both the "rise" and the "fall" of that
group of farmers he called the peasantry: production for the
market had begun much earlier; some of his evidence for massive increases in production was not typical; a significant
peasantry survived well after World War I.   Nevertheless, the
thrust of his thesis found general acceptance among historians.
(see also AGRICULTURE.)

BUSHMEN see SAN, KHOISAN.

BUSINESS CYCLES. The 18th-century Cape economy was lifted
from its almost constant depression by booms caused by the
Seven Years War (early 1760s) and the American Revolution
(1776-83) and, at the end of the century, by the coming of the
BRITISH.   The British occupation meant not merely a considerable increase in shipping but a revival of economic activity
generally.   A collapse in the wool trade (see ECONOMIC
CHANGE) helped bring on the depression of the mid 1860s,
from which the Cape only emerged as a result of the opening
up of the DIAMOND mines at Kimberley.   The most severe
depression of the 19th century occurred between 1882 and 1886.
There were various causes: an excessive speculation in diamond
mining shares; a severe drought; and the depression in England
and America.   The post-SOUTH AFRICAN WAR boom of 1901-02
was followed by a recession which lasted until 1909, caused in
large part by the legacy of destruction in the interior left by the
war.   Another recession, following the post World War I boom
of 1918-1919, lasted to about 1922.

The greatest depression of all, which hit the country in the
early 1930s, was closely linked to the European and American
one.   Had it not been for GOLD South Africa would probably
have had to devalue before Britain.   HERTZOG's decision to
remain on the gold standard after Britain had abandoned it in
1931, largely to demonstrate South Africa's independence,
caused great difficulties.   Once the South African pound lost
its parity with gold (December 1932), the consequent increased
price of gold stimulated the economy and began the recovery.
The depression had important political effects, being a major
factor in the coalition between SMUTS and Hertzog (see FU-
SION), and it greatly speeded up URBANIZATION, especially
of Afrikaners.

A mild recession in 1952-1953 was followed by a much more
serious one in 1960-1962, caused by the SHARPEVILLE shootings, the consequent international outcry and a crisis of confidence in the stability of the South African regime.   The government's tough measures to meet the crisis helped produce a
decade of spectacular economic growth.   The most serious

recession since the 1930s began in 1974. It was partly a result of the world recession following the rise in oil prices, but
it was greatly exacerbated by the crisis caused by the SOWETO
REVOLT and the new situation in Southern Africa after the
withdrawal of the PORTUGUESE and the advent of Marxist regimes in MOZAMBIQUE and ANGOLA. The crisis of confidence
was greater than that after Sharpeville, but once again the crisis was followed by a spectacular boom, this time fuelled by a
dramatic rise in the gold price. In 1980 South Africa's rate of
economic growth--8 percent--was probably the highest in the
world. From late 1981, with a steeply falling gold price, the
country once again, following the world trend, moved into recession.

BUTHELEZI, Mangosutho Gatsha (1928-). Descended from both
CETSHWAYO himself and Cetshwayo's chief minister at the time
of the Anglo-ZULU war (1879), Buthelezi is also a nephew of
Pixley SEME. Expelled from FORT HARE in 1952 for AFRI-
CAN NATIONAL CONGRESS Youth League activities, he became
an adviser to two Zulu kings, one his cousin, the other his
nephew. Having attempted unsuccessfully to resist the imposition of the BANTUSTAN system on his people, Buthelezi decided to work through it, becoming Chief Minister of KWAZULU
in 1972. He continued to make clear his opposition to SEPA-
RATE DEVELOPMENT, and emerged as the most outspoken of
the BANTUSTAN leaders, rejecting independence for his fragmented and impoverished territory. Accused of lending credi-
bility to the Bantustan policy, he argued that use must be made
of any platform to fight apartheid, even a platform created
by apartheid itself.
His role, then, was an ambiguous one. He revived INKATHA
as a mass organization which he claimed as the successor to the
banned ANC. He went to London in 1979 to meet the ANC leadership in exile. But on the other hand he was prepared to advocate federalism as a device which would allow for some redistribution of power to Africans while allaying white fears, and
he encouraged foreign investment in South Africa on the grounds
that it provided jobs for blacks. During the SOWETO REVOLT
he came out on the side of order, and helped limit the disturbances in Natal. Committed to non-violence, he showed no sign
of being ready to use the potential power of Inkatha as a weapon
of struggle. BLACK CONSCIOUSNESS supporters who condemned
him as a collaborator forced him to leave Robert SOBUKWE's
funeral in March 1978. And soon after the 1979 meeting, the
ANC was once again calling him a government stooge.

BYWONER (Dutch: bijwoner: "one who lives with another"). Landless white tenant farmer. There had been bywoners from the
late 17th century, but they came into public notice as a group in
the late 19th century, as land grew increasingly scarce and their
numbers consequently increased. The Roman-Dutch system of
partible inheritance frequently led to sub-division continuing until land was no longer economically viable, and men had to work

for others. Bywoners were given the use of land in exchange
for either a share of the crop, or seasonal labor service, or
both. Some were virtually independent farmers, others little
distinguished from wage laborers. As demand for foodstuffs
increased in the late 19th century and agriculture became more
commercialized, bywoners were ejected from many farms.
Some went into transport riding, but the completion of the
RAILROADS to the WITWATERSRAND in the 1890s put most
transport-riders out of business. Many bywoners were hard
hit by the Rinderpest epidemic among their cattle in 1897, and
then the SOUTH AFRICAN WAR escalated the process by which
they were transformed into an urban Afrikaner proletariat. In
the early 20th century "bywoner" became virtually synonomous
with "POOR WHITE."

CAPE COLONY. The DUTCH EAST INDIA COMPANY settlers in
    1652 called their new colony "the Cape," the name first given
    to the south-western tip of the African continent by the PORTU-
    GUESE. By the time the British occupied the Cape in 1795, it
    covered almost 200,000 square miles--thanks to periodic exten-
    sions of the colonial boundaries, as the TREKBOERS moved
    further and further afield--and was one of the largest political
    units anywhere in Africa. During the 19th century the Cape
    again doubled in size, expanding to the ORANGE RIVER and
    beyond in the north, and to meet NATAL'S southern boundary
    in the northeast. From 1871 to 1884 the Cape included
    BASUTOLAND. In 1880 it annexed Griqualand West, the
    DIAMOND fields territory which Britain had ruled from 1871;
    in 1895 it took over the administration of the southern portion
    of BECHUANALAND.
        Until the late 1880s the Cape overwhelmingly dominated the
    weak states of the interior. But then the political and economic
    balance shifted very quickly towards the GOLD-rich TRANSVAAL,
    ruled by Afrikaner republicans. After the SOUTH AFRICAN
    WAR, power was returned to these Transvalers, and the Cape
    entered a Transvaal-dominated UNION in 1910.

CAPE SEA ROUTE   see BRITISH RULE; SIMONSTOWN.

CAPE SLAVERY. The first commander at the Cape, Jan van
    Riebeeck (1619-1677) proposed enslaving the indigenous
    KHOIKHOI, but that was contrary to DUTCH EAST INDIA
    COMPANY policy and the Khoi were useful as cattle traders.
    The first slaves, from Guinea and Angola on the west coast
    of Africa, were introduced in 1658. Though a regular slave
    trade to the Cape never developed, by 1721 there were 2,480
    slaves, 2,100 whites. In all, more slaves came from Asia
    than from Africa, and of the Asian slaves the bulk came from
    India. In the 18th century slaves were widely distributed
    among the arable farmers of the southwestern Cape, and a
    considerable number worked in semi-skilled occupations in

Cape Town.   The pastoral farmers of the interior (TREKBOERS)
kept hardly any slaves, using KHOISAN labor instead.   The
grants of land made to the British settlers of 1820 carried a
prohibition against the use of slave labor.

Though there was no plantation economy at the Cape, the
slaves performed much of the manual work in the southwestern
parts of the colony, where the slave system would seem to have
been a relatively efficient and profitable one.   One farmer would
often hire out his slaves to another, and the slaves would move
from wine to wheat farms at different times of the year as they
were needed.   That all slaves were black strengthened WHITE
RACISM.   Arduous manual labor came to be regarded as something beneath the dignity of the white man; "KAFFIR work" it
would later be called.

It has often been said that Cape slavery was "milder" than
slavery elsewhere.   Some slaves in Cape Town lived as part of
the family and were well-treated.   But the vast majority of
field-hands were treated much as slaves were elsewhere.   In
theory they had access to the courts, but few complaints were
brought, and even fewer masters punished as a result of such
complaints.   Only one master was ever executed for killing a
slave.   On isolated farms, slaves were at the virtual mercy of
their masters.   Because Cape slaves were mostly males, and
had been brought to the colony from a wide variety of places,
there was little stable family life and no development of a distinctive slave culture at the Cape.   The only two rebellions occurred in 1808 and 1825, when freedom was in prospect; they
were both small-scale affairs.   Many slaves escaped in the
18th century, however, and communities of runaway slaves existed for long periods of time on Table Mountain, behind CAPE
TOWN, and at nearby Cape Hangklip.   Very few slaves were
manumitted (see FREE BLACKS).

Slaves became even more valuable after the end of slave
imports in 1808, following the British Act of 1807 abolishing
the slave trade.   The slaveowners' freedom to act as they
wished towards their slaves was increasingly limited as a
consequence of the humanitarian movement against slavery in
the British empire as a whole.   Masters were angered that
measures drafted for the West Indies were applied to the Cape,
and its special circumstances ignored.   Eventually a British
Act of 1833 emancipated all the slaves in the empire.   Though
freed on 1 December 1834, the 39,000 Cape slaves were forced
to enter four-year APPRENTICESHIPS with their former masters, and for many of them conditions of service did not alter
during this period.   The masters were further aggrieved when
the compensation money was paid in London, and they failed to
get what they thought due to them.

CAPE TOWN.   The place of the first permanent European settlement
--and therefore the "Mother City" to white South Africans--the
site was chosen because water was available on the north-facing
Table Bay, which was somewhat protected by Table Mountain
from the storms that often battered the southern end of the Cape

Peninsula.   A fort and small settlement were established on
land the KHOIKHOI had used as pasturage, and passing ships
were supplied with fresh fruit and vegetables and salted mutton
or beef.   As the houses grew, from 155 in 1710 to about 500
in 1770 and 1,200 in the early 19th century, so De Kaap became Kaapstadt and then Cape Town.   By 1806 the population,
not including government employees and the British garrison,
had grown to 16,500, of which almost 10,000 were slaves and
another 800 were FREE BLACKS.   The number of slaves declined after the end of the slave trade in 1808 and, with growing British immigration, whites became a majority of the
town's population in about 1840.

Cape Town was military headquarters, administrative center
for a vast hinterland (the seat of parliament from 1854), and
marketing center for the wine and wheat farmers of the south-
west Cape, but it remained chiefly dependent on the trade of
passing ships and its position as port of entry to the interior.
With the wool boom in the eastern Cape in the 1840s and 1850s,
Cape Town lost its pre-eminent commercial position, but its
merchants provided the capital for commercial expansion in the
east.   It was not until the days of sail were passing that a
breakwater and dock were built (begun 1860, opened 1870) to
give protection from the fierce gales that often struck Table
Bay.   In 1869 the opening of the Suez Canal reduced the strategic importance of the route round the Cape, but with the discovery of DIAMONDS and then GOLD, Cape Town became one of
the main ports of entry to a wealthy interior (see RAILROADS).
During the SOUTH AFRICAN WAR another £2 million was spent
on the harbor, and during World War II extensive reclamation
made possible the building of a new dock, further greatly enlarged in the 1970s to cope with tankers and then containeriza-
tion.

Cape Town's population, which approached 25,000 in 1850,
rose to 33,000 in 1875 and over 77,000 in 1904.   It was not
until the last years of the 19th century that Africans began to
arrive in large numbers; before that, whites, under the influence of British LIBERALISM, were confident enough to be liberal to people of color.   Not long after emancipation of the
slaves (1834), Cape Town became a municipality (1840), with
a non-racial suffrage based on property.   The ex-slaves lived
on the fringes of the city, in the Malay Quarter and in what
became DISTRICT SIX, but there was no enforced residential
segregation until 1901, when plague hit Cape Town and provided
an excuse for the African population to be shunted out en masse
to a LOCATION outside town.   For Africans Cape Town had
been, and remained, most closely associated with Robben Island, seven miles offshore in Table Bay, which housed political prisoners from the eastern Cape in the 19th century, and
would continue to house such prisoners into the 1980s (see,
e.g., UMKHONTO WE SIZWE).

From 1910 Cape Town was the seat of the Union parliament, but gradually decisions taken in Pretoria began to shape
the life of the city.   In World War II and its aftermath, in

particular, large numbers of people poured in from the rural
areas.   Afrikaners, often employed by largely greater Cape
Town-based Afrikaner capital, settled mainly in the northern
suburbs.   After 1948 Cape Town was subjected to the GROUP
AREAS ACT, and within 30 years the most integrated of South
African cities became the most segregated.   With the removal
of "Coloureds" from DISTRICT SIX and elsewhere, new slum
areas were created on the crime-ridden Cape Flats.   Cape
Town received international attention when violence erupted on
the Flats in 1976 and again in 1980, and for the treatment of
its outcast peoples, such as those expelled from District Six,
and the Africans who lived in the CROSSROADS camp in defiance
of the INFLUX CONTROL regulations (see also "COLOURED"
LABOR PREFERENCE POLICY).

CATTLE-KILLING (1856-1857).   The "national suicide" of the
XHOSA.   By 1856 Xhosa society had been devastated by a long
series of FRONTIER WARS with the Cape colonists.   An epidemic of lungsickness was wiping out many of their cattle herds.
The Xhosa knew that the British had suffered reverses in the
Crimean war at the hands of the Russians, whom they understood
to be black.   A long tradition of Xhosa prophets included Nxele
(Makanna) (before 1790-1820), who led the unsuccessful Xhosa
attack on Grahamstown in 1819, and Mlanjeni (c. 1830-1853), who
had given his name to the hard-fought frontier war of 1850-1853.
Now a sibyl, Nongqause (1841-1898) began to see visions in a
pool just north of the Kei river.   If cattle were killed and no
crops cultivated, she said, a new age would dawn, in which cattle would be plentiful and the ancestors would return.   Because
Sarhili (Kreli) (c. 1814-1892), the Xhosa paramount, believed
the prophecy, many others did, and there was great pressure
on unbelievers to participate in the killing.   When the great day
finally came (16 February 1857) and nothing happened, those who
had killed their cattle turned on those who had not, blaming
them.   Perhaps 20,000 starved to death, and at least as many
entered the Cape colony to look for work.   Sir George GREY
(1812-1898), the Cape governor, who accused both Sarhili and
Moshweshwe (see BASUTOLAND) of instigating the cattle-killing
so that the Xhosa would in desperation turn on the colony, took
advantage of the situation to clear parts of BRITISH KAFFRARIA
for white settlement.   Sarhili and his starving people were
driven out of their country east of the Kei, most of which was
a few years later settled with MFENGU and other Africans from
the Ciskei.   The incorporation of the Xhosa within the colonial
economy was greatly speeded up, the MISSIONARIES began to
gain large numbers of converts, and the ability of the Xhosa to
wage war against the colony was destroyed for almost a genera-
tion.   In the 20th century Africans generally believed either that
Grey had instigated the cattle-killing, or that the traders had,
wishing to benefit from the large number of hides that came on
the market.   In reality, the cattle-killing must be understood as
a millenial response by desperate people.

CENSORSHIP.   Though censorship has a long history in South
   Africa--for censorship in the 1820s see under PRESS--the
   modern system of censorship for political reasons is intimately
   connected with the rise of the APARTHEID state.   The Suppression of Communism Act (1950) and later amendments (see COM-
   MUNIST PARTY) prevented BANNED and listed people being
   quoted, or anything they wrote being published.   Radical newspapers were suppressed.   While such censorship fell under the
   Ministry of Justice, the Publications and Entertainments Act of
   1963 created a government-nominated Publications Control Board
   under the Ministry of the Interior.   This Board banned publications for a number of reasons, which included "harming relations
   between sections of the community."   Appeals against its decisions went--in rare cases, because of the costs involved--to the
   Supreme Court.   New legislation in 1974 provided for decisions
   on banning to be taken by local committees of censors, with appeals not to the Supreme Court but to a Directorate of Publications.   A new category of "possession prohibited" was added to
   earlier bans on distributing material, so that mere possession
   became a crime, whether or not the publication had been acquired legally and in good faith, and whether or not the owner
   knew of the findings of the censor board.
      In the early 1960s many of South Africa's black writers had
   their works proscribed.   By the late 1970s a total of some
   20,000 works had been banned.   Of the over 1,000 publications
   then being banned under the Publications Act each year, over
   half were for "endangering the state."   They included a large
   number of publications by students.

CHINESE LABOR.   With the SOUTH AFRICAN WAR over, the mineowners found themselves unable to attract the necessary African
   MIGRANT LABOR for the GOLD mines.   They therefore asked
   MILNER, who was governing the Transvaal, to obtain labor for
   them from China.   Recruiting began in North China among the
   refugees from the Russo-Japanese war in early 1904, and the
   first 10,000 workers arrived in South Africa in May.   Over a
   four year period 63,296 were sent to the WITWATERSRAND.
   The mineowners argued that by bringing in the Chinese the
   mines would boom and create more jobs for whites.   Certain
   jobs were reserved for whites (see JOB COLOR BAR) to allay
   white fears.   But HET VOLK campaigned for the repatriation of
   the Chinese, and "Chinese slavery" became a major issue in the
   British general election of 1906.   Once returned to power in
   Britain, the Liberals insisted that recruiting end and repatriation begin.   Repatriation was relatively easy because the Chinese were housed in COMPOUNDS (unlike the INDIANS working
   on the sugar plantations).   The last Chinese introduced under
   the scheme left South Africa in 1910.
      The Chinese not only helped the post-war recovery of the
   gold mines, they undercut the bargaining power of Africans.
   Their three- or four-year contracts had provided that they were
   to live in compounds and receive low wages.   The Chinese made

some attempt to protest, most notably in the go-slow strike at the North Randfontein mine in March 1905. From 1906, with the post-war boom over, Africans were desperate enough to work on the mines again, even for the lower wages now offered, and for them too compounds now became the customary form of accommodation.

CHRISTIAN INSTITUTE of Southern Africa (CI). Ecumenical, independent Christian organization for promoting dialogue and witnessing to reconciliation, founded by Beyers NAUDE in 1963. As it became more and more involved in work with Africans, it grew more radical, promoting the study of the Christian role in apartheid society and reacting sympathetically to the development of Black Theology, one wing of the BLACK CONSCIOUSNESS MOVEMENT. The CI was declared an "affected organisation" in 1975, which meant it could no longer receive financial aid from outside the country. Then in October 1977 it and its journal Pro Veritate were BANNED, as also were Beyers NAUDE and other officials.

CISKEI (land "this side," i.e. west, of the Kei River). A BANTUSTAN which was granted "independence" in December 1981, when it had a de facto population of 650,000, almost all XHOSA-speakers. As with the other Bantustans, independence meant the loss of South African citizenship for a much larger number of Africans--1½ million--classified Ciskeian but not living within the territory. Like the other Bantustans it was totally dependent on South Africa for the bulk of its revenue, for markets and raw materials, and for job opportunities. In the 1970s the Ciskei served as the dumping ground for at least 150,000 people relocated under MASS REMOVALS. An additional 250,000 Africans were moved from the port city of East London and settled within the Ciskei at Mdantsane, which was by 1980 the second largest dormitory town for Africans in the country after SOWETO. By independence half the Ciskeian population lived below the poverty datum line, and well over half of all earnings came from migrant labor outside the Bantustan. Malnutrition was rife and it was estimated that half of all children born died before the age of five. The Ciskei was run by an authoritarian oligarchy headed by Lennox Sebe, who had become its second Chief Minister in 1973 with the aid of the votes of nominated members of its legislature. Before the 1978 elections there was a wave of detentions and arrests, after which Sebe's Ciskei National Independence Party won every seat. He accepted independence against the advice of a commission he had himself appointed. In a referendum on the issue in 1980 almost everyone who voted supported independence but only 60 percent voted and wide-spread intimidation was alleged.

CIVILISED LABOR. The labor policy of the PACT GOVERNMENT after 1924 purported to be based on the provision of jobs to "civilised persons." "Civilised" in fact meant white, and the policy was an extension of an earlier white labor one begun

before Union.   It involved employing whites in unskilled and
semi-skilled jobs, mostly in the public sector (the Post Office
and the Railways in particular) at protected rates of pay, so
that there was a considerable wage differential between the lowest paid white worker and the highest paid African worker.
This helped solve "POOR-WHITEISM" and divided the working
class on racial lines, removing the white worker from the mass
of the working class.   (See also JOB COLOR BAR; MANUFAC-
TURING INDUSTRY.)

COLOR BAR.   The term has often been used to mean the JOB
    COLOR BAR, racial discrimination in access to employment.
    In Class, Race and Gold (1976), F. R. Johnstone broadened the
    usage and spoke of "exploitation colour bars," which included
    the PASS laws, the COMPOUND SYSTEM and other mechanisms
    to keep African wages low.   He argued that these exploitation
    color bars were more significant than the JOB COLOR BAR,
    for they were the chief guarantor to capital of cheap labor.

"COLOURED" LABOR PREFERENCE POLICY.   The government an-
    nounced in 1954 that workers classified "Coloured" were to be
    given preference over Africans in the western Cape.   It was
    claimed that unskilled "COLOUREDS" were being undercut by
    Africans, who were said to be newcomers in the western Cape
    (they were, but only relatively; there were 10, 000 Africans in
    Cape Town by 1900).   Policy-makers may have thought of a
    time when the western Cape might be a white "HOMELAND"
    (though whites would be outnumbered in it by "Coloureds").   A
    decade later there was a further announcement: the number of
    African workers in the western Cape was to be frozen, and no
    further homes built for them there.   Many Africans living in
    the eastern part of the area began to be moved out of it (see
    MASS REMOVALS), while INFLUX CONTROL was applied ex-
    tremely rigorously in Cape Town, the main magnet for African
    labor.   Employers had to justify hiring Africans rather than
    "Coloureds."   Despite these measures, the number of MIGRANT
    LABORERS in Cape Town increased, and many of them sought
    to settle and bring their families.   Large shanty towns grew up
    on the outskirts of the city.   Some were bulldozed before the
    international attention focussed on CROSSROADS led the govern-
    ment to rehouse its people.   But Africans in the western Cape
    continued to have less assurance of permanent rights than those
    elsewhere; when the government introduced 99-year leasehold
    for urban Africans in the late 1970s, the western Cape was ex-
    cluded from the scheme.

"COLOURED" POLITICS.   In the late 19th century the Cape's non-
    racial FRANCHISE enabled "COLOUREDS" with the necessary
    qualifications to obtain the vote, but they were not active with-
    in the political parties that emerged.   The first "Coloured" po-
    litical organization--an AFRIKANER League--was formed in
    Kimberley in 1883, but the first of importance was the African
    Political (from 1919, People's) Organization (APO), founded in

September 1902.   From 1905 its history was inextricably linked
with the person of Dr ABDURAHMAN, its president for 35
years.   With others, it protested the color bar in the Act of
UNION, but Abdurahman continued to support one or another of
the whites-only political parties, giving his backing in the 1930s
to the UNITED PARTY.   Some young radicals including his own
daughter, Cissie Gool, set up a National Liberation League in
December 1935 which rejected the APO and any involvement
with white politics.   As the Africans lost their common roll
franchise (1936), MALAN and other members of the NATION-
AL PARTY made it clear that they wanted to put the "Coloureds"
on a separate voters roll as well.   In 1939 a draft Cape Provincial Ordinance empowered local authorities to segregate public places; Cissie Gool led a mass protest and it was dropped.
A turning point came in 1943, when the SMUTS government
decided to create a nominated Coloured Advisory Council, which
many "Coloureds" feared would prove the precursor of a Coloured Affairs Department (CAD), which they associated with
second-class citizenship.   Radicals took over the APO, which
expelled those who, believing in a separate "Coloured" identity,
were willing to serve on the new body.   An umbrella Anti-CAD
movement came into being, which drew together all those who
opposed the new council, and adopted a policy of total boycott
of it.   Others, while critical of the council, rejected the tactic
of boycott as negative and worthless.   The Anti-CAD was in
turn affiliated to the NON-EUROPEAN UNITY MOVEMENT.
After the "Coloureds" in the Cape lost their common roll
vote in 1956 (see "COLOURED" VOTE ISSUE), they were given
the right to elect four white members to parliament on a separate roll.   The Anti-CAD movement organized a boycott of
these elections, and relatively few "Coloureds" voted.   Three
years later the anticipated Coloured Affairs Department was
created, with its own Minister of Coloured Affairs.   Some National Party ideologues believed that VERWOERD's SEPARATE
DEVELOPMENT vision could be extended from Africans to
"Coloureds" and they too be given a territorial "HOMELAND."
Though the government rejected this as impractical, it abolished
the representation of "Coloureds" by whites in parliament in
1968 and established a Coloured Persons Representative Council (CRC), which was empowered to administer "Coloured" affairs in such fields as local government, finance, education,
welfare, and pensions.   Once again, those on the left of "Coloured" politics advocated a total boycott of the new institution.
The Labour Party, however, founded in 1965, agreed to contest
elections to the CRC, though rejecting the body as an apartheid
creation, and announcing its intention of working to close it
down.   In the first CRC election in September 1969 Labour
gained a majority of the 40 elected seats, but the twenty nominated members kept it from power.   In the 1975 election there
was a very low poll, but Labour won 31 seats and an absolute
majority on the council.   It then refused to appropriate budget
moneys and a government nominee was made chairman of the
executive.   This proved unworkable and the CRC was disbanded.

By that time the government had decided that the "Coloureds" were to be brought within the central political system in some way and the Presidents' Council--in which the Labour Party refused to participate because it excluded Africans--was given the task of working out some form of incorporation which would not threaten white supremacy (see CONSTITUTIONAL CHANGE).

"COLOURED" VOTE ISSUE (1951-1956). The NATIONAL PARTY's desire to remove the "COLOUREDS" from the common voters' roll produced a major constitutional crisis in the early 1950s. MALAN was given legal advice that he could remove the "Coloureds" to a separate roll by a simple majority vote in the House of Assembly, despite the entrenchment of the Cape FRANCHISE in the constitution, because the Statute of Westminster (1931) had given South Africa sovereign independence. A Separate Representation of Voters Act was passed in 1951, putting the "Coloured" voters on a separate roll, with power to elect four white members to the Assembly, one to the Senate and two to the Cape Provincial Council. Four "Coloured" voters then contested the Act, and the Appellate Division of the Supreme Court ruled in 1952 that despite the Statute of Westminster an amendment of the entrenched clauses still required a two-thirds majority of a joint sitting of both Houses of Parliament. As the National Party did not have such a two-thirds majority, an Act was passed setting up parliament as a High Court to review cases in which legislation was declared invalid. This too was struck down by the Appellate Division. The matter then became an issue in the 1953 general election. The National Party won an increased majority but still did not have the necessary two-thirds. An attempt to persuade UNITED PARTY members to support a compromise Bill failed. Malan's successor, STRIJDOM, then proceeded both to increase the number of appeal judges needed to hear constitutional issues and to enlarge the Senate from 49 to 89 members. In the new Senate 77 of the 89 seats were held by Nationalists. The necessary two-thirds majority was then obtained, and the "Coloureds" removed from the common voters' roll (1956).

"COLOUREDS." In the early 19th century Cape whites distinguished themselves from "people of color." This category included FREE BLACKS, KHOIKHOI and people of mixed descent, but not Africans, then not found within the Cape Colony in any number. Long before they were classified by APARTHEID laws as nonwhite, non-African, and non-Asian, people of mixed descent regarded themselves as "Cape Coloureds," or were called by whites "Cape boys." An attempt by the African People's Organisation (see "COLOURED" POLITICS) to popularize the term "Eurafrican" failed. In 1911 the Cape Supreme Court found that there was no clear way in which whites and light-skinned "Coloureds" could be distinguished. With the implementation of APARTHEID, a Population Registration Act (1950) emphasized association and ancestry rather than color to establish who was "Coloured." Those classified in that way increasingly came to identify themselves as "so-called Coloureds," members of the black oppressed. Apartheid legislation recognized Malays (see ISLAM) and GRIQUAS as separate sub-groups among the "Coloureds."

The "Coloureds" emerged, then, from the intermixing of the 18th century, from MISCEGENATION between whites (not all of whom were passing sailors, as would be later alleged), slaves, and Khoisan peoples. As Africans became incorporated in the colonial society in the 19th century, "Coloureds," speaking the same languages as whites (more Afrikaans than English), found that they occupied an intermediate position, a middle role in the racial hierarchy. Compared to Africans, they were relatively privileged; they did not have to carry PASSES (see ORDINANCE 50) and could enter the cities as they wished. Light-skinned "Coloureds" were able to "pass" into white society. But the Cape School Board Act of 1905 had the effect of excluding most "Coloureds" from the new system of general public education, while other forms of segregation were dictated by social convention rather than law.

White supremacists divided on whether the "Coloureds" belonged on the white or African side of the main racial divide. HERTZOG was prepared to accept them as allies of the whites against the SWART GEVAAR ("African menace") and advocate a measure of assimilation. But after 1948 the whites distanced themselves from the "Coloureds," who were stripped of their common roll vote (see "COLOURED" VOTE ISSUE), forced to live in their own GROUP AREAS, and humiliated through a wide range of PETTY APARTHEID regulations. Whites on the far right even spoke of finding a "HOMELAND" for them. The more conservative "Coloureds" continued to emphasize their "Coloured" identity and their cultural and biological links with whites, but younger ones joined Africans in mass protest at the time of the SOWETO REVOLT. After that, the governing party moved slowly to reincorporate the "Coloureds" in some new way within the political process (see "COLOURED" POLITICS; CONSTITUTIONAL CHANGE).

In the mid 20th century nine-tenths of "Coloureds" lived in the Cape Province, one third in the Cape Peninsula itself, though in the late 1970s there was a considerable movement of "Coloureds" to the Transvaal, where prospects were brighter than in the Cape. Many of the elite "Coloured" families left for Australia or Canada in the decades after SHARPEVILLE, during which "Coloureds" suffered immensely from the implementation of the GROUP AREAS ACT in particular. There was much poverty among the 2.5 million "Coloureds" in 1982, especially in the rural areas, where long traditions of servility remained unbroken.

COMMANDOS. As white settlement moved away from Cape Town, FREEBURGHERS began to organize their own mounted militia units and these were officially sanctioned by the DUTCH EAST INDIA COMPANY in 1715. The Company supplied ammunition to the commandos, whose service was unpaid. Under the command of elected leaders, the farmers undertook expeditions, often punitive in character, against SAN, KHOISAN, and then, from the late 18th century, BANTU-SPEAKING people. The San were hunted down like vermin. The commandos on their own were unable to dislodge the Khoisan groups from the Sneeuberge and Nieuwveldberge in the last quarter of the 18th century, or the Bantu-speakers from the ZUURVELD; in both cases it was only BRITISH aid that established white supremacy. In the late 1830s the VOORTREKKERS took the commando system into the interior, where it was used extensively against African enemies. In 1880-1881, and again in 1899-1902, commandos fought the British in the TRANSVAAL WAR OF INDE-PENDENCE and then the SOUTH AFRICAN WAR. In the 20th century the commando was seen in new guises, in the RAND REVOLT and the TORCH COMMANDO. Local citizen units in the South African Defence Force were known as commandos.

COMMONWEALTH. South Africa played an important role in the evolution of the British Empire into the Commonwealth. It was largely in response to pressure from HERTZOG that the Imperial conference of 1926 declared that Britain and the Dominions, including South Africa, were "autonomous communities within the British Empire, equal in status, in no way subordinate the one to the other in any aspect of their internal or external affairs." South Africa then adopted its own nationality and flag (see FLAG CONTROVERSY). Though Hertzog favored South Africa becoming a REPUBLIC, he did not consider that practical politics. Once South Africa took full power to alter or amend any legislation by the Status of the Union Act (1934), he accepted the relationship with Britain, and on that basis entered FUSION. In the NATIONAL PARTY under MALAN there was strong support for a republic, eventually achieved under VERWOERD in 1961.

After the white voters had voted in favor of a republic, Verwoerd went, as he had promised he would, to the Commonwealth Prime Ministers' conference in London in March 1961 to ask that South Africa remain a member of the Commonwealth after the change in status. But when it became clear that South Africa's continued membership would result in others leaving the Commonwealth, he formally withdrew South Africa's application. From 31 May 1961, when it became a republic, South Africa ceased to be a member of the Commonwealth. Its departure was a major step towards greater international isolation, and South Africa gradually lost its privileged access to markets in Britain. But when Verwoerd returned from the London conference, he told his supporters that the country's exclusion had been a miracle willed by God, and many of them rejoiced in what had happened.

COMMUNIST PARTY OF SOUTH AFRICA (CP). Founded in July 1921 as a result of the amalgamation of the International Socialist League, which had been formed by those who broke with the LABOUR PARTY in 1915 over its support for the war effort, and other left groups. A section of the Communist International, the CP from the beginning maintained relatively close links with Moscow. During the RAND REVOLT, some of its members attempted to combine radicalism and racialism, their slogan in support of the strikers being "Workers of the World Unite and Fight for a White South Africa." Three communists on the executive of the INDUSTRIAL AND COMMERCIAL WORKERS UNION were expelled in 1926, but the communists won recruits in the AFRICAN NATIONAL CONGRESS in the late 1920s before it too swung to the right. The party had only 200 African members in 1927, 1,600 in 1928, out of a total membership of 1,750. Orders then came from Moscow that it should work for a "Native Republic" in South Africa. S. P. Bunting (1873-1936), the general secretary, and other leading white members opposed the new policy because they still hoped to radicalize the white working class and make it the vanguard of a class-conscious proletariat. But Bunting's group was expelled from the party as deviationists (1931) and the party committed itself to what it termed "national liberation." In the 1930s it did pioneering work in organizing African workers. Some of its African members served on the executive of the ANC. Africans were to elect three white communists to parliament as "Native Representatives" (see FRANCHISE), two of whom were prevented from taking their seats.

The Suppression of Communism Act (1950), progressively tightened up in later years, and renamed the Internal Security Act in 1976, included a very wide definition of communism: it was any doctrine aiming at political, industrial, social, or economic change by, or partly by, promoting disturbances or disorder or unlawful acts. The Minister of Justice was given wide power under the Act to name members of unlawful organizations, and to prohibit such persons from belonging to any other political or trade union organization. Knowing that it would be declared unlawful under this Act, the CP went underground (1950). Its newspaper, The Guardian, which had appeared in Cape Town from 1937, was suppressed, but reappeared under new names until finally extinguished in 1963. Many members of the CP were active in the Congress of Democrats, formed for white sympathizers of the other congresses (see CONGRESS ALLIANCE) in the 1950s. In the early 1960s the SECURITY POLICE infiltrated the leadership of the underground CP and a number of its officials were tried and convicted (see FISCHER). In exile, leading members of the tightly-knit party, which continued to adopt a strongly pro-Soviet line, served on the executive of UMKHONTO WE SIZWE and helped co-ordinate the ANC's military strategy. From its exile base in London, the party published The African Communist.

COMPOUND SYSTEM. The compound system introduced on the Kimberley DIAMOND fields in 1885 was an extended variant on the use of prison labor from the Kimberley convict station. Between 1885 and 1889 the bulk of the African mine labor force of 10,000 men was placed in twelve large closed compounds, in which they had to remain for the six to twelve months they

stayed at the mines. The mineowners justified the system as a
measure to prevent the theft of diamonds, and argued that the
miner would save more and return home with a larger proportion of their earnings. But the compound system also served
other purposes: it gave the mineowners total control over the
laborers, who could be forced to undertake underground work,
which many tried to resist. Before laborers were allowed to
leave, they were stripped naked and searched.

On the Witwatersrand GOLD mines, CHINESE and then African workers were required to live in large barrack-like, single-
sex hostels for the duration of their contracts. Theft was not a
problem, and these hostels were not totally closed as at Kimberley. The early ones were extremely spartan, with the workers sleeping on double-decker concrete bunks. As at Kimberley, the compounds served to limit the workers' independence,
isolate them from other workers and the society around them,
and give the mineowners maximum control of the labor-force
If the laborers struck, the compounds could be surrounded and
they then became virtual prisons.

The term "compound" was also used more loosely from the
late 19th century to include any living quarters for a number of
African workers, whether or not there were any restrictions or
controls over the residents. In Cape Town, for example, there
was at the beginning of the early 20th century a large harbor
compound, as well as other, smaller "compounds" housing African workers for private concerns.

CONCENTRATION CAMPS. During the last quarter of 1900, in an
attempt to bring the SOUTH AFRICAN WAR to a conclusion, the
British began to herd both Afrikaners and Africans into concentration camps. With their women and children forced from the
farms into camps, it was hoped the guerillas in the field would
surrender. Many of the over 40 camps for whites had not been
properly prepared to receive their inmates, and disease spread
rapidly. Almost 28,000 died in these camps, including more than
22,000 children under the age of 16. This loss of life did much
to bring the Boers to negotiate in 1902. It also left an indelible
scar on the Afrikaner consciousness.

Africans, too, were cleared from the countryside to prevent
the Boer COMMANDOS receiving assistance and supplies. Over
100,000 African refugees were placed in 66 camps, half in the
Transvaal, half in the ORANGE RIVER COLONY. Over 14,000
deaths were recorded in these very over-crowded and often un-
sanitary camps.

(In the two World Wars "enemy aliens" and those suspected
of working to subvert the war effort were placed in internment
camps. Those interned during World War II included John
VORSTER.)

CONFEDERATION. Sir George GREY was the first to advocate, in
the late 1850s, a federal South Africa. In 1867 Lord Carnarvon
(Henry Molyneux Herbert, 1831-1890), as British Colonial Secretary, steered the British North America Act through the

British parliament. On becoming Colonial Secretary again in 1874, he hoped he could do for South Africa what he had done for Canada. Until recently it was argued that Carnarvon's search for political unity in South Africa was motivated by strategic considerations relating to the defense of the British Empire; he hoped that a self-governing white-ruled, united South Africa within the Empire would be able to defend itself, while guaranteeing British control of the sea-route to India. In the mid 1970s considerable evidence was brought forward to show that among Carnarvon's advisers were men, most notably SHEPSTONE, concerned to promote South Africa's economic development in the new age ushered in by the discovery of DIAMONDS, and in particular to secure a regular flow of MIGRANT LABOR.

Carnarvon first attempted to arrange a conference at which representatives of the various white South African states would meet to discuss political unity. When this proved a failure, he authorized Shepstone to annex the Transvaal, sent out FRERE as the new HIGH COMMISSIONER to bring about confederation, and carried legislation permitting such a confederation through the British parliament in 1877. But Carnarvon resigned from the Disraeli government early the following year over the Eastern Question involving Russia and Turkey. The search for a confederation continued under his successor, but the ZULU defeat of British arms at Isandhlwana in January 1879 was one major setback, the Cape parliament's rejection of the idea in June 1880--after which FRERE was recalled--another. When the Transvalers rose in revolt later in 1880 (see TRANS-VAAL WAR OF INDEPENDENCE) the hopes of achieving confederation were finally laid to rest. Circumstances just were not propitious for it in the 1870s, but the attempt to bring it about did much to transform South Africa. It was to be another thirty years before the goal was won (see UNION).

CONGRESS ALLIANCE. Joint opposition front of congresses of Africans (the AFRICAN NATIONAL CONGRESS), Indians, "Coloureds" and whites (the Congress of Democrats, for which see COMMUNIST PARTY). From early 1955 it also included the SOUTH AFRICAN CONGRESS OF TRADE UNIONS and the FEDERATION OF SOUTH AFRICAN WOMEN. Its activities culminated in a Congress of the People, held on 26 and 27 June 1955 at Kliptown south of Johannesburg. Some 3,000 attended, and the FREEDOM CHARTER was adopted clause by clause. Many of the leading figures involved were subsequently charged with high treason (see TREASON TRIAL).

CONQUERED TERRITORY. Name given to the lands west of the Caledon River which were conquered by the Free State from Moshweshwe's SOTHO in the war of 1865-66 (see BASUTOLAND). Boer COMMANDOS destroyed the Sotho crop and forced the Sotho to yield over half their arable land. The result was that the Sotho were confined to a largely mountainous territory east of the Caledon, while the Free State

obtained the most fertile strip of land within its borders. In
the 1970s LESOTHO took its claim to this territory to the
UNITED NATIONS, but its extreme dependence on South Africa
made it unable to press the claim.

CONSERVATIVE PARTY (1982-). Party formed by Andries
TREURNICHT and his supporters after they had broken with the
NATIONAL PARTY in March 1982. The new party took up an
ideological position between that of the NP and that of the
HERSTIGTE NASIONALE PARTY. Among its supporters was
Dr Mulder (see MULDERGATE).

CONSTITUTIONAL CHANGE. In terms of the South Africa Act,
passed by the British parliament in 1909, South Africa became
a unitary state with a Westminster-style constitution. Parliamentary power was virtually unlimited, though the equality of
the two official languages and the franchise rights of black voters in the Cape were entrenched and could be altered only by
agreement of two-thirds of the members of both Houses of
Parliament--the Assembly and the Senate--sitting together.
The Prime Minister, the leader of the majority party in the
Assembly, formed his cabinet--the executive--from among his
supporters in parliament. A Governor-General was formal
head of the executive. In the four provinces (the four colonies
before Union), provincial councils had limited areas of responsibility, and no ordinance made by them had effect if repugnant
to an Act of Parliament.
    All members of parliament had to be "of European descent,"
i. e. whites. Members of the House of Assembly were elected
on a one member per constituency, winner-take-all system;
senators were mostly elected by members of the Assembly and
provincial councillors. By the South Africa Act, the constitution of the Senate could not be altered for ten years. In 1926
the PACT GOVERNMENT, which did not have a majority in the
upper House, provided that the Senate should be dissolved at the
same time as, or shortly after, the Assembly. This ensured that
the government of the day would have a majority in the upper
House. At the time of the constitutional crisis over the "COL-
OURED" VOTE ISSUE, the Senate was enlarged (1955) to give
the government a two-thirds majority of both houses sitting together; its size was reduced again in 1960.
    Thanks to redefinition of the imperial relationship, in which
HERTZOG played a major role, the Union parliament took the
power to alter or repeal British legislation applicable to South
Africa, including the South Africa Act itself (Status Act, 1934),
after which the Hertzog government claimed equality with Britain
as a member of the COMMONWEALTH.
    The REPUBLIC Constitution Act (1961) retained the constitu-
tional framework of the South Africa Act, merely changing the
name of the country to "Republic" and creating the new office
of State President to take over the duties of the British sovereign and the Governor-General. The State President was
elected by members of the legislature, and was therefore the

nominee of the majority party.

Parliament's importance declined in the years after 1948.
Debates often had little influence on legislation, and the executive was given a vast array of discretionary powers.   Parliament was not recalled when the SOWETO REVOLT occurred.
And executive power was extended beyond the cabinet: a National Security Council, established in 1972 to advise on security matters and including military and other officials as well as
parliamentarians, became increasingly important in decision-
making.

From the mid 1970s there was much talk about the inappro-
priateness of a Westminster-style constitution for South Africa.
In 1977 the government put forward proposals for a new constitution, which were submitted to and approved by the NATIONAL
PARTY.   They provided for three separate parliaments for
whites, "Coloureds" and Indians (African aspirations were supposed to be met through SEPARATE DEVELOPMENT).   The
maintenance of white domination was to be secured by the device
of a powerful "cabinet council" on which whites would have an
ensured majority.   A parliamentary committee was then given
the task of considering constitutional reform.   In 1980, following its recommendations, the Senate was abolished and an advisory President's Council established, on which nominated
whites, "Coloureds" and Indians served.   The constitutional
proposals were then referred to this Council, which reported
on them in May 1982 (see also COMMONWEALTH; FRANCHISE).

CORY, George Edward (1862-1935).   Historian of the 1820 BRITISH
settlers.   Educated at Cambridge, he went to South Africa in
1891 as vice principal of Grahamstown Public School and was
Professor of Chemistry at Rhodes UNIVERSITY College from
1904 until his retirement in 1925.   His multi-volume history of
the British settlers was misleadingly entitled The Rise of South
Africa; volume 6 was published posthumously.

COTTESLOE CONSULTATION.   A closed meeting of church leaders
organized by the World Council of Churches and held in December 1960 in the aftermath of SHARPEVILLE.   The Cape and
Transvaal DUTCH REFORMED CHURCH (DRC) delegations accepted the final statement, which rejected unjust racial discrimination and spoke of the need for consultation between all on
matters of common concern.   But VERWOERD and conservatives
within the DRC rallied that church to reject the statement, after
which the DRC left the World Council of Churches.   (See also
Beyers NAUDE; Andries TREURNICHT.)

CRESWELL, Frederic Hugh Page (1866-1948).   Labor leader.
Trained as a mining engineer in England, he arrived in South
Africa in 1893 and became a mine manager.   After the SOUTH
AFRICAN WAR he was the main champion of a white labor policy on the GOLD mines, attempting unsuccessfully to put this
into practice at the Village Main Reef mine.   Elected to the
first Union parliament, he became leader of the new LABOUR

PARTY. After World War I, during which he gave full support
to the war effort and saw Labour split, he grew increasingly
friendly with HERTZOG. This led to an understanding between
them in 1922 to form a joint opposition against SMUTS. In
1923 a PACT was announced and when the Pact came to power
in 1924 Creswell became Minister of Labor and of Defence.
When he opposed the right of the National Congress of his party
to dictate policy to the members of parliament, he was ousted
as leader, but Hertzog kept him in his cabinet until coalition
with Smuts in 1933.

CROSSROADS. A squatter town which grew up near CAPE TOWN's
main airport in the mid 1970s, and received international attention in 1978 when the police raided it and there were fears it
would be bulldozed, as other nearby shanty towns had been. It
came to symbolize the failure of the government's attempt,
through INFLUX CONTROL, to prevent African families becoming new permanent settlers in the greater Cape Town area.
Many MIGRANT workers, wishing to live with their families
but unable to find suitable accommodation in the LOCATIONS,
built their own homes made of corrugated iron and hessian
(coarse cloth) at Crossroads. After international attention had
been focussed on its 20,000 residents, the cabinet minister responsible visited the area and forestalled its demolition. It was
then agreed to build a new African township for those Crossroads families whose breadwinners were legal residents or gain-
fully employed. The government made it clear that it regarded
this departure from previous policy as a special case, and influx control was applied with greater rigor than ever from 1979
on. (See also "COLOURED" LABOR PREFERENCE POLICY.)

DE BEERS CONSOLIDATED MINES. Nicholaas de Beer (1830-before
1894) was the farmer who owned the land on which the Kimberley and De Beers DIAMOND mines were discovered. Bought
from De Beer by a syndicate of merchants and members of the
Cape parliament, the land was later taken over by the government of Griqualand West. A De Beers Company was formed by
Cecil RHODES in 1880 with an issued capital of £200,000. By
1885 it had capital of almost £850,000 through consolidation of
claims in the De Beers mine. With a loan of £1 million from
the Rothschilds, Rhodes then bought a large holding in the Kimberley mine. De Beers Consolidated was formed in 1888, and
by 1891 had effective control of the industry. De Beers then
made an agreement with a powerful group of dealers, the Diamond Syndicate, who bought the entire output. From 1902 profits from sales were divided between De Beers and the Syndicate.
    Having a monopoly on production, De Beers could control the
output to avoid over-production and so to realize high prices.
It bought up land it thought might contain diamonds, fearing a
major new source of supply it could not control. In 1902 the
Premier Diamond Mine was formed to exploit the rich Cullinan

mine near Pretoria. Competition from that source hurt De
Beers, especially in the recession of 1907-08. Rich alluvial
discoveries in German South West Africa (NAMIBIA) also undermined its monopoly. But by the end of World War I De Beers
had bought a controlling holding in the Premier Diamond Mines,
and in the early 1920s Ernest Oppenheimer (1880-1957), chairman of the holding company ANGLO-AMERICAN, gained control
of the South West mines. In the 1930s the producers themselves
took over the distribution and marketing of diamonds through the
London-based Central Selling Organisation.

DEFIANCE CAMPAIGN. Civil disobedience campaign launched by
the AFRICAN NATIONAL CONGRESS (ANC) and the South African INDIAN Congress on 26 June 1952. The two congresses
called for the defiance of laws relating to PASSES, GROUP
AREAS, separate representation, and Bantu Authorities (see
BANTUSTANS), and also for the ending of "land rehabilitation"
schemes, which involved the culling of cattle. The defiers were
to court arrest and so clog the judicial machinery that the system would break down. Of the 8,500 protestors arrested, most
were Africans, but they included some Indians and "Coloureds"
and a few whites (see Patrick DUNCAN). The government's
response was to pass a Criminal Laws Amendment Act (1953)
which prescribed severe penalties for breaking laws by way of
protest. When some demonstrators, accused of occupying prem-
ises reserved for whites, won cases in the Supreme Court on
the grounds that separate facilities were not equal, the government passed a Separate Amenities Act (1953) which explicitly
provided that separate facilities need not be equal. A number
of the leaders of the campaign were BANNED. Though the campaign increased repression, it did raise the ANC to new heights
of prestige, and it helped stimulate the establishment of both the
CONGRESS ALLIANCE and the LIBERAL PARTY.
    For the Gandhian ideas on which the campaign was based,
see under INDIANS.

DE KIEWIET, Cornelis (1903-). Taken to South Africa from Holland when young, he studied at the University of the Witwatersrand in the early 1920s, where he fell under the influence of
W. M. MACMILLAN, for whom he worked on the PHILIP papers.
Against Macmillan's advice that he study South Africa's social
and economic history, he went to London to work on imperial
policy, work that led to British Colonial Policy and the South
African Republics and then The Imperial Factor in South Africa,
which carried the story from the early 1870s to the mid 1880s.
Taking a teaching post in the United States, De Kiewiet was cut
off from South African materials, but did write his History of
South Africa Social and Economic (1941), a masterly survey. A
greater stylist than Macmillan, his History made him even more
influential than his mentor. In later life he was a university
administrator in America, and in 1982 he was living in retirement in Washington, D. C.

DELAGOA BAY.   The PORTUGUESE traded from the shores of this
excellent natural harbor, on which today Maputo, capital of
MOZAMBIQUE, is situated, from the 1540s.   Trading routes
ran from the Bay to the mining areas of the eastern Transvaal
and the elephant hunting lands of present Natal.   Some historians believe that trade with Delagoa Bay above all explains that
process of political centralization leading to the emergence of
the ZULU kingdom.   An exploratory trek, sent out from the
Cape under Louis Trichardt in 1834 to investigate conditions in
the interior, eventually reached Delagoa Bay, where most of
the party died of fever (GREAT TREK).   Britain disputed ownership of the Bay area with Portugal; the French President decided in Portugal's favor in 1875.   The Transvaal government
then made an agreement with Portugal for a RAILROAD to link
the Bay with the WITWATERSRAND.   After the discovery of
GOLD, this idea was revived, and the line completed in 1895.
Until the mid 1970s it was used to transport large numbers of
Mozambican MIGRANT LABORERS to the mines.   In the 20th
century much of the Witwatersrand's exports left southern
Africa via Lourenço Marques, the later Maputo.

DETENTION WITHOUT TRIAL.   Its history in South Africa goes
back at least as far as the famous diarist Adam Tas (1668-
1722), who was arrested in 1706 for criticizing the DUTCH
EAST INDIA COMPANY officials at the Cape.   During both
world wars active supporters of Germany were interned without trial.   But it was not until the 1960s that detention without
trial became part of the ordinary law of the land.
      In the aftermath of SHARPEVILLE a state of emergency was
proclaimed and almost 20,000 persons detained (1,800 political
detainees, 18,000 so-called "idlers").   VORSTER, Minister of
Justice from 1961, introduced detention without trial as a rou-
tine measure, and allowed the SECURITY POLICE latitude in
its use.   The time limit for such detention was first set at 12
days.   Then an Act of 1963 allowed police officers without warrant to arrest and detain persons for up to 90 days at a time
if they suspected them of committing, intending to commit, or
having information about, a specified range of political offenses.
Ninety-day detainees were often redetained when the first period
was up.   They were subjected to solitary confinement and there
was no judicial review of any kind.   Only some were subsequently charged and tried.   The maximum period was extended
to 180 days at a time in 1965.   The legal charade of "releasing" detainees every 180 days and immediately redetaining them
was largely ended by the Terrorism Act of 1967 which gave the
police power to detain indefinitely for interrogation (section 6).
Between 1967 and the end of 1981 over 4,000 people were detained under that Act.   An Internal Security Act of 1976 sanctioned preventive detention of anyone whose activities were, in
the government's opinion, thought to endanger the security of
the state or the maintenance of public order.   Such powers were
a constant threat to any who contemplated extra-parliamentary

opposition, and the government's use of them drove such opposition underground and helped crush it.

Detainees frequently alleged torture, inquests revealed injuries, and in the period 1963 to 1977 at least 44 people detained for political reasons died while in police custody. The outcry over the brutal treatment of Steve BIKO by the police in 1977 seems to have led to instructions being given them that further deaths should be avoided. But another political detainee died in 1978, and in February 1982 Neil Aggett, a prominent white trade union official, died in detention.

DIAMONDS. Alluvial diamonds were found along the ORANGE RIVER in 1867, but it was not until 1870 that digging began in the great pipes of blue ground running into the earth at what developed into the town of Kimberley. Work began on the Kimberley mine itself, soon the richest diamond mine in the world, in mid 1871.

Ownership of the fields was much disputed. The Orange Free State, the Transvaal and the GRIQUA state ruled by Nicolaas Waterboer (c. 1820-c. 1885) all claimed the area. Waterboer's agent David Arnot (1821-1894) had for years been pressing flimsy Griqua claims with great skill. In October 1871 the British HIGH COMMISSIONER extended British protection to the Griqua and annexed the diamond fields. With the Cape unwilling to assume the burden of ruling them, they became the separate Crown Colony of Griqualand West. The Free State was compensated by a cash payment of £90,000 in 1876--which was also an unsuccessful bribe to get BRAND to discuss CONFEDERATION --and in 1880 the Cape was finally persuaded to incorporate Griqualand West.

In the first years of digging, the ground extracted was loaded onto buckets, hauled out and dry-sorted. But accumulation of water in the 3,000 small claims, and the collapse of the reef, soon created problems. From the mid-1870s amalgamation of claims began to take place on a large scale. The steam machinery used from the late 1870s required considerable capital, while falling prices--initially because demand dropped with the great depression from 1873, but in the early 1880s because of overproduction--intensified competition among those with capital, and led to further amalgamation. By 1888, when DE BEERS CONSOLIDATED MINES was formed, underground mining had become the norm. In 1891 De Beers finally won control of all the Kimberley mines. As other diamond mines were discovered --in the Transvaal and then South West Africa--De Beers sought to control them as well, and was ultimately successful in that aim. By 1936 diamonds valued at over £320 million had been produced.

South Africa's first industrial community, Kimberley suddenly acquired 50,000 people, and by 1872 was second only to Cape Town in size in the sub-continent. Some 13,000 whites employed over twice that number of African laborers, who journeyed to the fields from as far away as the PEDI country of the northeastern Transvaal or the DELAGOA BAY hinterland (see THONGA). At Kimberley Africans worked long enough to

earn a rifle before returning home (see MIGRANT LABOR).
Africans living closer, such as the southern SOTHO, supplied
the mines with foodstuffs, and peasant production of cereals in
BASUTOLAND in particular boomed. Extensive illicit diamond
buying on the fields was used to deny Africans, who were
blamed for it, their own claims. The few diggers who were
not white were soon put out of business. A strict PASS LAW
was introduced as early as 1872 to control the African labor
force on the fields. A much tighter system of control was
instituted through the COMPOUND SYSTEM of the mid 1880s.
   Capital accumulation on the diamond fields made possible the
rapid exploitation of the GOLD of the WITWATERSRAND; many
of the RANDLORDS had links to Kimberley. The discovery of
diamonds did not merely transform a backward, poverty-stricken
part of the interior; it brought new prosperity to the ports that
served the fields--Cape Town, Port Elizabeth--and pulled RAIL-
ROADS into the interior. (See also CONFEDERATION.)

DIFAQANE see MFECANE.

DISTRICT SIX. The sixth district in the municipality of CAPE
   TOWN, it lay on the slopes of Devil's Peak overlooking Table
   Bay harbor and was in the early 20th century the most multi-
   racial residential area in South Africa. After the passage of
   the GROUP AREAS ACT (1950) there was uncertainty about its
   future, and it grew increasingly squalid. In 1966 it was declared a white area under that Act. It then had about 30,000
   "Coloured" people living in it, 1,300 Indians and 600 "others."
   Despite much protest, and continued opposition from the Cape
   Town City Council, the MASS REMOVAL of these people began
   in 1968, and the demolition of the houses they vacated. By
   early 1982 all but a few families had been forced out of the
   area, 40,000 people had been resettled on the Cape Flats, on
   the outskirts of the city, and District Six resembled a waste-
   land. Immense bitterness had been caused, especially among
   "Coloureds," who had had great sentimental attachment to the
   area.

DITHAKONG, battle of (1823) see GRIQUA; MANTATEES;
   MFECANE; TSWANA.

DOMINION PARTY. Founded in 1934 by C. F. Stallard (1871-1971) (cf.
   STALLARD DOCTRINE) and a group of ENGLISH-SPEAKING
   Natalians who would not follow SMUTS into FUSION. They
   mistrusted HERTZOG's "South Africa First" policy and believed that FUSION endangered the imperial connection. They
   voted against the HERTZOG BILLS on African land and FRAN-
   CHISE in 1936 and supported Smuts in 1939 over the question
   of entering WORLD WAR II. Largely NATAL-based, the
   Dominion Party marked a reversion to the earlier UNIONIST
   approach.

DRAKENSBERG (Afrikaans: "dragon mountain"). To BANTU-

SPEAKING peoples the spectacular central portion of this 650
mile long chain, which reaches over 11,000 feet, was known
as the Qathlamba, "the mountain of spears." These mountains
separate the coastal corridor from the interior plateau or highveld (see VELD), the NGUNI-speaking peoples from the SOTHO-
speakers. But only in their central portion, which today divides
LESOTHO both from the TRANSKEI and from NATAL, and again
in the eastern Transvaal, are they a very formidable barrier.
Where today they form the boundary between the Orange Free
State and Natal, they were relatively easy to cross, whether by
those scattered by the MFECANE in the early 1820s, or by the
VOORTREKKERS moving in the opposite direction in 1837. SAN
retreated into these mountains; LANGALIBALELE fled into them
in 1873; and they were the scene of fighting in both the TRANS-
VAAL WAR OF INDEPENDENCE and the SOUTH AFRICAN WAR.

DU TOIT, S.J. (1847-1911) see AFRIKAANS; AFRIKANER BOND.

DUBE, John Langalibalele (1871-1946). "Mafukuzela" (Zulu: "he
who struggles against obstacles") was the first president-general
of the AFRICAN NATIONAL CONGRESS (ANC). The son of one
of the first ordained pastors of the American Board ZULU mission, he was educated in Natal and the United States. After becoming a Congregational minister, he established the Ohlange
Institute, modelled on Booker T. Washington's Tuskegee, in the
Inanda district of Natal. Like Washington, Dube stressed the
virtues of thrift, industry, education, and capital accumulation.
In 1903 he launched Natal's first African newspaper, Ilanga lase
Natal, and remained its editor until 1915. He went on deputa-
tions to London to protest the South Africa Act (1909) and the
NATIVES LAND ACT (1914). Though he resigned as President-
general of the ANC in 1917, he ran the Natal branch of Congress
until 1945. He was increasingly seen as a conservative figure,
closely linked to the Zulu royal house, spurning the ICU and opposing radicals in the ANC. Elected to the executive committee
of the ALL-AFRICAN CONVENTION (1935), he was the target of
widespread criticism when he supported the HERTZOG BILLS on
the grounds that they would enlarge the RESERVES. He represented Natal on the NATIVES REPRESENTATIVE COUNCIL from
its establishment (1937) until his death.

DUNCAN, Patrick (1870-1943). Civil servant, politician and governor-
general. MILNER, for whom Duncan had worked in London after leaving Oxford, called him out to South Africa in 1901 to
help in the reconstruction of the Transvaal after the SOUTH
AFRICAN WAR (see KINDERGARTEN). From 1903 to 1907
Duncan was an efficient Colonial Secretary for the Transvaal.
Then, while a lawyer in Johannesburg and leading figure in the
PROGRESSIVE PARTY, he campaigned for UNION, serving as
legal adviser to the Transvaal delegates to the NATIONAL CON-
VENTION. He sat in Parliament as a UNIONIST for ten years,
then as a minister in SMUTS' cabinet of 1920-24 was one of the
Prime Minister's chief advisers. He played a leading role in

the events leading to coalition, FUSION and the founding of the
UNITED PARTY in 1934. Appointed Minister of Mines and Public Works in the coalition cabinet of 1933, he left the cabinet
when appointed Governor-General in November 1936, the first
South African to hold that post. On 4 September 1939 he refused HERTZOG's request that he dissolve parliament and call
an election, and instead asked Smuts to form a cabinet. He
believed that in the circumstances parliament, and not the white
electorate, should decide on South African participation in
WORLD WAR II.

DUNCAN, Patrick (1918-1967). Educated at Winchester and Oxford,
son of a governor-general (see Patrick DUNCAN, 1870-1943),
this man of passionately-held beliefs resigned from the British
Colonial Service in BASUTOLAND in 1952 to join the DEFIANCE
CAMPAIGN and put into practice his Gandhian beliefs. On
crutches, he led the defiers through the gate of the Germiston
location east of Johannesburg, was arrested and served time in
jail. A strong anti-communist, he then became national organizer for the LIBERAL PARTY, and editor of its unofficial
journal Contact. In late March 1960 he played a critical role
in defusing tension between the police and the leaders of a
PAN-AFRICANIST CONGRESS-organized march by over 20,000
Africans on Cape Town. He was BANNED soon after, but later
escaped to Basutoland, resigned from the Liberal Party, and
worked for the PAC in its Dar es Salaam and Algiers offices,
its only white member.

DURBAN. White settlement began at the large natural harbor
known as Port NATAL in 1824, when a small party from the
eastern Cape arrived to trade. Gradually a city, called after
Sir Benjamin D'Urban (1777-1849), governor of the Cape in the
mid 1830s, grew up round the bay. When it received its municipal charter in 1854 it contained 1200 whites and fewer Africans. In the early 1870s Theophilus SHEPSTONE introduced
an early form of INFLUX CONTROL: Africans were to wear
badges and be registered; violators were to be banished from
the town. Durban's importance as a port was vastly increased
by the discovery of GOLD in the Transvaal, and the building of
the RAILROAD which by the mid 1890s linked it to the WIT-
WATERSRAND. In the 20th century it handled more cargo each
year than any other South African port. By mid century, when
its population comprised Africans, Indians and whites in almost
equal numbers, it was the country's third largest city, and attracted large numbers of tourists to its famous beaches.

DURBAN RIOTS (1949). A minor incident involving an INDIAN shop
assistant and an African boy led to a riot in which 142 people
were officially reported dead (87 Africans, 50 Indians, 1 white,
4 unidentified). Over 1,000 persons were injured and many
buildings, especially Indian shops, destroyed. Africans re-
sented the Indians' dominant role in commerce, their freedom
from PASS laws and their ability to buy white man's liquor.

Whites said the riots showed the need for further URBAN SEG-
REGATION, and government spokesmen used them to justify the
GROUP AREAS ACT. In the aftermath, the AFRICAN NATION-
AL CONGRESS and the Indian National Congress, which had
formed a pact in 1947, agreed to work more closely together.

DURBAN SYSTEM. A system of urban African administration pioneered in DURBAN, the key element in which was the financing
of that administration out of the profits obtained from the municipal monopoly of the production and distribution of "KAFFIR
beer" (utshwala in Zulu). The Natal Native Beer Act of 1908
provided the Durban municipality with the necessary powers to
implement the system. Though justified in terms of the removal of the evils of illegal liquor and drunkenness, it drew
extra revenue from African workers, and meant that they funded
the state apparatus by which they were controlled. The 1923
Natives Urban Areas Act enabled other municipalities to copy
the Durban system if they wanted to. In the 1970s most of the
revenue of the Administration Boards responsible for the African urban areas came from the sale of beer. (See also URBAN
SEGREGATION.)

DUTCH. The language of the Cape under the DUTCH EAST INDIA
COMPANY and under BRITISH RULE until the 1820s, when the
British governor proclaimed English the language of government
and justice. English increasingly became the sole medium of
instruction in Cape schools. In the Afrikaner republics established as a result of the GREAT TREK, Dutch was the language
of government, law, the schools, and the church. From the
1870s J.H. Hofmeyr (1845-1909), then editor of De Zuid Afrikaan
newspaper in Cape Town, began to campaign for the restoration
of the rights of Dutch in the government, courts, and schools of
the Cape. He succeeded in having Dutch recognized as an official language of the Cape parliament in 1882, and thereafter
Dutch gradually gained equal recognition with English as an
official language in the colony. When the Transvaal and Free
State came under British administration during the SOUTH
AFRICAN WAR, English became the official language, but the
South Africa Act, creating UNION, provided that Dutch and English should both be official languages and be treated equally. In
1925 the Union parliament passed legislation declaring that
"Dutch" was to be understood as including AFRIKAANS. Afri-
kaans in effect became the other official language from that date.

DUTCH EAST INDIA COMPANY (Verenigde Oostindische Compagnie
(VOC); Jan Compagnie). A private commercial undertaking,
founded in 1602, it was in the early 18th century the largest
shipping and commercial company in the world. In the second
half of the 17th century it sent out on average 22 Indiamen a
year via the Cape to Batavia, on the island of Java, and its
other eastern possessions. The Cape station it founded in 1652
was to supply fresh meat, fruit, and vegetables to the passing
ships; it was not planned as a colony of settlement. Until 1732

the Cape was governed both from Holland and from Batavia;
thereafter from Holland alone. The company was declared
bankrupt in 1794, the year before the Cape was taken over by
the BRITISH. The DEIC was formally dissolved in 1798, and
when the Cape was handed back by the British in 1803, the
colony came under the rule of the new Batavian regime in Holland.

DUTCH REFORMED CHURCH (DRC). The Nederduitse Gereformeerde Kerk (NGK) was the official church in the Cape Colony
during the DUTCH EAST INDIA COMPANY period. After the
British took over the Cape, it gained its autonomy from the
Calvinist church in Holland, to become the first independent
church in South Africa. Its life was invigorated by a number
of Scottish Presbyterian ministers who joined it from the 1820s.
The son of one of them, Andrew Murray the younger (1828-
1917), was the major figure in an evangelical revival that
swept the NGK in the 1860s and 70s. One result was that the
NGK began to enter mission work on a large-scale, both in the
Transvaal and further afield in tropical Africa. In 1857 the
NGK Cape synod had decided that though not desirable nor
scriptural, due to "the weakness of some" (whites), separate
services could be held for whites and blacks. Separate congregations became the rule, leading to separate mission or
"daughter" churches: the sendingkerk (mission church) for
"Coloureds," founded in 1881, the NGK in Afrika for Africans,
and the Indian Reformed Church.
    The NGK was not sympathetic to those who left on the
GREAT TREK, but nevertheless began work among the Transvaal trekkers in the 1840s. In the early 1850s, however, the
trekkers at Potchefstroom in the western Transvaal decided
against links with a church associated with the British-ruled
Cape, and formed their own conservative Nederduitsch Hervormde Kerk, which was given official recognition in the republican constitution of 1856. Religious dissension continued,
with those who objected to the singing of hymns in public worship forming a separate, even more conservative Gereformeerde
Kerk at Rustenburg in 1859. The members of this strict Calvinist church, much influenced by the neo-Calvinism of Holland,
were known as Doppers, perhaps from "dorper" meaning vil-
lager, or because of the short jackets they wore. The theological school of this church was to develop into the Potchefstroom
University for Christian Higher Education. In its centenary
year, the Gereformeerde Kerk boasted 214 congregations, with
91,000 members.
    In the early years of the 20th century the NGK churches in
the four colonies sought to create a federal structure, with a
single country-wide synod, but it took over 50 years to achieve
that goal. In the 1970s the NGK was by far the largest of the
DRC churches, claiming $1\frac{1}{2}$ million white members. The DRC
generally found no difficulty in finding scriptural support for
APARTHEID, especially when conceived as SEPARATE DEVEL-
OPMENT, and it was only very hesitantly that the NGK voiced

unhappiness with some of the results of that policy, such as the effect of MIGRANT LABOR on African family life.

ECONOMIC CHANGE. It is usually assumed that the transition from a hunting and gathering economy to one based on pastoralism was associated with the movement of KHOIKHOI into South Africa, and the transition from pastoralism to a mixed pastoral and vegecultural economy with the arrival of BANTU-SPEAKERS. The introduction of AGRICULTURE is in turn associated with the diffusion of an iron technology (see IRON AGE).

Both the Khoikhoi pastoralists and the Bantu-speaking mixed farmers were involved in considerable trade--in cannabis, iron, cattle, beads--over long distances before the coming of the whites. The establishment of a colony of white settlement (see DUTCH, FREEBURGHERS) greatly increased the exchange of commodities, in particular cattle and the products of hunting bartered for beads, iron objects and other European goods. Besides the fruit and vegetables grown to supply the passing ships, the production of wheat and wine became increasingly important at the Cape. Viticulture, introduced by Jan van Riebeeck (1619-1677), the first Dutch commander, and stimulated by the arrival of the Huguenot refugees in 1688, became the main industry of the southwestern Cape in the early 19th century. A lowering of British tariffs in 1813 encouraged exports, which rose to over 1 million gallons by 1822. The raising of the tariff subsequently led to the virtual collapse of the export trade in wine, while infection of the vines by the phylloxera disease virtually destroyed the industry in the 1880s.

From the 1830s wool began to overtake wine as the major Cape export. Woolly-fleeced merino sheep were introduced into the eastern Cape in 1827 and within a few years hides and skins, the other main export from the eastern Cape, had fallen far behind wool exports. Thanks to the expansion of the British woollens manufacturing industry, the demand for wool continued to increase, and production rose from 144,000 pounds in 1834 to 491,000 in 1838 to over 1 million in 1841 to almost 5 million in 1851, while in 1862 as much as 25 million pounds was exported. Though the price of wool slumped after the American civil war, and a severe drought in the 1860s greatly reduced production, wool remained the country's most important agricultural export.

Much of the history of NATAL from the 1860s is the story of sugar. While white farmers were attracted to its production, black peasants supplied a large proportion of the grain market. As the demand among Africans for European-produced commodities, and especially guns, increased, so great merchant houses grew up in both the eastern Cape and Natal. These mercantile capital interests played an important role in the first years of the DIAMOND fields. The discovery of diamonds, followed soon after by GOLD, set in motion changes that transformed much of the country's economy, and shifted its economic

center of gravity away from the coastal ports to the interior
highveld.   Foreign capital poured in: of the total of £200 million absorbed by the mining sector between 1887 and 1934,
three fifths came from abroad.   New industries were started to
supply the mines, and a huge new market for food opened up.
For a time, American grain had to be imported to meet the demand on the Witwatersrand.   But white farmers, aided by the
transfer to them of revenues obtained from mining, began to
commercialize, and competition from African peasant farmers
was eliminated (see AGRICULTURE, BUNDY THESIS).   As mineral production expanded and diversified (see DIAMONDS, GOLD,
MINING), MANUFACTURING grew apace and South Africa's position as the economic giant of the continent was further entrenched.
In the post-World War II period perhaps the most notable development was the increasing monopolization of capitalist production (for the leading example, see ANGLO-AMERICAN COR-
PORATION).

ENGLISH-SPEAKING WHITES.   There were some 5,000 English-
speaking whites in the Cape in 1820, when another 5,000 arrived and were settled in the Albany district of the eastern
colony.   The BRITISH government, responsible for the scheme,
had led the settlers to believe that they would be agricultural
smallholders in an empty territory reminiscent, in the words of
the then British governor of the Cape, of an English parkland.
In fact, the scheme was designed to provide an inexpensive buffer on the frontier, and they were deliberately settled in contested territory.   Agriculture on the small plots they were given
proved very difficult, and many soon moved into Grahamstown
and the other small towns that grew up in the eastern Cape.   By
the 1840s Grahamstown had become a major center for trade between the colony and the XHOSA further east.
     While the eastern Cape acquired a British character, the
western portion remained predominantly DUTCH-speaking, though
leading Cape Dutch families, wishing to participate in the new
British administration, became fully anglicized.   Despite the
rise of the AFRIKANER BOND from 1880, the English-speaking
minority continued to dominate Cape politics in the 19th century.
English culture was dominant, especially in the cities, and
though English-speakers were often critical of the distant imperial authority and its local agents, British power buttressed
their position.
     NATAL, in contrast to the Cape, became a British colony in
which the white settlers were mostly English-speaking.   The
second major settlement of English-speakers in South Africa
took place in 1849-1852, when some 5,000 government-assisted
English and Scottish immigrants arrived in DURBAN, and made
their homes either there or in Pietermaritzburg or on allot-
ments in the countryside.
     With the discovery of DIAMONDS and then GOLD in the in-
terior, British artisans and skilled workers--many Cornish
miners, for example--were attracted to the country.   Some of
those who came to South Africa to fight on the British side in

the SOUTH AFRICAN WAR decided to stay. Sporadic immigration continued until SMUTS, in the aftermath of World War II,
embarked on a large-scale state-organized immigration scheme.
Of the 29,000 immigrants who arrived in 1947 and the over
35,000 in 1948, 88 percent were British nationals. On assum-
ing office, however, the NATIONAL PARTY government quickly
ended the program, fearing the immigrants would vote against
the party of AFRIKANER NATIONALISM. By 1961, with the
REPUBLIC achieved, and the government secure in power,
white immigration was again encouraged. The decolonization of
tropical Africa meant a considerable immigration of whites, especially from ZIMBABWE, which continued into the early 1980s.
Immigration from Britain itself reached 20,000 per annum in
the late 1970s. Immigrants from the ex-Portuguese territories
and from Mediterranean Europe--many of whom became small
shop-keepers--were absorbed, as other non-British immigrants
had been, into the English-speaking community. Few of these
recent immigrants took out South African citizenship; in 1982
one fifth of all English-speaking whites in the country were not
citizens.

The English-speaking whites never developed their own national identity or culture. Nor did they--except during a brief
jingoistic phase before the SOUTH AFRICAN WAR--adopt an
aggressive political stance. In the UNION they constituted only
40 percent of the white population, and so were politically im-
potent on their own. They attempted to forge alliances with
moderate Afrikaners to secure access to power, being willing
to accept Afrikaner political leadership which allowed a broad
South Africanism and a retention of the imperial connection (see
BOTHA; SMUTS; SOUTH AFRICAN PARTY; UNITED PARTY).
English parties could not survive (see UNIONIST PARTY;
DOMINION PARTY). With the rise of an exclusive Afrikaner
nationalist party to power in 1948, the English-speaking whites
were left in the political wilderness, and criticized by Afrikaners for not giving their undivided loyalty to South Africa. Dominant in the commercial and industrial life of the country, en-
joying their material prosperity, disillusioned with Britain itself and the Commonwealth, they continued to support the parliamentary opposition, the white supremacist UNITED PARTY
and then the more liberal PROGRESSIVE PARTY. Many of the
strongest critics of APARTHEID came from their ranks, and
liberal values were more deeply entrenched among them than
among any other group. Leading members in 1982 included
Harry Oppenheimer of ANGLO-AMERICAN, Nadine GORDIMER,
and Alan PATON.

ETHIOPIANISM. African independent church movement. The first
separatist church, the Thembu Church, was founded in 1884 in
the TRANSKEI by Nehemiah Tile (c. 1850-1891), who rejected
the white control he encountered in the Methodist Church and
broke with it. The separatist movement grew rapidly in the
late 19th century, both in the rural areas and in the cities.
In 1892 Mangena Mokone, a minister in the Methodist Church

in Pretoria, founded the Ethiopian Church, taking the name
from Psalm 68 verse 31 ("Ethiopia shall stretch out her hands
unto God"). In 1896 he was joined by James Mata Dwane
(1848-1916), who had quarreled with the Methodist Church over
how funds he had raised in England should be used. Dwane
went to America later that year and established a link between
the Ethiopian Church and the African Methodist Episcopal Church
(AMEC), a black church founded in Philadelphia in 1816, which
made him its general superintendent in South Africa. Then when
the AMEC Bishop H. M. Turner visited the country in 1898, he
was consecrated a Vicar-Bishop. But Dwane soon became disillusioned with the AMEC and led a large body of followers into
the Anglican Church as a separate Order of Ethiopia (1900).
The AMEC remained active in South Africa, but sought to dis-
tance itself from other independent churches.

In his classic Bantu Prophets in South Africa (1948), Bengt
Sundkler, a Lutheran missionary in Zululand, used the term
Ethiopianism for those independent churches--such as the Thembu and Ethiopian churches--that retained the outward form,
structure, and much of the theology of their parent churches.
Those he termed Zionist were also an expression of African
independence, but they blended African tradition with Christian
beliefs, and laid more emphasis on prophecy, healing, and
purification rites. If independent churches were a response to
racism and paternalism in the mission churches, the Zionist
ones in particular were also a response to the suppression of
African culture in those churches.

In the late 19th and early 20th centuries whites did not know
what to make of the new movement, and suspected it might
have political purposes, emphasizing as it did blacks acting on
their own. The LAGDEN COMMISSION investigated it, and it
was suspected of playing a major role in the BAMBATHA RE-
BELLION. Whites gradually came to realize, however, that the
independent church movement had become largely apolitical, an
alternative channel to political activity (though a few independent
church ministers were active in the AFRICAN NATIONAL CON-
GRESS). The potential power of the movement was weakened
by constant fission; by the 1970s there were over 3,000 separate independent churches in the country, largely because men
sought power and prestige through the leadership roles otherwise denied them in apartheid society. Many of these churches
comprised a single congregation of a few score followers. Attempts to bring the independent churches together, in particular
through a nation-wide Interdenominational African Ministers' Association, met with no longterm success.

FAGAN COMMISSION (1946-1948). The Native Laws Commission,
    appointed by the SMUTS government under the chairmanship of
    Henry Fagan (1889-1963), a former Minister of Native Affairs.
    Its response to the influx of Africans into the cities during
    World War II was to assert that the permanence of a settled

African labor force in the towns must be accepted. Though it
rejected the STALLARD DOCTRINE, the Fagan Report assumed
that MIGRANT LABOR would continue. Urban Africans should
administer their own affairs; in all other matters, they should
be consulted. The PASS laws should remain, but should be enforced more leniently. Though equivocal, its recommendations
did add up to a change of direction in African policy. But its
report was not published until February 1948, when the NA-
TIONAL PARTY seized upon it as evidence of the dangers to
whites were the SMUTS government to be returned to office and
to implement it. In this way the report contributed to Smuts'
defeat in the general election of that year.

FANAGALO (from the Zulu: "be like this"). A pidgin language, a
mixture of Zulu, Afrikaans and English, used--and sometimes
taught--to allow communication, especially between Africans who
spoke different languages on the mines and their European super-
visors. In the early 20th century, it was often known as "mine
KAFFIR."

FEDERATION OF SOUTH AFRICAN TRADE UNIONS (FOSATU) see
TRADE UNIONS.

FEDERATION OF SOUTH AFRICAN WOMEN. Non-racial women's
organization founded in 1954 by Helen Joseph (1905-   ) and
others. Soon claiming 10,000 members, mostly Africans,
through affiliated organizations, it became part of the CON-
GRESS ALLIANCE in 1955. It proved to be most successful in
mobilizing mass demonstrations, most notably the march of
20,000 women to the Union Buildings, Pretoria, to protest
against the extension of PASSES to African women (9 August
1956). Mainly an urban movement, it was hard hit by official
repression, including the BANNING of a number of its leaders.
Helen Joseph, one of those involved in the TREASON TRIAL,
was first banned, and then, after she had travelled around the
country to investigate the plight of those Africans banished to
remote areas, placed under house arrest. By 1982 she had
endured sixteen years under various banning orders.

FINGO see MFENGU.

FISCHER, Abram (Bram) (1908-1975). Grandson of a Prime
Minister of the Orange River Colony and son of a Judge-
President of the Orange Free State, he studied law at Oxford,
where he became a communist. In the 1940s he was a member of the Central Committee of the COMMUNIST PARTY OF
SOUTH AFRICA (CP) and in the 1950s, after the CP had been
banned, a member of the Congress of Democrats (see CON-
GRESS ALLIANCE). A brilliant lawyer, he led the defense in
a succession of political trials, including that of the leaders of
UMKHONTO WE SIZWE. In 1964 he was arrested and charged
with membership of the banned CP. Jumping bail, he went
underground to continue working for it. Arrested after ten

months underground, he was sentenced to life imprisonment in
1966 and was released only when in the terminal stage of can-
cer.

FLAG QUESTION.   A fierce controversy erupted among whites in
    1926-27 over a new national flag for South Africa.   In 1925,
    MALAN, a minister in the PACT GOVERNMENT, proposed a
    new flag to replace the variant of Britain's Red Ensign that had
    become South Africa's flag in 1910.   The matter of most con-
    tention was whether or not the Union Jack--for Afrikaners a
    symbol of former injustice, for English-speaking whites a part
    of their heritage--should form part of the new design.   In the
    end it was agreed that the flags of the former republics as well
    as the Union Jack should be included in the center of the new
    flag.   The controversy damaged the LABOUR PARTY, many of
    whose supporters believed their leaders should be concerned
    with more important issues than a new flag.   It helped distract
    the attention of English-speakers from the HERTZOG BILLS.
    No attempt was made to consult black opinion on the new flag.
    After the establishment of the REPUBLIC in 1961 there was
    periodic talk about the need for another flag.   That nothing was
    done about the matter was probably mainly a result of the mem-
    ory of the bitterness the question had provoked in the 1920s.

FORT HARE.   University College for Africans.   Support for the es-
    tablishment of such a college came from the LAGDEN COMMIS-
    SION (1905) after a considerable number of Africans had left to
    be educated in the United States.   DUBE and JABAVU both cam-
    paigned for it.   Attempts to get the new UNION government to
    finance it met with little success, but it opened as the South
    African Native College in 1916 on land given by the Church of
    Scotland adjacent to Lovedale, the leading mission high school
    for Africans.   Those who attended Fort Hare included BUTHE-
    LEZI, MANDELA, and MATANZIMA, as well as a number of
    Africans who rose to prominence in neighboring countries, such
    as Robert Mugabe in ZIMBABWE.   Affiliated to Rhodes Univer-
    sity in 1949, it was after 1959 taken over by the government and
    became an ethnic college for XHOSA-speaking students.   In the
    late 1960s it was one of the main centers of the BLACK CON-
    SCIOUSNESS MOVEMENT (see also UNIVERSITIES).

FRANCHISE.   The constitution granted the Cape in 1853 gave the
    colony a non-racial franchise with a low qualification: every
    male citizen over 21 years who owned property valued at £25,
    received a salary of £50 per annum, or received a salary of
    £25 plus free board and lodging, was entitled to vote.   It was
    another thirty years before blacks began to acquire the vote in
    significant numbers.   As more and more Africans were included
    within the colony with the progressive annexation of the TRANS-
    KEI, steps were taken to limit the number of African voters.
    Legislation of 1887 provided that land held on communal tenure
    did not count towards the property qualification.   In 1892 the
    property qualification was raised from £25 to £75, the wage

qualification was eliminated, and voters were required to sign
their name when registering. Though by 1909 only 10 percent
of all registered voters at the Cape were "Coloureds," and just
under 5 percent Africans, these black voters were able to influence results in several constituencies. In Natal, though the
franchise was in theory color-blind, legislation of 1864-65 kept
it from all but a few Africans, while INDIANS were debarred
from the franchise in 1896. In the Transvaal and Orange Free
State the franchise was limited to white men. The TREATY
OF VEREENIGING (1902) provided that there would be no change
in this regard before the restoration of self-government to the
ex-republics. Once self-government had been restored to the
whites, there was no possibility of votes being given to blacks.
    The NATIONAL CONVENTION (1908-09) decided that in the
Union each province would retain its existing franchise provisions. Cape delegates hoped that in time their non-racial
franchise would be extended to the northern provinces. Instead, the Cape franchise came to be seen as anomalous. In
1930 the vote was given to white women only, and in 1931 educational and property qualifications were removed for whites
only. The effect of these two measures was drastically to reduce the proportion of black voters in the Cape, which fell from
20 percent in 1929 to 8.5 percent in 1935. When the African
voters were removed from the common voters' roll by the 1936
Representation of Natives Act (one of the HERTZOG BILLS),
they constituted a mere 10,000 voters, making up only 1.4 percent of the total. The main reason for their removal was not
the threat they posed to white supremacy, but the fact that
while Cape Africans enjoyed the common roll franchise they
could not be made subject to the coercive labor system which
the government wished to impose on all Africans throughout the
country.
    The 1936 legislation provided for Cape Africans to vote on a
separate roll for three "Native Representatives," who had to be
whites. This token African representation in parliament was
abolished in 1960 (see Margaret BALLINGER).
    The first one-man/one-vote election for Africans to take
place in South Africa was held in the TRANSKEI in 1963. Other
BANTUSTANS held similar elections when they were given elected legislatures.
    In 1936 the NATIONAL PARTY had wanted the "COLOUREDS"
to be removed from the common voters' roll along with the Africans. When they came to power in 1948, the Nationalists
were determined to remove the "Coloureds," who posed a possible threat to their continued hold on power: when the UNITED
PARTY recaptured some provincial seats in 1949, it seemed
that if the "Coloureds" voted en bloc against the Nationalists
they might be ousted at the next general election. The attempt
to remove the "Coloureds" from the common roll provoked a
bitter constitutional crisis and was not achieved until 1956: see
"COLOURED" VOTE ISSUE; CONSTITUTIONAL CHANGE.

FREE BLACKS (Dutch: vrijzwarten). During the DUTCH EAST

INDIA COMPANY period, "Free Blacks" were free persons of
African or Asian descent, but the term did not include KHOI-
KHOI, BANTU-speaking people beyond the colony, or BASTARDS,
the offspring of unions between whites and Khoikhoi. Most
Free Blacks, then, were freed slaves. Only a few Africans
or Asians entered the colony as free persons. As manumission
was relatively infrequent--compared, say, to Spanish America--
there were never many Free Blacks. They constituted 7.4 percent of the total free population in 1670, but only 4.4 percent in
1770, when they numbered not many more than 1,000. Some
Free Blacks made a brief attempt at agriculture in the Stellenbosch area in the late 17th century, but that failed, and in the
18th century most were to be found in Cape Town, living in
poverty. They suffered statutory discrimination (cf. PETTY
APARTHEID): a curfew, for example, applied to "slaves and
people of color." ORDINANCE 50 of 1828 removed the legal
disabilities from which they suffered, and thereafter they were
gradually absorbed, with the emancipated slaves, into the wider
"COLOURED" population.

FREEBURGHERS (Dutch: vrijburgers. The term came to be used
   generally for all whites who were not company officials during
   the DUTCH EAST INDIA COMPANY (DEIC) period). In 1657
   nine company officials were released from their contracts of
   service and given smallholdings on land that had been KHOIKHOI
   pasturage a few miles from the site of the first permanent
   European settlement. These first freeburghers bound themselves to supply the company with foodstuffs at fixed prices.
   The company believed that this was the cheapest way to obtain
   the agricultural commodities needed for the passing ships.
   The total number of freeburghers increased, thanks in part to
   immigration (e.g. 180 Huguenot refugees arrived from France
   in 1688), to 1,334 by 1700. But there was little immigration
   in the 18th century and it was mainly because of freeburghers'
   marrying young and having very large families that their number rose to 15,000 by 1795. It was not until about 1755, however, that the number of adult male freeburghers exceeded that
   of DEIC officials.
      Recent work has shown that even in the arable south-western
   Cape in the 17th century there were considerable differences of
   wealth among freeburghers. The wealthier ones were in frequent conflict with the company officials in the 18th century.
   At the beginning of the century a petition went to the directors
   of the company suggesting that the governor and his leading officials were incompetent, and demanding reforms. The governor was recalled and the freeburghers were made the sole suppliers of food to Cape Town and the passing ships. In 1779 a
   group of freeburghers in and around Cape Town, who called
   themselves the Cape Patriots, sent a delegation to the Netherlands to present their grievances to the directors. They sought
   freedom to trade with foreign ships themselves, better prices
   for the goods they sold the company, participation in the government of the colony, codification of the laws, and a prohibition

on officials engaging in economic activities. Their complaints
continued, stimulated by ideas from the European enlightenment,
as the directors would only make limited concessions: seats on
the high court and the freedom to trade with foreign ships. Relations between the freeburghers and the government of the Cape
remained strained in the last years of DEIC rule. At the very
end (1795), the freeburgher TREKBOERS in the interior district
of Graaff-Reinet, angered by the company's inability to protect
them against the indigenous people, rose in revolt against rule
from Cape Town and declared their independence, a revolt put
down by the new BRITISH administration.

FREEDOM CHARTER. Document approved by a Congress of the
People organized by the CONGRESS ALLIANCE in June 1955.
It affirmed that South Africa belongs to all those who live in it,
black and white, and that no government can justly claim authority unless based on the will of the people. It demanded a non-
racial democratic government; equal protection before the law;
nationalization of the banks, mines, and heavy industry; land
redistribution; and equal work and educational opportunities.
The AFRICAN NATIONAL CONGRESS adopted it in March 1956.
From the late 1970s it again became a rallying point for non-
racial opposition groups within the country.

FRERE, Henry Bartle Edward (1815-1884). After a distinguished
career in India, Frere was offered the post of governor of the
Cape and HIGH COMMISSIONER in 1877 as the man best able to
bring about CONFEDERATION. Frere went to South Africa determined to achieve that goal, expecting to become the first
governor-general of the new British dominion. At the Cape
Frere soon found himself involved in another war with the
XHOSA (1877-1878). In the midst of it, he took the almost un-
precedented step of dismissing the Cape Prime Minister, ap-
pointing in his place a man more favorably disposed to confederation. Frere believed that before a self-governing white
dominion could be left to defend itself, white supremacy had to
be established throughout South Africa. This meant crushing
black resistance, at the heart of which lay--and in this view
he was encouraged by SHEPSTONE--the ZULU. Hence the
Anglo-Zulu war (1879), which opened with the British defeat at
Isandhlwana. After that the High Commission was divided, and
Frere kept in South Africa only to see whether he could further
the confederal cause. But Shepstone's annexation of the Transvaal had aroused Afrikaners against the British, and the Cape
parliament was hostile to confederation when the issue was
finally raised there in June 1880. After that Frere was recalled, to die a broken man.

FRONTIER TRADITION. In a lecture delivered at Oxford University in 1930, entitled The Frontier Tradition in South Africa
the historian Eric WALKER argued that WHITE RACISM, orig-
inating on the frontier in the 17th and 18th centuries, was an
important part of the ideology taken from the Cape to the re-

publics by the VOORTREKKERS. Since UNION the "frontier
tradition" had been responsible for the JOB COLOR-BAR, UR-
BAN SEGREGATION and opposition to the Cape's non-racial
FRANCHISE.   Picking up Walker's thesis, the psychologist I.D.
MacCrone, in his Race Attitudes in South Africa (1937) provided
detailed evidence from the 17th and 18th centuries to show that
the white race attitudes of the 20th century originated on the
early frontier.   In an influential paper presented in London in
1970, Martin LEGASSICK presented a critique of the "frontier
tradition" thesis, arguing that some of the least color-conscious
interaction between peoples of different societies occurred on
the frontier, and that for the origins of white racism one must
look to ideas imported from Europe and to the influence of
CAPE SLAVERY.   Legassick and other radical historians (see
HISTORIOGRAPHY) further argued that 18th-century racism was
quite different from the systematic and overt racism of the late
19th century, which they linked to the beginnings of industrial
capitalism at Kimberley (see DIAMONDS) and then on the WIT-
WATERSRAND.

FRONTIER WARS.   During the process of WHITE INTRUSION numerous armed conflicts occurred between the advancing whites,
sometimes aided by black allies, and those Africans whose lands
the whites occupied.   After two small wars in the late 17th century, resistance by the KHOIKHOI chiefly took the form of raiding.   The XHOSA attempted to hold back white intrusion onto
their lands through one hundred years of sporadic warfare.
From 1811 the colonists were aided in five major wars against
the Xhosa by the BRITISH army.   In 1819 a massive Xhosa assault on the garrison town of Grahamstown in what had been the
ZUURVELD failed, and after that they very successfully employed the tactics of guerilla warfare.   Adept at bush-fighting,
the Xhosa were conquered more through the destruction of their
crops and the loss of their herds than through defeat in battle.
The VOORTREKKERS engaged in major conflicts with the
NDEBELE in the Transvaal and the ZULU in Natal.   For fourteen years after its establishment in 1854, the Orange Free
State was involved, on and off, in warfare with Moshweshwe's
SOTHO (see BASUTOLAND), much of whose territory was taken
before they gained safety from further attack through being
granted BRITISH protection.   The Zulu suffered overwhelming
defeat at the hands of the Voortrekkers at BLOOD RIVER in
1838, but the Zulu polity survived north of the Tugela River,
and it was not until 1879 that British and colonial forces, after
the initial defeat at Isandhlwana, went on to conquer the Zulu
kingdom.   Unlike the Xhosa, the Zulu never altered their
method of fighting in fixed formation.   Having defeated the
Zulu, the British army humbled the PEDI of the eastern Transvaal whom the Transvalers themselves had been unable to subject to white control.   By 1880 the major frontier wars were
over--though military campaigns were necessary to subject the
VENDA of the northern Transvaal as late as 1898--and the next
phase of armed struggle took the form of ANTI-COLONIAL RE-
BELLIONS.

FUGARD, Athol (1932-). South Africa's foremost dramatist, who
sometimes acted in and directed his own plays. A number of
these are autobiographical, or set in the Port Elizabeth world
that is his home. They make powerful anti-apartheid statements. A Lesson from Aloes, in particular, won international
acclaim.

FUSION (1934). The merger of the NATIONAL PARTY under
HERTZOG and the SOUTH AFRICAN PARTY under SMUTS to
form the UNITED PARTY. Fusion, flowing from coalition
(1933), was born of a desire to pull the country out of its economic plight (see BUSINESS CYCLES) and to forge a new unity
after the constitutional relationship with Britain had been ad-
justed (see COMMONWEALTH). Hertzog believed that South
Africa's independence from Britain had been secured by the
Statute of Westminster (1931) and the Status Act (1934), and
that white unity was now possible on the basis of "South Africa
First" and full equality between the two white language groups.
The followers of MALAN, on the other hand, who rejected fusion, believed that real independence had not been attained, that
big capital was behind the merger, and that Afrikaners should
be further consolidated so that they could rule. Only the institution of a REPUBLIC would demonstrate South Africa's real
independence.
    Fusion ended in 1939, when Smuts broke with Hertzog and
took the country into WORLD WAR II.

GANDHI, M. K. (1869-1948) see INDIANS.

GAZANKULU. BANTUSTAN for the Shangaan/THONGA people in
the north-eastern Transvaal. Its creation involved the MASS
REMOVAL of some hundreds of thousands of people in the late
1960s and 1970s, increasing its population by over 50 percent
within a decade. By the end of the 1970s 43 percent of
Thonga-speakers domiciled in South Africa lived within Gazankulu, its population was almost 900,000, and 80 percent of its
income was earned outside its borders.

GLEN GREY ACT (1894). Introduced into the Cape parliament by
Cecil RHODES, it was initially designed for the Glen Grey district of the eastern Cape, now part of TRANSKEI, but Rhodes,
hoping it would become a blueprint for southern Africa as a
whole, spoke of it as a "Bill for Africa." It was extended
from Glen Grey into what was then the Transkei from 1898.
    It had three main elements. Firstly, it altered the system
of land tenure, replacing communal tenure by small individual
surveyed lots on a one-man/one-lot basis. Land held under
the new system could not be alienated without special permission and did not count towards the qualifications for the Cape
FRANCHISE. As there were not enough lots to go around,
some Africans found themselves permanently landless. Secondly,

as a further "gentle stimulus" to labor (in Rhodes' words), a
tax of ten shillings was imposed on all men who could not prove
that they had been in bona fide wage employment for at least
three months in any one year.   (The tax was strongly resisted,
proved cumbersome to apply and was soon found unnecessary,
so it was withdrawn in 1905).   Thirdly, a system of district
councils was introduced to provide for African participation in
local government on an advisory basis.   These councils were
extended within the Transkei until they embraced the entire region, and in 1931 a central United General Council (Bunga) was
created for the Transkeian territories, as a whole.

GOLD.   Pre-colonial gold-mining was undertaken by Africans at
various places in the Transvaal: Lydenburg and Pilgrim's Rest
in the eastern Transvaal; Zoutpansberg in the north; and along
the LIMPOPO river.   In the early 1870s considerable alluvial
gold was found and worked by white prospectors in the eastern
Transvaal.   Small amounts were also found at Rustenburg and
on the WITWATERSRAND before the discovery of the main reef
at the end of 1885.   The first ore from the Witwatersrand was
crushed in 1886.   The extent of the fields was not really appre-
ciated until the early 1890s, and it was only the introduction of
a new cyanide process that made possible the exploitation of the
deep level ores.   In 1930 new prospecting methods revealed vast
new reefs at a great depth to the south-west, and after World
War II a number of new mines in the northern Free State were
opened up.
     Though the Witwatersrand gold deposits were the largest in
the world, the average gold content per ton of rock mined was
very low.   Because of this, and because the gold-bearing reef
sloped downwards and went deep underground, large-scale mining operations were required, needing huge amounts of capital.
An oligopolistic industry emerged in which a few mining houses
drew on capital formed in Kimberley (see DIAMONDS) or attracted from overseas.   Of the £200 million invested between
1887 and 1934, 60 percent was from foreign sources.   With the
price of gold fixed, and mostly stationary, and with high devel-
opmental costs inevitable, attempts were made to keep labor
costs as low as possible.   Certain skilled jobs went to whites,
mainly immigrants from Europe, who were able to demand high
wages.   Wages for the vast army of unskilled African MIGRANT
workers were pushed down to a minimum.
     The discovery of gold turned the Transvaal, which had been
the poorest state in South Africa, into the wealthiest within a
few years.   By 1896, gold accounted for 97 percent of the value
of its exports.   It enabled KRUGER, for example, to complete
the railroad from DELAGOA BAY.   Gold played a major part
in bringing about the SOUTH AFRICAN WAR and then UNION.
It has remained the backbone of the South African economy,
contributing massively to state revenue and earning large quantities of foreign exchange.
     In 1933 South Africa's departure from the gold standard in-
creased the price by 65 percent, causing an immediate upturn

in economic activity (see MANUFACTURING INDUSTRY) and the
opening up of new mines.   From 1934 to 1968 the international
price was fixed at $35 (U.S.) a fine ounce.   A second-tier free
market in gold was then introduced and by the end of 1971 the
price had begun to move up: by 1972 the free market price
rose to $70 and in 1974, after the dramatic oil price increase,
it climbed towards $200.   Now for the first time since Union
the real wages of the African mineworkers were increased, and
the increased price enabled mines that otherwise would have
been marginal to be brought into production.   By 1978 36 active
mines were producing nearly 700 tons a year, roughly half the
total world production.   Gold auctions by the International Monetary Fund took the price down to under $80 again in 1976, but
at the end of the 1970s it shot up to peak at $875 an ounce in
January 1980, after the Russian invasion of Afghanistan.   With
an average price of $613 for 1980, the South African economy
achieved a record rate of growth.   High interest rates in the
United States and Soviet sales of gold then brought the price
down again: the 1981 average was $460 and in June 1982 gold
fell below $300 again.   See also RANDLORDS; WERNHER,
BEIT--H. ECKSTEIN; and, for labor on the gold mines see
CHINESE LABOR; CRESWELL; JOB COLOR BAR; MIGRANT
LABOR; RAND REVOLT; STRIKES.

GORDIMER, Nadine (1923-   ).   Leading novelist and writer of short
stories.   From The Lying Days (1953), set in the first years
of NATIONAL PARTY rule, through A World of Strangers
(1958), which told of the multi-racial CONGRESS ALLIANCE
era in Johannesburg, to The Late Bourgeois World (1966),
which concerned white involvement in SABOTAGE, to Burger's
Daughter (1979), which encompassed the SOWETO REVOLT, to
July's People (1981), set in the South Africa of the future,
Gordimer's sensitive writing reflected the changing moods of
white liberals and radicals.

GRAY, Robert (1809-1872).   After the BRITISH occupied the Cape,
the Church of England was introduced to serve the spiritual
needs of colonial officials and the military, but it was left to
Gray, who arrived in Cape Town in 1848 as the first Bishop,
to organize and expand the work.   A man of great energy and
determination, he created four more dioceses, in so doing
clashing with his church in England.   A high Churchman, he
believed in the apostolic authority of bishops.   When John
Colenso (1814-1883), Bishop of Natal, a polymath who had introduced critical biblical scholarship to South Africa, was accused by Gray of heresy, the issue soon became that of the
autonomy of the Anglican Church in South Africa.   Gray deposed Colenso, but the British Privy Council reinstated him
(1865).   Gray then refused to recognize him, rejected the
authority of English tribunals, and created an autonomous
Church of the Province of South Africa (1870).   A small
splinter Church of England in South Africa remained outside
it, but the Church of the Province was recognized by the

Anglican Church in England itself.

Gray encouraged mission work--the new bishop of Grahamstown, with financial help from the governor, George GREY, established four mission stations beyond the colonial border in the
mid 1850s--and did much for education. Among the schools he
founded was Zonnebloem College, Cape Town, where sons of
African rulers were trained to be Christian, English gentlemen.

GREAT TREK. Of the many organized treks (journeys by ox-wagon)
that took place in the 19th century, the mass migration of Afrikaner farmers, with their "Coloured" servants, from the eastern
Cape into the interior was by far the most important. Small
exploratory parties, which went out from the Cape in 1834 to
survey conditions in the interior reported vacant land in Natal
and on the highveld. The Great Trek itself got underway in
1836, and within a few years over 4,000 of the Cape's 68,000
whites had left, with perhaps an equal number of servants.
Over the decade from 1836 14,000 joined the Trek.

The VOORTREKKERS--those who went on the Great Trek--
were essentially rebelling against a British government at the
Cape whose interference in their lives they regarded as intolerable. But the Trek was also a response to the shortage of
land in the eastern Cape and the fear of a shortage of labor.
By outflanking the XHOSA and settling in the interior, the trekkers hoped to obtain all the land and labor they wanted, and to
be able to rule themselves and their laborers as they wished.
One of the trekkers (Anna Steenkamp) declared that they did not
so much object to the British freeing the slaves (see CAPE
SLAVERY) "as their being placed on an equal footing with
Christians, contrary to the laws of God and the natural distinctions of race and religion, so that it was intolerable for
any decent Christian to bow down beneath such a yoke." They
did not so much seek to create a new way of life in the interi-
or as recreate the old (see also ORDINANCE 50; BRITISH
RULE).

In the interior the Voortrekkers dispossessed vast numbers
of Africans, for the land was by no means empty. Those
trekkers who followed Piet Retief (1780-1838) over the Drakensberg mountains into Natal clashed with the ZULU, while those
who went north of the Vaal River fought the NDEBELE. Various of the new states they set up, including the Republic of
Natalia (see NATAL), proved short-lived. After the British
annexed Natal in 1843, most of the trekkers there soon returned again to the highveld. By 1860 two republics had
emerged: one north of the Vaal--the trekkers there having
been recognized as independent by Britain by the Sand River
Convention of 1852 (see TRANSVAAL)--and one between the
Orange and the Vaal, the independence of which the British
had recognized in 1854 (see ORANGE FREE STATE). White
South Africa then remained politically divided until the conquest of both republics by Britain at the turn of the century
(see SOUTH AFRICAN WAR), despite attempts at reunification
(see GREY; CONFEDERATION).

GREY, George (1812-1898). He was appointed Cape Governor and
HIGH COMMISSIONER in 1854, having been Governor of South
Australia (1841-1845) and New Zealand (1846-1854). After his
experience with Maoris and aborigines, he believed the Xhosa
should be brought within the Cape Colony and gradually "civi-
lized" through "assimilation." He therefore encouraged their
participation in the money economy, reduced the power of the
chiefs in BRITISH KAFFRARIA and put money into education
and a hospital. He exploited the CATTLE-KILLING (1856-7)
to further this policy, settling German immigrants among those
XHOSA who survived.

Disapproving of the conventions that had recognized the independence of the TRANSVAAL and ORANGE FREE STATE (see
also GREAT TREK), Grey believed that a federal South Africa
should be created so that a common "native policy" could be
applied. When he urged federation contrary to the wishes of
the British government, which wanted to cut its costs in South
Africa, he was recalled (1859), but he was reappointed by a
new government and returned to the Cape in 1860 for another
year before going back to New Zealand. He presented a unique
collection of books and manuscripts to the South African Library
in Cape Town.

GRIQUA. One of the many groups of KHOIKHOI and people of mixed
descent who moved out of the Cape colony and settled along the
middle reaches of the ORANGE RIVER in the late 18th century,
the Griqua were initially those people whom a London Missionary Society (LMS) MISSIONARY in 1813 persuaded to change
their name. Until then they had called themselves, with pride,
BASTARDS (Basters), regarding themselves as superior to their
unacculturated neighbors, but the missionary pointed out that the
term was offensive to whites and they agreed to call themselves
Griqua instead, because some of them were descendants of the
Chariguriqua Khoi. Their first leader, Adam Kok I (c. 1710-
c. 1795), the son of a white man and a slave, was born a slave
but was freed and obtained land in the Piketberg north of Cape
Town in the 1750s. Probably in response to discrimination, he
and others of mixed descent moved further north, first to Little
Namaqualand and then to the middle reaches of the ORANGE
RIVER, not far from its junction with the Vaal. From the beginning of the 19th century they began settling near some
springs north of the Orange. Their settlement, encouraged by
the LMS missionaries who worked among them, was the nucleus
of the later Griqualand West. A small armed and mounted
Griqua force played a key role in the battle of Dithakong (1823),
in which invading "MANTATEES" were defeated, saving the
TSWANA from further disruption during the MFECANE.

Some Griqua remained semi-nomadic, including, for a time,
those under Adam Kok II (c. 1790-1835), who lived by raiding
and hunting and were known as Bergenaars (mountain people).
But in 1825 Adam Kok II's people were allowed to settle at the
LMS's Philippolis mission in what was to become the southern
ORANGE FREE STATE. Adam Kok III (1811-1875) assumed

control there in 1837.   At Philippolis many Griqua became successful commercial farmers.   Quick to respond to the new economic opportunities opened up by merino sheep farming (see
ECONOMIC CHANGE), they put some of their new wealth into
the acquisition of wagons, with which they traded far and wide.
Griqua played an important role in the opening up of the ROAD
TO THE NORTH.

Both east and west Griqua organized themselves politically
much as the VOORTREKKERS were to do in their republics.
The west Griqua, however, suffered from the increasing dessication of their land from the 1830s, the loss of game to hunt,
and cattle diseases.   David Arnot (1821-1894), a man of
Scottish-Griqua descent, in order to resist trekker encroachment asserted a Griqua claim to land which, it transpired, was
rich in DIAMONDS.   When BRITAIN sought to take over the diamond fields, it accepted this claim, granted the west Griqua
British protection, and annexed the fields (1871).   Thereafter
Griqua were given individual tenure, but most of them rapidly
sold their farms to whites, while others lost their land when
they went into rebellion in 1878.   By the end of the century
only a few impoverished Griqua remained in the territory.

From the 1840s the Griqua at Philippolis began to face first
TREKBOER and then Voortrekker encroachment on their lands,
for after the BRITISH annexation of NATAL in 1843 many Natal
trekkers returned to the Free State.   In 1843 Adam Kok entered
into treaty relations with the Cape government, promising to
keep order along the frontier.   Three years later another such
treaty divided the Griqua lands into a leasable portion, in which
the Griqua could lease their farms, and an unleasable RESERVE
in which no whites were to have access to land.   But when the
ORANGE RIVER SOVEREIGNTY was proclaimed in 1848, Kok
was stripped of jurisdiction outside the reserve, and the Griqua
lost the leasable lands, while white farmers steadily moved onto
the reserve itself.   Not being white, the Griqua were unable to
assert their claim to equality of status.   As more and more of
them were persuaded by whites to sell their farms, Kok decided
to move away, across the DRAKENSBERG to what was called,
not entirely accurately, Nomansland.   Over 2,000 Griqua went
on their "great trek" in 1861-1862, suffering great privations on
the way.   In the early 1870s they were still recovering from the
trek and establishing themselves in the new territory as a new
ruling class over the Africans living there.   Before this process
was complete, they lost their independence.   With the Cape
eager to establish its control over the TRANSKEI, and because
the Griqua had received a bad press in Cape Town, the British
HIGH COMMISSIONER announced the "annexation" of Griqualand
East in 1874.

Much traumatized by this, and by Kok's death (1875), many
of the east Griqua began selling off their farms to whites, and
they became large-scale consumers of alcohol.   Some staged a
rebellion against the new Cape administration at their capital,
Kokstad, in 1878, but Cape forces were able quickly to suppress it, and the territory was formally incorporated within

the Cape in 1879. By the 1880s the Griqua there were a demoral-
ized people, resentful of the loss of their land and their independence.
    In thd 20th century a revivalist figure, Andrew Abraham Stock-
enström Le Fleur (1861-1941) sought to revive Griqua fortunes. In
1917 he corganized a trek from Kokstad to the south-western Cape.
That venture ended in disaster, but other treks led to permanent
Griqua settlements being established north of Cape Town and near
Knysna along the coast to the east. Officially, the Griqua were
classified as a sub-group within the "COLOUREDS." Efforts by
Le Fleur's successors to persuade the government to create a
Griqua "HOMELAND" were unsuccessful.

GROUP AREAS ACT (1950). It provided for the establishment in cities,
    towns and villages, of separate areas for each race group, and pro-
    hibited occupation or ownership of property in such areas by mem-
    bers of other groups. Most Africans had long been segregated in
    urban areas (see URBAN SEGREGATION); Group Areas extended
    the process to include the segregation of "Coloureds" and Indians.
    Much of the machinery devised for the restriction of INDIANS in
    the Asiatic Land Tenure Act (1946) was incorporated in the
    Group Areas Act.
        The government claimed that race mixing led to friction,
    citing the DURBAN RIOTS (1949) as proof, but the Act had other
    purposes: it furthered the process of racial definition so dear
    to APARTHEID theorists, while making control easier, for if
    necessary all-"Coloured" suburbs could be isolated. As towns
    and villages were divided into markedly unequal, racially sepa-
    rate areas, large numbers of "Coloureds" and Indians, forced to
    vacate their homes and businesses, were relocated far from
    city centers. Family, community and religious networks were
    broken, and many of the new areas almost totally lacked ameni-
    ties, while getting from them to work often involved crippling
    transport costs. Whites frequently made quick profits from
    properties vacated under the Act and then gentrified. Much
    Indian commerce was destroyed. Cape Town's DISTRICT SIX
    was perhaps the most notorious case of injustice, suffering, and
    bitterness engendered by application of the Act. By the end of
    1978, 374,990 "Coloureds," 172,156 Indians and 8,299 whites
    had been required to move under the Act. The Act was also
    used in the 1960s and 1970s to prevent a wide range of multi-
    racial activity, from education to sport. An amendment passed
    in 1982 provided that sports functions would no longer be sub-
    ject to the Act. This removed restrictions on non-racial sport.
    (See also MASS REMOVALS.)

HERSTIGTE NASIONALE PARTY (HNP) (Afrikaans: Re-established
    National Party; 1969-). Party formed after a small right
    wing in the NATIONAL PARTY (NP)--Dr Albert Hertzog, son
    of the former Prime Minister (HERTZOG), and three others--
    had been expelled from the party in 1969. The name of the

new party implied that the NP under VORSTER had not remained true to the earlier tradition from MALAN to VERWOERD. The dissidents opposed Vorster's OUTWARD POLICY, and in particular the appointment of a Malawian ambassador to South Africa, and the decision to allow a New Zealand rugby team, which included Maoris, to tour the country. To them, the NP had become dominated by an Afrikaner establishment that had "gone soft" on race issues, and they disliked Vorster's attempts to woo the English vote.

After the breakaway, Vorster advanced the general election a year, and eliminated the HNP from Parliament before it had time to organize (1970). It did as badly in subsequent elections in the 1970s, but in April 1981 won 192,000 votes, an estimated one third of all Afrikaner votes cast in the election, but still no seat in parliament. Its call for a return to BAASSKAP policies and for undiluted Afrikaner hegemony over English-speaking whites appealed particularly to Afrikaners in lower-income brackets.

HERTZOG, James Barry Munnik (1866-1942). Having gained fame as a field general in the SOUTH AFRICAN WAR, he was a co-founder of the Orangia Unie party (1906), the ORANGE RIVER COLONY equivalent of HET VOLK. He served in the ORC government from 1907 to UNION, participated in the NATIONAL CONVENTION, and was a minister in the first BOTHA cabinet. Breaking with Botha, he formed the NATIONAL PARTY (NP). After the PACT with LABOUR, HERTZOG became Prime Minister in 1924. The 1929 election gave the NP an absolute majority in the Assembly, but with the depression, and the changing status of South Africa vis à vis Britain (see COMMONWEALTH), Hertzog was by 1933 prepared to enter a coalition with Smuts' SOUTH AFRICAN PARTY. He remained Prime Minister when coalition became FUSION in 1934. His "HERTZOG BILLS," providing for political segregation for Africans and a new land deal, were eventually passed in 1936. He lost office when he opposed South Africa's entry into WORLD WAR II. He then joined Malan's Nationalists (1940), but was unhappy with Malan's rejection of English co-operation, so withdrew again. With N.C. Havenga (1881-1957), who had been his Minister of Finance from 1924 to 1939, he founded the AFRIKANER PARTY in 1941.

HERTZOG BILLS. Legislation on African land and labor and franchise matters, first proposed in 1926 and eventually passed, in altered form, in 1936-1937. The two-thirds majority in parliament required because the Cape African FRANCHISE was entrenched under the UNION constitution was not achieved until February 1936. The legislation made possible a Union-wide coercive labor system; as long as Cape Africans enjoyed access to the common roll franchise, such a system could not be elaborated.

In the draft legislation of 1926 and 1929, African SQUATTERS were to be forced to work for farmers for at least three months a year; the Native Trust and Land Act of 1936 provided that labor tenants were to work for 180 days, all squatters were to be registered and licensed, and squatting was to be phased out over 30 years. Enforcement of these provisions gave rise to massive RURAL RESISTANCE, especially in the Transvaal, but they could not be enforced in their entirety and in many areas the transition to a fully proletarianized labor force on the farms did not gather momentum until after the middle of the century (see MASS REMOVALS). For the land provisions of the Act see under NATIVES LAND ACT. The Representation of Natives Act (1936) removed the Cape Africans from the common roll, provided for their communal representation in parliament (see further under FRANCHISE) and created an advisory NATIVES REPRESENTATIVE COUNCIL. A Native Laws Amendment Act (1937) tightened INFLUX CONTROL to the urban areas.

HET VOLK (Dutch: the people). Political movement founded by Louis BOTHA in January 1905 to demand full self-government for the Transvaal and ORANGE RIVER COLONY, the immediate end of CHINESE LABOR, the end of restrictions on the public use of DUTCH, and relief for impoverished Afrikaners (see POOR WHITEISM). It rapidly gained support among Transvaal Afrikaners, and in the first general election held in the Transvaal under the new self-government constitution, it won a clear majority (February 1907). Under Botha and SMUTS, Het Volk then embarked on a program of "conciliation" (i.e. co-operation with English-speakers) which eased the path to UNION in 1910.

HIGH COMMISSION (1846-1964). The first High Commission was added to the new Cape Governor's charge in 1846. Devised to aid the Governor settle the colony's eastern frontier, it was in part instituted to give a particular individual extra pay. But the High Commission was renewed, and successive holders of the office used it as a cheap, informal means of extending British sovereignty. BRITISH KAFFRARIA was established under the High Commission at the end of 1847, the ORANGE RIVER SOVEREIGNTY at the beginning of 1848. Though it doubted whether the High Commission legally gave its holder power to act in this way, the Colonial Office in London nevertheless decided in both cases to accept the fait accompli. In 1868 BASUTOLAND was likewise annexed in terms of the High Commission, as were the DIAMOND fields in 1871. In 1877 the High Commission was enlarged, and Sir Bartle FRERE was sent out as Cape Governor and High Commissioner for all southern Africa, to aid in achieving the goal of CONFEDERATION. After the defeat of British forces at the outbreak of the Anglo-ZULU war, a separate High Commissioner for South-East Africa was appointed. The unity of the office was restored in 1881 and in 1884 the first official HIGH COMMISSION TERRITORY came into being, when BASUTOLAND was taken back from Cape rule.

    Cecil RHODES may have acted in the early 1890s as a kind of unofficial High Commissioner, but it was MILNER in the

last years of the century who actively used the High Commission
to magnify the crisis that led to the SOUTH AFRICAN WAR.
After that war he became the first High Commissioner to be
able to attempt to reshape all of South Africa.   Lord Selborne
(1859-1942), Milner's successor, gave public backing to closer
UNION. From 1910 the High Commissioner retained responsibility for the High Commission territories and until 1930 was
also governor-general, representing the Crown in South Africa.
After the declaration of the REPUBLIC (1961), and with the impending independence of the High Commission Territories, the
High Commission was abolished (1964).

HIGH COMMISSION TERRITORIES. The three British territories
    ruled in terms of the HIGH COMMISSION (sometimes, less ac-
    curately, known as the Protectorates). BASUTOLAND, BECH-
    UANALAND, and SWAZILAND were excluded from the new
    UNION because of Britain's special relationship with them and
    her fear that the white rulers of South Africa might not safe-
    guard the interests of its African inhabitants. Their ultimate
    transfer to the Union was envisaged in the South Africa Act
    (1909) but Britain pledged that the wishes of the African people
    of the territories would be considered before such transfer was
    effected. Every Union Prime Minister sought their transfer,
    HERTZOG most vigorously in the inter-war period, for he
    strongly disliked this constant reminder of Britain's continued
    direct involvement in southern African affairs. The inhabitants,
    however, made known their opposition to transfer, and Britain
    was unhappy with the thrust of South Africa's policy toward its
    African peoples. After the NATIONAL PARTY election victory
    in 1948 transfer became highly unlikely; after the inauguration
    of the REPUBLIC in 1961 it was out of the question. In 1963
    VERWOERD made a final appeal to Britain to let South Africa
    lead them to a BANTUSTAN-type independence. When Britain
    made it clear that it would grant them independence, Verwoerd
    became the first Prime Minister to accept that they would not
    be incorporated and to speak of a friendly neighbor policy to-
    wards them. When referring to South African land in African
    hands, Nationalists often added the three territories to the
    RESERVES to obtain a more impressive, but misleading figure
    (for they were not part of South Africa, while much of BECH-
    UANALAND was semi-desert). Locked into the MIGRANT
    LABOR system, their history one of increasing impoverishment,
    they had become by the mid-1960s so heavily dependent on South
    Africa that "South Africa's hostages" was an apt description for
    them. (Cf. LESOTHO.)

HISTORIOGRAPHY. In the mid-19th century, English-speaking white
    settlers began producing accounts of the founding and develop-
    ment of the Cape and Natal. Mainly narrative in form, they
    tended to be written from a British imperial perspective. An
    anti-imperial historiography began with a history in AFRIKAANS
    by S. J. du Toit (1847-1911) published in 1877, and was seen in
    most blatant form in the multi-authored A Century of Wrong

(1899), which chronicled the wrongs done by Britain in the 19th
century to the Afrikaner people. At roughly the same time, a
local settler tradition emerged that sought to be even-handed
in its treatment of British settlers on the one hand and Afrikaner trekkers on the other. The key figure was George McCall
THEAL, the first to spend long hours in the archives, and the
first to attempt a general history of South Africa. In his multi-
volume History, Theal baldly told the story of settler expansionism in great detail. Sympathetic both to those who had gone on
the GREAT TREK and those colonists who had remained in the
Cape colony, Theal was critical of the missionaries and of the
British government in London, both of whom he believed had
interfered unwisely in South African affairs. Though initially
interested in the history of Africans, Theal became increasingly racist in his writing, and much of his History was designed
to justify white conquest of the bulk of the land.
    In the early 20th century, posts in history began to be es-
tablished at the South African universities, and a new profes-
sionalism entered history writing. Afrikaner historians tended
to focus their attention on the GREAT TREK and the later history of Afrikaners, and their histories were usually highly de-
scriptive and unimaginative. P. J. van der Merwe (1912-1979)
wrote with great insight on the history of the TREKBOER.
Eric WALKER was the first professional historian to attempt a
general survey of South African history (1928), and he wrote
prolifically on numerous aspects of that history. But it was
W. M. MACMILLAN who in the 1920s pioneered what became
known as the "liberal" approach, which recognized relations
between white and black to be the central theme of South African history, and attempted to understand black history as well
as white. Of those who followed in the Macmillan tradition,
C. W. DE KIEWIET, one of his students, was the most brilliant.
    In the 1960s there emerged a new generation of liberal his-
torians, aware of the historiographical revolution that had transformed the writing of the history of tropical Africa and anxious
to use anthropology and other disciplines to understand African
societies. The doyen of these "liberal Africanists" was Leonard
THOMPSON, one of the editors of The Oxford History of South
Africa (2 volumes, 1969, 1971). In an influential collection of
papers published in 1969, Thompson argued that the history of
African societies was the "forgotten factor" in South African
history.
    It was in large part through their critical reviews of the
Oxford History that a new school of "radicals" or "revisionists"
gained prominence in the early 1970s. Mostly younger scholars,
many of them political exiles from South Africa, some themselves Marxists (e. g., LEGASSICK) and all influenced by Marxist historiography, they developed a critique of the liberal tradition from a materialist perspective. They pointed out that
liberals had played down, or ignored material factors. They
accused liberals of arguing that had ideological factors like
racism and Afrikaner nationalism not intervened, the capitalist

market place would have produced a non-racial society. The revisionists showed that racial oppression and capitalist exploitation had gone hand in hand, and that the relationship between capitalist industrialization and racial segregation had been an essentially complementary one. Apartheid policies, instead of imposing constraints on profit-maximization, had aided it. Segregation was essentially a response to capitalist demands for cheap labor. Against the liberal view that irrational race prejudice lay at the root of apartheid, the radicals argued that class rather than race had shaped the history of industrial South Africa. Some of them got round the central problem of a racially divided working class by calling white workers a new petty bourgeoisie.

By the end of the 1970s there was intense, and sometimes acrimonious, debate among radicals about such matters. Liberal Africanists, few of whom had remained uninfluenced by the new writing, agreed with much of it. But if radicals emphasized material factors to the exclusion of any others, or had a dogmatic belief in the primacy of class, then liberals parted company with them.

HLUBI see MFECANE; MFENGU; LANGALIBALELE AFFAIR.

HOFMEYR, J. H. (1845-1909) see AFRIKANER BOND; DUTCH; RHODES.

HOFMEYR, J. H. (1894-1948) see PATON; UNITED PARTY.

HOMELANDS. Term used by the South African government (e. g. in the Bantu Homelands Citizenship Act (1970)) for the former RESERVES. It implied that the territory of the BANTUSTANS (as they are called in this book) constituted the historical area of African occupation. The corollary was that Africans living outside these areas could be denied political rights where they lived and be made a citizen of one or another "homeland." In reality, the Bantustans were mere fragmented remnants of the lands Africans had once occupied, and for millions of Africans were in no sense "homelands." Because it was so historically misleading, and was used to justify a denial of rights, most critics of the Bantustan policy deliberately avoided using the term.

HOTTENTOTS. Name given the KHOIKHOI by the Dutch in the 17th and 18th centuries. It was derived onomatopoeically from what to the Dutch seemed their unintelligible speech. By the 19th century it had become a general term for all KHOISAN people and their descendants at the Cape, i. e. all people of color who were not slaves, FREE BLACKS or XHOSA. When the ex-slaves and "Hottentots" together came to be called "COLOUREDS," "Hottentot" (or "Hotnot") often meant one who had not become acculturated. "Hottentot" gradually acquired a strong perjorative connotation; even within the "Coloured"

community itself, it was used as a term of abuse. (Cf. also
BASTARDS; SAN.)

HUNTER-GATHERERS see SAN.

IMBUMBA YAMA NYAMA (Xhosa: "strong union," from a phrase
    allegedly used by Ntsikana [c. 1760-1820], the first African
    convert to Christianity in South Africa). Also known as Imbumba
    yama Afrika ("Union of Africa"), it was the first modern African
    political organization. Its establishment in the eastern Cape in
    1882 was an African response to the new AFRIKANER BOND,
    the first formal political party at the Cape. But the Imbumba
    did not last, and was followed by a number of equally ephemeral
    African political organizations in the years before the founding
    of the AFRICAN NATIONAL CONGRESS. John Tengo JABAVU
    was to claim that the Imbumba he founded in 1912 was heir to
    the first Imbumba, but there was no organizational link between
    them.

IMMIGRATION see, e.g. ENGLISH-SPEAKING WHITES; INDIANS.

INDEPENDENT CHURCHES see ETHIOPIANISM.

INDIANS. In the 1850s Sir George GREY, the Cape governor, sug-
    gested Indians be imported to work on the Natal sugar planta-
    tions, for Indians had been the key to the prosperity of the
    Mauritius sugar industry. Between 1860 and 1911 laborers re-
    cruited on contract entered Natal, the majority to work on the
    sugar cane plantations, but others on the railways and coal
    mines. Their indentures provided that after five years they
    could hire out their services on the labor market; after ten
    years they were entitled either to a free passage back to India
    or a free grant of land equal in value to the passage money.
    Though conditions, especially on the sugar plantations, were
    harsh, few took advantage of the opportunity to return to India.
    Some became itinerant hawkers, petty shopkeepers, or artisans,
    others suppliers of market produce.
        Besides the indentured laborers, so-called "passenger Indi-
    ans," mainly Gujerati-speaking Muslims from the Bombay
    Presidency, arrived independently to trade. By 1893, of an
    estimated Indian population of 46,000 in Natal, 5,500 were pas-
    senger Indians. White colonists knew them as "arabs," as
    distinct from "coolie" laborers, because they were mostly Mus-
    lims. Astute traders, the passenger Indians provided leader-
    ship to the Indian communities in Durban, Pietermaritzburg,
    and the other towns. A Natal Immigration Restriction Act of
    1897 required an education test in a European language, and
    so drastically reduced the number of Indian immigrants. Union
    legislation of 1913 prohibited the entry of any new immigrants
    besides the wives and children of those Indians already settled
    in South Africa.

Between 1893 and 1914 the central figure in Indian politics was Mohandas Karamchand Gandhi (1869-1948), who after obtaining legal training in England was retained as a lawyer by a Natal Indian trading firm. Almost immediately after arriving in Durban in 1893, he became the spokesman for the middle class passenger Indians. Having founded the Natal Indian Congress (1894) and becoming its first secretary, he led an unsuccessful protest against legislation which barred Indians from the vote (1895), even though there were only 251 registered Indian voters in Natal. During the SOUTH AFRICAN WAR he organized an Indian ambulance corps, which was used again during the BAMBATHA REBELLION. In 1903 he started the influential weekly Indian Opinion.

As early as 1885 the Transvaal had passed a law barring Indians from citizenship rights and the right to own fixed property, providing that they should live in separate areas set aside for them, and imposing a £25 registration fee. After the discovery of GOLD, significant numbers of Indians moved into the Transvaal despite the discrimination to which they were subjected there. The post-war British administration sought to limit the numbers of Indians entering the Transvaal by requiring that fingerprints be taken. Having developed his famous philosophy of satyagraha ("keep to the truth"), Gandhi launched a non-violent resistance campaign in September 1906, which led to an agreement that the registration be voluntary. His second campaign was broader, focussing on the poll tax that Indians had to pay and the non-recognition of marriages solemnized under Indian rites. He organized strikes on the Natal coal-fields and sugar plantations, and led a Great March from Natal to the Transvaal (1913). The lower-class indentured Indians, who had been critical of Gandhi because of his background and class position, now briefly rallied behind him. After Gandhi himself had spent time in jail, the poll tax was abolished and Indian marriages recognized. An exchange of letters between SMUTS and Gandhi--the "Smuts-Gandhi" agreement--appeared to settle other matters of dispute. Gandhi then left South Africa (July 1914) to fight for freedom in India itself.

Long after Union the Indian community was still regarded by the government as being resident in the country on a temporary basis. The Cape Town Agreement (1927) between the governments of South Africa and India provided for voluntary state-aided repatriation, but few Indians availed themselves of that. Many passenger Indians had done very well for themselves as traders, and acquired substantial property. During the depression of the 1930s a number bought properties from whites along the lower slopes of the line of hills known as the Berea in Durban. Smuts' war-time government appointed two commissions into Indian "penetration" of white areas. The Pegging Act of 1943 then prohibited the purchase by Indians of property from whites in Durban for three years. After a third commission, a more far-reaching Asiatic Land Tenure and Indian Representation Act (1946) divided Natal into exempted and unexempted areas; in the latter no Asiatics were permitted to buy or occupy

fixed property without permission. Under the influence of a
younger, more radical leadership, the Natal Indian Congress
launched another passive resistance campaign against this
"Ghetto Act" while the government of India withdrew its High
Commissioner, broke off trade relations, and raised the issue
in the UNITED NATIONS. After the failure of the passive resistance campaign, the Natal Indian Congress established closer
ties with the AFRICAN NATIONAL CONGRESS and Indians played
an important role in the DEFIANCE CAMPAIGN and CONGRESS
ALLIANCE of the early 1950s. Indian leaders suffered BAN-
NING and other harassment, and while the Indian Congress was
not itself banned, it was rendered ineffective. There was no
significant opposition when large numbers of Indians were forced
out of the cities under GROUP AREAS and resettled in small,
overcrowded Indian suburbs, where they often had to pay in-
flated prices for accommodation.

In 1961, the year of the REPUBLIC, the Indian community
was finally given full official recognition as a permanent part of
the South African population. A nominated Indian Council was
established (1964), which in 1968 became the statutory South
African Indian Council. Ten years later provision was made
for 40 of its 45 members to be elected. After further delays,
caused mainly by Indian opposition to the Council, the first
elections were held in November 1981. Thanks to a successful mass boycott, only 6 percent of the voters went to the polls.
A collaborationist group was, however, prepared to operate it,
and Indian representatives served on the President's Council
(see CONSTITUTIONAL CHANGE).

Despite religious (70 percent Hindu, 20 percent Muslim),
linguistic, and class divisions, the Indian community remained
a relatively cohesive one. 800, 000 strong, it was just under
3 percent of the total population in 1980; well over 40 percent
of all Indians in the country lived in Durban. Indian exclusiv-
ity and relative economic privilege had bred African resistance
in the past (see DURBAN RIOTS) and it was uncertain how far
Indians in general saw their struggle against discrimination as
bound up with that of the Africans.

INDUSTRIAL AND COMMERCIAL WORKERS UNION (ICU). Formed
in Cape Town in January 1919 by Clements Kadalie (c. 1896-
1951), a Malawi-born laborer, it spread from the African dock-
workers there to become a general union as well as a political
pressure group and populist movement. By 1927 the ICU
claimed 100, 000 members, the first nationwide movement with
a mass following among Africans (there were not many "Coloured" or Indian members). In the early 1920s most ICU activity was centered in the cities, but its expansion in the mid
1920s was mainly a rural phenomenon (the African labor force
in manufacturing was very small at this time). Many of its
members seem to have faced eviction from white-owned farms,
and some were evicted because they were ICU members.

The ICU played some role in obtaining wage increases in
Cape Town in 1920 and Bloemfontein in 1928, but otherwise

achieved very little. The hopes of its rural members were
disappointed, and from 1928 it gradually disintegrated. This
was in part a result of hostility from employers and from the
state, which passed new repressive legislation to counter it,
but it was also the result of internal weaknesses. An un-
structured organization, in which the funds collected were often
misused, it suffered from confusion and rivalry within its leadership. Kadalie, its national secretary and editor of its newspaper, The Workers' Herald, came under the influence of white
liberals, who persuaded him in 1926 to expel members of the
COMMUNIST PARTY and then to go to Geneva and Britain to
rally support. An autocratic leader, he fell out both with William Ballinger, an adviser sent out by the British Labour Party
in 1928 (see Margaret BALLINGER), and with his ambitious
lieutenant in Natal, who broke away with the important Natal
section. For organizing a strike in East London in 1930,
Kadalie was sent to jail, then BANNED, and the ICU survived
thereafter as merely a few independent branches of little significance.

INDUSTRIAL CONCILIATION ACT (1924). This legislation provided
    formal legal status for employers' organizations and TRADE
    UNIONS, but "PASS-bearing natives" (Africans) were not per-
    mitted to be members of registered unions. Coming soon after
    the suppression of the RAND REVOLT, the Act successfully
    incorporated unions of whites, "Coloureds" and Indians into a
    state-supervised system of control. Industrial Councils of em-
    ployer and employee representatives were set up to negotiate
    wages and conditions of work, and the Act is generally credited
    with helping to usher in an era of relatively harmonious labor
    relations. White labor saw it to be in its interests that Afri-
    cans be excluded from trade union rights, while the co-optation
    of white labor excluded any possible joint action by white and
    African workers.
        A 1956 Amendment required unions to be constituted on racial
    lines. In 1979 the Act was amended again after the first report
    of the WIEHAHN COMMISSION to allow for the registration of
    African unions (and also to remove the statutory JOB COLOR
    BAR). The registration of non-racial unions was permitted by
    further legislation in 1981.

INDUSTRIALIZATION see DIAMONDS; GOLD; MINING; MANU-
    FACTURING INDUSTRY.

INFLUENZA EPIDEMIC (1918). The Spanish 'Flu, which is thought
    to have killed 20 million people worldwide in 1918-1919, arrived
    in South Africa in September 1918. Its impact was uneven, with
    Kimberley's African compound being particularly hard hit, and the
    Transkei and Ciskei suffering severely, while Natal went rela-
    tively unscathed. The official deathtoll was 139,471 (11,726
    whites), but recent research suggests this was an under-
    estimate and that perhaps over a quarter of a million Africans
    died.

INFLUX CONTROL.   Control of the entry of Africans into the urban
areas.   In terms of the STALLARD DOCTRINE (1922), the urban areas were considered "white," and government policy aimed
to reduce the number of Africans in them to a minimum.   If
Africans were considered permanent residents and given freehold, then it was assumed that in the long run they could not
be refused voting rights.   Influx control also served to regulate
the distribution of African labor, in particular in the interests
of white farmers, who feared losing their labor to the towns.
Defenders of influx control claimed that it protected the jobs
and wages of those Africans in the urban areas, and that without it the towns would be "swamped" by Africans streaming in
from the poverty-stricken rural areas.
Control was exercised chiefly through the PASS LAWS and
provisions of other related legislation.   Some restrictions on
African women entering the towns were imposed in the 1930
amendment of the Natives Urban Areas Act (for which see also
URBAN SEGREGATION).   Legislation of 1937 attempted to restrict the number of Africans in town according to the availability of work, allowing the immigrant to the town 14 days to
find work, after which he had to leave.   But the most important tightening of influx control came as a result of 1952 legislation, which reduced the 14 day period to a mere 72 hours and
applied it to women as well.   Section 10 provided that Africans
not born in an urban area had no right to remain there, unless
they had lived there continuously for 15 years or had worked
continuously for one employer for 10 years.   These statutory
rights could be lost through, say, a criminal prosecution, which
might be for vagrancy or breach of contract.   Africans in the
urban areas consequently lived under the constant threat of being
"endorsed out."   In the Western Cape the "COLOURED" LABOR
PREFERENCE POLICY acted as an additional influx control device.
Despite all such measures, the number of Africans in the urban areas continued to increase (see URBANIZATION).   Yet
from the late 1960s the proportion of MIGRANT workers in
towns rose considerably.   There was no doubt that but for influx control there would have been far more Africans settled in
the towns.   In 1980 only 1.8 million Africans, 42 percent of
the urban African workforce, had Section 10 rights.

INFORMATION SCANDAL see MULDERGATE.

INKATHA (Zulu: grass coil placed on the head for carrying a load;
a ritual "grass coil of the nation" was kept at the Zulu royal
headquarters and was a symbolic object suggesting that the nation should stand firm).   An original Inkatha ya ka Zulu founded
in 1922-23 as a council to advise the ZULU king did not last
long.   In 1974 Gatsha BUTHELEZI formed Inkatha yeNkululeko
ye Sizwe (Zulu: National Cultural Liberation Movement) as a
political and cultural movement to give Africans pride in their
own culture and to work against racism and segregation.
Though open to all Africans from 1977, it remained in practice

Zulu-centered. By 1980 it claimed a paid-up membership of
over 300,000, making it the largest black organization ever to
have existed in South Africa. Opposing independence for
KWAZULU, it won every seat in that territory's first election in
1978. Despite its use of chiefly symbols, Buthelezi, its president, tried to promote it as the internal successor to the banned
AFRICAN NATIONAL CONGRESS. It accepted non-violence as
its strategy, on the grounds that white power made any other
strategy impractical. Radical blacks saw it as a divisive, ethnic and collaborationist organization.

IRON AGE. The first Iron Age culture was introduced into South
Africa early in the 1st millenium A.D. We know that those
who worked and used iron also raised cattle, made pots and
practiced AGRICULTURE. They may have been BANTU-
SPEAKERS as well. Evidence remains very tenuous and classification and periodization far from settled. Archaeologists
make a clear distinction between an Early Iron Age, which
lasted to about the 11th century, and a Later Iron Age. There
is a complete break in pottery styles. The Later Iron Age is
marked by a greater use of cattle, by a switch in site location
from valley bottoms, near water, to hilltops or the sides of
valleys, and by expansion of settlement from the wooded valleys of the coastal strip onto the interior grasslands. Across
the southern and central Transvaal and in the eastern half of
the Orange Free State there was in the later Iron Age a very
extensive use of stone building; in the southern Transvaal alone
over 6,000 stone ruins are known to exist. There was also
some GOLD mining in the eastern Transvaal and on the WIT-
WATERSRAND. Copper and tin were mined in the Transvaal
lowveld.

   In 1981 the oldest Iron Age site in South Africa was Silver
Leaves, east of Tzaneen in the foothills of the Transvaal
DRAKENSBERG. There iron slag and impressions of seeds
from cultivated cereals were found associated with charcoal
which was dated to the late 3rd century A.D. or the early 4th
century. At Broederstroom, west of Pretoria, the remains of
collapsed huts and traces of iron-working, associated with the
bones of domesticated animals, have been dated to the 5th century. It is presumed that an iron-using people displaced, and
perhaps to some extent also mixed with, an earlier indigenous
hunter-gatherer society ignorant of metal-working, stock-
breeding or plant domestication. The most striking Early Iron
Age materials to have survived in South Africa are the famous
LYDENBURG HEADS. Perhaps the best-known Later Iron Age
site is Mapungubwe, just south of the LIMPOPO RIVER in the
Transvaal, which is dated c. A.D. 1100. There burials were
accompanied by gold and copper jewelry and gold-plated figu-
rines of animals, suggesting that this was an important religious center in a state of considerable power and wealth. In
this case the skeletal remains suggest a non-Negroid and therefore perhaps non-Bantu speaking people. But in general there
is no doubt that the people who inaugurated the Later Iron Age

were the ancestors of those Bantu-speaking people who, many
centuries later, met Europeans.

ISLAM.   The first Muslims at the Cape were political prisoners,
convicts banished from the DUTCH EAST INDIA COMPANY's
possessions in the East, or slaves.   Of the slaves, most came
from Bengal, others from the west coast of India, or from the
Indonesian islands.   Many of the habits of the latter, whether
in clothes, food, or ritual, survived at the Cape.   Some of the
slaves who came from West Africa may have been Muslims.   A
remarkable growth of Islam occurred among the slaves at the
Cape in the late 18th century.   Not only did Islam appeal because it was color-blind, but masters welcomed the conversion
of their slaves to Islam, for it taught obedience and the avoid-
ance of alcohol.   Whereas there was a presumption that a slave
baptised a Christian would not be sold, there was no question
of an obligation to free a Muslim slave.   During the first
BRITISH occupation of the Cape, the Muslims in Cape Town
were able to persuade the authorities to allow them to practice their religion freely, and in 1804 the first mosque opened.
Because Malay was their lingua franca, the community, among
whom were many skilled artisans, became known as the Cape
Malays, especially after the emancipation of the slaves.   Today that name is rejected both as inappropriate and as an ethnic label, and "Cape Muslims" is used instead.   The majority follow the Shafi school, though a minority were persuaded by Abu
Bakr Effendi (1835-1880), sent to Cape Town by the Sultan of
Constantinople in 1862, to adopt Hanafi beliefs.   In 1980 the
Cape Muslims numbered some 160,000, just over half the total
number of Muslims in South Africa, for from 1860 on a new
wave of Muslims arrived from India, for whom see INDIANS.
(See also CAPE SLAVERY.)

JABAVU, John Tengo (1859-1921).   The son of MFENGU Methodists, he attended Healdtown Missionary Institution, where he
qualified as a teacher.   From 1881 he edited Isigidimi Sama
Xosa (Messenger of the Xhosa) at the Lovedale mission.   He
left there in 1884 to help organize the political campaign of a
white parliamentarian, who with other Cape liberals then helped
fund Imvo Zabantsundu (Native Opinion), a weekly newspaper
which Jabavu edited in King William's Town from November
1884.   Imvo gave Jabavu a powerful voice, and he remained
until the end of the century the most prominent Cape African
spokesman.   Though a strong critic of the 1887 FRANCHISE
legislation and the GLEN GREY ACT (1894), his belief that
Africans should support white political groups led him to back
the AFRIKANER BOND in 1898.   In 1909 he served on a delegation to London to protest the color bar in the South Africa
Bill (see UNION) and he returned there in 1911 for the Universal Races Congress.   When the South African Native National
Congress (later AFRICAN NATIONAL CONGRESS) was formed,

he would not join it, rejecting an all-black political organization, especially one that he did not dominate. The South African Races Congress he founded a few months later was not a success. In 1913 he came out in support of the NATIVES LAND ACT because it was introduced by one of his white friends, and his image among Africans was further damaged when he stood for the Cape Provincial Council in 1914 and prevented the re-election of the only African ever to serve on that body, Walter Rubusana (1858-1936). He did much to promote the cause of a university college for Africans and served on the council of the South African Native College, later FORT HARE, from its establishment in 1916 until his death.

His son Davidson Don (1885-1959) was president of the ALL-AFRICAN CONVENTION from 1936 to 1948 and the most prominent African member of the Fort Hare faculty until he retired as Professor of Bantu Languages in 1944.

JAMESON RAID (December 1895). With the aim of overthrowing KRUGER's Transvaal government, RHODES, Prime Minister of the Cape, secretly commissioned his close friend Leander Starr Jameson (1853-1917), then an administrator in Rhodes's British South Africa Company, to lead a force of mounted men from BECHUANALAND into the Transvaal. Joseph Chamberlain (1836-1914), the Colonial Secretary in London, knew something was afoot, though was later to deny it. The expected uprising of UITLANDERS did not materialize and the raiders were soon captured. Rhodes had to resign as Cape Premier and Jameson was sent to Britain to be tried (sentenced to 15 months imprisonment, he served less than four). A telegram from the German Kaiser to KRUGER, congratulating him on repulsing the Raid, aroused British ire and led the Kruger government to hope for German support in a future clash with Britain. The Raid seemed to bear out those who argued that the British record in dealings with the republics had been one of bad faith and injustice, and it pushed the Transvaal towards a firm alliance with the Free State. At the Cape, the Raid destroyed the alliance between Rhodes and Jan Hofmeyr of the AFRIKANER BOND.

JEWISH COMMUNITY. It was not until the BRITISH occupation of the Cape that Jews arrived in any numbers. Some became merchants in Cape Town, where the first permanent Hebrew congregation was founded in 1841, others traded in the interior, where they formed an accepted constituent of the white rural population in the Afrikaner republics. By 1880 there were some 4,000 Jews in South Africa. Then in the last two decades of the century there was a large influx from eastern Europe, especially from Lithuania. A literacy test, introduced by the Cape in 1902 to restrict INDIAN immigration, threatened to cut off this flow, but in 1906 Yiddish was recognized as a European language, and by 1914 over 40,000 Lithuanian Jews had entered the country. The Immigration Quota Act of 1930 reduced the flow of immigrants from eastern Europe to a trickle. Then after Hitler's accession to power in Germany, some 7,000 refugees fled to South Africa before an Aliens Act (1937) closed the door to further German Jewish immigration. Explicit anti-Semitism emerged in the 1930s in right-wing Afrikaner circles, opposed to any further immigration and viewing Hitler as a hero. But after World War II SMUTS and then MALAN supported the Zionist cause, with which South African Jews closely identified themselves. In the early 1960s relations between South Africa and Israel grew strained, and VERWOERD warned the Jewish community that Israel's criticism of apartheid was imperiling its position. After the 1967 Middle East war relations were normalized. VORSTER visited Israel in 1976, and the two "pariah" nations developed close economic, technological, and political links.

The Jewish population, which in 1936 had formed 4.5 percent of the white population, declined proportionately thereafter, because of immigration restrictions, a low birth rate, and some emigration and intermarriage. Though only 100,000 strong in 1980, the Jewish community played a major role in commerce and industry and in the professions.

JOB COLOR BAR. The use of the law to reserve certain jobs for whites, or to bar Africans from them. Most firmly entrenched in the mining industry, it spread from there to other fields of employment. In terms of a Mining Act passed by the Cape parliament in 1883, regulations were promulgated in 1885 providing that Africans should not handle blasting. A Transvaal law of 1893 prohibited Africans, Indians, and "Coloureds" from preparing charges, loading drills, or lighting fuses. From 1896 a skilled gold miner had to have a blasting certificate; it was understood that only whites would be able to obtain such a certificate. The Transvaal Boilers and Machinery Act of 1898 provided that no person of color could be an engine driver. These color bar provisions remained in force under the post-SOUTH AFRICAN WAR British administration. When the importation of CHINESE LABOR was authorized, a Transvaal Labour Importation Ordinance (1904) restricted over 50 specific occupations and trades for whites. After UNION the Mines and Works Act (1911) empowered the government to make regulations to control the grant of certificates of competence needed for skilled and semi-skilled jobs. In the regulations made under the Act, 51 occupations were reserved for white workers by 1920.

An attempt by mine management to adjust the job color bar and employ Africans in semi-skilled jobs previously reserved for whites led to the RAND REVOLT. With the REVOLT suppressed, the Chamber of Mines instigated a test case before the Transvaal Supreme Court, which found that the Mines and Works Act did not expressly sanction racial discrimination, and therefore regulations discriminating on that basis were ultra vires. When the PACT GOVERNMENT came to power, the 1911 Act was amended to provide expressly for racial discrimination in the issue of certificates of competence. The amended Act (1926) was often referred to as the "Color Bar Act."

The function of the job color bar has been the subject of much controversy. Mine owners often said that to save costs they would like to employ Africans, at lower rates of pay, in jobs reserved for whites. Liberal analysts, on the other hand, have seen the job color bar as impeding economic growth. Radicals argued that economic growth was underpinned by cheap African labor and that, by dividing the working class along racial lines, the job color bar helped keep African wages low.

After the NATIONAL PARTY was returned to power in 1948 it took further steps to secure the position of white workers. An Act of 1951 prevented skilled African building workers from working in "white" urban areas. The INDUSTRIAL CONCILIA-TION ACT was amended in 1956 to empower the Minister of Labour to reserve any work for people of a particular racial group. While not more than 2 percent of jobs were ever reserved in terms of determinations under this Act, most job reservation was implemented through state-enforced industrial council agreements between employers and white craft unions operating a closed shop. Besides the apprenticeship system, such measures as GROUP AREAS, INFLUX CONTROL and the "COLOURED" LABOUR PREFERENCE policy in the western Cape all served to restrict job opportunities on a racial basis.

Both international pressure and the growing shortage of skilled and semi-skilled labor worked to undermine statutory job reservation in the late 1970s. In 1979 the government accepted a recommendation from the WIEHAHN COMMISSION that the principle of such job reservation be rejected. Existing work reservation determinations were to remain in force, however, until they could be phased out with the assent of the relevant white union. It was not until February 1982 that resistance by a white union to the ending of job reservation in Cape Town's municipal services was overcome, and they were opened to people of all races. But the powerful white Mine Workers' Union continued to oppose the scrapping of job reservation in the mines, the last area where determinations remained in force. (See also COLOR BAR, CIVILISED LABOR.)

JOHANNESBURG. Today the largest city in South Africa, the land it occupies was in 1885 bare VELD. With the discovery of the main GOLD reef of the WITWATERSRAND, in 1886 a town was laid out, named for Johann Rissik, a surveyor, and Christian Johannes Joubert (1834-1911), a Transvaal politician. The diggers camp which in 1887 contained 3,000 people soon had on three sides of it yellow dumps of waste material from the mines. By 1899 its population had shot up to 120,000. After the BRITISH took over its administration, they increased its area from 5 square miles to 82 square miles (1903). By 1914 its population was over a quarter of million, and that figure did not include those Africans living illegally on the outskirts of the town.

The rapid development of this ultra-materialistic city from a mining camp of one-story buildings with galvanized-iron roofs to what was the single largest concentration of whites on the

African continent left Johannesburg a city of immense inequali-
ties of wealth: in the early 20th century, while Jan Note was
building up an "army" of Ninevites on the fringes of the city
which survived by robbing fellow Africans who had come to
"Egoli" (from "gold") to work, in the northern suburbs the
RANDLORDS lived in the greatest affluence. By the mid 20th
century, Johannesburg had become the center of a ribbon of
towns along the golden Rand, and the hub of the largest industrial and commercial concentration in the country. From the
1960s, as air travel replaced sea travel, it was also the main
gateway to and from South Africa.

KAFFIR (also Caffre, Caffer, Kaffer and other variants). Originally an Arabic noun meaning "the ungrateful," it came to be used
for those who did not believe in Allah. Muslim traders took it
down the east African coast, where it was applied to the indigenous African peoples. In 18th-century Cape Town the much
despised officials whose task it was to inflict punishments as
offenders were known as "Caffres." Though the Portuguese on
occasion used "Kaffir" for KHOIKHOI, it was most commonly
used for BANTU-SPEAKING Africans. The Dutch and then the
British applied it to the XHOSA, despite evidence from at least
as early as the 1820s that the latter disliked being called by
that term. From the mid 19th century it came to be applied
more generally to all Cape NGUNI, or even all Bantu-speaking
Africans. The pejorative connotation attached to the word led
to its being replaced, from about the end of the 19th century,
by "Native" (in turn later replaced by BANTU). In the 1970s
there were a few cases of Africans being awarded damages in
the courts because whites called them "Kaffir."
     "Kaffir" was used in various combinations with other words,
e. g. , Kaffir farming (a system of tenant farming in which Africans paid rents to live on white-owned land).

KANGWANE (land of the Ngwane, from whom the SWAZI emerged).
A small BANTUSTAN created for the Swazi within South Africa.
When it was given a legislative assembly in 1978, only 100, 000
of the estimated 600, 000 Swazis in South Africa lived in the territory, which was divided into a portion adjoining the northern
Swaziland border and another bordering the Kruger National
Park. In the 1970s the South African and Swaziland governments entered into secret negotiations on the transfer of the
territory to Swaziland. In June 1982 the South African government announced that Kangwane was to be incorporated in Swaziland, along with a portion of KWAZULU, and the Kangwane
legislative assembly, which was known to oppose incorporation,
was dissolved.

KARROO (KHOI: "dry country"). Region of flat-topped hills and
tussocks of dry grass on open, treeless plains, which covers

half the Cape and the southwestern Orange Free State. Once
over the concentric mountains skirting the Karroo, there was
nothing to stop the advance of the white TREKBOERS, no place
for the SAN to group and resist. Because of its aridity, it was
not settled by BANTU-SPEAKERS before the 19th century. Sci-
entists believe that human activity in the past century and a half
has increased the area of dessication, enlarging the Karroo.
Splendid evocations of the region are to be found in The Little
Karoo [sic.], stories by Pauline Smith (1882-1959), and in Olive
SCHREINER's The Story of An African Farm.

KAT RIVER SETTLEMENT. The right of the KHOIKHOI and "other
free persons of color" to own land was recognized in ORDIN-
ANCE 50 (1828), but they then had no access to land outside the
mission stations. The Kat River Settlement was established for
them by the Cape government in 1829 in a relatively fertile valley from which the XHOSA ruler Maqoma (1789-1873) had been
ejected shortly beforehand. The government intended the settlement to serve as a buffer between the colony and the Xhosa, and
the new settlers were drawn in to fight on the colonial side in
the wars of 1834-35 and 1846-47 against the Xhosa. In the
second of these wars in particular, the settlement suffered severely. White settlers increasingly coveted the land, especially
when some of the settlers began to prove successful peasant
producers. Whites engaged in commercial sheep farming wanted
its lands for their sheep; others sought to employ the settlers
as laborers.
   Driven to rebellion, about half the settlers took up arms in
1851 against the colonial authorities, when the colony was involved in another war with the Xhosa. Andries Botha (c. 1790-
after 1852), a leading rebel, was convicted of high treason and
the rebels' land confiscated and given to whites. The loyalists
remained in the settlement, some retaining their titles into the
20th century. In 1981 the government announced that the Kat
River valley would be incorporated into the newly "independent"
CISKEI.

KHOIKHOI (or KHOI). Yellow-skinned pastoralists, they called
themselves "Khoikhoi," meaning "men of men," in their click
language, but were known to whites in the 17th and 18th centuries as "HOTTENTOTS" an insulting imitation of their stac-
cato, clicking speech.
   The Khoikhoi are thought to have originated in or near present northern Botswana. It is speculated that hunter-gatherers
who acquired livestock, probably early in the 1st millenium
A.D., moved south to the ORANGE RIVER, from where some
continued due south and then moved westward to the Cape Peninsula (the Cape Khoi), while others travelled west along the
ORANGE RIVER to near its mouth, then south into Namaqualand (the Nama). It is assumed that the Khoi were the first
to keep cattle, but whether they were responsible for introducing sheep into the southwestern Cape early in the 1st millenium A.D. is not known.

The Khoi were a relatively homogenous people who, when encountered by Europeans, kept cattle and sheep, but grew no crops besides dagga (marijuana). As their economy was fragile, they often had to revert to a purely hunter-gatherer existence. Semi-nomadic, they built more substantial huts from rushes than the SAN, made pottery and knew how to shape metal (the Nama south of the Orange River worked copper). They lived in weakly structured polities under rulers who seem to have had little power to prevent frequent disintegration. Sometimes the San robbed their cattle; sometimes they had San clients. There was much interaction, including intermarriage, between the Khoi and BANTU-SPEAKING PEOPLE, particularly the southernmost SOTHO, the Tihaping, north of the Orange, and the southernmost NGUNI, the XHOSA, east of the Bushman's River.

Van Riebeeck and other DUTCH officials asked that they be allowed to enslave Khoikhoi, but the Company refused this, insisting that good relations were necessary to obtain cattle from them. It was believed, too, that the Khoi would make poor slaves because they were lazy and unaccustomed to sedentary labor. At first the Khoi were ready to exchange their cattle for such goods as beads, buttons, and iron objects. But increasingly trade became raiding, as Europeans swept off the cattle they wanted. Two small wars were fought between the Europeans and the Khoikhoi in the early years of the settlement, but Khoikhoi society mainly disintegrated, not through armed conflict, but because of the gradual loss of land and cattle, which forced the Khoi to take work with whites. Khoi society was too fragile to cope with the unequal commercial relationship established by the Dutch. As their societies crumbled Khoi became herdsmen, ox-trainers, and wagon-drivers for the whites. Nevertheless, Khoi resistance must not be underestimated: some of those who lost their cattle became "Bushmen" raiders along the advancing frontiers of white settlement. In the last quarter of the 18th century bands of up to 1,000 of these raiders kept the whites at bay and prevented their further advance into the interior. Some of those Khoi who had been reduced to a landless proletariat in the eastern Cape took up arms in 1799 and joined the XHOSA in resistance to the colonists. It took the British over two years to suppress this great Khoi rebellion.

It is thought that there were some 200,000 Khoikhoi south of the Orange in the mid-17th century. By the late 18th century there were perhaps 20,000 within the Cape settlement. Vast numbers of Khoi in the south-western Cape died in the smallpox epidemic of 1713, and further epidemics followed in 1735 and 1767. Those who survived within the colony, working for whites, remained legally free, but in practice they were without rights, and their position little different from that of the slaves (see CAPE SLAVERY). The PASS laws to which they were subject at the turn of the century were swept away by ORDINANCE 50 (1828). Gradually the Khoi, now speaking proto-AFRIKAANS, became part of the "COLOURED" commun-

ity. But before the end of the 18th century others had sought
to escape white rule by trekking northwards to the middle
reaches of the Orange river, where some of them became
known as !Kora (Korana).

KHOISAN. Name used by the anthropologist Isaac Schapera in his
    The Khoisan Peoples of South Africa (1930), as well as by
    later scholars, for the KHOIKHOI and the SAN together. Lin-
    guists tell us that the Khoi language is quite distinct from the
    San ones, but the historical evidence available often does not
    make clear what language was being spoken or whether the peo-
    ple referred to were hunter-gatherers or herders. It would
    seem that Khoi who lost their cattle and reverted to a purely
    hunter-gatherer existence were often called "Bushmen" or
    "Bushmen-HOTTENTOTS." Khoisan is, then, a convenient
    composite term.

KHOLWA (Zulu: "believer"). Those Natal Africans who received
    some formal education, were Christian and had to some extent
    been "westernized." By the end of the 19th century there were
    an estimated 40,000 African communicants and 100,000 adhe-
    rents in Natal. Though often as critical as whites of the "bar-
    barism" of their fellows, the Kholwa were not accorded equal
    status with whites, most of whom feared the challenge posed by
    growth of a large Kholwa community. In the eastern Cape such
    Africans were known as "school people," as distinct from those
    non-Christians called either "red people" (because of the red
    clay with which they smeared their bodies) or "blanket people"
    (because they wore blankets instead of European clothes).

KINDERGARTEN. Contemptuous term used for the group of young
    Oxford graduates who helped MILNER administer the Transvaal
    and the ORANGE RIVER COLONY after the SOUTH AFRICAN
    WAR. Devoted to Milner and his imperial ideas, most of them
    went on to distinguished careers outside South Africa. Lionel
    Curtis (1872-1955) in particular played a key role in promoting
    the cause of UNION after Milner's departure. Patrick DUNCAN
    was to become a South African cabinet minister and governor-
    general.

KRUGER, S.J. P[aul] (1825-1904). His forefathers were TREK-
    BOERS in the northeastern Cape, but his immediate family
    became VOORTREKKERS in 1836, and he witnessed battles
    against Mzilikazi's NDEBELE and the ZULU. He soon made
    a reputation for himself among the Transvaal voortrekkers as
    a fearless soldier, and became military leader (commandant-
    general) in 1863. Dissatisfied with the "liberal" regime of
    President Burgers (1834-81), he almost left the Transvaal on
    another trek to the north in the early 1870s. When the Brit-
    ish annexed the Transvaal, he led the opposition and in 1877
    and again in 1878 served on protest deputations to Europe.
    After Gladstone, on coming to office in England, refused to
    cancel the annexation, Kruger agreed to lead an armed revolt

(see TRANSVAAL WAR OF INDEPENDENCE), but at the same time continued negotiations, which helped secure the return of self-rule under "British suzerainty" in 1881. After his election as State President in 1883, he persuaded the British to negotiate a new convention, which omitted reference to such "suzerainty." His efforts to secure a "road to the sea" were thwarted, but a RAILROAD from DELAGOA BAY to Pretoria was opened in 1895. The JAMESON RAID fiasco increased his prestige in the Transvaal, and in 1898 he won re-election as president for the fourth time by a large margin. After negotiations with MILNER on the UITLANDERS failed, and Kruger realized that the British wanted to rule the Transvaal, he decided to take the initiative and with Free State support sent the British an ultimatum which led to the outbreak of the SOUTH AFRICAN WAR.

With the approach of British forces in May 1900, Kruger was forced to leave Pretoria. A few months later it was decided that he should go to Europe to seek foreign support for the Boer cause. He failed to secure material aid, and died in exile in Switzerland. His career was later a source of great inspiration for resurgent AFRIKANER NATIONALISM.

KWANDEBELE. Implementation of the government's BANTUSTAN policy in the 1970s increased ethnic tensions between the Ndebele of the Transvaal who were of NGUNI origin but had no connection with Mzilikazi's NDEBELE STATE, on the one hand, and the North SOTHO of LEBOWA and the TSWANA of BOPHUTATSWANA on the other. The Ndebele persuaded the government to institute a separate "HOMELAND" for them on some farms northeast of Pretoria, on which 100,000 of the half million Ndebele were settled. In May 1982 there was talk of "independence" for this minute, impoverished state, which was little more than a sprawling mass of tin shanties. Such "independence" would mean that a casino could be established within close reach of Pretoria, casino gambling being illegal in "white" South Africa.

KWAZULU (land of the ZULU). When the BANTUSTAN became "self-governing" in 1977, it consisted of over forty blocks of land in Zululand and NATAL, separated from each other by patches of white-owned land, and it stretched from Mozambique and Swaziland in the north to the Transkei in the south. Consolidation proposals, put forward in 1975 but not implemented by 1982, would have made Kwazulu ten separate pieces of land, but involved the relocation of half a million people. Though Kwazulu formed only 38 percent of the area of the former Natal province, it had, in 1980, 57 percent of the region's population but produced only 6 percent of the gross regional product. Of its income, 80 percent came from remittances from MIGRANT workers, or those who commuted daily from the Bantustan into "white" South Africa. As the Zulu formed the largest single African people, the refusal of the Kwazulu chief minister, Gatsha BUTHELEZI, to consider accepting "independence" for

his impoverished territory, constituted a major obstacle to the
accomplishment of the APARTHEID grand design.

LABOUR PARTY. The leading figures in the early labor movement
were skilled artisans who had come from Britain or Australia.
The South African Labour Party was launched at a series of
meetings in the years before Union. The industrial militancy
before World War I (see STRIKES) and the political disarry after HERTZOG's break with the SOUTH AFRICAN PARTY boosted
support for Labour, which in 1914 won control of the Transvaal
Provincial Council. But while the right wing of the party, led
by CRESWELL, supported the war effort, a smaller pacifist section under William (Bill) Andrews (1870-1950) broke with the
party to form an International Socialist League, a forerunner of
the COMMUNIST PARTY. As a result of this split, Labour did
poorly in the 1915 election. It had early favored racial segregation; with the loss of its left wing, it more than ever pandered
to WHITE RACISM.
    After the UNIONISTS joined the SOUTH AFRICAN PARTY,
that party took a number of seats from Labour in the 1921 election, reducing its strength to nine. But Creswell then entered
into a PACT with Hertzog and in the 1924 election Labour won
18 seats and a place in government. Labour then began to die
a slow death. Overwhelmingly English in its ethos, it never
attracted Afrikaner workers in any numbers and those who had
voted for it now switched to the NATIONAL PARTY. Many of
its English supporters were critical of its leaders for spending
so much time on the FLAG QUESTION. Its main achievement
in office was the Mines and Works Amendment Act (see JOB
COLOR BAR), which protected skilled white artisans in their
jobs. When one of the Labour leaders developed close ties
with Kadalie of the INDUSTRIAL AND COMMERCIAL WORKERS
UNION, he was dismissed from Hertzog's cabinet in 1928. This
further divided the party, which lost 10 seats in the 1929 election. With the outbreak of WORLD WAR II, Labour backed
SMUTS and the war effort, and a Labour member was included
in Smuts' coalition ministry. With UNITED PARTY help, Labour
maintained a toehold in parliament until 1958. Though it came
out with a statement on fundamental rights for all races in 1946,
coupled with a call for a NATIONAL CONVENTION, it realized
that such liberalism appealed more to middle class than working
class white voters. That the party never sought to win support
for itself through a strong trade union base was not the least of
the reasons for its decline into insiginificance.

LAGDEN COMMISSION (1903-1905). The South African Native Af-
    fairs Commission under Sir Godfrey Lagden (1851-1934), then
    in charge of African administration in the Transvaal, was ap-
    pointed by MILNER after the SOUTH AFRICAN WAR to provide
    guidelines for a uniform African policy in the new South Africa.
    In its report (1905), it came out in favor of an essentially

segregationist policy: the Cape system of clearly demarcated RESERVES and Africans voting on a separate roll for a fixed number of white members of parliament.   It recommended that SQUATTING on white farms should be checked, that Africans should be able to acquire freehold title in urban LOCATIONS, and that a college be established for the higher education of Africans.

Many of its recommendations were implemented after UNION: see NATIVES LAND ACT; FRANCHISE; FORT HARE.   Others, such as freehold for Africans in urban areas, were not (see URBAN SEGREGATION).

LANGALIBALELE AFFAIR.   In 1873 Langalibalele (1818-1889), ruler of the Hlubi people living under the DRAKENSBERG mountains in north-western Natal, both refused to have registered some guns his men had obtained on the DIAMOND fields and ignored various summonses to explain his conduct.   That his people were acquiring prosperity as peasant farmers was causing concern among nearby white farmers.   When an armed force was sent to arrest Langalibalele, a skirmish occurred as he fled, in which three whites and two blacks were killed.   This so-called "rebellion" shocked white Natalians.   Langalibalele was soon captured.   Given a mockery of a trial, he was banished for life to Robben Island off Cape Town.   Thousands of his Hlubi people and their neighbours were dispossessed of their lands.

The panic reaction of the Natal colonists to this petty episode showed their insecurity.   CARNARVON took advantage of it to push Natal into support for his CONFEDERATION scheme. Natal's lieutenant-governor was recalled, and Carnarvon refused to allow Langalibalele to remain on Robben Island.   He was kept a prisoner on the mainland near Cape Town until 1887, when he was allowed to return to Natal.

LEBOWA (SOTHO: the north).   BANTUSTAN created for the North Sotho, including the PEDI.   When it obtained "self-government" in 1972, it consisted of a number of pieces of territory in the central northern Transvaal and its population of just over one million constituted some 56 percent of all North Sotho within South Africa.   In the late 1970s and early 1980s its leading politician, Cedric Phatudi, resisted pressure on him to accept "independence" for Lebowa.

LEGASSICK, Martin (1940-).   The most influential radical historian of the 1970s.   He grew up in South Africa and was educated at the universities of Cape Town, Oxford (first for physics), Ghana and California, Los Angeles, where his Ph.D. dissertation was on the early 19th-century frontier zone north of the Orange river.   He lectured in sociology at Warwick University from 1974.   His extremely influential papers included "The Frontier Tradition in South African Historiography," "The Making of South African 'Native Policy,' 1902-1923:   the Origins of 'Segregation'" (unpublished) and "South Africa: Forced Labor,

Industrialization, and Racial Differentiation. '' In 1979 he was
one of those suspended from the AFRICAN NATIONAL CON-
GRESS for advocating it strengthen its links with the proletariat.
(See also HISTORIOGRAPHY and see the bibliography).

LESOTHO. After it gained its independence in 1966 (see BASUTO-
    LAND; HIGH COMMISSION TERRITORIES), Lesotho initially es-
    tablished friendly relations with Pretoria, with Prime Minister
    Jonathan visiting VERWOERD in 1967. When the outcome of the
    1970 election went against him and Jonathan staged a coup, he
    was widely believed to have been aided by South Africa. But in
    the 1970s Jonathan became more militant and took a strong anti-
    apartheid line. He refused to recognize the ''independence'' of
    the BANTUSTANS, claimed part of the eastern Free State (see
    CONQUERED TERRITORY) and established diplomatic relations
    with Cuba and the Soviet Union despite South African objections.
    In the late 1970s he claimed that South Africa was giving aid to
    his main rival, the exiled Basutoland Congress Party under
    Ntsu Mokhehle. Lesotho remained heavily dependent on South
    Africa, and in particular on the earnings of MIGRANT LABOR-
    ERS in South Africa. The number of Lesotho workers on the
    gold mines increased after independence, but declined in the
    late 1970s as the mines obtained more workers from within
    South Africa itself. Nevertheless, in 1980 there were still
    150,000 Lesotho workers in South Africa, and they provided
    more than 80 percent of Lesotho's gross national product.
    Lesotho remained a member of the Rand currency zone, and
    all its exports went to South Africa.

LIBERAL PARTY (1953-1968). When the general election of 1953
    returned the NATIONAL PARTY to power with an increased
    majority, a group of whites unable to support the racial policy
    of the UNITED PARTY decided to form a non-racial party which
    stood for the maintenance of the rule of law and equal rights
    for all in a democratic South Africa. Fearing communist in-
    fluence, they would not participate in the CONGRESS ALLIANCE.
    Some Liberals argued that if the party stood for universal suf-
    frage it would totally alienate the white electorate. When the
    main advocates of a non-racial qualified franchise left to join
    the new PROGRESSIVE PARTY, the Liberal Party did adopt
    universal suffrage as its policy (1960). In the 1961 election it
    polled fewer than 2,500 votes. Its membership then was not
    much above 5,000, perhaps a majority of whom were Africans.
    The image of the party was damaged when some of its mem-
    bers were found to have turned to SABOTAGE in the early
    1960s. In 1963-64 over forty of its leading members were ar-
    rested or BANNED, and a number of others went into exile.
    The party dissolved itself in 1968 when the Prohibition of Po-
    litical Interference Act of that year made it illegal for politi-
    cal parties to continue to be non-racial.
        Among its distinguished members were Margaret BALLINGER
    and Alan PATON.

LIBERALISM. In the South Africa context, liberalism has meant
    not merely an adherence to liberal values, such as the rule of
    law and freedom of speech, but also being a "friend of the na-
    tive," and believing in the possibility of evolutionary change
    towards a more equitable society.
        The imperial connection brought liberal ideas to the Cape in
    the early 19th century. The humanitarianism introduced by the
    MISSIONARIES in the 1820s and 1830s included a rejection of
    distinctions based on race and a concern that people of color
    should be treated with justice. The Cape's BRITISH rulers in-
    sisted that the FRANCHISE be color-blind. But Cape liberalism
    was not merely an imperialist imposition; it took root in the
    colony and became the ideology of local interest groups. Mer-
    cantile interests, in particular, sought the formation of a pros-
    perous black peasantry and a black elite incorporated politically
    through the non-racial qualified franchise. There were limits
    to the enlightened paternalism found in Cape Town--a long way
    from a large African population--or in the Eastern Cape, where
    merchants sought trade and missionaries Christian converts:
    non-racialism was not extended to social relations, nor was it
    incorporated within the political parties that emerged in the late
    19th century. Nevertheless, there was a very real difference
    between the Cape tradition--which Cecil RHODES summed up in
    the dictum "Equal rights for every civilised man"--and the "no
    equality in church or state" of the Transvaal.
        With the mineral revolution, mining interests increasingly
    sought labor from the African reserves rather than agricultural
    produce and the African peasantry (see AGRICULTURE; BUNDY
    THESIS) was gradually undermined. But liberal values survived
    both in a segment of the white community and among the black
    elite. It can be argued that after Union, liberalism was sus-
    tained not only in the churches, the English-speaking universities
    and such white-dominated institutions as the Joint Councils of
    Europeans and Natives, which flourished in the 1920s, and the
    Institute of Race Relations (founded 1929), but also in the AFRI-
    CAN NATIONAL CONGRESS itself. It was perhaps only at the
    end of the 1940s that the "liberals" in the ANC lost their dom-
    inance. Liberal values were sustained in the 1950s chiefly by
    the LIBERAL PARTY, and after its demise, to a lesser extent
    in the--from 1968--uni-racial PROGRESSIVE PARTY.

LIMPOPO RIVER. The name may come from a SOTHO word mean-
    ing "river of the waterfall." Second in size of the African
    rivers that enter the Indian Ocean, the Limpopo, unlike the
    Zambezi, often carries little or no water, and it has never
    been a barrier to human movement (see ZIMBABWE). For
    many centuries before it became the Transvaal's northern and
    northwestern boundary, it was an important trade route between
    the interior and DELAGOA BAY. A road into Zimbabwe over
    Beit (cf. WERNHER-BEIT) Bridge opened in 1929; a rail link
    across the river at the same place began operating in 1974.

LOBOLO (NGUNI form; bogadi: TSWANA; bohali: SOTHO). Marriage payment made by the bridegroom's family to the father or guardian of the bride.   In both Sotho and Nguni society cattle were traditionally handed over, but from the late 19th century a wide range of goods--of which iron hoes were among the most common--or money took the place of cattle.   Whites, and especially MISSIONARIES, misunderstood the nature of the transaction, spoke of lobolo, "bride-price," as a way of buying a wife, and condemned it.   Missionaries also objected to it because it was part of a polygamous marriage system, and because it implied that the marriage was potentially dissolvable. To Africans, on the other hand, it strengthened the marriage and discouraged divorce.   (See also MIGRANT LABOR.)

LOCATIONS.   Though the 1820 BRITISH settlers went to locations in the ZUURVELD, the term came chiefly to be applied either to rural areas where Africans congregated or had exclusive rights of occupation (see also RESERVES) or to sections of urban or periurban areas set aside for blacks.   Urban locations (later called townships)--like Ndabeni, outside CAPE TOWN, to which the African residents of the city were forced to move in 1901--were usually separated from the white urban area by a cordon sanitaire, and were linked by rail to industrial sites. Most offered no employment and few or no amenities.   They were essentially places where workers, treated as commodities, slept and in which they could be controlled.   (See SOWETO and also URBAN SEGREGATION.)

LONDON MISSIONARY SOCIETY   see   MISSIONARIES; John PHILIP.

LUTHULI, Albert John (c. 1898-1967).   President-General of the AFRICAN NATIONAL CONGRESS from 1952 until his death, and recipient of the Nobel Peace Prize for 1960.   His grandfather was the first convert to Christianity at the Groutville mission on the Natal north coast, and Luthuli himself was a deeply religious man.   He came into prominence in 1952 when he backed the DEFIANCE CAMPAIGN and was dismissed by the government from his post as chief in the Groutville reserve.   He issued a statement saying "Who will deny that thirty years of my life have been spent knocking in vain, patiently, moderately and modestly at a closed and barred door?"   A succession of BANNING orders confined him to his rural home through most of his presidency of the ANC.   He was one of those charged in the TREASON TRIAL.   Six days after SHARPEVILLE, he publicly burnt his pass and was detained, tried, and fined.   In December 1961 he went to Oslo to receive the Nobel Prize, awarded for his commitment to non-violence in his opposition to apartheid.   With the money, he bought two farms in Swaziland to be used by political exiles.

LYDENBURG HEADS.   Seven modelled terracotta representations of life-sized human heads were discovered buried in a hillside a few miles from Lydenburg in the eastern Transvaal in the 1950s. From associated pottery they are thought to date to c. A.D. 500.

They constitute the most important single early IRON AGE find
in South Africa. They are now in the South African Museum,
Cape Town.

MACMILLAN, William Miller (1885-1974). Taken to South Africa
as a child, he returned to Britain to study at Oxford. In 1910
he accepted an appointment to the Department of History and
Economics at Rhodes University, Grahamstown, and moved
from there to the School of Mines, Johannesburg, soon to become the University of the Witwatersrand, in 1917. He remained at "Wits" until the early 1930s, when he resigned in
large part because of his dislike of the racial policies of the
government, and the failure of the University to support him in
his criticisms, but also because he wanted to spend time ex-
ploring the British colonies in the tropics. He returned to
South Africa only for short visits thereafter.

   Macmillan pioneered the writing of social and economic history in South Africa, and was also the founder of what became
known as the "liberal school" (see HISTORIOGRAPHY). His
first published pamphlets concerned social conditions in Grahamstown. As early as 1919 a set of lectures appeared on
The South African Agrarian Problem and its Historical Development. Then in 1920 he received the first batch of the papers
of John PHILIP of the London MISSIONARY Society. Through
Philip's eyes he became deeply interested in policies to people
of color in the early 19th century Cape, and in the history of
the "other side" of the frontier. On the Philip papers were
based his two seminal works, The Cape Coloured Question
(1927) and Bantu, Boer and Briton (1929; revised edition 1963)
and his chapters in volume 8 of the Cambridge History of the
British Empire (1936). Having moved from studying POOR
WHITES to poor Africans in the Herschel district of the Cape,
he produced his Complex South Africa (1930). Among his students in Johannesburg was C. W. DE KIEWIET and among his
colleagues Margaret BALLINGER.

MAFEKING (Tswana: Mafikeng: "place of stones"). The most
northerly town in the Cape Colony and the administrative capital of the BECHUANALAND protectorate, Mafeking became famous when besieged by the Boers during the SOUTH AFRICAN
WAR. Defended by Colonel R. S. Baden-Powell (1857-1941) and
white and African forces, it was relieved in May 1900, after a
siege that had lasted since the previous October. Successive
defeats of its forces in the early stages of the war had shocked
the British, and the relief of Mafeking bolstered national pride;
the news was greeted with tremendous enthusiasm in London.
Mafeking was much less important militarily than Ladysmith
(Natal), the siege of which was a much larger and more costly
affair. In 1980 Mafeking was transferred to BOPHUTHATSWANA.

MALAN, Daniel François (1874-1959). A DUTCH REFORMED

CHURCH minister from 1905, he worked for the upliftment of
POOR WHITES and for the recognition of AFRIKAANS as a
written language. Supporting HERTZOG and the new NATIONAL
PARTY, Malan was appointed editor of its Cape Town newspaper
Die Burger in 1915. He entered parliament in 1919 and became
a member of Hertzog's cabinet in 1924. Mainly because of his
uncompromising stance during the FLAG QUESTION, he came
to be regarded -as the leader of extreme Afrikaner nationalism.
When Hertzog formed his coalition with SMUTS, Malan refused
to accept a seat in the coalition ministry, but continued to support Hertzog as a coalition candidate in the 1933 election. But
when coalition led to FUSION, he broke with Hertzog and formed
the Gesuiwerde Nasionale Party (The Purified National Party),
becoming the leader of the opposition in the Assembly. In the
mid 1930s he advocated that the "Coloureds" as well as Africans
be removed from the common voters' roll. With help from the
AFRIKANER BROEDERBOND, which he had joined in 1933, and
the emotional centenary VOORTREKKER celebrations in 1938,
Malan sought to establish his party as the vehicle of Afrikaner
nationalism.

After the outbreak of WORLD WAR II ended FUSION, he was
prepared to try to forge a new alliance with Hertzog, but on his
own terms. During the war, the major challenge to Malan came
from his right, from the OSSEWABRANDWAG and others who rejected the path of constitutional change. After a bitter conflict,
Malan eliminated this opposition, and before the 1948 election
concluded an election agreement with the AFRIKANER PARTY.
Having united enough of Afrikanerdom behind him to win that
election, he remained Prime Minister until his retirement in
November 1954.

MANDELA, Nelson Rolihlahla (1918-   ).   AFRICAN NATIONAL
CONGRESS leader. Born into the Thembu (TRANSKEI) royal
household, he was suspended from studying at FORT HARE after a student protest. In Johannesburg he played an increasingly important role in the ANC Youth League. From 1953 to
1961 he was BANNED, but tried to continue his joint law practice with Oliver Tambo (1917-   ), later external leader of the
ANC, while also organizing for Congress. He was one of those
who stood trial for TREASON from 1957 to 1961. In 1961 he
went underground to organize a mass STAY-AWAY on REPUB-
LIC day and then to work for the new military organization
UMKHONTO WE SIZWE. After travelling abroad, he returned
to South Africa, was arrested by the police in August 1962 and
sentenced to five years' imprisonment. After the Umkhonto
headquarters was raided, he stood trial again, and this time
received life imprisonment. His statement from the dock at
the close of the trial received wide publicity. He was then
kept on Robben Island off CAPE TOWN. As ANC leader he
remained the leading symbol of repression in South Africa.
"Free Mandela" campaigns in 1971 and 1980-81 received support from members of the PROGRESSIVE PARTY leftwards.
His wife, Winnie, a woman of great force of character, suffered

continual government harassment. This included, in the 1970s, being banished from SOWETO to Brandfort, a remote Free State town, and BANNED.

MANTATEES. A name given the SOTHO at the time of the MFECANE. It was derived from Mnanthatisi (c. 1780-after 1835), the female regent of the Tlokoa, one of the Sotho peoples set in motion in about 1822 by the arrival of the Hlubi in the Caledon Valley in what is now the eastern ORANGE FREE STATE. The fearsome reputation of Mnathatisi spread far and wide and many groups--most notably that which attacked the town of Dithakong, near Kuruman, in 1823--were known to whites as "Mantatees," whether or not Mnanthatisi's people were among them. The tens of thousands of Sotho refugees who moved south to escape the upheavals were also known as Mantatees when they arrived in the Cape.

MANUFACTURING INDUSTRY. Though there were some seventy small manufacturing concerns at the Cape by the 1860s, it was the development of the DIAMOND and GOLD mines that provided the first large-scale market for manufactured products. Dynamite, miners' boots, and other necessities were soon being produced locally, but the growth of manufacturing industry was slow before World War I because the mines drew off skilled labor and capital, while the large earnings of foreign exchange from the export of diamonds and gold enabled the country to pay for industrial imports. Output of the manufacturing sector was valued at under £20 million in 1904, at £35 million by 1915. During World War I imports were difficult to obtain, which did much to boost local manufacture, the output of which had risen by 1920 to £75 million. A Federated Chamber of Industries was founded in 1917. When the post-war depression arrived (see BUSINESS CYCLES) the LABOUR PARTY pressed for protection, to provide employment for whites in local industry. Mineowners, on the other hand, opposed protection because tariffs would increase their costs. After the PACT government came to power, protection was extended by the Tariff Act of 1925. Thanks to the government's CIVILISED LABOR policy the proportion of whites in manufacturing industry, which had been 37.5 percent in 1919, rose to 40.6 percent in 1936.

After South Africa went off the gold standard at the end of 1932, sending the price of gold soaring, a large part of the increased profits went to stimulate manufacturing. This occurred through direct investment, state subsidization and expanded consumer spending. In 1943 the value of output from manufacturing overtook that of the mining sector. World War II then provided extra protection from foreign competition and further stimulated production. The number of manufacturing establishments, which had risen from 6,543 in 1933 to 8,505 in 1939, increased to 9,999 by 1946, and output, which had increased by 140 percent between 1933 and 1939, rose another 141 percent during the war. Well over three quarters of the country's factories were located in the four main metropolitan

regions, three of which were on the coast, the most important
one inland: the southwestern Cape; Port Elizabeth-Uitenhage;
Durban-Pinetown; and the Pretoria-Witwatersrand-Vereeniging
(PWV) triangle, with its mines and heavy industry as well as
light secondary industry.   In the 1960s there was a large flow
of foreign capital into manufacturing industry; by 1973 40 percent of all foreign capital was invested in that sector.   By then,
along with food, clothing, textiles and wood and paper products,
much machinery, chemical and metal products, and electronic
equipment was being produced, some for defense requirements
(see MILITARY).   There was a considerable export sector.
The proportion of whites employed in the labor force in the
manufacturing sector, which fell to 21 percent in 1976, continued to fall thereafter.

MARKS, Shula (1936-   ).   Historian.   Educated at the University of
Cape Town and London University, where she completed a doc-
toral thesis subsequently published as Reluctant Rebellion (1970),
a study of the BAMBATHA REBELLION.   In the 1970s she ran
a Societies of Southern Africa seminar at the Institute of Commonwealth Studies, University of London.   This seminar brought
together historians from South Africa itself and those in exile,
and much of the new work on South African history (see HIS-
TORIOGRAPHY) first appeared there.   She wrote or co-authored
a number of seminal articles on such diverse topics as Khoisan
resistance, the role of the Imperial Factor in the 19th century,
and Milner and the South African state, and she was a major
contributor on South Africa to the Cambridge History of Africa.
In 1982 she was Reader in History at the School of Oriental and
African Studies, University of London.

MASS REMOVALS ("resettlement").   While the forced relocation of
people had a very long history before 1950, it was massively
stepped up as a result of government policy in the 1950s.   Between 1950 and 1980 over 2 million people, almost all blacks,
were forced to move, for ideological and economic reasons.
Forced removals of non-Africans within urban areas took place
under the GROUP AREAS ACT; only African removals are considered here.
    The process of forcing Africans into LOCATIONS in the ur-
ban centers, begun in the early years of the 20th century (see
URBAN SEGREGATION) was continued after 1948.   Sophiatown,
for example, a vibrant community of more than 60,000 four and
a half miles from downtown Johannesburg was destroyed, and the
white suburb of Triomf (Afrikaans: "triumph") created in its
place.   African residents of Sophiatown, some with freehold title, were forced to move out to SOWETO, where no freehold
was allowed.   In Alexandra township, too, on Johannesburg's
northeastern boundary, Africans and "Coloureds" had been able
to acquire freehold titles from 1912.   Well over half its population was ejected in the 1960s and 1970s before the government
announced that the remaining families might stay (1979).   In
other urban centers Africans were moved out to "dormitory

towns," devoid of industrial or other work opportunities, in
adjacent BANTUSTANS. The people of Duncan Village, for example, in the port city of East London, were relocated in
Mdantsane in the CISKEI, over twenty miles away, from where
they had to commute to work in East London.

There were many other types of forced mass removal. Some
Africans held freehold land in rural "black spots" surrounded by
white-owned farmland, or they farmed mission-owned land.
There were over 200 such "black spots" in Natal in the 1950s;
by 1980 most had been "cleared." Well over 150,000 Africans
were forced out of the Western Cape under the "COLOURED"
LABOR PREFERENCE POLICY. Larger numbers were relocated
because of the ending of SQUATTING on white-owned farms, or
under INFLUX CONTROL measures controlling entry to, and
residence in, metropolitan areas. People considered surplus to
production requirements--the unemployed, the old, the young,
women--were dumped in the BANTUSTANS. There, in remote
rural areas, already overpopulated and overgrazed, without employment opportunities, they were usually given temporary accommodation in tents or bare corrugated-iron rooms. Sometimes there were no facilities at all. Sporadic publicity was
focussed on the shocking conditions in resettlement camps, especially in northern Natal, the western Transvaal and the Ciskei. Some improvements were made, as at Dimbaza in the
Ciskei (after the adverse publicity from the film "Last Grave
at Dimbaza"), but the process of relocation had not slackened
as South Africa entered the 1980s.

MASTERS AND SERVANTS ORDINANCE (1841). Passed seven years
after the end of CAPE SLAVERY and three years after the re-
lease of the ex-slaves from their compulsory APPRENTICESHIP,
this Cape legislation was designed to tie the ex-slaves to their
masters, especially on the farms. Oral contracts were made
binding, and stringent penalties laid down for desertion. Early
in the life of the Cape Parliament the legislation was tightened
up (1856), and it remained in force until 1974, by which time
other forms of labor control had made it superfluous.

MATANZIMA, Kaiser Daliwonga (1915-). Educated at Lovedale
and FORT HARE, he was appointed to the Bunga (see TRANS-
KEI) in 1942. An attorney by profession, he gathered enough
support among the chiefly elite in the Transkei to become
Chief Minister in 1963. The Transkei National Independence
Party he organized then won elections in 1968 and 1973. A
tough, shrewd politician, who ruled autocratically, he yet created the appearance of popular support for "independence,"
which was granted in October 1976, when he became Prime
Minister of the new state. In 1979 he became President, allowing his brother George Matanzima (1918-), who had been
his Minister of Justice, to take over as Prime Minister. In
October 1981 Kaiser Matanzima announced that he would retire
in 1982. (See also BANTUSTANS; SEPARATE DEVELOPMENT.)

MAYIBUYE I AFRIKA ("Africa, come back!"). Slogan popularized
by the AFRICAN NATIONAL CONGRESS newspaper Abantu-
Batho, then used by the COMMUNIST PARTY in the 1930s, and
employed as an ANC freedom cry in the DEFIANCE CAMPAIGN
and after. It meant, not a return to the old order, but the return of the land to those from whom it had been taken, i.e.
(South) Africa for the Africans. (Cf. AMANDLA.)

MFECANE (ZULU: the crushing; coined as an NGUNI form of the
SOTHO Difaqane or Lifaqane. The Mfecane in the Sotho area
west of the DRAKENSBERG is usually known as the Difaqane).
The time of revolutionary change associated with the rise of
the ZULU empire in the early 19th century. Beginning in the
coastal corridor between the Drakensberg and the Indian Ocean,
it spread until almost all the peoples living in the northern half
of what became South Africa were involved.
    Various explanations have been advanced to account for the
process of political centralization that led to the emergence of
a large, militarized, authoritarian Zulu state by the 1820s:
pressure on scarce resources in the limited coastal corridor
as a result of population increase following the introduction of
maize in the 18th century; a severe ecological crisis brought
on perhaps by the great madlatule drought of c. 1806; or the
effects of the growing trade in the late 18th century between
the northern NGUNI and the PORTUGUESE at DELAGOA BAY
to the north. On a less profound level, some historians have
stressed military innovations, the age-regiment (AMABUTHO)
system, the short stabbing spear and the "bull's-horns" formation.
    By the second decade of the 19th century two states were in
competition among the northern Nguni: the Ndwande state under
Zwide (c. 1775-1825) and the looser Mthethwa confederacy led
by Dingiswayo (c. 1770-c. 1818). Towards the end of that decade the Mthethwa suffered a crushing defeat at the hands of the
Ndwandwe. The Ndwandwe were then in turn defeated by the
Zulu under Shaka (c. 1787-1828) in about 1819, and Zwide
forced northwards. To escape the turmoil and Shaka's ruthless
rule, many groups fled, spreading warfare and dislocation west
across the Drakensberg and south into the Transkei. With much
destruction of crops, there was considerable resort to cannibal-
ism. Long-established settlement patterns on the highveld were
disrupted. The Hlubi of Natal, moving across the mountains in
1821-22, attacked the Sotho-speaking Tlokoa led by Mnanthatisi
(see MANTATEES) west of the Caledon river, the Tlokoa in turn
attacked others, and so it went on. The disruption might have
spread even further west had it not been for the defeat of an
invading army of Sotho by a force of Africans and GRIQUA at
Dithakong, near present Kuruman, in June 1823. The marauding
Ngwane, having moved through what became the eastern Free
State, were only dispersed in a clash with an expeditionary
force from the Cape in the central TRANSKEI (battle of Mbholompo, 1828). Out of the disruption of the Mfecane emerged a

number of major new states, including Mzilikazi's NDEBELE
STATE and the BASUTOLAND of MOSHWESHWE. Other states,
such as those of the PEDI or the Tlokoa were radically recon-
structed. Large areas were depopulated, so that the VOOR-
TREKKERS could believe they would easily be able to establish
themselves in the interior or in Natal. Perhaps most importantly, the Mfecane gave to millions of Africans new identities
--Zulu, Swazi, Ndebele--which would be long-lasting.

The effects of the Mfecane on Central and East Africa can
be traced in the other volumes in this series.

MFENGU (Fingo). It is said that the scattered remnants of various
NGUNI groups (Hlubi, Zizi, Bhele and others) broken up and
disrupted by the MFECANE, introduced themselves to the
XHOSA of the TRANSKEI in the 1820s by saying "siyamfenguze"
("we are hungry and seek shelter"). The Gcaleka (eastern)
Xhosa gave them large herds of cattle to look after. The pioneer Wesleyan Methodist MISSIONARY John Ayliff (1797-1862),
based at the Transkeian mission station of Butterworth from
1831, saw the Mfengu as potential converts, spoke of their
"slave" status among the Xhosa, and when the opportunity arose
during the FRONTIER WAR of 1834-1835, "emancipated" them
by leading them westward out of Xhosa territory. With vast
herds of cattle they took with them, 16,000 Mfengu were placed
under colonial tutelage east of the Fish river as a buffer between the colonists and the Xhosa. Many Mfengu, not being
subject to any traditional leaders, were quick to accept Christianity and eager to acquire western education; numbers became
prosperous peasant-farmers (see also AGRICULTURE; BUNDY
THESIS). Whites called the Mfengu "the Jews of Kaffirland."
They fought in the frontier wars of 1846-1847, 1850-1853 and
1877-1878 on the colonial side, and were rewarded with the
grant of considerable land taken from the defeated Xhosa. After Sarhili (c. 1814-1892), the Xhosa paramount, had been expelled from his territory because of his involvement in the
CATTLE KILLING, part of it was allotted the Mfengu and came
to be known as "Fingoland." In the 1870s Fingoland itself was
the springboard for a new wave of migration into the deep
Transkei, especially East Griqualand, over which the Cape government was then extending its control.

In the late 19th century the most prominent Mfengu, John
Tengo JABAVU, tried to work to overcome the Mfengu-Xhosa
division. But "Fingo day" celebrations, held on 14 May each
year since 1907, helped maintain their separate identity, and the
government's imposition of the Bantu Authorities system (see
BANTUSTANS) in the 1950s greatly increased ethnic tensions.
As the CISKEI moved towards "independence," the Mfengu supported the opposition to the ruling Xhosa elite.

MIGRANT LABOR. Africans worked as migrants--left home to
work for periods ranging from a few weeks to several years--
in the ZUURVELD before the end of the 18th century. By the
1840s PEDI travelled south from the eastern Transvaal to take

jobs in the Cape colony for long enough to earn a gun. In the
1850s Africans from south of DELAGOA BAY (see THONGA)
began working in Natal. The substantial migrancy of Pedi from
the 1850s has been explained by their need to arm against Zulu,
SWAZI, and VOORTREKKER military threats. In Thonga society, migrancy was regulated by chiefs who used it to enhance
their control over the young men who through migrant labor
earned the bride-wealth (see LOBOLO) necessary for marriage.
    Those societies already engaged extensively in migrant labor
were the main suppliers of labor to the DIAMOND fields in the
early days, where the Pedi were known as "Mahawas" and the
Thonga as "Shangaans" (from Soshangane [c. 1790-1858], founder
of the Gaza empire north of DELAGOA BAY). In the early
1870s some 50-80,000 Africans went to work at Kimberley each
year. Those who lived closest--the GRIQUA or TSWANA--
provided little labor, preferring to supply foodstuffs. There
was soon a shortage of labor, and active steps began to be
taken to obtain migrants. As African societies were brought
under white control in the 1870s and after, taxes were imposed,
some deliberately designed to force men out to work. With the
opening of the GOLD mines, requiring a larger labor supply,
came greater coercion (see, e.g., GLEN GREY ACT).
    In the early years of gold mining, there was considerable
competition among the various companies for African labor,
which helped push up costs. To eliminate such competition and
bring down wages, a centralized and monopsonistic recruiting
system was established. The Native Labour Supply Association,
founded in 1896, became the Witwatersrand Native Labour Association (Wenela) during the SOUTH AFRICAN WAR and supplied labor from non-British territories, most importantly
MOZAMBIQUE. The Native Recruiting Corporation was established by the Chamber of Mines in 1912, to handle recruiting within South Africa itself and in the HIGH COMMISSION
TERRITORIES. In the late 1970s the two organizations were
combined under the new name of the Employment Bureau of
Africa Limited.
    In the 1890s between 50 and 60 percent of the Africans who
worked on the gold mines of the Witwatersrand--70,000-100,000
at any one time--went there from Portuguese East Africa (Mozambique). But the SOUTH AFRICAN WAR disrupted that flow,
and within South Africa itself competition from public works and
other sectors pushed up wage rates. Africans disliked underground work and knew conditions on the mines to be deplorable,
so they chose other options. As the mineowners were unable
to get the required labor, they turned to CHINESE LABORERS,
who were paid less than Africans were prepared to accept during the post-war boom. But by 1906, when the Chinese began
to be withdrawn, the boom was over, options on the labor market had closed, and many Africans found that to survive they
had to go to the mines.
    Mineowners, however, continued to argue that Africans were
target workers and did not respond to economic incentives as
whites did: they worked to meet some particular need, and to

pay them higher wages would merely mean that they would leave the mines sooner. But what had initially been a preferred form of labor by workers wishing to return to their own societies became a system imposed on workers who had constantly to oscillate between their home base and their place of work, where they were not permitted to settle with their families (for the legal and administrative controls erected to prevent a stable labor force emerging see especially INFLUX CONTROL; PASSES).

The mineowners, wanting large numbers of unskilled workers at the lowest possible rates of pay, claimed that the migrant labor system was crucial to their continued profitability. Wages for migrants were set at the level of the basic needs of "single" workers: they and their families were assumed to be supported by subsistence agriculture in the rural areas, while the young, the old, and the ill were supposed to be taken care of by the kinship group in the RESERVES or the foreign country from which the migrant came. The mineowners claimed that were they to have to pay family wages, their mines would have to close. Wages paid migrants on the gold mines dropped in the first two decades and real wages remained static for some forty years. It was not until 1969 that they surpassed the 1911 level. (During the same period the gap between white and black earnings on the mines increased from 9:1 in 1911 to over 20:1.) Migrancy also meant COMPOUND housing, saving the mines the capital costs of even rudimentary family housing for their workers. It also weakened Africans' bargaining power on the labor market, for it was difficult for migrants to obtain any skills with which to bargain, and employers had little incentive to provide migrants with training. Where in secondary industry some skill was required, employers sought stablized labor, but in construction or service industries based on manual labor migrancy remained the norm.

There were political reasons, too, for continued migrancy: as segregationist philosophies gained ground among white policymakers in the 20th century, so a permanent, stabilized African work force, either on the mines or elsewhere in the metropolitan areas, seemed less and less desirable. Not only were migrants housed in compounds subject to greater control than stabilized workers, but it could also be argued that migrants from within South Africa exercized political rights of some kind in their own areas, the RESERVES or, as they became, the BANTUSTANS.

From the 1930s there was a widening of the catchment area for the mines to countries as far north as Tanganyika. But soon after obtaining their independence in the 1960s, Tanzania and Zambia closed their doors to South African recruiters. The flow of migrants from Malawi increased until 1974, when it too was suddenly cut off. Following the transfer of power in Mozambique the following year, the number of migrants from that country declined sharply. The proportion of foreign migrants had gone up from 68 percent in 1970 to 78 percent in 1974, but by 1977 had fallen to under 50 percent and by 1980 of the over

500,000 migrants employed on the mines only about 40 percent were from outside South Africa, with LESOTHO the single largest supplier. As the mining industry increasingly looked for labor within South Africa, so the wages it paid had to be competitive with those paid in other sectors. With a dramatic rise in the gold price in the 1970s, wages paid to African migrants on the gold mines trebled.

The elaboration of the internal migrant labor system in recent decades was carried out chiefly in terms of the Native Laws Amendment Act of 1952, which provided for the establishment of labor bureaus. By 1971 almost 800 of these had come into existence, and were channeling labor from the rural areas to where it was needed.

MILITARY. Though the South African Defence Force (SADF) was created in 1912, soon after UNION, it was not until WORLD WAR II that the army, the air force, and the navy gained their modern separate identities. The SADF shrank after that war, but expanded rapidly after 1960. In that year expenditure on defense was less than $50 million. This constituted under 1 percent of Gross National Product and less than 7 percent of total government spending. Though there had been considerable local production of weapons during World War II, by 1960 there was little emphasis on local manufacture. By 1964-65, however, the arms budget had increased to over $210 million. In response to a non-mandatory arms embargo imposed by the UNITED NATIONS, an Armaments Development Corporation of South Africa (Armscor) was established in 1966 to promote increased self-sufficiency. Jets and trainer aircraft were built under French and Italian licenses. After 1972 there were further large increases in the arms budget; national service obligations (the draft) were extended and the permanent force enlarged. By the time the mandatory arms embargo was imposed by the UN Security Council in 1977, in the wake of BIKO's death and the clamp-down on black organizations, South Africa had a powerful armory and significant arms industry. By 1982 South Africa produced well over 80 percent of its arms and was a major arms exporter. Military cooperation continued with Israel and Taiwan, other "pariah" states, and some arms were supplied "under the counter" from other sources. Defense spending was then over $2 billion a year (the NAMIBIA war costing $1 million a day), 20 percent of the government's total expenditure and over 5 percent of GNP.

(Military aspects of white expansionism in the 18th and 19th centuries can be traced through BRITISH RULE; COMMANDOS; FRONTIER WARS; see also, e.g., SOUTH AFRICAN WAR.)

MILNER, Alfred (1854-1925). Educated in Germany, London, and at Balliol College, Oxford, Milner held important financial posts in Egypt and London before he was sent out to South Africa in 1897 as Cape governor and HIGH COMMISSIONER. A doctrinaire social engineer, he aimed to create a self-governing white dominion in which a well-controlled African labor force would

help ensure the continued supply of GOLD to Britain. In negotiations with KRUGER, Milner focussed on the position of the
UITLANDERS in the Transvaal. There was the possibility that
were they enfranchised, the political balance would swing against
Kruger. But the Transvaal president was essentially right in
saying (in 1899) that it was not the franchise Milner wanted but
his country. For that Milner was prepared to go to war. He
hoped that after the Transvaal had come under British rule the
expansion of mining and related activities would draw thousands
of workers from Britain. But he made no attempt to alter the
racial order in the conquered republics, while post-war British
immigration fell far short of expectations. Not only did his efforts to outnumber the Afrikaners fail, but so did the steps he
took to destroy their culture, which stimulated the growth of
AFRIKANER NATIONALISM. The mining industry remained in
the doldrums after the war, and had to be rescued through the
importation of CHINESE LABOR, which was highly unpopular
both in the Transvaal and in Britain. Nevertheless, it has been
argued recently that in replacing the Kruger regime with a more
efficient one, Milner served the longterm interests of mining
capital. He left South Africa in March 1905.

MINING. The importance of the mineral discoveries in the 19th
century for the economic development of the country may be
followed through the entries on DIAMONDS and GOLD. Gold
in particular remained of central importance in the South African economy, but a significant development in the 1960s and
1970s was a dramatic growth in the non-gold mining sector.
Two new deep-water harbors--at Richards Bay, north of Durban, and Saldanha Bay on the west coast--were built specifical-
ly for the bulk exports of minerals. Richards Bay was linked
by rail to the eastern Transvaal highveld, the major coal-
producing region. Coal production trebled in the 1970s, and
became second only to gold as a foreign-exchange earner. By
1980, 29 million tons were being exported annually. Saldanha
was opened primarily for the bulk export of iron ore from the
Sishen open-cast mine in the northwestern Cape. Of those
minerals of special strategic significance, chrome and manganese were probably the most important; the bulk of the known
world reserves of both lay in South Africa. Uranium was important for South Africa's NUCLEAR PROGRAM. Though the
presence of uranium oxide in the gold-bearing ores of the Witwatersrand was known from the early 1920s, the separation of
uranium from such ores did not begin until 1952. By 1982 over
100 million tons had been produced.

MISCEGENATION. Though interracial marriages, such as that between Eva, a KHOI convert and a Dutch surgeon in 1664, were
rare in the DUTCH EAST INDIA COMPANY period, extensive
miscegenation occurred. Children produced of extramarital
liaisons were not usually regarded as white (see BASTARDS).
When a number of London Missionary Society MISSIONARIES
married women of color in the early 19th century, they were

much criticized for doing so by white settlers.

The Cape Morality Act of 1902 was an early attempt to restrict sexual relations across the color line: harsh penalties
were laid down for white women (prostitutes) having such relations with African men. The much more important Immorality
Act of 1927 prescribed heavy penalties for sex between any
whites and Africans. After the NATIONAL PARTY came to
power in 1948 it was quick to pass further legislation. First,
a Mixed Marriages Act (1949) forbade marriages between whites
and members of all other groups, though there had been fewer
than 100 such mixed marriages a year. Secondly, an amendment to the Immorality Act in 1950 prohibited sexual relations
between whites and "COLOUREDS." The police then engaged in
widespread snooping to see whether crimes were being committed under the amended law. A number of whites took their
own lives when faced with the prospect of being tried under this
legislation. Convictions in terms of it, numerous in the first
two decades, declined somewhat at the end of the 1970s, and
P. W. BOTHA spoke of possible "adjustments" to the Immorality
and Mixed Marriages Act.

MISSIONARIES. The first European missionary sent to minister to
the indigenous people at the Cape was the Moravian (Lutheran)
George Schmidt (1709-1785), who began work at Genadendal,
about 100 miles east of Cape Town, in 1737. He returned to
Europe in 1744 and it was not until the 1790s that mission work
was resumed, both at Genadendal and elsewhere. The most important of the new missionaries was Johannes van der Kemp
(1747-1811) of the interdenominational London Missionary Society
(founded 1795), who arrived in the colony in 1799.

Van der Kemp first tried to work among the XHOSA of the
eastern Cape, but when that proved unsuccessful turned his attention to the KHOIKHOI, for whom he established the most famous of the Cape mission stations, Bethelsdorp (now within
Port Elizabeth). His plea for equality for Khoi aroused the
anger of the colonists, who feared that his station would draw
laborers from their farms. But the LMS persevered, and
throughout the first half of the 19th century had more missionaries in the field, scattered over a wider area, than any other
society. In the north the dominant figure was Robert Moffat
(1795-1883), whose base from 1825 was the Kuruman station,
about 120 miles northwest of Kimberley. Translator of the
bible into the TSWANA language and author of Missionary La-
bours and Scenes in Southern Africa (1842), Moffat made Kuruman the center of a vast missionary work. From there David
Livingstone (1813-1873) was to move into the far interior. The
Superintendent of the LMS in the 1820s, 30s and 40s, John
PHILIP, was a central figure in the history of his times. The
LMS did not work much among the settler population, instead
moving ahead of the expanding colonial frontiers. Most of its
stations in the settled colony were gradually incorporated in the
Congregational Church.

The other great Protestant missionary society active in South

Africa in the early 19th century was the Wesleyan Methodist
Missionary Society. William Shaw (1798-1872), who arrived as
a chaplain to some Methodist families among the 1820 BRITISH
settlers, did not only work among the settlers--he was responsible for establishing a chain of mission stations beyond the Cape's
eastern border stretching almost to Port NATAL. Like the
LMS, the Methodists also did pioneering missionary work among
the SOTHO in the north. In time the Methodist became the
largest of the English-speaking churches, and the one with the
most African members.

Of the other missionary societies, Scottish missionaries were
most active in what became the CISKEI, where they founded
Lovedale in 1824, which in the late 19th century was the leading missionary educational institution in South Africa. The
Berlin Missionary Society, a Lutheran organization, began work
in the eastern Cape in the 1830s, but its stations were destroyed
during the War of the Axe (1846-47) and it moved its attentions
first to Natal and then, from the 1860s, to the eastern Transvaal, where it persevered in work among the PEDI despite the
opposition of Sekhukhune (1814-1882). The Rhenish Mission
worked in the western Cape and Namaqualand, the Norwegian
Missionary Society in Zululand. The most successful of the
Zulu missions was that of the American Board, the Boston-
based counterpart of the LMS. In 1853 it founded Adams College which, before it was closed down by the government in
1956 (see BANTU EDUCATION), educated a considerable number of Natal's African elite.

It was not until the mid-1850s that the Anglicans began mission work on the eastern Cape frontier (see GRAY). As a result of the evangelical revival in the DUTCH REFORMED
CHURCH in the 1860s, it began mission work in the Transvaal
as well as further afield, while the ROMAN CATHOLIC
CHURCH's mission work did not enter its main age of expansion until this century.

In the first half of the 19th century the missionaries made
relatively little progress. By 1850, 10,000 Africans lived on
32 mission stations in the eastern Cape, but not all were converts. The first converts were mostly fugitives, rebels or
social rejects. Among the southern NGUNI the main body of
converts were MFENGU, uprooted from their societies during
the MFECANE. Missionary intolerance of African customs
aroused opposition to their work. Many Africans saw Christianity as a subversive ideology, part of the general threat
posed by whites to African societies. It was only after the
CATTLE KILLING (1856-57) that the Xhosa became Christians
in considerable numbers.

Initially criticized by the colonists as interfering busybodies,
too sympathetic to people of color, the missionaries have more
recently been seen as agents of conquest who promoted capitalist and colonial expansion. Some did double as agents for white
governments, and missionaries were often accepted by Africans
as unofficial brokers between them and white authorities. The
"Christianity and civilisation" that missionaries brought involved

weaning Africans from pre-capitalist modes of production, draw-
ing them into the market-oriented colonial economy, and creating "artificial wants." While some missionaries did what they
could to halt settler expansion, others, often bitterly divided
themselves and rivals for converts, were led to advocate the
overthrow of independent African societies in the interests of
the extension of Christianity. In 1982 there were an estimated
13 million practicing Christians in South Africa, 80 percent of
whom were black.

MOSHWESHWE (Moshoeshoe in the official orthography of LESOTHO;
    c. 1786-1870), SOTHO statesman. He acquired his name--an
    onomatopoeic praise-name meaning "the shaver"--after he had
    "shaved off" another ruler's cattle. The son of a minor Sotho
    ruler in the upper Caledon valley, he owed much of his success
    to his skill in holding his followers together during the upheaval
    of the 1820s (see MFECANE). He exploited the flat-topped
    mountains east of the Caledon, and especially that known as
    Thaba Bosiu (Sotho: "mountain of the night"), which he made
    his capital in 1824. He built up his herds of cattle--in large
    part through very successful raids on the Thembu south of the
    DRAKENSBERG, in what became the TRANSKEI--and then re-
    cruited followers through loaning out cattle (see SISA). Mag-
    nanimous to his enemies, he was the humane and tolerant ruler
    of a relatively loosely-knit federal state.
        Having created that state, he had, after 1848, to try to pre-
    serve it in the face of new pressures. In 1843 the British had
    recognized that his lands extended well west of the Caledon;
    attempts to restrict his land after the proclamation of the
    ORANGE RIVER SOVEREIGNTY (1848) caused him to lose much
    of his faith in them. But after the establishment of the inde-
    pendent ORANGE FREE STATE, and especially after the incon-
    clusive war with that state in 1858, he realized that the best
    hope of escaping being swallowed by the Boers lay in British
    protection. The Seqiti War of 1865-66 (war of the noise of
    cannon) left the Sotho in desperate plight, and it was fortunate
    for them that in March 1868 the Cape governor and HIGH COM-
    MISSIONER agreed to extend British protection. But the west-
    ern boundary demarcated at the meeting between the high com-
    missioner and commissioners appointed by the Free State
    Volksraad (parliament) at Aliwal North in February 1869 left
    the Sotho without land west of the Caledon (see further under
    CONQUERED TERRITORY).

MOZAMBIQUE (Portuguese East Africa). For over eighty years the
    most important foreign source of African MIGRANT LABOR for
    the GOLD mines. In the 1890s over half the labor force on the
    mines came from there. Contracts with "East Coast natives"
    (as Mozambicans were called) were for longer periods than
    those with Africans within South Africa, and employing them
    pushed down African wage rates in South Africa. The stream
    of Mozambicans to the mines continued, with an average of
    100,000 men a year working there during the 30 years after

World War II.   But after the independence of Mozambique in
June 1975, the supply began to dry up and was soon a fraction
of that number.   But other strong economic ties continued to
bind the two countries.   South Africa had invested about £115
million in the Cabora Bassa hydroelectric scheme on the Zambesi, and was the obvious market for some of the electricity it
produced.   Nevertheless, in 1980 and 1981 power supplies were
disrupted, thanks to sabotage by the Mozambican Resistance
Movement, which was said to have South African backing.
Though South Africa had initially established "business as usual"
relations with the Frelimo government in Maputo, it raided the
AFRICAN NATIONAL CONGRESS quarters in one of Maputo's
suburbs in January 1981.   Large numbers of South African
tourists had visited the Mozambican capital prior to independence, but that traffic ended completely after the new government came to power.

MULDERGATE.   Name given by the press to the scandal in the Department of Information, in which the responsible minister was
Dr Connie Mulder (1925-   ).   There were some similarities to
the U.S. Watergate affair.   After being appointed Secretary for
Information in 1972, Eschel Rhoodie advanced a plan to put the
government's case by establishing front organizations and buying
friends around the world.   VORSTER, Mulder, and others agreed
to establish a secret fund to bankroll Rhoodie's schemes.   Individuals and organizations abroad were given money, and efforts
made to buy influential newspapers and journals.   The largest
sum went to establish an English-language pro-government newspaper in Johannesburg, the Citizen.   By 1978 there had not only
been serious "irregularities" in the use of the secret funds, but
R64 million had been transferred from Defence and other depart-
ments to the secret fund without statutory authority.   Infighting
within the NP helped bring the matter into the open, as did able
investigative journalism and the courage of a judge.   When the
scandal began to come out, those involved sought to cover up
what had happened.   Mulder denied in parliament that any government money had gone to finance the Citizen.
    Worry about the scandal led to VORSTER's resignation as
Prime Minister in 1978.   Mulder's involvement in it cost him
the premiership, which went to P.W. BOTHA.   Two months
later Mulder was forced to resign from the Cabinet, and he
later left the NP in disgrace.   After a government commission
of enquiry found that Vorster had known about the Citizen, he
resigned as State President.   The Department of Information
was disbanded.   Of those directly involved in the scandal, only
Rhoodie was prosecuted, and he was acquitted on appeal.   (See
also OUTWARD POLICY).

MZILIKAZI see NDEBELE STATE; TRANSVAAL.

NAMIBIA.   Formerly South-West Africa (SWA), a large sparsely

populated territory on South Africa's northwestern flank, occupied by the Germans after 1884 and conquered by South African
forces in 1915.   South Africa claimed it at the Versailles peace
conference (1919), but outright annexation was forbidden and it
became a C-class mandate under the League of Nations.   This
permitted South Africa to administer it as an integral part of
the Union, subject only to a few limitations designed to safeguard the interests of the indigenous people, and the duty of
reporting annually to the Permanent Mandates Commission of
the League.

In 1946 SMUTS proposed to the first session of the new
UNITED NATIONS (UN) that SWA be regarded as an integral
part of South Africa.   This was rejected, and South Africa was
asked to place the territory under the trusteeship system, which,
unlike the mandate one, explicitly envisaged progress of the
territory towards self-government.   South Africa in turn rejected this, denying that it was legally bound to place the territory under UN trusteeship.   In 1949 the new NATIONAL PAR-
TY government gave SWA whites representation in the South
African parliament; it also refused to submit further reports
on the territory to the UN.

The UN General Assembly then asked the International Court
of Justice at the Hague for an advisory opinion on SWA's international status.   In 1950 the Court decided that South Africa
need not place the territory under UN trusteeship, but that the
mandate was still effective and the obligation to continue to submit reports (now to the UN) still existed.   The South African
government not only refused to accept this but from 1954 even
"Native affairs" in the territory were transferred to Pretoria's
direct control.   In 1962 the International Court decided that it
was competent to hear a complaint brought by Ethiopia and Liberia, which had both been members of the League, that South
Africa had violated the mandate through the practice of APAR-
THEID in the territory.   But after protracted litigation the
Court in 1966 decided by eight votes to seven that Ethiopia and
Liberia did not after all have locus standi in the case.   With
that, the UN General Assembly voted to terminate South Africa's
mandate.   Another application was then made to the International Court, which in 1971 ruled that South Africa's continued occupation of the territory was illegal.

All this time South African rule of the territory had meant
closer and closer links between the two countries.   VERWOERD
said there was no difference between them, while a government
commission recommended (1964) that a full BANTUSTAN system, on the South African model, be created in SWA.   But the
collapse of Portuguese power in Africa in 1974 led South Africa
to rethink its strategy.   For one thing, it was realized that the
South West African People's Organisation (SWAPO) which had
been engaged in a low-intensity guerilla campaign against South
African rule from 1966, would be able to use ANGOLA as a
base of operations if that country had a pro-SWAPO government.
South Africa's first response was to summon an ethnically
based consultative council which met at the Turnhalle building

in Windhoek. By 1977 the Turnhalle conference had drafted a proposal that provided for independence for the territory by the end of 1978. South Africa then came under pressure from the five Western countries on the UN Security Council--the United States, Britain, France, West Germany and Canada--not to transfer power to an internal group. Wanting international recognition for the new government in Namibia, and also credit from the West, South Africa agreed in 1977 to go along with a plan put forward by negotiators from the five Western countries, which provided for an election under UN auspices, in which SWAPO would participate. At the same time, a South African-appointed Administrator General of the territory abolished a number of racially discriminatory laws. In April 1978, South Africa formally agreed to the Western plan, subsequently embodied in UN resolution 435 of 1978.

Then followed years of tortuous negotiations on the way the UN plan would operate. At first the questions at issue were the size and composition of the UN Transitional Assistance Group (UNTAG), the number and location of South African and SWAPO bases during the transitional period, and a possible demilitarized zone. When agreement on these seemed to have been reached, South Africa raised the issue of UN bias towards SWAPO, and demanded proof of its "neutrality." The advent of President Ronald Reagan's administration in Washington which seemed likely to be more sympathetic made South Africa dig in its heels, and a conference of the major parties organized by the UN in Geneva in January 1981 proved abortive. Later that year the Western initiative was revived under the leadership of the Assistant Secretary for African Affairs in the Reagan administration. The Western five now decided to negotiate in three phases. The first laid out constitutional guarantees designed to safeguard minority rights in the territory after independence, and provided for a complex electoral system. The second phase was to concern the transitional arrangements, the third the implementation of the package. Early in 1982 negotiations were still proceeding on the first phase. It remained uncertain whether the South African government was prepared to see a free and fair election take place, which would almost certainly return a SWAPO government. It was known that right-wingers in South Africa were ready to accuse the government of selling out the whites in the territory if it allowed a SWAPO government to come to power.

While negotiations continued with the Western contact group, South Africa continued to hand over power gradually to the Democratic Turnhalle Alliance, which had won an internal election organized by South Africa at the end of 1978 and which subsequently dominated the Ministerial Council established in Windhoek. By late 1981 only foreign, defense, and constitutional matters remained under South Africa's direct control. At the same time, a massive South African military presence occupied the northern part of the territory and fought a bush war with SWAPO there and in southern ANGOLA. A few days after it accepted the Western plan for the territory in 1978,

South African forces attacked SWAPO's Cassinga base well inside Angola, and such attacks continued, until by late 1981 the
South African army had created a virtual cordon sanitaire along
the Angolan-Namibian border.   The South African military
sources claimed 1479 SWAPO guerillas killed (1981), against
the loss of 29 South Africans.   Another 1000 SWAPO supporters
had been killed during Operation Protea (August 1981) on a
SWAPO base in southern Angola.   In 1982 both the South African and American governments tried to link a settlement in
Namibia with a withdrawal of Cuban forces from Angola.   (See
also UNITED NATIONS; WALVIS BAY.)

NATAL.   Lying between the great chain of the DRAKENSBERG and
the Indian ocean, Natal was given its name by the first European to pass along its shores, Vasco da Gama (see PORTU-
GUESE).   Before the rise of the ZULU empire in the early
19th century, it was the home, according to Theophilus SHEP-
STONE, of 94 small NGUNI chiefdoms.   From their mountain
fastnesses SAN raided Nguni cattle, which to them were game.
     The small trading post of Port Natal (see DURBAN) was es-
tablished in 1824, but the first large group of whites to enter
Natal crossed the Drakensberg in 1837 (see GREAT TREK).   By
1839 some 6, 000 trekker pastoralists were living in their Republic of Natalia between the Tugela river in the north and the
Mzimkulu in the south.   After the BRITISH annexation of 1843--
largely for strategic reasons, to prevent any hostile power gain-
ing a foothold on the southern African coast--most of the trekkers left for the highveld.   Then 5, 000 new immigrants came
from Britain in 1849-1852 (see ENGLISH-SPEAKING WHITES)
and helped give Natal its English character.   By the mid 1850s
there were still fewer than 10, 000 whites.   Over 100, 000 Africans, housed in RESERVES totalling almost 2 million acres,
were administered by Theophilus SHEPSTONE through a system
of indirect rule and paternalism.   Thanks to indentured INDIAN
labor, sugar, most of it grown in the sub-tropical coastal belt
north of Durban, became the mainstay of Natal's economy.
     Natal remained an autonomous district of the Cape Colony
until 1856, then was separated from the Cape and given its own
legislative council, which the colonists used as a platform from
which to berate Shepstone for his reserve system and to appeal
for the reserves to be broken up so that they might enjoy more
African labor.   Though Natal's FRANCHISE was in theory non-
racial, like the Cape's, in practice it was closer to that to be
found in the trekker republics.   With a powerful ZULU state to
the north, and large numbers of Africans in their midst, Natal's
fearful whites were not inclined towards LIBERALISM.   Steps
were taken in the mid 1860s to bar Africans from the franchise,
by making exemption from customary law a necessary requisite.
Such exemption was very difficult to obtain.
     After the LANGALIBALELE rebellion, an attempt was made
to reduce Natal to Crown colony status, in part so that Natal
could give its support to CARNARVON's CONFEDERATION
scheme.   In reaction, a movement grew for responsible govern-

ment, finally achieved in 1893.   Long before then the white
community's chief fear, the Zulu military machine, had been
dismantled, and Zululand, after ten years of British rule
through the HIGH COMMISSIONER, was, with adjoining Tonga-
land (see THONGA), incorporated into Natal in 1897.
More MISSIONARIES worked in Natal than in any other African territory of comparable size in the 19th century.   The
American Board took the lead in producing a significant KHOL-
WA Christian community, many members of which became prosperous peasants and acquired western education.   Men like
DUBE, LUTHULI, and SEME came from this class.   Leading
whites were quick to accuse kholwa members of ETHIOPIAN
churches of being behind the BAMBATHA REBELLION (1906).
That revolt, showing Natal's weakness, helped push it into
UNION (1910).   Within Union, Natal's conservative ENGLISH-
SPEAKING WHITES disliked Afrikaner domination, and occa-
sionally spoke of secession (see SEPARATIST MOVEMENTS).
In the 1970s over forty separate pieces of African land were
excised from the province and constituted as the KWAZULU
Bantustan.   Many hundreds of thousands of Africans living on
white farms were forced to move into Kwazulu (see MASS RE-
MOVALS).   The BANTUSTAN included major dormitory towns,
within a few miles of DURBAN, from which hundreds of
thousands commuted daily to work.   That there was a single
Natal-Kwazulu economy, and that therefore the region should be
governed as one, was the main thrust of the report of a commission appointed by Gatsha BUTHELE ZI of Kwazulu, which
made public its findings in early 1982.

NATIONAL CONVENTION.   The body which drafted the UNION constitution.   It assembled in Durban on 12 October 1908, nine
years to the day after the outbreak of the SOUTH AFRICAN
WAR.   Thirty whites from the four colonies participated, the
numbers being roughly proportionate to the white populations:
twelve from the Cape, eight from the Transvaal, and five each
from the Orange River Colony and Natal.   The Convention met
behind closed doors in Durban and Cape Town between October
1908 and February 1909.   Differing over the key issue of the
FRANCHISE, the delegates agreed to let the existing systems in
the various colonies continue under Union, but only whites were
to be members of the new parliament.   Unable to agree on the
choice of a capital, the delegates proposed that Cape Town be
the seat of parliament, Pretoria the administrative capital, and
Bloemfontein the seat of the appellate division of the Supreme
Court.
It has often been suggested that there should be another National Convention to draw up a new dispensation for South Africa,
and that this time it should include representatives from all
groups of the population.   The call for such a Convention was
made strongly after SHARPEVILLE.   That there should be such
a Convention is an important plank of PROGRESSIVE PARTY
policy.

NATIONAL PARTY (NP) (1914-). General HERTZOG, the leading
representative of republican sentiment in the first Union Cabinet,
was forced out of office in 1912 after he had asserted a "South
Africa First" policy, which seemed to English-speakers to question the imperial relationship with Britain. In January 1914,
with a group of mainly Free State supporters, he formed a new,
exclusively Afrikaner party, which stood for dual-medium education and compulsory bilingualism in the civil service. Its first
program of principles stated: "In our attitude towards the Native the fundamental principle is the supremacy of the European
population in the spirit of Christian trusteeship, utterly rejecting
any attempt to mix the races." Its original support was mainly
rural and agrarian. The NP benefitted from the AFRIKANER
REBELLION, which BOTHA and SMUTS put down with force,
and from the increasingly close ties between their SOUTH AFRI-
CAN PARTY and the English UNIONIST PARTY. More and more
of the newly urbanized Afrikaner workers supported the NP.
Thanks to the PACT made with the LABOUR PARTY, Hertzog
and the NP gained power in 1924. After the 1929 election, it
had 78 seats to the SAP's 61 and Labour's 8. But then came the
depression (see BUSINESS CYCLES) and Hertzog's decision
(March 1933) to form a coalition government with Smuts. The
following year the FUSION of the NP with the SAP ended the
first phase of NP history.
    As the old NP died, a new one was born. Malan's response
to Fusion was to form a Gesuiwerde Nasionale Party (Purified
NP), accusing Hertzog of selling out the principles of the NP.
Malan's party, which became the official opposition, was strongest in the Cape, where it enjoyed the support of Die Burger
newspaper and the Nasionale Pers publishing house. Initially it
had only one member of parliament in the Transvaal (see
STRIJDOM). But in the 1938 general election it increased its
strength to 27 in the country as a whole.
    After SMUTS had taken South Africa into World War II,
Hertzog and Malan came together in a brief "hereniging" (re-
union). Their new Reunited National Party was committed to
a REPUBLIC, but membership was not denied Afrikaners who
were against trying to establish a republic "in the existing circumstances." Hertzog's faction soon broke away again (see
AFRIKANER PARTY) and the NP was decisively beaten by
SMUTS in the 1943 general election. But at the end of the war
the NP and Afrikaner Party came together, enabling the NP,
with Afrikaner Party support, to form a majority after the 1948
general election, even though it had won only 37.2 percent of
the votes (the United Party gained 47.9 percent).
    That election was a major turning-point in recent South Afri-
can history. The NP campaigned on a platform of APARTHEID,
its answer to the large influx of Africans to the towns (see UR-
BANIZATION). It wanted to tighten up the MIGRANT LABOR
system and prevent large numbers of Africans entering "white"
urban areas. In this way it sought to deny the African proletariat any means to bargain for incorporation in the political

system.   But apartheid was only one reason for the NP's success.   More than a political party, the NP presented itself as
the party of volkseenheid ("unity of the people") and was for its
supporters one arm of a movement that sought to comprehend
all spheres of activity.   It was closely linked to the DUTCH
REFORMED CHURCH, the Afrikaner PRESS and a wide range
of cultural, academic, professional, and business organizations
and societies.   The secret AFRIKANER BROEDERBOND played
a major role in its victory.   When its supporters heard they
had won, they said that they had "got the country back" (from
the English-speakers and their allies).

Once in office, the NP took steps to ensure it would not lose
power at the next election.   South West Africa (NAMIBIA) was
given six seats in the Assembly, all won by Nationalists in
1950.   The attempt to remove the "COLOUREDS" from the common voters' roll provoked a constitutional crisis (see "COL-
OURED" VOTE ISSUE), but did not harm the NP in the 1953
election.   At each successive election in the 1950s and 1960s
the NP increased its share of the votes cast by the white electorate.   Though it attracted some English-speaking support in
the late 1960s and the 1970s, the NP remained fundamentally
an ethnic party, with its primary concern the protection of
Afrikaner interests as it saw them.

After VORSTER became Prime Minister in 1966, the right-
wing in the party soon became restive with the direction of his
policy, which seemed to them contrary to Verwoerdian policy.
They opposed multi-racial sport, diplomatic relations with black
African countries, and appeals for English-speaking support.
The discontent gradually came to a head, and at the September
1969 Transvaal congress of the NP, the dissidents were expelled (see HERSTIGTE NASIONALE PARTY).   Vorster managed to prevent them posing a real threat to the unity of the
NP.   The specter of a major division was a powerful deterrent
and the memory of the internecine strife of the 1930s and early
1940s was still vivid.   Many right-wing Nationalists, such as
TREURNICHT, chose to remain within the NP and attempt to
influence it from within.   But after BOTHA became Prime Minister the right wing again grew increasingly unhappy with the
direction of policy: the removal of aspects of "PETTY APART-
HEID" and the move towards the admission of "COLOUREDS"
and Indians to the same political system with whites, which implied multi-racial government.   In the April 1981 election,
though the NP won 131 seats, the HNP none, the NP share of
the vote dropped to 57 percent, while the HNP gained 191, 000
votes, 14. 1 percent of those cast.

NATIONAL UNION OF SOUTH AFRICAN STUDENTS (NUSAS).
Formed in 1924 with the aim of bringing together students at
all the UNIVERSITIES in South Africa.   But Afrikaans-speaking
students disliked the dominance of the English-speakers in the
organization and in 1933 three of the four Afrikaans campuses
disaffiliated and formed a rival Afrikaanse Studentebond (ASB).
The fourth, Stellenbosch, left NUSAS in 1936.   NUSAS then

became based in the four English-medium campuses of Cape
Town, Witwatersrand, Rhodes, and Natal. The proposed admission of the African college of FORT HARE had been an issue in the Afrikaans breakaway, but it was not until 1946 that,
with the more radical students in NUSAS in a majority, Fort
Hare students were admitted. NUSAS's multi-racialism and its
radical politics were anathema to the ASB.

In a move similar to the withdrawal of the Afrikaner students, African students in 1969 formed their own SOUTH AFRI-
CAN STUDENTS ORGANISATION, claiming NUSAS was paternal-
istic. NUSAS was one of a number of organizations investigated
by a parliamentary commission appointed in 1972. As a result
of its report, eight of its leaders were BANNED. NUSAS then
became the first organization to be declared an "affected organisation," under an Act which prevented such organizations obtaining funds from abroad (see also CHRISTIAN INSTITUTE).
Despite all the government actions taken against it, NUSAS remained the main student organization on the English-speaking
campuses and continued to be one of the most radical opposition
groups operating legally within the country.

NATIVES LAND ACT (1913). An attempt to obtain uniformity in land
policy after UNION, this Act acquired great symbolic significance.
In the Cape and Natal before Union, there were no restrictions
on Africans buying land outside the RESERVES. In the Transvaal, on the other hand, land owned by Africans had had to be
registered in the name of the chief African administrator. A
Supreme Court case of 1905 found that Africans could hold land
in their own right outside the reserves. As African purchase,
often through a syndicate, increased--78 farms or portions of
farms were acquired in 1910-12--alarm grew amongst whites.
The 1913 Act froze the existing racial distribution of land:
Africans could not buy or obtain title to land outside the reserves (the "scheduled areas"); non-Africans could not acquire
title to land within them. It also envisaged land being added to
the reserves, especially in the Transvaal and the Orange Free
State, where there was little reserve land. A commission under Sir William Beaumont (1851-1930), a retired Natal judge,
was set up to assess African needs for extra land and to recom-
mend where such land could be found. Its report (1916) was in
turn referred to local committees, the findings of which were
accepted by the SMUTS government in 1921. But the additional
land was not provided for until the Native Trust and Land Act
(1936), and then the land released (15.3 million acres) was
much less than that allocated by the Beaumont Commission.
The land scheduled in 1913 was a mere 7 percent of the total
area of the country; with the additional land released in 1936,
the reserves were to constitute just over 13 percent of the
total area. By the end of the 1970s, however, not all this
"quota" land had been acquired, and added to the reserves (by
then called "national states").

The Land Act did not only provide for a grossly inequitable
division of land between Africans and non-Africans. It was

also concerned with the eviction of African SQUATTERS.
White farmers wanted them turned into either labor tenants,
working for a set number of days, usually 90 per year, in
return for access to land, or wage laborers. But eviction was
not to take place in Natal and the Transvaal "until parliament
has made other provision," and in 1913 that was a long way
off (see HERTZOG BILLS). For the Free State, however,
previous anti-squatting provisions were confirmed, and share-
croppers--disliked in part because of the equality implicit in
their relationship with the farmer--were forced off the land as described in the vivid pages of PLAATJE's classic Native Life in
South Africa (1916).
     The Land Act could not be applied to the Cape, for to inter-
fere with Africans' land rights was to interfere with their access to the qualified franchise. Uniformity of policy, then, had
to await the removal of the Cape Africans' common roll vote in
1936: see HERTZOG BILLS.

NATIVES REPRESENTATIVE COUNCIL. Advisory body established
     in terms of HERTZOG's Representation of Natives Act of 1936.
     (See FRANCHISE; HERTZOG BILLS). AFRICAN NATIONAL
     CONGRESS leaders and others decided to participate in it, and
     between 1937 and 1946 it regularly passed moderate resolutions
     calling for the redress of African grievances. These were con-
     sistently ignored by the government. In 1946 it decided to ad-
     journ in protest over the suppression of the African minework-
     ers' STRIKE. After becoming Minister of Native Affairs in
     1950, VERWOERD convened it but merely to tell it of the need
     for APARTHEID. It was abolished under the Bantu Authorities
     Act of 1951, which provided for the establishment of local, re-
     gional, and territorial African councils in the RESERVES.

NAUDE, Beyers (1916-   ). Director of the CHRISTIAN INSTITUTE
     (CI) 1963-1977. Son of a founder of the AFRIKANER BROEDER-
     BOND, of which he himself became a member. A DUTCH RE-
     FORMED CHURCH minister, it was as acting moderator of his
     church that he participated in the COTTESLOE CONSULTATION
     after SHARPEVILLE. Dismayed by his church's subsequent re-
     jection of the statement that came out of that meeting, Naudé
     founded the CI and became an increasingly radical opponent of
     APARTHEID. Forced to resign his ministry, he was shunned
     as a traitor to the Afrikaner volk. Eventually he and the CI
     were both BANNED in October 1977. He subsequently left the
     white Dutch Reformed Church and joined a congregation of the
     African branch of that church.

NDEBELE STATE (c. 1822-1838). During the wars fought by
     Shaka of the ZULU in his rise to power, a small group of
     members of the Khumalo clan fled north of the Drakensberg
     mountains under Mzilikazi (Moselekatse, Silkaats, and other
     variants; c. 1790-1868). He was probably an independent ruler,
     in a tributary relationship to Shaka, before he moved away.
     The story that he defied Shaka by refusing to surrender booty

is almost certainly apocryphal. In the late 1820s Mzilikazi built up a powerful, highly militaristic state with its capital just north of the present Pretoria. Many of the SOTHO-speaking peoples of the central Transvaal were absorbed into the new state, either through marriage or conquest. In about 1832 the raiding state moved west, into the modern Rustenburg area of the western Transvaal. There Mzilikazi still found himself challenged by various enemies, including GRIQUA and then VOORTREKKERS from the south, besides the Zulu, who remained a threat under Shaka's successor Dingane (ruled 1828 to 1840). After a party of trekkers had repulsed an attack by his forces in October 1836, the trekkers went on to destroy the large Ndebele town at Mosega in January 1837. Mzilikazi then withdrew his people to the north, and eventually succeeded in recreating his state in what was later to become known as Matabeleland in southwestern ZIMBABWE.

NEUMARK THESIS. In his Economic Influences on the South African Frontier, 1652-1836 (Stanford, California, 1957), S. D. Neumark criticized the notion that the TREKBOERS of the interior were self-sufficient subsistence farmers, and that frontier expansion occurred either because whites were unable to obtain land in the arable areas or because they disliked DUTCH EAST INDIA COMPANY rule and desired freedom and independence. In his view the trekboers were crucially linked to markets at the coast, and he supplied evidence to show the extent to which they supplied cattle, hides, and skins to Cape Town in exchange for guns, ammunition, and other commodities. He believed that it was the profitability of the cattle trade that led men to take up pastoral farming. But his thesis has been criticized by those who deny that the expansion of white settlement was a response to the demand for the produce of the interior. Such critics argue that the authorization of new loan farms in the interior does not reflect increased demand for inland produce measured by the number of foreign ships that called at the Cape. Neumark's critics suggest instead, as earlier writers had, that the very large families of the white settlers, and their Roman-Dutch system of partible inheritance, were the chief motors of frontier expansion, and they stress the extent to which the trekboers in the remote interior lived a subsistence existence, with no need to convert their cattle to cash.

NGUNI. A group of southeast BANTU languages spoken by AFRI-CANS of the coastal belt from Zululand to the CISKEI. These Bantu-speaking peoples were known as "Abingonei" (perhaps from the TSWANA "koni" meaning easterners) from at least the 1830s. The Nguni may in turn be divided into the Cape Nguni or XHOSA-speaking people and the Northern or Natal Nguni, who were incorporated into Shaka's ZULU empire and came to speak Zulu. For a group of Nguni origin in the Transvaal see KWANDEBELE.

That Nguni languages contain more clicks than SOTHO ones is an indication of greater interaction with KHOISAN people.

Extensive intermarriage between Nguni and Khoisan people is
also suggested by physical appearances and the incorporation of
religious and medical ideas from the Khoi in Nguni culture.
Pastoralism played an even more important role in Nguni than
Sotho culture and economy.   Traditionally the Nguni lived in
beehive huts around their scattered cattle kraals.   The accounts
of PORTUGUESE sailors shipwrecked along the eastern coast in
the 16th and 17th centuries describe people whose rulers were
known as "inkosi," the Nguni word for ruler, living in what is
now northern Natal and the TRANSKEI.

NKOSI SIKELEL'I-AFRIKA (Xhosa: "God Bless Africa").   The African national anthem, sung by the ANC and adopted as their national anthem by the TRANSKEI and CISKEI BANTUSTANS.
Composed by Enoch Sontonga in 1897, it was first sung publicly
in 1899.   It was completed by Samuel Mqhayi (1875-1945), the
greatest figure in XHOSA literature, who was journalist, teacher
and praise-singer as well as novelist and poet.

NON-EUROPEAN UNITY MOVEMENT.   Founded in 1943, it emerged
out of efforts, mainly led by "Coloured" intellectuals in Cape
Town, to form a united front of the oppressed against racial
discrimination in the late 1930s.   It brought together both those
"Coloureds" who rejected SMUTS' Coloured Advisory Council
and the idea of a Coloured Affairs Department (see "COL-
OURED" POLITICS) and members of the ALL AFRICAN CON-
VENTION.   NEUM policy was non-collaboration and total boycott of the institutions of the oppressor.   The first point on its
ten-point program was full franchise rights for all.   In the late
1940s it began to attract considerable support in the rural
TRANSKEI, but in the early 1950s it opposed the DEFIANCE
CAMPAIGN and CONGRESS ALLIANCE and was kept alive only
by a group of "Coloured" theoreticians of a Trotskyite persuasion.   By 1959 it was riven by feuds, and it disintegrated in
the early 1960s, when a number of its leaders were BANNED
or forced into exile.   An exile wing was formed in Zambia.
Within South Africa, its views continued to be propagated in the
Educational Journal, a newsletter published by the Teachers'
League of South Africa, an affiliate of the NEUM.

NUCLEAR PROGRAM.   Two small research reactors at Pelindaba,
near Pretoria, went critical in 1965 and 1967.   In 1970 it was
announced that the South African Atomic Energy Board had pioneered a new process to enrich uranium, of which the country
had abundant supplies (see MINING).   A pilot plant, at Valindaba, began operating in 1975.   The following year a French con-
sortium won a contract to supply two light-water reactors at
Koeberg, thirty miles north of Cape Town, to become opera-
tional in 1982 and 1983.   As the pilot plant could only produce
minute amounts of enriched uranium, the South African Electricity Supply Commission signed a contract with the United
States Department of Energy in terms of which raw uranium
would be enriched in the United States for Koeberg.   But then

the American Nuclear Non-Proliferation Act (1978) required international inspection of nuclear facilities before nuclear fuel could be exported from the U.S. South Africa refused to allow inspections or to sign the Nuclear Non-Proliferation treaty, on the grounds that the inspections required would expose the secrets of the country's enrichment process. Some thought the government wanted ostentatiously to reserve the right to develop nuclear weapons as a last resort defense against external pressures to change its policies. Speculation about a South African nuclear bomb increased in 1977 when the Russians claimed that a satellite had detected preparations for a nuclear test in the Kalahari desert. Two years later an American satellite detected a mysterious flash of light in the South Atlantic which was thought might have been from a nuclear test.

In 1981 South Africa was able to buy the enriched uranium it needed for the Koeberg power plant from Europe. At the same time, it agreed to permit the International Atomic Energy Agency to inspect Koeberg, but not the Valindaba enrichment plant.

ORANGE FREE STATE. The hundreds of stone ruins that dot the northern Free State attest to a long history of African occupation (see IRON AGE). As the 19th century opened, SOTHO-speakers lived across all but the southernmost portion of the lands between the ORANGE RIVER and its tributary the Vaal. The 1820s saw this country in turmoil, but out of the disruption of the MFECANE two major states emerged on either side of the Caledon valley: that founded by MOSHWESHWE east of the Caledon (see BASUTOLAND) and the Tlokoa state ruled by Sekonyela (c. 1804-1856) from his capital just west of that river. The rivals eventually clashed in 1853, Moshweshwe's forces were victorious, and the bulk of Sekonyela's followers fled south of the Orange.

The VOORTREKKERS passed through the eastern Free State in the late 1830s. Wishing to put as much territory as possible between themselves and the British, they trekked beyond the Vaal or the DRAKENSBERG. But after the British annexation of NATAL, many returned to the highveld and settled among the TREKBOERS already between the Orange and the Vaal. Some began to infiltrate the lands of the GRIQUA around Philippolis to the south. Early in 1848 the HIGH COMMISSIONER, concerned with stability on the Cape's northern border, proclaimed the ORANGE RIVER SOVEREIGNTY, which brought all the Orange-Vaal territory under British rule. Six years later, however, the British government, tired of bearing the burden of administering the Sovereignty, agreed to recognize the independence of the whites in the area (Bloemfontein Convention, 1854). In the new Orange Free State, the constitution was modelled on that of the United States, but only whites could be citizens.

In 1858 and again in 1865 Free State forces were launched against Moshweshwe's Sotho in a contest for possession of the

fertile lands along the Caledon valley.   In Cape Town and London British officials believed the Free State government might
be seeking a route to the sea through the Sotho territory and
the TRANSKEI.   In 1868 Britain annexed Basutoland, which the
following year was given a common boundary with the Cape,
preventing Free State expansion eastward.   With the Sotho under British rule, the Free State contained no large African
settlements other than that at Thaba Nchu, east of the capital,
which was incorporated in 1884.   A census taken in 1890 found
the Free State contained 77,000 whites and 128,000 Africans.

Under its able President BRAND, the Free State was hardly
a "model republic," but it was far less ramshackle than the
TRANSVAAL, and had close ties to the Cape.   Wool was the
main export (see ECONOMIC CHANGE).   Free State farmers
were slow to respond to the new demand for foodstuffs from
the DIAMOND fields, in part because transportation remained
so primitive, but between 1880 and 1891 agricultural production
doubled, most of it coming from the CONQUERED TERRITORY
taken from the Sotho, where soils were fertile and rainfall good.
The Free State claim to the diamond fields failed, but Brand
collected £90,000 compensation from the British.   With the discovery of GOLD on the WITWATERSRAND, followed soon after
by Brand's death, the Free State moved away from the Cape
and into the Transvaal's orbit.   After the JAMESON RAID there
was a strong feeling that all Afrikaners should stand together
against the British, and the Free State entered into an alliance
with the northern republic which brought it into the SOUTH
AFRICAN WAR in 1899.

Bloemfontein, founded at the site of a spring in the center of
the territory in 1846, was occupied by the British army in May
1900, and the Free State became the Orange River Colony.   But
it recovered its name as a province in the UNION, and Bloemfontein became the new national judicial capital (see NATIONAL
CONVENTION).

After the devastation wrought during the SOUTH AFRICAN
WAR, sharecropping spread rapidly, Africans commonly giving
half their crop to the landowner in return for seed and the use
of the land.   But sharecropping came under strong attack
from white farmers who now wanted to commercialize, and who
argued that sharecropping left them without adequate labor and
was inimical to proper master-servant relationships.   After
passage of the NATIVES LAND ACT (1913), many Africans were
ejected from white-owned farms.   The northeastern portion of
the province became the heart of the country's highly productive
"maize triangle."   The opening up of the Free State gold-fields
after World War II brought vast new wealth to the north of the
province.

ORANGE RIVER.   Named by a Scottish employee of the DUTCH
EAST INDIA COMPANY in 1779 for the Dutch prince of the
House of Orange.   The Nama and Korana KHOIKHOI, who had
lived along its banks from early in the Christian era, knew it
as the Gariep ("Great River").   Longest of South Africa's

rivers--1,200 miles from LESOTHO to the Atlantic--it is also
the least navigable major river; in the dry winter months it becomes a mere chain of pools. Individual TREKBOERS began
crossing it from the 1760s, and they were followed by MIS-
SIONARIES and traders. In stages (1835, 1847), it became the
Cape's northern boundary. The VOORTREKKERS crossed it via
the main fords near its junction with the Caledon river. In
1868 and then again in 1878 wars broke out between the Korana
Khoi pastoralists living in loosely organized bands along the middle Orange and white farmers encroaching on their lands from
south of the river. In 1878-79 Cape mounted forces and local
whites suppressed the resistance with great brutality, after
which the Khoi were sent into service in the colony. From
1880, with its annexation of Griqualand West (the DIAMOND
fields country), the Cape gained a considerable territory north
of the Orange, which was further enlarged with its annexation
of British BECHUANALAND in 1895.

ORANGE RIVER COLONY. Name given to the conquered ORANGE
    FREE STATE when it came under British rule in 1900. When
    the area became a province in the new Union of South Africa in
    1910, its name reverted to Orange Free State.

ORANGE RIVER SOVEREIGNTY (1848-1854). In February 1848 Sir
    Harry Smith (1787-1860) used his HIGH COMMISSION to pro-
    claim the Queen's sovereignty over the land between the
    ORANGE RIVER and its major tributary, the Vaal. He justi-
    fied this to London in terms of the need to create order on the
    Cape's northern border; TREKBOERS and GRIQUA had clashed
    just north of the Orange. Attempts to establish or define a
    border between the white farmers and the SOTHO of MOSHWESHWE
    (see BASUTOLAND) failed, the British government grew restless
    at the expense of the administration north of the Orange, and in
    1854 the Sovereignty came to an end when the British formally
    recognized the independence of the Boers between the Orange and
    the Vaal and, temporarily, left Moshweshwe to fend for himself.

ORDINANCE 50 (1828). Cape ordinace which removed legal inequal-
    ities suffered by "HOTTENTOTS and other free persons of col-
    or," including restrictions on freedom of movement. Since its
    passage, "COLOUREDS" have not had to carry PASSES. When
    emancipated, the slaves (see CAPE SLAVERY) fell heir to it,
    and a draft vagrancy law of 1834, designed to undo much of
    Ordinance 50, was vetoed in London.
        Pressure exerted by John PHILIP of the London Missionary
    Society in London was one reason for the Ordinance. But hu-
    manitarian concern for justice for the KHOI meshed with the
    desire of Cape officials to see both a freer labor market and
    the emergence of a Khoi "Coloured" elite. Beyond the estab-
    lishment of the KAT RIVER SETTLEMENT, however--an at-
    tempt to give substance to that clause of the Ordinance which
    recognized the right of the Khoi to own land--no positive steps
    were taken to lift the "Coloureds" from their impoverished,

inferior and servile position. The evidence suggests that the Ordinance had little effect on master-servant relationships in the eastern districts of the colony. The Afrikaner frontier farmers, however, saw it as a clear sign that the BRITISH regime sought to alter those relations in the direction of great-er equality between master and servant. In this way Ordinance 50 became a cause of the GREAT TREK.

OSSEWABRANDWAG (OB) (Afrikaans: "Oxwagon firewatch").
Formed as a cultural movement of Afrikaners inspired by the emotions generated by the centenary celebrations of the GREAT TREK in 1938, it became in the early years of WORLD WAR II an avowedly national-socialist organization working for a totali-tarian Afrikaner republic. After J. F. J. van Rensburg (1878-1966), an admirer of Hitler who hoped the Germans would win the war, became its commandant-general in 1940, it organized on para-military lines and sought to usurp the role of the NA-TIONAL PARTY (NP) as the organizational expression of Afri-kaner nationalism. It had an estimated 400,000 members by early 1941, but then state employees were barred from belong-ing to it, MALAN launched a bitter attack on it, and in Decem-ber 1941 an OB plot was uncovered and the ringleaders arrested. But neither the OB nor the anti-Semitic Greyshirts (or South African Nationalist Union), founded in 1933, were banned, though some of their meetings were, nor was Van Rensburg arrested or interned. The NP consolidated its position and emerged from the 1943 election as the sole political voice of Afrikaner-dom. After that, support for the OB dwindled.

OUTWARD POLICY (also known as "dialogue" or "detente"). In the late 1950s and early 1960s South Africa was critical of the co-lonial powers for leading their African countries to what it said was premature independence. But as black African countries became independent, VERWOERD realized that it was in South African interests to develop friendly relations with neighbouring countries, which might otherwise assist guerillas operating against South Africa. In 1963 he announced that South Africa had abandoned its claim to incorporate the HIGH COMMISSION TERRITORIES and added that, with Britain's impending with-drawal from direct responsibilities in southern Africa, the way was open for South Africa, with its economic and technical ex-pertise, to aid and cooperate with other countries. From that year South African Prime Ministers periodically spoke of a southern African common market, commonwealth or constella-tion of states. While the political aim was to create a buffer of dependent states, ruled by compliant regimes, industrialists hoped that important new markets would be opened up for South Africa's manufactured goods.
        In the late 1960s and early 1970s South Africa also looked further afield, searching for friends in order to lessen interna-tional pressure against the universally condemned apartheid sys-tem. Considerable aid, some of which helped build a new capi-tal, went to Hastings K. Banda's Malawi, which sent large

numbers of MIGRANT LABORERS to South Africa. Banda established diplomatic relations with South Africa--the only African country to do so--in 1967, and in 1970-71 VORSTER and Banda made official visits to each other's country. Despite an Organisation of African Unity declaration against contacts with South Africa in 1971, South Africa would claim unofficial relations with a dozen countries, including Mauritius, Malagasy, Gabon, Ivory Coast, Zaire, Liberia, Ghana, and the Central African Republic. Secret funds from the Department of Information (see MULDERGATE) were used to try to win friends and make deals.

Such contacts continued until 1975. Vorster's "friendly neighbour" policy to the new Frelimo regime in Mozambique won him some credit, as did his steps to push Ian Smith towards a settlement in ZIMBABWE. Vorster met Kaunda of Zambia at a conference at the Victoria Falls in August 1975 to discuss Zimbabwe, and also in that year secretly met President Tolbert in Liberia. But then South Africa's military intervention in ANGOLA destroyed most of the goodwill built up in black Africa. The brutal way the SOWETO REVOLT (1976) was suppressed helped destroy all illusions north of the Zambesi that apartheid was being liberalized. Despite the collapse of the "outward policy," however, countries such as Zambia still found it necessary to continue to conduct extensive trade with South Africa, and use its ports for the export of their minerals. In April 1982 Kaunda again met the South African Prime Minister. (See also ANGOLA; LESOTHO; MOZAMBIQUE; SANCTIONS; ZIMBABWE.)

PACT GOVERNMENT (1924-33). In terms of an election agreement made between HERTZOG of the NATIONAL PARTY and CRESWELL of the LABOUR PARTY in 1923, the two parties agreed not to oppose each other in the next general election, but to support each other's candidates against those of the SOUTH AFRICAN PARTY. If the Pact parties came to power, Hertzog was not to bring up the question of South Africa's secession from the British Empire during the life of the first parliament, the two parties were to retain their separate identities, and together they would work for economic reform.

The Pact government, formed under Hertzog after the 1924 election, sought to further the interests of white farmers, white labor, and infant Afrikaans business. This was done through diverting revenue from the mines to agriculture and local industry, while a wide range of protective tariffs was imposed to protect local MANUFACTURE. The public sector grew rapidly, with white supremacy entrenched through the government's CIVILISED LABOR policy. The Mines and Works Amendment Act (1926) reinforced the JOB COLOR BAR in the mining industry.

To those who in the 1970s reinterpreted 20th-century South African history in terms of the changing dominance of fractions

of capital, the advent of the Pact government marked a shift in
hegemony from international mining capital to national capital.
But the mines did not lose all the gains they had made after
the RAND REVOLT (1922); white workers' wages remained relatively low, for example, under the Pact government.

After the June 1929 election the NP held an absolute majority of seats in the Assembly, but the Pact continued in a nomi-
nal sense until the Hertzog-SMUTS coalition of 1933 (on which
see FUSION).

PAN-AFRICANIST CONGRESS (PAC). In the mid 1950s those who
called themselves "Africanists" within the AFRICAN NATIONAL
CONGRESS grew increasingly unhappy with the multi-racialism
of the CONGRESS ALLIANCE. They accused the ANC leaders,
many of the ablest of whom were BANNED, of being out of
touch with the African masses. Robert SOBUKWE and other
Africanists were stirred by the way in which Kwame Nkrumah
led Ghana to independence, and once Ghana was independent they
heard Nkrumah call for the freedom of all Africa. They believed that the Africans of South Africa would have to work for
their own liberation, but they identified their struggle with the
continental one for African freedom. More militant tactics,
they believed, would give Africans greater self-confidence in
their ability to overthrow apartheid on their own. Their belief that Africans were oppressed as a people attracted to them
some who were anti-white and others who were anti-communist.
Though the PAC goal was "an Africanist socialist democracy in
a non-racial polity," their radicalism was more racial than
socialist.

The Africanists broke away from the ANC at a Transvaal
congress in November 1958, and organized themselves into the
PAC at a meeting in Orlando, Soweto, in April 1959. Sobukwe,
the leading theoretician, was elected president. Quickly gathering support, especially in the southern Transvaal and among
migrant workers in Cape Town, the PAC leadership realized
that if it were to seize the initiative from the ANC it must get
in first with a defiance campaign. Protesters were to leave
their passes at home and present themselves for arrest at their
local police stations. The PAC hoped that the campaign would
escalate, that defiers would stay away from work and the economy be brought to a halt. When the campaign began on 21
March 1960, the police opened fire both at SHARPEVILLE and
at Langa outside Cape Town, and Sobukwe was arrested. On 8
April the PAC found itself BANNED. An exile headquarters was
then established in Maseru, LESOTHO, under Potlako Leballo
(1924-).

PAC supporters in the Cape organized an underground military
wing which they called Poqo (Xhosa: "pure"). This engaged in
a number of acts of terrorism, including the murder of five
whites in the TRANSKEI in February 1963. Two months later
Leballo announced that a general uprising was imminent. The
BASUTOLAND police raided his headquarters and passed a list
of names found there to the South African police, who arrested

thousands of Poqo members.   By mid 1965 it had ceased to
exist as an effective organization.

The PAC survived in exile, developing ties with Peking,
operating offices in such places as Cairo, Algiers, and Dar es
Salaam, and receiving recognition as a liberation movement
from both the Organisation of African Unity and the UNITED
NATIONS.   Efforts to draw closer to the ANC failed, and the
PAC itself was riven with factionalism.   Some BLACK CON-
SCIOUSNESS adherents were briefly attracted to it when they
went into exile in the 1970s, but in 1978 it suffered a major
setback when its cadres in SWAZILAND were rounded up and
deported.   The following year Leballo was finally ousted as
leader.   After a brief rule by a triumvirate, John Pokela, recently released from imprisonment on Robben Island, emerged
as the new leader.   (See also Patrick DUNCAN.)

PASS LAWS.   From 1709 Cape slaves were required to carry passes
if they moved about, and by the end of that century such a requirement had been extended to KHOIKHOI laborers, tying them
to the farms.   The new BRITISH administration consolidated
these early provisions in a code of 1809.   But under humanitarian pressure, the Cape administration in 1828 freed Khoikhoi
labor (see ORDINANCE 50) and from that time "Coloured" people have not had to carry passes.   As Africans entered the
Cape Colony from the east to work after 1828, however, they
were required to have pass(ports).   Permanent African residents were given certificates to show that they were excluded
from the pass laws.

With the establishment of the first industrial center at Kimberley in the 1870s (see DIAMONDS) a more rigid pass system
was introduced, enforced by nightly police raids, mass arrests,
and token trials.   The Griqualand West Proclamation 14 of 1872
made no mention of race, but provided that any person without
a pass and without being able to give a good account of himself
might be arrested by a police officer without warrant and taken
before a magistrate.   Such a person was then liable for a fine,
imprisonment, or corporal punishment.   Justified in terms of
countering illicit diamond buying, this law served in fact both
to control the flow of African labor to the diamond fields and
to regiment the African workers there.   Transvaal legislators
subsequently enacted similar, but overtly racial, legislation.
By a law of the mid 1890s all Africans had to wear a metal
plate or badge on their arms to indicate their employment.   Not
having a pass, which might cost one shilling to obtain, meant
arrest and imprisonment.   Pass laws were used to try to stem
the high rate of desertion among African workers on the gold
mines (in 1910 15 percent of all workers deserted).   Then with
Union, a Native Labour Regulation Act (1911) required all male
African workers, including foreigners, to carry passes.   Di-
recting labor where employers needed it, the pass system
helped keep labor cheap.

Africans repeatedly protested against the "dompas" (dom:
"stupid" in Afrikaans), the most humiliating badge of their

inferior status.   In 1913 African women in the Free State
waged an extensive passive resistance campaign against a local
requirement that they carry passes.   Another such campaign by
both men and women in the Transvaal in March 1919 achieved
nothing, and the 1923 Natives (Urban Areas) Act (see URBAN
SEGREGATION) extended the pass system.   The AFRICAN NA-
TIONAL CONGRESS continued to protest through petition, while
the COMMUNIST PARTY organized occasional pass-burnings, as
in December 1930, but the tightening-up continued.   The most
important Act was one of 1952, which stipulated that all Africans
over sixteen had to produce a pass (renamed a reference book)
on request by any member of the police or any administrative
official at any time.   The pass carried details of employment
and other personal data.   The extension of passes to African
women produced widespread protests, culminating in a march
by 20,000 women on the Union Buildings in Pretoria in August
1956 (see FEDERATION OF SOUTH AFRICAN WOMEN).   The
PAN AFRICANIST CONGRESS anti-pass campaign in March 1960
was met by the shooting at SHARPEVILLE and a few days after
that Albert LUTHULI of the ANC burnt his pass in symbolic defiance of the law.   For a few weeks the pass laws were suspended, only to be reimposed and enforced with new vigor as
government efforts to prevent more Africans settling in the urban areas intensified (see INFLUX CONTROL).
     Parallel to the main police force and law courts, a special
police and court system emerged to enforce the pass laws.
Pass raids on township residents by armed inspectors took
place in the early hours of the morning.   Anyone without a
valid pass was arrested; in the decade 1965 to 1975 there were
on average over half a million pass law arrests a year.   Those
brought before the Commissioners' Courts (as they were known
in the early 1980s) were deemed guilty until they proved their
innocence; the vast majority of cases under the pass-laws--of
which there were an estimated 5.8 million between 1965 and
1975--were undefended, and were often dealt with in court at
over thirty cases an hour.   From 1981 those arrested, instead
of being tried, were sometimes deported to an "independent"
BANTUSTAN, in terms of an Act of 1972 allowing for the sum-
mary deportation of foreigners.

PATON, Alan Stewart (1903-   ).   Born and educated in Natal, he
     was principal of Diepkloof Reformatory for Africans near Johan-
     nesburg from 1935 to 1948, transforming it from a prison to a
     school.   He began writing his famous novel Cry the Beloved
     Country when on a tour of Norway in 1946.   A founder member
     of the LIBERAL PARTY, he became its most prominent figure
     and its president in the late 1950s.   His books include a biog-
     raphy of J.H. Hofmeyr (1894-1948), Smuts' more liberal deputy,
     a volume of autobiography entitled Towards the Mountain and the
     novel Ah, But Your Land is Beautiful (1981).

PEDI.   In the 18th century a small SOTHO group from the south-
     western Transvaal moved across to the Steelpoort river valley

in the east, gained control of the trade-routes running to the
Mozambique coast, and established its supremacy over the Sotho
of the area. The zenith of early Pedi power was reached under
Thulare (c. 1780-1820). After his death, the polity was disrupted by succession disputes and then, more severely, by the
MFECANE, during which the Pedi were attacked by Mzilikazi's
NDEBELE and others. Its power was revived under Sekwati
(c. 1780-1861), who took refugees from the upheaval under his
protection and built a new capital at a good defensive point between the Olifants and the Steelpoort rivers. After beating back
a ZULU attack, Sekwati was ready to pay tribute to Mpande (c.
1798-1872) as a peace offering. Relations with the VOORTREK-
KERS deteriorated as they began to encroach on territory the
Pedi claimed. An expedition they sent against Sekwati in 1852
unsuccessfully laid siege to his capital, but Sekwati agreed in
1857 to sign a treaty with them by which the Steelpoort river
was recognized as the boundary of his lands. Already by this
time numerous Pedi were going out to work as MIGRANT LA-
BORERS, for which they earned guns.
Sekwati's successor Sekhukhune (1814-1882) had first to deal
with a serious challenge to his succession, but he then built up
the power of his state further, and the many of his people who
went to the DIAMOND fields in the 1870s brought back great
numbers of firearms. By the 1870s the polity controlled a
large part of the eastern Transvaal. But, weakened by many
years of drought, the Pedi then had to face a series of attacks
from Transvaal COMMANDOS, aided by their Swazi allies.
That the Transvaal government had been unable to humble the
Pedi was a reason the BRITISH gave to justify their annexation
of the territory in 1877. Having dealt with the ZULU, the
British then turned against the Pedi. Two British regiments,
aided by a large Swazi force, under the overall command of
Garnet Wolseley (1833-1913) attacked Sekhukhune's capital in
November 1879 and quickly put an end to Pedi independence.
Sekhukhune was taken captive and his half-brother and rival
installed in his place. Soon after being released, Sekhukhune
was stabbed to death by his rival. The Transvaal government
divided the Pedi country, expropriated much of their land, and
forced many of the Pedi to work as APPRENTICES for Afrikaner farmers. In the late 1950s Sekhukhuneland, as it was
then called, saw some of the strongest opposition anywhere to
the imposition of Bantu Authorities (see BANTUSTANS; RURAL
RESISTANCE).

PETTY APARTHEID. Term used for Jim-Crow style segregation.
As often pointed out, such discrimination was hardly petty to
those on the receiving end of it, but it was "petty" compared
with the "grand apartheid" of BANTUSTANS and INFLUX CON-
TROL. Much international criticism of APARTHEID focussed
on "petty apartheid."
Its long history goes back at least as far as discriminatory
regulations directed against FREE BLACKS in the 18th century
Cape. As in the southern United States, the late 19th century

saw a great increase in such discrimination, not only in the
republics--Africans were not permitted on the sidewalks of
Johannesburg--but also in the Cape, where, for example, special trains were laid on for African workers in Cape Town in
1901. Nevertheless, there was much less of such discrimination at the Cape, and especially in Cape Town itself, with its
large "Coloured" population, than in other parts of the country.
After the NATIONAL PARTY victory in 1948, however, there
was a great increase in "petty apartheid": in the Cape Peninsula full train apartheid was introduced (1949) and, later, bus
apartheid. In the early 1960s segregation was extended to en-
trances to public buildings, elevators, beaches, and even li-
braries (blacks and whites at the South African Library in Cape
Town had to read its rare books at separate tables).

Beginning in the late 1960s there was a relaxation of some
aspects of "petty apartheid." Envoys from black states were
excluded from it, and as South Africa came under international
criticism for its racial discrimination in sport, so certain fix-
tures were called "multi-national" or "international" when blacks
participated, the suggestion being that blacks were members of
other "nations." A permit system allowed certain hotels and
restaurants to admit local blacks on a similar pretense.

"Petty apartheid" has usually been explained in terms of
crude WHITE RACISM. It has been suggested that its function
is largely symbolic, and not directly related to economic or
political domination. Recently some historians have sought to
argue that it did serve an economic purpose: by isolating and
"de-civilizing" blacks, it promoted their exploitation.

PHILIP, John (1777-1851). Congregational minister from Aberdeen,
Scotland, who arrived at the Cape in 1819. He soon became an
extremely influential superintendent for the London Missionary
Society (LMS) in South Africa. Besides consolidating and expanding the work of the LMS, he campaigned for full legal
equality for the colonial KHOIKHOI. A vigorous polemicist, he
had close connections with Exeter Hall, the center of British
philanthropy, and he returned to England to use his influence,
publishing his Researches in South Africa there in 1828. Later
that year the House of Commons recommended that the free
people of color at the Cape should enjoy equal status with
whites; this coincided with the passage of ORDINANCE 50 at
the Cape. Besides preparing the ground for that measure,
Philip was responsible for the disallowance of a draft vagrancy
law (1834) that would have reimposed on the Khoi many of the
former restrictions.

Back at the Cape, Philip tried to persuade the Cape Governor to adopt a new approach to frontier affairs based on a system of treaties with African and GRIQUA rulers. He approved
the extension of British authority, but wanted indigenous people
to remain in possession of their land. He envisaged a Chris-
tianized "Coloured" and African elite along the colonial borders
working harmoniously with the British authorities. Condemned
by the white settlers of the time for his "interference," Philip's

stature was placed beyond doubt by the two books W. M. MAC-
MILLAN wrote in the 1920s based on Philip's private papers,
which were shortly afterwards destroyed by fire (1931). (See
also MISSIONARIES.)

PLAATJE, Solomon Tshekisho (1876-1932).   Writer and politician.
An interpreter and magistrate's clerk in MAFEKING during the
siege, and author of a diary of that event which remained unpublished until the 1970s, he became editor of a Sechuana
(TSWANA language)-English newspaper and wrote prolifically in
his newspaper and elsewhere.   One of the founders of the South
African Native National Congress (later the ANC, q. v.) in 1912,
and its first general secretary, he accompanied its deputation
to Britain to appeal against the NATIVES LAND ACT.   His
slashing polemic against that Act, Native Life in South Africa
(1916), survives as a classic, while his novel Mhudi, set
against the background of the intrusion of Mzilikazi's NDEBELE
into the lands of Plaatje's own Tswana people, spoke of the dispossession of his own day.   Written about 1917 but not published
until 1930, Mhudi was the first novel in English to be published
by a black South African.

POOR WHITEISM.   Land shortage caused by the end of expansion
into new territory and the subdivision of farms into uneconomic-
ally small units under Roman-Dutch inheritance law had begun
to drive Afrikaners (see BYWONERS) off the land in large numbers before the SOUTH AFRICAN WAR.   It was in the 1890s
that the existence of a "poor white problem" began to be a matter of major public debate, when it was regularly discussed at
AFRIKANER BOND congresses.   The burning of farms by the
British army during the South African war increased the process, as did such natural disasters as the drought of 1903-08.
Forced to the towns, landless Afrikaners found that Africans
were prepared to accept a wage considered to be below that
needed to sustain a white family.   The Transvaal Indigency
Commission (1906-08) defined "poor whites" as able-bodied
whites without skills who were unable to obtain employment in
competition with Africans.   By 1917 the government estimated
that there were over 100, 000 such people.
     The DUTCH REFORMED CHURCHES at first hoped that they
could be resettled on the land, but from WORLD WAR I began
pressing the government to provide sheltered employment for them.
It was not until after the 1922 RAND REVOLT, however, when
the possibility existed that in another such revolt white workers
might join Africans in a working class alliance, that the state
intervened in a major way to tackle the "problem. "   The PACT
GOVERNMENT that came to power in 1924 greatly stepped up
the policy of giving preferential treatment in the public sector,
and especially the railways, harbors, and postal services, to
unskilled white workers, and paying such workers higher than
usual wages.   Where there was deliberate job creation for poor
whites, there was also protection from wage competition from
blacks (see CIVILISED LABOR).   On the initiative of the churches

a commission funded by the Carnegie Corporation of New York
was set up to investigate the "problem" throughout the Union.
After it had in its five volume report (1932) stressed the importance of social care, the HERTZOG government set up a
Department of Social Welfare (1934).   Many poor whites were
absorbed into the new MANUFACTURING INDUSTRY established
in the 1930s.   By the end of that decade the "problem" was
widely considered to have been "solved."

POPULATION.   The first general census of the Cape, taken in
1865, estimated the population of that colony at 500,000.   Further censuses were taken in 1875 and 1891, the first simultan-
eous census of all South Africa in 1904 and the first Union census in 1911, when the total population was found to be just under 6 million.   Further general censuses were taken in 1921,
1936, 1946, 1951, 1960, 1970 and 1980.   Censuses of whites
only were taken in 1918, 1926, 1931 and 1941.
   The proportion of whites in the total population reached
21.9 percent in 1921, the largest anywhere in Africa.   Since
then, despite continued immigration, the white proportion has
fallen steadily, and in 1970 was 16.4 percent.   The white population, just over one and a quarter million in 1911, was
4,603,000 in 1980.   While the white rate of increase in 1980
was 0.9 percent that of Africans was about 2.4 percent.   The
total population, which in 1911 was estimated to be just under
6 million, was just under 7 million in 1921, over $9\frac{1}{2}$ million
in 1936, and by 1980 was 28 million.   Of that latter figure,
Africans comprised 72 percent (20 million), Asians 3 percent
(800,000), "Coloureds" 9 percent ($2\frac{1}{2}$ million) and whites 16
percent.   Since Union (1910) the proportion of the total population living in the Cape Province and the Orange Free State has
declined markedly, and that living in the Transvaal increased,
until by 1980 44 percent lived there.
   For the Population Registration Act (1950) see under
"COLOUREDS."

PORT ELIZABETH.   Named after the wife of an acting governor of
the Cape, it was the place where the BRITISH 1820 Settlers
landed (see ENGLISH-SPEAKING WHITES).   It became the chief
outlet for the export of wool (see ECONOMIC CHANGE) and the
Cape's second port after CAPE TOWN.   After World War I it
developed into an important industrial center, concerned especially with automobile assembly: both General Motors and
Ford built assembly plants there.   A UNIVERSITY for whites,
the only dual-medium (English and Afrikaans) one in the country, was established in 1975.   Port Elizabeth had been an important center of AFRICAN NATIONAL CONGRESS activity in
the 1950s, which may partly explain why in the 1970s it was
notorious for the harshness of its local SECURITY POLICE
(see BIKO).

PORTUGUESE.   Though Portuguese navigators were the first to
discover the sea-route round the Cape in the late 15th century

(see CHRONOLOGY, p. xiii), the Portuguese made no attempt
to establish a permanent settlement on South African soil, and
their ships preferred instead to call at St. Helena in the Atlantic ocean.   The Portuguese presence at DELAGOA BAY, the
end of a number of important trade-routes from within what became South Africa, was eventually to lead to the incorporation
of that good natural harbor and its immediate hinterland within
MOZAMBIQUE.   Portuguese rule in Mozambique and ANGOLA
provided South Africa in the 1960s with a cordon sanitaire, lost
after the military coup in Lisbon in 1974 and the swift decolonization of the two territories.   That decolonization, which led to
the arrival of 20,000 Cuban troops in Angola and made continued
white rule in ZIMBABWE impossible, helped produce a major
crisis of confidence among white South Africans in 1976 (see also
SOWETO REVOLT; OUTWARD POLICY).

PRE-CAPITALIST MODES, DEBATE ON.   The work of French
Marxist anthropologists inspired an intense debate in the 1970s
on the nature of pre-capitalist modes of production.   Attempts
were made to apply this debate to South Africa at a number of
conferences of historians held in southern Africa in the late
1970s.   Some historians sought to distinguish a lineage or homestead mode, based on subsistence production, from a tributary
mode in which captives were forcibly incorporated through raiding and in which the relations of production reflected a desire
for luxury consumption.   Others argued that the homestead mode
remained dominant until its suppression by the capitalist mode
of production.   Many "liberal Africanists" (see HISTORIOGRA-
PHY), pointing to problems with the very concept of mode of
production, regarded much of the debate as too theoretical to
be useful in furthering understanding of what actually happened
in these societies.   By the end of the 1970s even those working
within the new paradigm seemed to realize that more empirical
work was needed before the concepts could be further refined.

PRESS.   In the first decades of the 19th century the only regular
publication at the Cape was the Government Gazette.   The first
newspaper, the South African Commercial Advertiser, appeared
in 1824.   The governor closed it down and it was only in 1828
that it resumed publication with the promise of freedom to pub-
lish subject only to the law of libel.   In 1830 a Dutch-language
newspaper was started in opposition to the Advertiser.   The
first Afrikaans-language newspaper was Die Patriot (1876), the
first daily newspaper the Cape Times (Cape Town 1876).   The
formation of the Argus Printing and Publishing Company in
1866 began the era of managerial newspapers; the two leading
papers in its stable were The Cape Argus (Cape Town) and The
Star (Johannesburg).   More popular journalism was ushered in
by The Rand Daily Mail (Johannesburg, 1902) and the Sunday
Times (Johannesburg, 1906), both papers becoming part of the
South African Associated Newspapers (SAAN) group in 1955.   In
1915 the NATIONAL PARTY acquired a party organ with the establishment of Die Burger, a daily Cape Town newspaper owned

by the Nasionale Pers. Die Transvaler was started in 1937
(see VERWOERD).

The first journals to aim at a black readership emerged
from the missions of the eastern Cape in the mid-19th century,
in both English and XHOSA. An independent black-controlled
press began with the establishment of Imvo Zabantsundu (Native
Opinion), edited by J. T. JABAVU from King William's Town
from 1884. It was followed by Izwi Labantu (East London) and
Ilanga lase Natal (Durban). Indian Opinion, founded by Gandhi
(see INDIANS), remained financially independent, but from the
1920s the African press was taken over by white business interests, attracted to the market it served and concerned about protest journalism.

The Guardian, founded by members of the COMMUNIST PAR-
TY in 1937, survived its BANNING in 1950 by changing its name,
but after four such changes was finally suppressed in 1963. The
World, which had over 150,000 African readers, was banned in
1977, and The Post, which took its place, in 1981. By then
over 100 laws and regulations restricted press freedom, especially in the reporting of matters concerning the military,
the prisons, the police, "national security," and exile politics.
The English press still enjoyed a measure of freedom because
the government sought to present a "democratic" image in white
politics, and because of its "responsibility," for despite its increasing black readership it was restrained in its coverage of
the black struggle.

PRETORIA see TRANSVAAL. Because Pretoria was administrative capital of the country after 1910, "Pretoria" is often used
to mean the South African government.

PROGRESSIVE PARTY. Cape: The JAMESON RAID polarized politics at the Cape as J. H. Hofmeyr (see AFRIKANER BOND) broke
with RHODES, while among the English-speakers a Progressive
party was formed to challenge the Bond. Rhodes automatically
became its unofficial leader. In the 1898 election there were
for the first time two well-defined parties, with colony-wide
constituency organizations, opposing each other. After the election the Progressives formed the opposition, led by Sir Gordon
Sprigg (1830-1913), a veteran parliamentarian. With the outbreak of the SOUTH AFRICAN WAR, criticism of the Raid les-
sened and Jameson (1853-1917), who was elected to parliament
in 1900, emerged as leader of the Progressives by 1903. This
made him Prime Minister when that party won the election of
1904. Jameson re-enfranchised those Afrikaners who had rebelled during the war, but they did not vote for him and he fell
from office in 1908. A strong supporter of federal union for
South Africa, he persuaded the party in that year to change its
name to UNIONIST PARTY. Transvaal: In the 1890s Afrikaners
opposed to KRUGER, led by General Piet Joubert (1831-1900),
were known as the Progressive Party, though they were not an
organized political grouping. The Progressive Association
formed in 1904 after the war was a totally different body, led

by prominent Johannesburg RANDLORDS. After the election of
1907, the Progressives formed the main opposition to HET
VOLK in the Transvaal.

PROGRESSIVE PARTY (1959-). At the Bloemfontein congress of
the UNITED PARTY (UP) in 1959 eleven of its 53 members of
parliament broke with the party on the issue of the allocation of
land to the RESERVES. The UP argued that if VERWOERD was
to balkanize the country no more land should be transferred to
the BANTUSTANS; the Progressives believed that there was an
obligation to provide additional land under the 1936 HERTZOG
legislation. The Progressives soon adopted a constitutional
policy based on a qualified franchise, rigid constitution, and
entrenched bill of rights. The central plank of their platform
was the abolition of racial discrimination. In the 1961 general
election only one of them, Helen Suzman (1917-), retained
her parliamentary seat. The continued existence of the party
in the 1960s and early 1970s was due in large measure to
Helen Suzman's parliamentary performance as critic of government policy, and to the continued financial support of Harry
Oppenheimer, head of the ANGLO-AMERICAN CORPORATION.
When the Prohibition of Political Interference Act (1968) outlawed multi-racial political parties, the LIBERAL PARTY dissolved itself, but the Progressive Party protested, shed its
"Coloured" and African supporters and carried on. In the 1970
election it won only 3.5 percent of the vote, but in 1974 the
tide turned and it won six seats. The following year certain
"Young Turks" who had been forced out of the UP formed a
short-lived Reform Party, which then merged with the Progressives to create the Progressive Reform Party. In September
1977 another merger took place with a breakaway group from
the UP, and the name changed again to Progressive Federal
Party (PFP). After the November 1977 election the PFP inherited the UP's role as Official Opposition. In 1978 it adopted
a new constitutional policy, which abandoned the qualified franchise for universal suffrage within a federal framework, but
laid much stress on the promise to call a new NATIONAL CON-
VENTION. The PFP firmly rejected the constitutional proposals
(see CONSTITUTIONAL CHANGE) put forward by the government
in 1982.

QWA QWA (formerly Witzieshoek). BANTUSTAN created in 1974
for the southern SOTHO. It comprised some 200 square miles
of mountainous, barren territory bordering LESOTHO, Natal
and the Orange Free State. Its de facto population, which had
been 20,000 in 1960, was by 1980 estimated at 300,000, most
living in the capital Phuthaditjhaba. Almost all its income
came from the remittances of migrants working in the Transvaal or Orange Free State. It was thought that because the
territory was such an unlikely candidate for "independence,"
the government would seek to transfer it to Lesotho one day.

RACE QUESTION.   In the 1870s there was much fear among whites
of a possible "war of the races" in which Africans would present a united front against the whites.   After the conquest of
the African societies had been completed, whites commonly
meant by "race question" relations between AFRIKANERS and
ENGLISH-SPEAKING WHITES.   This seemed the crucial cleav-
age, especially after the SOUTH AFRICAN WAR, whereas white-
black relations were so hierarchical that it could be supposed
that they did not involve any competitiveness or potential for
conflict.   "Race question" was used in that way as late as the
1950s, but by then the dominant use had again become white-
black relations.   The South African Institute of Race Relations,
founded in 1929, had always been primarily concerned with relations across the color-line.

RACIAL SEGREGATION.   Much of South African history is the story
of the attempts by whites to exclude others from belonging to or
having rights in a common society, and of the failure of these
attempts.   Soon after the establishment of the first European
settlement in Table Bay, Van Riebeeck attempted, by growing a
hedge, to keep stock-keeping KHOIKHOI out of the settlement.
As white TREKBOERS moved east and came into contact with
BANTU-SPEAKING Africans, the Cape government repeatedly
issued orders designed to prevent such contact, fearing that it
would lead to conflict.   After the first conflict occurred in the
ZUURVELD in the late 1770s, Cape Governor Van Plettenberg
(1739-1793) established the Fish River as the border between
the colony and the XHOSA.   But there were Xhosa west of the
Fish, the Fish was easy to cross, and there was no agreement
on the line of the Fish anyway, so contact and conflict continued.
With the aid of British troops, the expulsion of the Xhosa from
west of the Fish was effected in 1812, and in 1819 the Cape
Governor created a belt of territory east of the Fish as a buffer to hold the two sides apart.   Once again, segregation failed;
in numerous ways contact increased.
    A second form of segregation involved incorporating African
peoples but keeping them separate within a white-controlled
state.   John PHILIP of the London Missionary Society favored
this, and Theophilus SHEPSTONE put it into effect in Natal,
creating large African RESERVES.   Later, segregation took
other forms; in the towns URBAN SEGREGATION meant separate residential areas; Jim Crow-style segregation meant separate facilities in hotels, restaurants, trains, buses, and a
host of other places and activities (see PETTY APARTHEID);
political segregation meant separate political institutions for
blacks (see, e.g. "COLOURED" POLITICS; NATIVES REPRE-
SENTATIVE COUNCIL); educational segregation meant separate
schools; the JOB COLOR BAR reserved jobs for whites; and so
on.   Inevitably, separate meant unequal.   "No equality in church
or state" proclaimed the constitution of the SOUTH AFRICAN
REPUBLIC (Transvaal).   When a century later the Supreme
Court suggested that separate facilities should be equal, the
legislature quickly stepped in to declare that separate facilities

need not be equal (Separate Amenities Act, 1953).

While one may look back, for the origins of racial segregation in South Africa, to racist ideas brought by the early European settlers from Europe, and to the influence of Cape slavery,
which strengthened the link between blackness and inferiority,
and of the frontier, where blacks came to be seen as the enemy, it was not until the 20th century that a philosophy of segregation was elaborated. It found expression in the report of
the LAGDEN COMMISSION (1905), was adopted in the program
of principles of the LABOUR PARTY (1910) and formed the
topic of much discussion among English-speaking intellectuals
in the 1920s and 1930s, before being taken over by Afrikaner
intellectuals in the 1940s and developed into the philosophy of
APARTHEID. Justified by reference to the assumed superiority
of "European civilisation" and the need to protect the "identity"
of both whites and Africans, segregation was an ideology, radical historians have argued, serving the material interests of industrial capital, especially in the mining and agricultural sectors. The reality was the creation of a coercive labor system
in which African labor was ultra-exploited. (For the mechan-
isms see INFLUX CONTROL; MIGRANT LABOR; BANTUSTANS;
and crossreferences under those headings.) Others have seen
apartheid as the political ideology of Afrikaner supremacy, a
device to maintain that supremacy over at least the greater
part of South Africa (for the Bantustan policy as it evolved provided for the end of formal white domination over limited areas
of the country). As most whites were Afrikaners, if those who
were not white could be excluded from effective participation in
the political process, and Afrikaner unity be secured, then continued Afrikaner domination was assured.

RAILROADS. A private company began building a railroad from
Cape Town to Wellington, fifty miles away, in 1859, and in
1860 a line of two miles was opened in Durban. It was with
the growth of Kimberley (see DIAMONDS) that major construction began. Because of the long distances to the diamond fields,
and the absence of any intermediate traffic, the new lines were
state ventures. Competition between the coastal towns for the
interior trade led to separate lines being built from Cape Town,
Port Elizabeth, and East London to the diamond fields. After
1886 the Cape and Natal both pushed lines on towards the WIT-
WATERSRAND, while KRUGER sought the rapid completion of a
line built by the Nederlansch Suid-Afrikaansche Spoorwegmaat-
schaapij (Netherlands-South African Railroad Company) between
the Rand and non-British DELAGOA BAY. Kruger's line ran
into financial difficulties, RHODES had to aid it, and as a result the Cape line was able to reach JOHANNESBURG in 1892.
By the end of 1895 the Rand was connected by rail to Delagoa
Bay and Durban as well. In 1894 a Cape line bypassing the
Transvaal and heading for Central Africa through BECHUANA-
LAND had reached MAFEKING. By the end of the century, a
considerable portion of the country's present network had already been completed. During the First World War a line was

swiftly carried north into NAMIBIA.

Once the railroad systems began to be integrated, they helped bind the country together, underpinning UNION and providing the essential infrastructure for the later development of MANUFAC-TURING INDUSTRY. Railraod rating policy greatly aided white farmers, especially those who produced maize. The railroads carried hundreds of thousands of MIGRANT LABORERS to the urban centers each year. They also transported coal and other export ores to the coast; the line from Sishen to Saldanha for the bulk transport of iron ore (see MINERALS), completed in the early 1970s, carried nothing else.

RAND REVOLT (March 1922). A violent episode in a struggle be-tween the mining companies and the white workers over the operation of the JOB COLOR BAR in the GOLD mining industry on the WITWATERSRAND. Because of a crisis of profitability in the industry--15 of the 35 gold mines were operating either at a loss or at minimal profit by late 1921--the Chamber of Mines announced its intention of reducing white miners' pay and of moving Africans into semi-skilled jobs previously reserved for higher-paid whites. This meant the repudiation of a formal commitment by the industry in 1918 that the status quo in the ratio of white to black miners would be maintained. The white mine unions struck in January 1922 in protest, joining other white workers already on strike against wage cuts. Afrikaner mineworkers organized themselves into paramilitary "COMMAN-DOS" to enforce the strike, and when the strikers had by early March gained virtual control of the east Rand, Prime Minister SMUTS declared martial law and sent in the army. After four days of bitter street fighting, the strikers had been crushed, but at least 153 people, and probably many more, had been killed, including 72 soldiers and policemen. The strike lead-ers were arrested and four executed. The mining companies then proceeded to cut white wages and substitute lower paid African workers for whites in a number of semi-skilled jobs, laying off white workers to do so. The Chamber of Mines en-gineered a test case and the Transvaal Supreme Court found that the legally enforced JOB COLOR BAR was ultra vires (be-yond the legal authority).

But the white miners had another card to play. Thanks largely to his brutal suppression of the Revolt, Smuts lost the 1924 election. The PACT GOVERNMENT appointed a commis-sion of inquiry into mine labor, which found that in the inter-ests of "health and safety" Africans should be confined to un-skilled jobs. A "Color Bar Act" (1926) then permitted racially discriminatory regulations to be issued, and the mining color bar was re-enacted. White miners' wages remained relatively low in the late 1920s, however. (See also COMMUNIST PAR-TY; STRIKES; TRADE UNIONS.)

RANDLORDS. Mining magnates, the lords of the WITWATERSRAND. They had various complaints against the KRUGER government. Its dynamite monopoly and grant of a railway concession to the

Netherlands-South African RAILROAD Company increased their
costs.   It promoted liquor sales to the African mine-workers,
reducing their productivity.   Though it could suddenly increase
its taxes on the mines, as it did in 1898, it could not guaran-
tee a stable supply of African labor.   J. A. Hobson's contemporary account suggested that the Randlords were responsible for
the JAMESON RAID and the SOUTH AFRICAN WAR.   J. S. Marais, in The Fall of Kruger's Republic (Oxford, 1961) pointed
out that some supported Kruger, others MILNER, and this division he ascribed to whether or not they went along with British imperial objectives.   But in an article in the Economic History Review (1965) the eminent Australian historian Geoffrey
Blainey suggested that owners of deep-level gold mines supported the Raid, seeking to replace Kruger's government with
one more amenable to their interests, while the owners of
purely outcrop mines, which required less capital, did not.
Later research showed this to be too simple, but revealed that
those implicated in the Raid had longer-term commitments to
the industry, and were more development orientated, than those
not involved.   The former, after the failure of the Raid, hoped
for reform from the Transvaal government, but Kruger's defeat
of his less conservative rival in the 1898 election made them
doubt that peaceful reform was possible.   Propagating the view
that the UITLANDERS were an oppressed group, they pushed
for war.   British victory would, they hoped, bring them a regime which would promote their interests, and in particular
provide both a steady flow of African labor and free trade.   Yet
the extent of the influence of the Randlords on the British policymakers in the last years before the SOUTH AFRICAN WAR remains controversial.   That their interests came to coincide with
British imperial interests does not mean that the Randlords
determined British policy.   (See also WERNHER, BEIT--H.
ECKSTEIN.)

REBELLIONS   see   AFRIKANER REBELLION; ANTI-COLONIAL
    REBELLIONS; BAMBATHA REBELLION; BLACK-FLAG RE-
    VOLT; GREAT TREK; LANGALIBALELE AFFAIR; and also
    FREEBURGHERS and SEPARATISM.

RELIGION   see   CHRISTIAN INSTITUTE; COTTESLOE CONSULTA-
    TION; DUTCH REFORMED CHURCH; Robert GRAY; ISLAM;
    MISSIONARIES; Beyers NAUDE; ROMAN CATHOLIC CHURCH.

REPUBLIC.   From the time of the conquest of the TRANSVAAL
    and ORANGE FREE STATE republics during the SOUTH AFRI-
    CAN WAR there were those Afrikaners who hankered after a
    return to republican independence.   For them the monarchy
    was a symbol of imperial domination.   Those who had partici-
    pated in the AFRIKANER REBELLION of 1914 were mostly re-
    publicans.   After the redefinition of the imperial relationship in
    the late 1920s and early 1930s (see COMMONWEALTH), Hert-
    zog was satisfied that South Africa was independent of Britain
    and he no longer believed a republic was practical politics.

MALAN remained committed to a republic, though not as an immediate goal, and republicanism intensified after Hertzog failed to keep South Africa out of WORLD WAR II. VER-WOERD saw the republic as the natural constitutional form for the Afrikaner, and in 1942 Die Transvaler newspaper, which he edited, published a draft constitution for a future South African republic.

After coming to power in 1948 (see NATIONAL PARTY), the Nationalists realized that they did not have majority support among the white electorate and Malan shelved the issue, as did STRIJDOM, who still hoped to persuade Britain to allow South Africa to incorporate the HIGH COMMISSION TERRITORIES. But not long after becoming Prime Minister, Verwoerd decided to take the gamble of holding a referendum of white voters on the republican issue. He promised that the republican constitution would not be drastically different from the existing one, and that he would work for South Africa's continued membership of the COMMONWEALTH. India had become a republic and remained within the Commonwealth, so there was some hope that South Africa could also stay in that organization. The "winds of change" speech by the British Prime Minister Harold Macmillan to the South African parliament in early 1960, dissociating Britain from South Africa, did not help the anti-republic cause. In the referendum held on 6 October 1960, 52 percent of the white voters supported the republic (both opposition parties had urged their supporters to vote "No"). The Union then became a republic on 31 May 1961; see CONSTITUTIONAL CHANGE.

RESERVES. Relatively little land was reserved by whites for KHOIKHOI and people of mixed descent. By the end of the 18th century the Khoikhoi had been dispossessed of all their land within the Cape Colony. Their only access to land was at mission stations, or, from 1829, in the KAT RIVER SETTLEMENT. As the Cape expanded, the bulk of the land reserved for "COLOUREDS" lay in the semi-arid northwestern Cape (little Namaqualand).

Dispossession of Africans was not nearly so total, thanks to their numerical and military strength. As whites extended their control over African territories, land was set aside for Africans, in large part to keep them away from areas of white settlement for security reasons. Later in the 19th century, the reserves became reservoirs of labor, from which MIGRANT LABORERS could be drawn and to which they could be returned when their contracts expired. White farming interests often demanded the break-up of the reserves, for they provided a refuge for workers who deserted from the farms, and locked up labor that might otherwise be exploited. Some whites believed they could put the land to much better use. Mining interests, on the other hand, usually argued for the enlargement of the reserves, for they were the source of the supply of migrants. As early as the 1870s the TRANSKEI was used as a dumping ground for "surplus" Africans, i.e., those surplus to labor requirements in "white" areas (see MASS REMOVALS).

The first reserves for Africans were demarcated as the Cape extended its control eastward from the 1830s. After the Cape-XHOSA war of 1834-5, 15,000 MFENGU were settled east of the Fish river by the Cape governor. In Natal, SHEPSTONE established large reservations in the late 1840s. As other areas were annexed but not settled by whites, they became reserves: the bulk of Zululand, parts of the Ciskei, most of the Transkei, and pockets of the northern Transvaal, while in the Free State the only reserves were the minute Thaba Nchu and Witzieshoek (now QWA QWA). Most of the African reserves lay in a great arc round the northern periphery of the country, from the northwestern Cape through the western, northern and eastern Transvaal into Zululand and Natal and down the eastern Cape to the Fish River. The NATIVES LAND ACT (1913) restricted African rights of access to land outside the reserves, which then comprised 7.8 percent of the country. Additional land was released in 1936 and very gradually added to the reserves (or BANTUSTANS), so that by 1980 they comprised 13 percent of the land surface of South Africa.

In many African areas there had been a rapid response to market opportunities in the middle and late 19th century. African peasant production flourished in the Ciskei in the 1860s, in the western and southern Transkei in the 1870s and 80s, and in the north-eastern Transkei in the following two decades. But then cash-crop production went into rapid decline. From the mid-1920s government commissions repeatedly commented on the decline of the reserves and the critical state of agricultural production there. Some anti-erosion measures were introduced; "betterment schemes" concentrated scattered homesteads into villages, and fenced arable and grazing lands. But there was no large capital investment, and by the 1940s it was clear that the reserves were not able to support those not working as MIGRANT LABORERS, even on a subsistence basis. Overstocked, congested, denuded, overgrazed, and eroded, the reserves were also increasingly overpopulated. Population density rose from over fifty per square mile in 1916 to almost sixty per square mile in 1940. As productivity declined, more and more people sought work outside them as migrants. By 1947 30 percent of Ciskeian farmers were landless, and 60 percent owned less than five cattle. The decline in agricultural productivity accelerated after about 1955 as a result of a further leap in their population, in turn a consequence of the commercialization of white farms and the MASS REMOVAL of SQUATTERS, and a tightening up of INFLUX CONTROL. In the 1960s and 1970s, as the government moved the reserves--renamed BANTUSTANS--towards self-government and then "independence," more money was pumped into them, which financed a little industry and some agricultural improvements. But the general picture remained one of squalid misery, and an almost total dependence on migrant labor.

RETIEF, Pieter (1780-1838) see GREAT TREK; ZULU.

RHODES, Cecil John (1853-1902). He followed his brother Herbert
from England to Natal in 1870, where he grew cotton, and then
to the DIAMOND fields, where he began working his brother's
claims in November 1871. From the mid 1870s he began to
acquire his vast fortune, initially through a pumping contract
for the removal of water from submerged claims. This brought
him a steady income, from which he bought up submerged
claims in the De Beers mine. By 1880 he was able to form a
De Beers Mining Company, which owned 90 claims. Seven
years later it had secured sole ownership of the entire De
Beers mine. When DE BEERS CONSOLIDATED MINES was
registered the following year, Rhodes, a life governor, was a
millionaire. Though less personally involved on the WIT-
WATERSRAND GOLD fields, his Consolidated Gold Fields company was nevertheless by 1895 an even larger source of his
income than De Beers.

When the Diamond fields were incorporated in the Cape
(1880), he successfully stood for one of the new parliamentary
seats, which he then held until his death. His first years as
a parliamentarian were much involved in attempting to secure
the ROAD TO THE NORTH for the Cape, for the imperialism
Rhodes represented and furthered was the imperialism of Cape-
based mining capital, not metropolitan imperialism. Though
Britain and not the Cape took over BECHUANALAND, that territory was at least, from Rhodes' perspective, denied to KRU-
GER. But then came the discovery of gold and the sudden turn
of economic fortunes in the Transvaal's favor. By the end of
the decade the Cape's agrarian interests--which found political
expression in the AFRIKANER BOND--and its mining interests
came together in the face of this challenge, and, with Bond
backing, Rhodes, the man of action as well as wealth, became
Prime Minister (1890).

Much of his time in the years of his greatest influence was
taken up with the European settlement of the country north of
the Transvaal which was to bear his name for over 80 years
(see ZIMBABWE). But, taking on the portfolio of Native Affairs at the Cape, he piloted the GLEN GREY ACT, his "Bill
for Africa," which was designed in part to provide labor for
the mines, through the Cape parliament (1894). The same
year he was responsible for the Cape taking over Pondoland,
the last remaining independent area between the Cape and Natal,
completing the annexation of the TRANSKEI to the Cape colony.

From mid 1895 he planned a military uprising by UITLAND-
ERS in the Transvaal to overthrow the Kruger government and
make the Transvaal a British colony. Though he did not give
prior approval to the JAMESON RAID, his support for Jameson
meant he had to resign as premier. The break with Hofmeyr
and the Bond was final. In the polarized politics of the post-
Raid period, Rhodes got English-speaking support and by early
1898 was de facto leader of the new PROGRESSIVE PARTY.
But from 1897 his health deteriorated, and he died in the last
months of the SOUTH AFRICAN WAR.

ROAD TO THE NORTH.   Also called the Missionaries' Road, it was
the passage through the territory annexed by Britain as BECHUANA-
LAND in 1885.   Linking the Cape to central Africa, and various
TSWANA trading centers one with the other, it lay on the outer
western limits of pastoral farming, just within the rainfall belt
averaging 15 or more inches per year; further west lay the dry
Kalahari desert.   Transvaal TREKBOERS had moved into the
area by the early 1880s, when two small republics, Stellaland
and Goshen, were formed across the western border of the
Transvaal.   Cecil RHODES realized the value of the road as a
route into the interior--that taken by MISSIONARIES such as
Moffat and Livingstone four decades earlier.   Were the Transvaal farmers to secure their hold over it, further British expansion would be checked, a route which MIGRANT LABOR took
to Kimberley threatened, and territory which might include un-
discovered DIAMOND mines lost to his control.   Rhodes was
not successful in acquiring it for the Cape, but officials in London were persuaded that Transvaal westward expansion should
be checked to prevent a possible later link-up with the territory
Germany had acquired in South-West Africa.   So the Road was
placed in British hands, and Rhodes in the early 1890s pushed
a railroad from Kimberley north along it, to skirt Kruger's
Transvaal.

ROCK ART.   South Africa possesses the richest treasury of rock
art in the world, the legacy of its Stone Age peoples (see SAN).
It is especially to be found in the southwestern Cape, in the
mountains north of Cape Town; in the eastern Cape; and in the
great DRAKENSBERG chain of mountains.   It has been suggested,
but not proved, that the simpler style of the Cape paintings
means they are older than those of the Drakensberg.   In the
late 19th century white travellers found San still painting in the
Drakensberg area.   Very recent attempts to date organic material associated with engraved rocks suggest that some of the
paintings go back at least 10,000 years, but many are relatively recent, depicting white TREKBOERS, soldiers, or horses.
Though a wide range of animals are depicted, the eland, the
largest of the antelope, is far the most common, probably because of its role in San mythology.   Much of the art probably
had a spiritual significance to those who painted it.

ROMAN CATHOLIC CHURCH.   Catholics were prohibited from public worship at the Cape until 1804 and the first vicar apostolic
for South Africa was not consecrated until 1837.   Protestant opposition helped delay Catholic mission work among Africans until the late 19th century.   The most famous Catholic mission
center was Mariannhill, in Natal, which the Trappists ran on the
lines of a medieval European monastry.   In the 20th century
there was considerable Catholic expansion, both among whites
and Africans, and the growth of an indigenous ministry.
    The DUTCH REFORMED CHURCH, in particular, was
strongly anti-Catholic, and the cry of "Die Roomsegevaar"

("the Roman danger") was often heard.   Immigration from
Catholic countries was discouraged into the 1970s.   The hierarchy of the Catholic Church, for its part, was cautious in its
criticism of state policies before the 1970s.   In that decade its
protests grew stronger, and it took the lead in disregarding the
law and opening its schools to children of all races.   By then
the number of Catholics was thought to be approaching two million.

RURAL RESISTANCE.   From c. 1920 to the early 1960s there was
great ferment in many rural areas, as Africans protested
against various forms of state intervention.   Between 1926 and
1928 the membership of the INDUSTRIAL AND COMMERCIAL
WORKERS UNION soared, and most new members were labor
tenants and others in the rural areas.   There was a brief attempt to rally farm workers, especially in the Cape, by local
members of the AFRICAN NATIONAL CONGRESS before the
conservative wing took over in 1930.   As labor tenants were
removed under the HERTZOG legislation of 1936, resistance
grew, especially in the northern Transvaal, with Alpheus Maliba
the leading figure.   Taxes were not paid, government surveys
disrupted, marches held.   Under the influence of the COMMU-
NIST PARTY, an attempt was then made to use the courts to
resist the state.   The state in turn used massive repression,
and by 1945 this resistance had petered out.
    From 1939 betterment schemes were introduced to improve
the land in rural areas: grazing was controlled, fencing
erected, and stock culled.   Resistance to this in Witzieshoek
(later QWA QWA) culminated in the police shooting 14 protesters.   In the Transkei, too, there was resistance to the clust-
ering of people into so-called rehabilitated villages.   A secret
armed movement in the Mount Ayliff district, the Kongo, affiliated to the ALL-AFRICAN CONVENTION in 1948.   A new phase
of rural struggle opened with the government's attempt to implement Bantu Authorities in the RESERVES (see also BANTUS-
TANS).   In the 1950s the urban-based organizations began again
to pick up the rural demands; the DEFIANCE CAMPAIGN, for
example, was in part directed at stock culling.   The extension
of the PASS laws to African women was a further cause of
rural resentment in the late 1950s.   Rural violence intensified,
especially in the eastern and western Transvaal and in both
Thembuland and Pondoland in the Transkei.   The most spectacular rural revolt occurred in east Pondoland in 1959-1960.   Rebelling against the imposition of Bantu Authorities, peasants
withdrew into the hills and sought to burn the homesteads of
collaborators.   A state of emergency was proclaimed and police
and troops, aided by armored vehicles and helicopters, suppressed the revolt.   From the early 1960s state control was
too great, and the impoverishment and the consequences of
MASS REMOVALS too debilitating, for further revolts of that
kind to occur.

SABOTAGE. The OSSEWABRANDWAG engaged in sabotage as part
of its campaign against the country's involvement in WORLD
WAR II. But the offense of sabotage was not created in law
until 1962, in response to a new wave of sabotage that began
the previous year. UMKHONTO WE SIZWE and a mainly white
African Resistance Movement used explosives designed to dis-
rupt government, police and parastatal operations. At the
same time, Poqo, an offshoot of the PAN-AFRICANIST CON-
GRESS, engaged in acts of terrorism against whites. The 1962
legislation provided for the death penalty for sabotage, and within a year or so of its passage, with most of the people involved
having been arrested, acts of sabotage ceased. A new era began after 1977, this time the work of UMKHONTO alone. Again,
targets of strategic or economic importance were attacked, most
notably the SASOL oil from coal plant (1980), power stations in
the eastern Transvaal (1981) and the Voortrekkerhoogte military
base (1981). The sabotage campaign took a new turn with bomb
explosions in commercial areas of Durban, East London, and
Port Elizabeth in 1981, and at PASS-system courts and offices
in Cape Town. The main purpose seemed to be, in the words
of a captured saboteur, "armed propaganda" for the AFRICAN
NATIONAL CONGRESS.

SAN. Hunter-gatherers, the descendants of the aboriginal inhabitants of the region, they lived in quite distinct communities,
with discrete click languages and no conception of a common
identity. "San" was the KHOIKHOI word for those who gathered
food. Whites called them Sonqua HOTTENTOTS or, more commonly, "bushmen" (bosjesmans, bosiemans, and other variants),
whether because of the environment in which they were found or
because their shelters were made of bushes is not clear.
    The typical San band was thought to have comprised no more
than 20 persons, and to have moved seasonally within a limited
area in search of food to gather, game to kill, or fish. Recent
work has suggested that gathering was usually far more important to their survival than hunting. They used small stone arte-
facts as scrapers, missile tips and drills, and they fashioned
bows and arrows and fish traps. Over thousands of years they
developed the art of painting on rocks (see ROCK ART).
    Scattered thinly in the 17th century over much of what is
now South Africa, some San became clients of KHOIKHOI or
BANTU-SPEAKING Africans. Those who hunted for the TSWANA
were known as Masarwa. San were renowned for their rainmak-
ing skills, and also engaged in trade. At least one XHOSA clan
was partly San in origin. But relations between the San and
these other peoples were frequently hostile. To the San, the
cattle of Khoikhoi, Bantu-speakers, and trekboers must have
appeared as game fit to hunt. The whites often behaved with
extreme savagery towards the San, sending out COMMANDOS
to exterminate them, though their children were sometimes
captured and kept as APPRENTICES. Many in the face of
such attacks retreated into the mountains and the more arid
areas. Mission work among the San began in 1799, when a

London Missionary Society station was opened on the Sak river,
but it had little success.   Together with cattle-less Khoi, San
put up major resistance to the white advance when it reached
the Niewveldberge and the Sneeuberge on the fringes of the
KARROO in the late 18th century.   When that resistance was
finally broken, after three decades, the San fell back either
into the foothills of the DRAKENSBERG mountains or into the
semi-desert lands south of the ORANGE.   In that latter region,
still called Bushmanland today, a Cape inquiry of the 1860s
found they had been mercilessly treated.   Some retreated further into NAMIBIA or Botswana.   The last survivors within
South Africa died in the early 20th century.

SANCTIONS.   In the aftermath of SHARPEVILLE, the UNITED NA-
TIONS General Assembly called for economic and diplomatic
sanctions to be imposed against South Africa (1962).   Later
General Assembly resolutions called for even more wide-
ranging sanctions, including the end of cultural and sports ties.
South Africa was excluded from the 1964 Olympic Games because of racial discrimination in its sport (see SPORTING
CONTACTS).   Though the United States abided by a non-
mandatory arms embargo approved by the UN Security Council
in 1963, other countries did not, and France in particular continued to supply South Africa with a wide range of weapons (see
MILITARY).   One of the most effective actions taken against
South Africa in the early 1960s was the decision by African
states to refuse South African aircraft overflying or landing
rights.   This forced South African Airways to fly "round the
bulge" of the African continent to get to Europe.
As the South African economy boomed in the mid-1960s, talk
of economic sanctions faded.   South Africa openly flouted the
UN call for international sanctions against the illegal regime in
ZIMBABWE from 1965.   No attempt was made to impose sanc-
tions against South Africa for this.   It was clearly in South
Africa's interest that sanctions not be seen to work in the
Zimbabwe case.   With the independence of MOZAMBIQUE and
ANGOLA, however, when it seemed to the South African gov-
ernment that the continuation of white rule in Zimbabwe was
not viable, VORSTER did put pressure on Ian Smith to bring
Africans into his government.
After the sanctions debates of the early 1960s, South Africa,
not having oil of its own, took the threat of an oil embargo
seriously.   From the mid-1960s oil was stockpiled, in disused
mines and elsewhere.   The government set up a Southern Oil
Exploration Corporation (SOEKOR) in 1965 to search for oil.
It found none, but the search, which mostly took place off the
southern coast, was stepped up after the Organisation of Petroleum Exporting countries raised the oil price dramatically
(1973) and imposed an embargo on the supply of oil to South
Africa.   It was decided to build a second, and then a third,
plant to produce oil from coal, of which South Africa had
abundant supplies, and there was also much experimentation
with petroleum substitutes.   South Africa did not have problems,

in the event, in obtaining oil.   In the 1970s Iran was its main
supplier, thanks to the Shah.   When that supply was cut off,
South Africa was able to buy the oil it needed on the spot market.
    After BIKO's death and subsequent repression, the UN Secur-
ity Council imposed a mandatory arms embargo against South
Africa (see MILITARY).   When it seemed that other sanctions
might be imposed were South Africa to continue to flout the UN
over NAMIBIA, it agreed to participate in negotiations for a
UN-supervised election there, negotiations which dragged on for
years.   In the early 1980s, with Ronald Reagan in the White
House and Margaret Thatcher in office in Britain, South Africa
was confident no further sanctions would be imposed.   Direct
United States investment in South Africa was then over $2 bil-
lion--17 percent of total foreign investment in the country--and
United Kingdom investment worth three times that amount.   Despite the Organisation of African Unity's mandatory boycott,
African countries were said to be conducting trade worth $1.2
billion with South Africa in 1981, 8 percent of the country's
total trade.   (See also OUTWARD POLICY.)

SCHREINER, Olive (1855-1920).   Novelist and polemicist.   At
    twenty-five, while governess on a KARROO farm, she com-
    pleted The Story of an African Farm (London, 1883), the book
    for which she is most famous.   The daughter of a German
    missionary, her upbringing was pious and harsh, but she early
    became a convert to Spencerian freethinking.   She went to Eng-
    land in 1881 but returned for long periods to South Africa,
    where she opposed Britain's participation in the SOUTH AFRI-
    CAN WAR, and then warned of the dangers were the two white
    groups to unite over the bodies of the blacks.   Her Woman and
    Labour (1911) was a powerful feminist tract.   The asthma from
    which she suffered most of her life and from which she died,
    was probably psychosomatic.   Some critics regard Thoughts on
    South Africa, written in the early 1890s but not published until
    after her death, as her finest work.
        One of her brothers, William Philip Schreiner (1857-1919),
    was Prime Minister of the Cape from 1898 to 1900 and then a
    strong opponent of UNION because of the color bar in the pro-
    posed constitution.

SECURITY POLICE.   After VORSTER became Minister of Justice
    in 1961 the Special Branch of the police concerned with "secur-
    ity matters" was enlarged and allowed free use of greatly en-
    hanced powers.   In the 1960s its agents successfully infiltrated
    the underground COMMUNIST PARTY; in the 1970s a member of
    the security police became Assistant Director of the Internation-
    al University Exchange Fund in Geneva, where he gathered in-
    formation on anti-apartheid activities.   The security police were
    most notorious for their treatment of political prisoners, and
    especially for their harsh methods of interrogation.   Between
    1963 and early 1982 at least 46 people died while in their
    custody (see also DETENTION WITHOUT TRIAL).

A Bureau of State Security, popularly known as BOSS even
after its name was changed to National Intelligence Service, was
created in 1969.   It gathered intelligence and undertook covert
operations, the budget for which was greatly increased in the
mid-1970s.   Though supposed to operate outside the country, it
was also active within it.   It clashed with Military Intelligence
on a number of occasions in the 1970s, and for a time, until
the uncovering of the MULDERGATE scandal revealed something
of BOSS's role, Military Intelligence was subordinated to it.

SEGREGATION.   See especially RACIAL SEGREGATION, but also
     APARTHEID; BANTUSTANS; RESERVES; URBAN SEGREGATION.

SEME, Pixley ka Isaka (c. 1880-1951).   The moving spirit behind
     the founding of the South African Native National Congress, later
     the AFRICAN NATIONAL CONGRESS, Seme was its president
     from 1930 to 1937.   He grew up in Natal, and was educated
     first in America, where he was much influenced by Booker T.
     Washington, then at Oxford and in London, where he was ad-
     mitted to the bar in 1910.   Returning to South Africa, he
     practiced as a lawyer in Johannesburg.   Besides organizing the
     founding meeting of SANNC, he established Abantu-Batho, the
     ANC newspaper.   But he did not hold high office in the ANC
     until the conservatives elected him president in 1930.   Ultra-
     cautious in his approach, he did nothing to revive its flagging
     fortunes.   He was one of the convenors of the first meeting of
     the ALL-AFRICAN CONVENTION in 1935, but he turned against
     that body when it became a permanent organization, seeing in
     it a potential rival to the ANC.

SEPARATE DEVELOPMENT.   Term used by VERWOERD from
     1959 to suggest that government policy was not mere domina-
     tion (BAASSKAP) but promoted the "separate development" of
     the different "races."   For Africans this meant the BANTUS-
     TAN policy, which was used to deny Africans any claim to
     rights in the core area of South Africa.   It also served to di-
     vide Africans along "ethnic" lines, and create a number of
     collaborative petty bourgeoisies.   Some Africans believed that
     in the absence of alternative legal channels for political action,
     they should use those offered by "separate development," even
     to the extent of accepting "independence" (see MATANZIMA);
     others that they should use the platform provided by "separate
     development" to thwart the implementation of the policy (see
     BUTHELEZI).   Still others rejected any form of collaboration.
        There were NATIONAL PARTY (NP) intellectuals and right-
     wingers to whom "separate development" also meant the terri-
     torial segregation of "Coloureds" and Indians.   Most Nationalists
     accepted, however, that, unlike the Africans, these groups had
     no "HOMELAND," and at most could be given a measure of
     control over their own affairs.   In 1977 the NP decided that
     they should be brought within the same constitutional framework
     as whites (see CONSTITUTIONAL CHANGE).

SEPARATISM.   In BANTU-SPEAKING societies, separatism was
fostered by the succession system: as the heir was son of the
"great wife," married usually late in life, the eldest son of the
"right-hand," the first married, usually became regent.   When
the heir came of age, the regent and perhaps other sons often
broke away to form their own chiefdoms.
    Separatism in white societies has taken very different forms.
White frontier farmers in 1795, 1799, 1801, and 1815 sought
unsuccessfully to create an independent republic on the eastern
Cape frontier.   A petition by the 1820 BRITISH settlers (see
ENGLISH-SPEAKING WHITES) began a new separatist agitation.
The leading settlers of Grahamstown in particular sought more
effective control over government, centered in distant Cape
Town.   Some concessions were won: a commissioner-general
for the eastern districts (1828-1833); a lieutenant-governor for
the east (1836-1847); and even the meeting of the Cape parliament in Grahamstown on one occasion (1864).   But the eastern
Cape separatists were confused in purpose and did not even enjoy the support of all easterners, let alone the midlands settlers.   From the 1870s the movement lost momentum.
    A recurrent theme in the history of English-speaking NATAL,
separatist sentiment came to a head there in 1960-1961 at the
time of the REPUBLIC referendum, when there was considerable
talk among Natal's whites of secession from Afrikaner-dominated
South Africa.   With the material prosperity of the 1960s, such
dreams were forgotten.

SHAKA see ZULU.

SHARPEVILLE.   African township at Vereeniging in the southern
Transvaal where undisciplined police in a panic reaction opened
fire on PAN-AFRICANIST CONGRESS (PAC) demonstrators on
21 March 1960.   Sixty-nine Africans died, mostly shot in the
back as they fled, and 186 were wounded.   The shooting
aroused universal condemnation and "Sharpeville" came to
symbolize the repression of the African majority in South
Africa.   Also on 21 March, violence erupted in the African
township of Langa outside Cape Town, where four PAC demonstrators were killed.   After the shootings the anti-pass campaign was accompanied by a national STAY-AWAY called by the
AFRICAN NATIONAL CONGRESS (ANC) and much general unrest, with numerous violent incidents not only in the major
centers but also in the smaller towns.   On 24 March meetings
were banned in many districts.   Two days later the PASS laws
were suspended, and on 29 March a state of emergency was
proclaimed.   The white citizen reserves of the army were then
mobilized, thousands detained, and the ANC and PAC both
banned.   The crisis led to a massive outflow of foreign capital;
within a year the gold and foreign exchange reserves had fallen
by half.   Many skilled and professional people left the country.
White control was not seriously threatened, however, and the
crisis gave the government the opportunity to use massive

repression, which virtually destroyed the African nationalist movement within the country, and through the new "stability" imposed, helped produce a decade of unparalleled economic growth.

SHEPSTONE, Theophilus (1817-1893). Son of an 1820 settler who became a missionary, Shepstone grew up on the eastern Cape frontier and from the late 1830s to 1845 was agent with the MFENGU settled at Fort Peddie east of the Fish river. He then became diplomatic agent with the African peoples of NATAL, and was from 1856 to 1876 its Secretary for Native Affairs. He first coaxed or coerced two-thirds of Natal's Africans into large LOCATIONS (i. e. RESERVES). There they were ruled through either their traditional authorities, or chiefs created by Shepstone. Customary NGUNI law was recognized, and the governor, as "Supreme Chief," given extensive powers, which Shepstone exercised on his behalf. Though his system was a pragmatic response to the situation he found in Natal, it accorded with his belief that Africans should be governed separately and should be protected in their occupation of land. He made several unsuccessful attempts to found a large African state which he would oversee, either in ZULU territory or south of Natal. In the 1870s he was responsible for an early form of INFLUX CONTROL designed to prevent permanent African settlement in Natal's cities. Some have seen in the Shepstonian system "the roots of segregation" in 20th century South Africa.

When LANGALIBALELE disobeyed him (1873), Shepstone determined he must be crushed. The farcical trial of the rebel and the brutal treatment of his people led to criticism of Shepstone in London, but the Colonial Secretary found a new role for him, sending him to the Transvaal to "persuade" it of the benefits of CONFEDERATION. Backed by only 25 men, Shepstone raised the Union Jack in Pretoria in April 1877; then administered the Transvaal for two years. In the months before the outbreak of the Anglo-ZULU war, he, more than anyone, urged on FRERE the merits of provoking that war. Through his brother, and then his son, who in succession were Natal's Secretary for Native Affairs, he kept a measure of control over Natal's African policy into the late 1880s.

SIMONSTOWN. A safe anchorage on the eastern side of the Cape Peninsula, 30 miles south of Cape Town, named after Simon van der Stel (1639-1712), DUTCH EAST INDIA COMPANY (DEIC) commander at the Cape. In 1743 after ships were lost in gales in Table Bay, the DEIC made Simon's Bay the official winter anchorage. It was there that BRITISH forces landed in June 1795 to capture the Cape. After the ending of the slave trade (1808), a small British naval squadron was stationed there to intercept slave ships rounding the Cape; many of the captured ships were brought in to Simonstown, where their cargoes of "Prize Negroes" were released. As the main naval base in southern Africa, it retained its importance after the opening of the Suez Canal (1869), for the Cape sea route

remained of immense strategic significance. Major extensions
to the port facilities were undertaken in the early 20th century
and opened in 1910.   In 1921 the Union took over responsibility
for the land defenses of the port.   During World War II, allied
vessels operated from Simonstown against German ships in the
South Atlantic and Indian Oceans.
    With the development of a South African navy, the South
African authorities pressed the British to hand over the base.
This was done in April 1957, when it became the headquarters
of the South African navy.   The Simonstown agreement gave the
British the right to use the base in peacetime and in war,
whether or not South Africa was also at war, and South Africa
agreed to buy British-made naval vessels.   But when the Labour
government came to power in Britain, it refused to sell South
Africa any weapons of war because of its racial policies, and
the agreement was suspended.   After the UNITED NATIONS'
mandatory arms embargo (1977), South Africa undertook further expansion of the naval dockyard, including the building of
a new tidal basin to accommodate submarines obtained from
France.   This was opened in 1980.
    In the early 1980s most of the oil shipped from the Persian
Gulf to the West went via the Cape, for the Suez Canal could
not take supertankers.   Of the 3,000 ships that passed the
Cape in 1980, almost half were tankers.

SISA (mafisa; ngoma).   Among both NGUNI and SOTHO, the practice
    of loaning out cattle.   The cattle or their milk could be re-
    claimed at any time; the person entrusted with the cattle had
    the use of them but did not obtain ownership.   It was a way to
    acquire dependents, and MOSHWESHWE in particular used it ex-
    tensively after the MFECANE to build up a large following:
    see BASUTOLAND.

SLAVERY see CAPE SLAVERY and cf. APPRENTICESHIP.

SMUTS, Jan Christian (1870-1950).   Cape born, Cambridge educated,
    State Attorney of the Transvaal (1898) and a senior officer dur-
    ing the SOUTH AFRICAN WAR, in which he led a BOER COM-
    MANDO into the Cape, Smuts was at the center of South Afri-
    can politics throughout the first half of the 20th century.   A
    founder of HET VOLK (1905), he became a Minister in the
    Transvaal government in 1907, played a major role in pushing
    unification at the NATIONAL CONVENTION, was Prime Minister
    from 1919 to 1924, Deputy Prime Minister from 1933 to 1939
    and Prime Minister again from 1939 to 1948.   In both World
    Wars he was active both with the South African forces and in
    the making of British strategy.   A proponent of the philosophy
    of holism, he was accepted as an international statesman as no
    other South African has ever been.   At home, he was much
    criticized by some Afrikaners for his role in the suppression
    of the AFRIKANER REBELLION and for selling out to British
    imperialism.   White workers knew him as the man who brutal-
    ly suppressed the RAND REVOLT, Africans as the one who had

authorized the massacre of BULHOEK and approved the removal
of the Cape African vote (see FRANCHISE). There is evidence
that in his last years in office Smuts was beginning to turn his
mind to moving the country away from segregationist policies,
but he believed there was plenty of time to make such changes
and he was shocked when swept out of office in 1948 (see NA-
TIONAL PARTY; UNITED PARTY).

SOBUKWE, Robert Mangaliso (1924-78). Born in Graaff-Reinet,
and educated at FORT HARE, where he was active in AFRICAN
NATIONAL CONGRESS politics, he taught African languages at
the University of the Witwatersrand from 1954. He came increasingly to question ANC strategy, believing its involvement
with non-Africans weakened it. In 1958 he urged the "Africanists" to break away, and in 1959 was elected first president of
the new PAN-AFRICANIST CONGRESS. Surrendering himself to
the police at the beginning of the PAC anti-PASS campaign on
the day of SHARPEVILLE, he was given a harsh three year
sentence for incitement, after which he was detained on Robben
Island off CAPE TOWN, under special legislation, for another
six years. He was then allowed to settle in Kimberley, and,
though still restricted, began his own law practice.

SOTHO. Used in the 1830s for the followers of MOSHWESHWE of
BASUTOLAND, it was later adopted by linguists as their name
for that group of BANTU languages spoken by Africans on the
highveld, the interior plateau west of the DRAKENSBERG mountains. The people who speak Sotho languages are usually divided into three main sub-clusters: the northern Sotho of the
northern and eastern Transvaal (including PEDI); the TSWANA
of the northern Cape, western Transvaal, BOPHUTHATSWANA
and BOTSWANA; and the southern Sotho of the Orange Free
State, QWA QWA and Lesotho.
    Despite considerable intermingling between Sotho and NGUNI
people over the centuries, cultural distinctions survived. Among
the Nguni there was a rigid taboo on marriage into one's mother's
or father's clan, but among the Sotho parallel and cross-cousin
marriage was common. To categorize distinctive settlement
patterns or forms of economic life is more difficult. The western Sotho (Tswana) often lived in large settlements, housing
five to ten thousand people, which were sometimes autonomous
polities. The first whites to visit the Tlhaping capital of Dithakong in 1801, for example, were impressed by the size and order of the city. It has been suggested that such large settlements were the product of environmental constraints, such as
lack of water and the need for defense in semi-arid regions.
But other Sotho lived in small villages, or even scattered homesteads like the Nguni. Unlike the Nguni, many Sotho used stone
extensively in their building, and the thousands of stone ruins
spread through the southern Transvaal and the northern Orange
Free State are testimony to the density of their settlement.
Some northern and western Sotho mined copper and GOLD as
well as iron.

SOUTH AFRICAN CONGRESS OF TRADE UNIONS (SACTU). Founded
in 1955 by critics of the decision by the TRADE UNION CON-
GRESS OF SOUTH AFRICA to restrict its membership to registered (non-African) TRADE UNIONS. SACTU joined the CON-
GRESS ALLIANCE as its trade union wing, and sought to mobilize the African working class. By 1961 it claimed 46 affiliated
unions and 53,000 members, the vast majority Africans. In the
early 1960s, following SHARPEVILLE, its leadership was banned,
and it was driven underground, though not BANNED.

SOUTH AFRICAN EXPANSIONISM. At the end of the 19th century,
Alfred MILNER envisaged "a self-governing" white community
supported by well-treated and justly governed black labor from
Cape Town to the Zambesi. BOTHA and SMUTS shared this
imperialist vision, hoping to incorporate southern Mozambique,
Southern Rhodesia (ZIMBABWE) and South West Africa (NAMIBIA),
as well as the three HIGH COMMISSION TERRITORIES, the incorporation of which was envisaged in the Schedule to the South
Africa Act (1909) which created the UNION. Mining interests
were concerned about the supply of MIGRANT LABOR and possible new mineral deposits, white agrarian interests with acquiring more land and prizing out more labor. With the rise
of the NATIONAL PARTY, Smuts in the early 1920s hoped that
the incorporation of Southern Rhodesia would mean new support
for his SOUTH AFRICAN PARTY. White supremacist interests
would be furthered by the acquisition of adjacent territory, it
was believed, and new markets were sought for South African
goods as its industrialization entered its MANUFACTURING
phase.
But none of the hopes of the expansionists were achieved.
The white settlers of Southern Rhodesia voted against joining
South Africa in 1922. South West Africa became a mandate
under the League of Nations in 1919, and though it was to be
ruled virtually as an integral part of South Africa itself, it was
never fully incorporated. The Africans of the High Commission
Territories made clear their opposition to South Africa's segregationist policies. So no further territory was acquired, and
South African expansion remained informal: neighboring countries were drawn into South Africa's orbit in a variety of ways.
The High Commission territories were linked in a customs'
union and common monetary zone. Most neighboring countries
supplied large numbers of migrant workers to South Africa.
South African goods and expertise flowed into the neighboring
countries, and the South African police and military were frequently active across South Africa's borders. (See also OUT-
WARD POLICY.)

SOUTH AFRICAN PARTY (1911-1934). Born in November 1911,
after the achievement of UNION, through the amalgamation of the
various parties represented in BOTHA's cabinet, including the
AFRIKANER BOND in the Cape and HET VOLK in the Transvaal.
Under Botha and then SMUTS, the South African Party stood for
"conciliation," the reconciliation of Afrikaners and English-

speakers on the basis of a common loyalty to South Africa.
After the breakaway of HERTZOG and the formation of his NA-
TIONAL PARTY, the South African Party found itself increasingly reliant on the jingoistic UNIONIST PARTY, and an informal alliance led to absorption of the Unionists in 1920. After
winning 79 seats in the 1921 general election, the South African
Party grew increasingly unpopular, not least because of Smuts'
brutal suppression of the RAND REVOLT, and it lost power to
the PACT in 1924. By then it had been depicted as the party
of mining capital and Smuts as the lackey of Hoggenheimer (i.e.
Jewish capitalism) and the tool of British imperialism. Many
Afrikaners remained bloedsappe, however (literally blood South
African Party men, i.e. those with a hereditary loyalty to
Botha and Smuts), and the policy of conciliation took on new
life when, at a time of economic crisis, Hertzog in 1933 agreed
to form a coalition with the South African Party. This led to
FUSION with Hertzog's party the following year, and the forma-
tion of the UNITED PARTY.

SOUTH AFRICAN REPUBLIC. For the republic established north
of the Vaal river in 1858 see TRANSVAAL; for 20th-century
republicanism see REPUBLIC; for the republic established in
1961 see also CONSTITUTIONAL CHANGE.

SOUTH AFRICAN STUDENTS' ORGANISATION (SASO). In 1967-68
Steve BIKO came to realize that the few African students in the
NATIONAL UNION OF SOUTH AFRICAN STUDENTS largely left
it to white students to articulate black grievances. Together
with other students from the ethnic UNIVERSITIES and the theological seminaries, students who had grown up since the banning
of the AFRICAN NATIONAL CONGRESS and the PAN-AFRICANIST
CONGRESS, Biko decided in 1968 that an all-black student organization should be formed. SASO was inaugurated at a conference
at Turfloop, the campus of the University of the North, in 1969,
with Biko as its president. Biko articulated its belief that
blacks should work on their own, and not under the guidance of
white liberals. Critics called SASO racist. Probably because
it was all-black, the segregation-minded government tolerated
its strong rhetoric for a time. Winning strong support on the
African campuses and also among Indian students in Durban
and "Coloured" students at the University of the Western Cape,
it helped establish the Black People's Convention (BPC) in 1972,
an umbrella political movement based on BLACK CONSCIOUS-
NESS, and became more militant, closing down the University
of the North and calling for a boycott on other black campuses.
From 1973 its leaders began to be BANNED and DETAINED
WITHOUT TRIAL. In 1975 some were charged under the Terrorism Act (see BLACK CONSCIOUSNESS). It remained active,
however, working closely with the BPC, until October 1977,
when both organizations were banned.

SOUTH AFRICAN WAR (1899-1902). Also known as the Boer war
or Anglo-Boer war, or, to Afrikaner historians, the Second

War of Freedom (the first being that of 1880-81; see TRANS-
VAAL WAR OF INDEPENDENCE).

Until recently most historians argued that MILNER was
chiefly responsible for the war, and that it was fought in the
interests of British supremacy in the sub-continent. Ronald
Robinson and Jack Gallagher in their Africa and the Victorians
(London, 1961) stressed British concern with the sea-route to
India: the Transvaal's new wealth gave it new opportunity to
attract all Afrikaners into a South African republic outside
British control, and this placed British supremacy, necessary
to secure the route to India, in jeopardy. In the 1970s historians returned to the idea, advanced by J. A. Hobson (1858-1940)
at the time of the war, that it was fought for essentially economic reasons. For Hobson, the RANDLORDS had been behind
the war, fought to ensure the supply of cheap African labor to
the GOLD mines. Clearly Britain's interests were not only political and strategic; the Transvaal was the largest single pro-
ducer of gold in 1899, responsible for between one-fifth and
one-quarter of the world's supply. It would be surprising had
gold not played an important part in British thinking, but its
significance as a cause of the war remains a matter of debate
among historians.

The decision by the Boers to strike first in October 1899
was taken in the hope that if the British garrison in north-west
Natal could be overwhelmed and the Cape be roused to rebellion,
a negotiated peace might be arranged on Boer terms. The
British, for their part, believed the war could be won before
Christmas. A series of British defeats ("black week"; December 1899) was followed by the appointment of Lord Roberts
(1832-1914) as Commander-in-Chief of the British forces, with
Lord Kitchener (1850-1916) as his Chief of Staff. On 27 February 1900, the anniversary of the Boer victory at Majuba in
1881, the Boers suffered a humiliating defeat when General
Piet Cronjé (1836-1911) and 4,000 men surrendered to Roberts
at Paardeburg. Roberts then captured Bloemfontein and
marched on to Johannesburg and Pretoria. The Orange Free
State was annexed in May, the Transvaal on 1 September 1900.

But the war was not over. Louis BOTHA and Christiaan de
Wet (1854-1922), the new military leaders, decided to adopt the
strategy of guerilla war, and a more ruthless phase opened.
In response to the casualties inflicted on them by the Boer
COMMANDOS, the British began burning farms and destroying
crops and livestock, in an attempt to deny the commandos the
means to continue the war. After Kitchener succeeded Roberts
as Commander-in-Chief in November 1900, the British created
a vast network of blockhouses connected by barbed-wire barri-
cades, while civilians, both white and black, were interned in
CONCENTRATION CAMPS. Captured Boers were sent to
prisoner-of-war camps in St. Helena, Bermuda, Ceylon, and
India. More and more Africans were used--nearly 10,000
were serving under arms on the British side by the end of the
war--despite the tacit agreement by both sides that the war
should remain a "white man's war."

By March 1902 the effective area of Boer resistance had become very restricted, with supplies hard to obtain and the commandos finding it more and more difficult to cross the British
lines. Almost 14, 000 Boers had surrendered voluntarily to the
British (the "hensoppers": hands-uppers) and almost 5, 500,
mostly landless BYWONERS, had joined the British forces (the
"joiners"). Among the "bittereinders" (bitter-enders: die-
hards), it was realized that to continue the war might mean
losing their bargaining position altogether. Peace talks with
Kitchener and MILNER were therefore opened, and these led to
the surrender of Boer independence on the terms laid down in
the TREATY OF VEREENIGING (May 1902). The war had cost
the British, who had put half a million men into the field, £191
million and over 7, 000 military deaths. Total losses on the
Boer side, including civilian deaths, amounted to almost 35, 000.
No one knows how many Africans died as a result of the war
(but see CONCENTRATION CAMPS). (See also MAFEKING.)

SOUTH WEST AFRICA see NAMIBIA

SOWETO (Acronym formed from "South-Western Townships"). A
vast sprawling African residential area southwest of Johannesburg. There were no houses for tens of thousands of Africans
who went to Johannesburg to work during the WORLD WAR II.
Most joined the SQUATTER population, living in shanties on the
outskirts of the city. After the War they were gradually provided with houses in the 28 townships eventually grouped into
Soweto, along with the bulk of the remainder of Johannesburg's
African population. Africans living in the suburb of Sophiatown,
much closer to the downtown area, were forced out to Soweto
in the mid 1950s, losing their freehold titles, as also were
many from Alexandra township in the 1970s.

The Soweto houses were mostly four-room "matchboxes" with
no electricity, ceilings, or running water. The miles and miles
of identical houses were laid out to make control by the police
as easy as possible. As in other African urban LOCATIONS,
the spartan conditions were partly a product of an unwillingness
to spend more money, but also partly a result of a belief that
better conditions might encourage permanent residence and
should not be provided for that reason. From 1955 an attempt
was made to zone individual townships on an "ethnic" basis--
NGUNI, SOTHO or "other"--but most of Soweto remained poly-
glot. As many of its residents were there illegally, its exact
population was never known, but in the mid 1970s it was probably over one million. Soweto had no industries, and a quarter
of a million of its people travelled on a single railway line
from it each day to work. The poverty and dreariness of the
place attracted adverse publicity during the SOWETO REVOLT,
leading the government to announce plans to provide electricity
to the houses and more entertainment and sporting facilities.

Soweto had been run by the Johannesburg City Council's Non
European Affairs Department, but was taken over by the West
Rand Administration Board, a nominated government body, in
1973. Residents of Soweto had served on an Advisory Board,

replaced by an Urban Council in 1968 which in turn became a
Community Council in 1978. Elections to these bodies consis-
tently produced minute polls, the vast majority of Sowetans rejecting them as powerless institutions of the oppressors.

SOWETO REVOLT. On 16 June 1976 the police fired into a large
crowd of schoolchildren marching through Orlando, one of the
townships making up SOWETO. Demonstrations and police retaliation continued in Soweto and spread from there to other
townships on the WITWATERSRAND and then to black urban
ghettos in Cape Town, Port Elizabeth, and East London. The
main targets of the rioters were government buildings, including schools and beer halls. A call by the students for a general strike in August met only slight success, and the police
were able to use MIGRANT workers against the demonstrators.
A boycott of classes in schools was extremely effective, especially in the Cape Town area; in early 1977 over 300,000
pupils were participating.
  The spark that set off the revolt was the insistence by the
educational authorities that AFRIKAANS be used as a medium
of instruction in Soweto's high schools. To Africans, Afrikaans
was seen as the language of the oppressors, and instruction in
it put them at a further disadvantage relative to white pupils.
But if Afrikaans was the trigger, the revolt was more broadly
directed against BANTU EDUCATION as a whole, an inferior
education designed to fit blacks for apartheid society, and also
against conditions in the ghettos. By 1976 BLACK CONSCIOUS-
NESS had made young Africans more assertive, and the independence of ANGOLA and MOZAMBIQUE had raised hopes of
change in South Africa. The brutality of the police response
may have been a deliberate way of "teaching the blacks a lesson," to dash such hopes for change.
  The revolt left at least 661 people dead, all Africans except
for some 50 "Coloureds" and a few whites. Many hundreds of
Africans were DETAINED WITHOUT TRIAL. Thousands of
young Sowetans fled the country; many of them were subsequently recruited by the AFRICAN NATIONAL CONGRESS as
guerillas. Like SHARPEVILLE, "Soweto" quickly became a
household name round the world for black resistance to apartheid and white repression. The police put down the revolt
without calling on the army, parliament was not recalled, no
state of emergency was proclaimed (the government had all the
powers it needed without one) and VORSTER said "There is no
crisis." There was nevertheless a crisis of confidence in
white society, and a large outflow of foreign capital.
  In the aftermath, the government dropped its insistence on
Afrikaans-medium instruction and took some steps to give
permanent residents of Soweto and other urban areas more to
lose--electricity in their houses, 99-year leasehold tenure (not
in the Western Cape), more amenities--in the hope that they
would not wish in future to jeopardize their privileged "insider"
status by pressing with violence any claim to effective political
rights or full South African citizenship.

SPORTING CONTACTS. In the 1950s the South African government
would permit no sports competitions involving people of different races, and separate administrations for individual sports
were set up on racial lines. Thanks to lobbying by the South
African Non-Racial Olympic Committee (SANROC), launched in
1963, the International Olympic Committee barred South Africa
from participating in the Tokyo Olympic games (1964) because
of racial discrimination in its sport. South Africa was later
expelled from the Olympic Movement, much to the distress of
the sport-loving white population in particular. In 1968
VORSTER refused to admit an English cricket touring team
which included a "Coloured" man from Cape Town who had settled in England. Two years later the South African cricket
tour to England was cancelled. As the country's sporting ties
diminished, so the government, in an attempt to restore them,
permitted special "multi-national" sports events, in which blacks
were allowed to play with whites. But the non-racial sports
movement within and outside the country continued to call for
the end of all racial discrimination in sport. As South African
sport became more integrated in the late 1970s, the non-racial
movement began to argue that non-racial sport could not be
played in an APARTHEID society. So South Africa remained
largely isolated in sport in the early 1980s. Visits by a South
African rugby team to New Zealand in 1981, and an English
cricket team to South Africa in 1982, both aroused great controversy.

SQUATTING. Term usually used for African cultivators in rural
areas who lived on, and had direct access to, white-owned
land, or for those people who built their own temporary shelters in urban areas.
    In the 19th century Africans often found themselves turned
into "squatters" as the land on which they lived passed into
white hands. In return for continued access to it, they then
usually had to pay rent in cash or kind, or work for the owner
for a period each year (labor tenancy), or do both. Some
squatters became such successful peasant farmers that white
farmers wanted their competition eliminated. As white farmers engaged in more commercialized farming, so they lobbied
for anti-squatting legislation. Various attempts to remove
Africans from white-owned land, such as the Cape Squatting
Act of 1879, or to limit the number of families per farm,
such as the Transvaal law of 1895 allowing only five African
families per farm, proved ineffective. The NATIVES LAND
ACT (1913) was in part an attempt to tackle the issue, and
was followed by the mass expulsion of squatters from farms
in the Free State. The Native Trust and Land Act (1936; see
HERTZOG BILLS) contained provisions to eliminate squatter-
peasants from white farmland, but they were not enforced
country-wide, and the agricultural lobby lost influence in the
SMUTS government of the early 1940s. It was not until after
the NATIONAL PARTY was returned to power in 1948 that the
first really effective machinery for removing squatters--the

Prevention of Illegal Squatting Act (1951)--enabled the ejection
of squatters to take place at a much greater pace (see MASS
REMOVALS).

Urban squatting resulted because people were unable to find
housing in the urban areas. Some POOR WHITES built their
own temporary shanties in the cities in the interwar depression
years, but the great bulk of squatters were blacks. Restrictions on the legal residence of African families in the urban
areas were an important cause of squatting (see INFLUX CON-
TROL). The urban African population trebled between 1921 and
1946, with the ratio of women to men increasing particularly
during WORLD WAR II. During the war years the African population of Johannesburg shot up by two-thirds, to reach almost
40,000 by 1946. The first major mass movement among urban
squatters emerged in 1944, when James "Sofasonke" (Zulu: "we
shall all die together") Mpanza (1889-1970), a charismatic figure, led homeless Africans to vacant ground in Orlando location, later part of SOWETO. There they built shacks of corrugated iron in what was then called Shantytown. Orlando had
been established as a model location during the early 1930s by
the Johannesburg municipality, which was embarrassed by the
squatter movement. Mpanza's 20,000 followers were mostly
given houses, and gradually his and the other squatter camps
around the city were destroyed as their populations were absorbed into the municipal housing provided. In the 1970s, the
most significant urban squatting occurred outside Cape Town,
where it was estimated in 1977 that there were between 120,000
and 180,000 "Coloured" squatters and 51,000 African squatters.
Because of the government's "COLOURED" LABOR PREFERENCE
POLICY, it was decided in the late 1960s not to build any more
family housing for Africans. Two large squatter camps--
Modderdam and Unibel--were bulldozed in 1977-78. For a time
it seemed that the 20,000 people living at CROSSROADS, many
of whom had come from Modderdam or Unibel, would suffer the
same fate. In April 1979 it was announced that Crossroads people with jobs and legal entitlement to urban residence would be
provided with new public houses. But the government proved
unable to prevent other Africans and "Coloureds" entering the
greater Cape Town area and squatting. One of the Johannesburg squatter leaders said in 1947 that the government was
"like a man who has a cornfield which is invaded by birds.
He chases the birds from one part of the field and they alight
in another part...."

STALLARD DOCTRINE. The Transvaal Local Government Commission of 1922, under the chairmanship of Colonel Stallard, declared that "The Native should only be allowed to enter urban
areas, which are essentially the White man's creation, when he
is willing to enter and to minister to the needs of the White
man and should depart therefrom when he ceases so to minister." The idea that the towns had been built by and for whites
lay behind subsequent urban African legislation and administration. (See also FAGAN COMMISSION; INFLUX CONTROL;
URBAN SEGREGATION.)

STAY-AWAYS.   The stay-away, which involved a general withdrawal
   of labor, not over a workplace dispute but for political purposes,
   emerged as a tactic of black resistance in December 1949, when
   it was one of the forms of action listed in the Program of Action adopted by the AFRICAN NATIONAL CONGRESS.   The first
   stay-away organized by the ANC took place on the Witwatersrand
   on 1 May 1950 as a protest against unjust laws, and was followed by a national stay-away on 26 June of that year.   The
   tactic was used, with varying degrees of success, in 1957,
   1958, 1960, 1961, 1976, and 1977.   In the most successful,
   500,000 workers stayed away from work for three days in 1976
   during the SOWETO REVOLT.

STOCKENSTRÖM, Andries (1792-1864).   An efficient landdrost (administrator) of Graaff-Reinet district from 1815 to 1828, he was
   commissioner-general of the Cape's eastern districts from 1828
   to 1933 (see SEPARATISM).   Having supported the passage of
   ORDINANCE 50, he established the KAT RIVER SETTLEMENT
   in 1829.   When he gave evidence to the select committee of the
   British House of Commons on the treatment of aborigines in
   1835, the colonists regarded his criticisms of them as betrayal.
   He returned to be a much reviled lieutenant-governor of the
   eastern districts from 1836 to 1839; from 1845 he lived in retirement on his farm Maasström near the modern town of Bed-
   ford.   In 1846 he played an important role in the frontier war
   of that year, and he served in the Cape parliament from its
   establishment in 1854 to March 1856.   No man in the 19th century Cape had greater breadth of vision, none gained the respect
   of a wider constituency, black as well as white.

STRIJDOM, Johannes Gerhardus (1893-1958).   Lawyer and farmer,
   who found himself, when he supported MALAN in his refusal to
   enter FUSION, the sole NATIONAL PARTY member of parliament in the Transvaal.   The "Lion of the North," as he was
   known, was chosen NP leader, and therefore Prime Minister,
   on Malan's retirement in 1954 because he was leader in the
   Transvaal and had built up the party there.   As Prime Minister
   he pushed through the removal of the "COLOURED" common
   roll franchise (see "COLOURED" VOTE ISSUE) and was an uncompromising believer in BAASSKAP.

STRIKES.   The earliest strike is thought to have been staged by
   "Coloured" boatmen and stevedores at the Cape Town harbor in
   1854 for an increase in wages to help compensate for a higher
   bread price.   Then African workers in Port Elizabeth harbor
   struck in 1856.   There have been very few cases of strikes in
   which both Africans and whites participated.
       The period 1907-22 was one of great militancy among labor
   on the Witwatersrand, with a series of major strikes on the
   mines.   The first such strike by white miners took place in
   1907 when the minewoners instructed the miners to super-
   vise three instead of two drills.   More than 4,000 struck and
   the army was called in.   Afrikaners were hired to take the

place of strikers, and the strike was broken. In 1913 19,000
white miners went on strike over union bargaining rights.
Again strong-arm tactics were used by both soldiers and the
police against the strikers. BOTHA and SMUTS intervened and
an agreement was reached. Following the strike, the Riotous
Assemblies Act (1914) was passed to give the government the
power to ban outdoor meetings and picketing. Massive force
was used against another strike in 1914 and the strike leaders
were deported. The most important strike by whites took
place in 1922. Faced with a crisis of profitability in the coal
and gold mines, the owners cut wages in the coal mines and
announced that they would do the same for the gold mines, and
also allow Africans to take over semi-skilled jobs from whites.
First the coalminers struck, then there was a general strike of
20,000 white workers on the gold mines. An armed revolt followed, put down by the army (see RAND REVOLT). White labor
was cowed, and then co-opted through the INDUSTRIAL CONCIL-
IATION ACT (1924).

The first strike by Africans on the gold mines took place in
1896. In 1913, 9,000 African workers on four gold mines struck
and the army was called in to force them back to work. A
subsequent commission of inquiry produced certain improvements in compound and work conditions. In 1918 the Johannesburg sanitation workers struck; arrested for breaking their contracts, the strikers were sentenced to two months' labor. Then
in 1920, at a time of rapid inflation and severe drought in the
rural areas, some 71,000 migrant workers on 21 gold mines
struck for higher wages. Again the army was called in, and
one by one the compounds were forced to resume work. Some
working conditions were improved, but the PASS laws tightened
up.

Massive strike action by Africans began again during WORLD
WAR II, when labor was in short supply. In 1942 some 8,000
workers in various Witwatersrand industries went out. A war
measure then outlawed strikes by Africans and provided severe
penalties for strike action. After the war, the African Mine
Workers' Union, formed in 1941, got over 60,000 workers on 19
mines to strike. The 1946 strike was forcibly broken up by the
police; twelve miners were killed. One of the consequences
was closer relations between the African trade union movement
and the ANC.

An Act of 1953 made strikes by Africans illegal, and in the
repressive post-SHARPEVILLE decade black labor was cowed.
But then from 1973 there was a dramatic change, which in part
followed a successful strike by Ovambo workers in NAMIBIA
the previous year. Early in 1973, seemingly spontaneously,
strikes spread from the brickmakers to textile and other workers in Durban; over a two-month period more than 61,000 workers were involved, and in most cases they were able to extract
increased wages. The government's first response was to try
to encourage the creation of liaison committees, but by the mid-
1970s, as major strike action continued, it was clear that such
committees were no substitute for representative and recognized

trade unions. Though Africans were allowed to form and join registered unions in 1979, strike action continued at roughly the 1973 level as South Africa entered the 1980s. In a number of cases strikers were effectively supported by a consumer boycott organized by community associations. (See also TRADE UNIONS; STAY-AWAYS; WIEHAHN COMMISSION; and under INDIANS.)

SWART GEVAAR (Afrikaans: "black peril"). Emotional appeal to whites, conjuring up visions of a danger similar to that the VOORTREKKERS were supposed to have faced during the GREAT TREK. In the eastern Cape, in Natal and on other 19th century frontiers, white settlers, insecure in the face of much larger numbers of Africans, regularly experienced "scares," moments of mass panic during which African attacks were feared. By the early 20th century, the only military threat was from an uprising such as BAMBATHA's REBELLION, and white fears expressed themselves in other ways. In 1910, for example, there was mass hysteria among the whites on the WITWATERSRAND and elsewhere over sexual assaults by Africans--male domestic servants were usually blamed--on white women. In the election of 1929, in particular, appeals were made to white voters on the basis of the alleged threat posed by those "soft" on Africans. SMUTS merely recommended that South Africa cooperate with other African territories, but he was dubbed "the apostle of a black KAFFIR state." Playing on the racial prejudices of the Afrikaner voters in this way, HERTZOG won the election. Similarly, in 1948 MALAN used "swart gevaar" tactics against the UNITED PARTY, which he suggested would permit Africans to settle in the urban areas in unlimited numbers. The United Party in turn used them in 1959 to suggest that VERWOERD's BANTUSTAN policy would give too much to Africans and was dangerous to white interests.

From 1917 the "black peril" had occasionally been linked to the "red menace," especially when the COMMUNIST PARTY was seen to be making headway in its work among Africans. After about 1977, appeals by the NATIONAL PARTY on "swart gevaar" lines diminished, and support sought instead on the basis of an alleged "total onslaught" against South Africa, spearheaded by the Soviet Union.

SWAZILAND. Under Sobhuza I (ruled c. 1815-c. 1838) and his son Mswati II (c. 1826-1865), a major state was constructed north of the ZULU kingdom, claiming the allegiance of both NGUNI and SOTHO-speakers, some of whom lived well to the south and west of the boundaries of modern Swaziland. In the mid 1840s Mswati, faced with continuing threats from the ZULU, entered into treaty relations with the VOORTREKKERS in the eastern Transvaal. After his death, the landlocked South African Republic (TRANSVAAL) searching for an outlet to the sea, claimed virtually all the Swazi country. The present western boundaries were demarcated during British occupation of the Transvaal, leaving much land inhabited by Swazis within that state. But

white encroachment did not stop there. After the discovery of
gold in north-west Swaziland in 1879, white prospectors sought
mineral and land concessions, which were freely granted by the
weak Swazi ruler. The Transvaal itself assumed the administration of Swaziland from 1895, leading the British to cut Swaziland off from the sea by the annexation of the adjoining THONGA
territory. When Britain took over Swaziland during the SOUTH
AFRICAN WAR, the Swazis themselves were left only 38 percent
of the territory; the rest had passed into the hands of individual
whites or the British Crown.

When the Transvaal obtained self-government, Swaziland became a HIGH COMMISSION TERRITORY (1907), and with the
two other such territories remained under direct British control
at the time of UNION. In 1968 Britain granted it independence.
The half million Swazi within South Africa were provided by the
South African government with their own "HOMELAND," KANG-
WANE. Many political refugees from South Africa fled to
Swaziland, but the Swaziland government came under pressure
not to allow guerillas to operate from its territory. In the late
1970s it deported many members of the PAN-AFRICANIST CON-
GRESS. Negotiations took place with the South African government on the incorporation of Kangwane within Swaziland, and
the addition to Swaziland of the Ngwavuma territory, the most
northerly part of KWAZULU, which would give Swaziland access
to the sea and a port at Kosi Bay.

THEAL, George McCall (1837-1919). The most prolific and probably most influential of all South African historians. Canadian-
born, he was an editor in BRITISH KAFFRARIA before starting
to write a general history of his adopted country, the first attempt at which he completed while teaching in Lovedale school.
He was then employed in various capacities by the Cape Native
Affairs Department, during which time he wrote the bulk of his
eleven-volume History. He was also given the office of Colonial
Historiographer. Among the works he prepared for publication
were 36 volumes in the Records of the Cape Colony series and
8 volumes of the Records of South-East Africa. While at Lovedale he had adopted missionary sympathies for people of color,
but after he moved to Cape Town he became increasingly racist in his writing. Though he proclaimed his objectivity, he
sought out evidence to justify white claims to occupy the bulk of
South Africa's land, and through his writings helped create the
mythology which underpinned apartheid ideology.

THOMPSON, Leonard Monteath (1916-). Educated at Rhodes and
Oxford universities, he joined the faculty of the UNIVERSITY of
Cape Town after World War II. There in the 1950s he wrote
his magisterial The Unification of South Africa (1960), which appeared as the 50th anniversary of UNION was celebrated. From
1961 he taught in the United States, first at UCLA and then,
from 1968, at Yale, where he is Professor of African History.

His publications include Survival in Two Worlds (1975), a biography of Moshweshwe of LESOTHO, but he is probably best
known as co-editor and co-author of The Oxford History of
South Africa, which appeared in two volumes in 1969 and 1971
(see further under HISTORIOGRAPHY).

THONGA (Tsonga, Tonga).   From a root meaning "east" and there-
    fore "people from the east." In the late 19th century Natal
    colonists used it for those BANTU-SPEAKING people north of
    the ZULU, to whom they had long paid tribute.   The
    small Thonga chiefdoms were, with the establishment of
    a Transvaal protectorate over the SWAZI kingdom in 1895, an-
    nexed by the BRITISH to prevent the Transvaal reaching the sea.
    The Swiss MISSIONARIES, and especially the pioneer ethnogra-
    pher Henri-Alexander Junod (1863-1934), extended use of the
    term to embrace all those people among whom they worked, and
    whom they claimed were linguistically related, whether south of
    DELAGOA BAY, in southern MOZAMBIQUE or in the eastern
    Transvaal, for considerable numbers of people from the Delagoa
    Bay hinterland had moved into the eastern Transvaal during the
    MFECANE.   The Swiss missionaries did much to impose a Thonga
    identity on people where none had existed before, and this
    process was carried much further by the South African govern-
    ment's BANTUSTAN policy, in terms of which a separate
    HOMELAND for the Transvaal Thonga was established (see
    GAZANKULU).
        The peoples of the Delagoa Bay hinterland hunted for ivory
    along the LIMPOPO RIVER and traded it with the PORTU-
    GUESE from at least the early 18th century.   They were the
    chief middlemen in the trade that grew between the Portuguese
    at the Bay and both the NGUNI and the SOTHO.   Their long in-
    volvement in such trade perhaps serves partly to explain why
    they, more than other African peoples, participated in MIGRANT
    LABOR at such an early date and on such an extensive scale.
    From the 1860s they began moving south through Zululand to
    seek work on the sugar plantations or elsewhere in Natal.   The
    Cape tapped this source and imported Thonga labor by sea; at
    the Cape they were known as "Mosbiekers" ("from Mozambique").
    Large numbers travelled overland to the DIAMOND fields in the
    1870s, where they were known as "Shangaans" (from Soshangane
    [c. 1790-1858], who had fled the ZULU country during the
    MFECANE to found an empire in southern MOZAMBIQUE).

TORCH COMMANDO.   Originally the War Veterans' Action Commit-
    tee.   A quasi-political ex-servicemen's organization, it staged
    a number of spectacular protests, some including torch-light
    processions, in May 1951 against the government's bill to re-
    move "Coloured" voters from the common roll (see "COLOURED"
    VOTE ISSUE).   Opening its membership to non-veterans, the
    Torch Commando had attracted, by late 1951, some 120,000
    members in 350 branches.   Though there were a few Afrikaners
    in the leadership, most of its members were English-speaking
    whites; whether "Coloureds" could become members was left

unclear, but it was made known they were not welcome. Besides opposing the government on the "Coloured" Vote Issue,
there was no agreement on what to do.   Some were for a new
NATIONAL CONVENTION to revise the constitution, others successfully pushed the Torch Commando into a united front with
the UNITED PARTY and the LABOUR PARTY. The NATIONAL
PARTY sought to depict the Torch Commando as dangerous and
unconstitutional.   After the NP, to the shock of Torch members,
won the general election of April 1953, some joined the new
LIBERAL PARTY, while others believed the Torch should dis-
band.   A very small majority of those at its congress in June
1953 decided to carry on, but by then the Torch was on its
deathbed, and attempts to revive it in 1955 came to nothing.

TRADE UNION CONGRESS OF SOUTH AFRICA (TUCSA).   Formed in
1954-55 as a federation of registered TRADE UNIONS, it was in
the early 1980s the largest such body in the country.   In 1956
it opposed legislation extending the JOB COLOR BAR, but excluded African unions from its membership, and SACTU was
set up as a rival body to mobilize the African working class.
In 1962 TUCSA decided to allow African unions to affiliate, but
under pressure from both the government and white unions those
that had joined were forced to withdraw in the late 1960s.   From
1974 TUCSA once again allowed African unions to affiliate.
Those that did so were mainly unions organized parallel to the
registered unions, and under white control.   Those on the left
criticized TUCSA for its narrow non-political approach.

TRADE UNIONS.   The earliest unions, formed among white immigrant workers, were craft unions.   Cape printers made an attempt to organize in 1838.   In 1881 typographical and carpen-
ters' unions were established in Cape Town.   Unionism greatly
increased with the mineral revolution.   An Artisans and Engine-
Drivers Association came into being on the DIAMOND fields in
1883 and a branch of the British Amalgamated Society of Engi-
neers was formed in 1886, the forerunner of the Amalgamated
Engineering Union established in 1920.   The Transvaal Miners'
Association brought together white miners in 1902, foreshadow-
ing the all-white Mine Workers' Union established in 1913.
     As mineowners sought to lower their labor costs by fragment-
ing craft operations and substituting semi-skilled or unskilled
Africans for whites, white trade unions were increasingly concerned not only to improve the economic position of their members against the employers and win union recognition, but also
to prevent Africans (or, for a few years, CHINESE) acquiring
jobs held by whites.   The two decades after the SOUTH AFRI-
CAN WAR were decades of great militancy by the white unions
(see STRIKES).   After the suppression of the RAND REVOLT,
however, trade union membership declined markedly and the
state stepped in to control industrial relations through the recognition of non-African unions and the provision of new conciliation
machinery (see INDUSTRIAL CONCILIATION ACT).
     With more and more Afrikaners joining the urban working

class, the AFRIKANER BROEDERBOND played a crucial role in
detaching them from English-controlled unions, or wresting control of unions from often corrupt English-speaking cliques. In
1933, for example, a new railwayman's union was set up for
Afrikaners. After a long battle, control of the powerful white
Mine Workers' Union passed into Afrikaner hands.

The first African trade unions of any significance were
formed at the end of World War I. The Industrial Workers of
Africa emerged out of classes run by the International Socialist
League (see LABOUR PARTY, COMMUNIST PARTY) for Africans in Johannesburg in 1917. Its slogan was Sifuna zonke
(Zulu: "we want all"), and it was hoped that it would grow into
a large union of the unskilled, along the lines of the American
union called the Industrial Workers of the World. But the police
infiltrated it, and it soon fell apart. The first large general
union on the African continent was the INDUSTRIAL AND COM-
MERCIAL WORKERS UNION, formed by Clements Kadalie in
1919.

In the late 1920s and early 1930s, as the ICU collapsed, a
number of short-lived industrial unions began to emerge among
African workers parallel to unions registered under the INDUS-
TRIAL CONCILIATION ACT. The latter included some unions
--the Garment Workers' Union most notably--that brought together Afrikaner and "Coloured" workers. It was not until
1956 that an amendment to the Industrial Conciliation Act prevented any further registration of such unions, but long before
that many of them had been hard hit by state action.

During World War II, when the African workforce in industry
grew rapidly and labor was short, African unionism entered a
militant phase, which culminated in the 1946 STRIKE, when the
African Mine Workers' Union, formed in 1941, brought out over
60,000 miners. The brutal suppression of the strike was followed by greater cooperation between the African trade union
movement and the ANC.

Between 1954 and 1960 40-odd unions affiliated with the
SOUTH AFRICAN CONGRESS OF TRADE UNIONS. But the
1960s was a decade of repression, with minimal union activity.
From the early 1970s, however, young whites, with close links
with the universities, helped organize unregistered unions, and
some of them suffered detentions and bannings as a result.
(The sixth trade unionist to die in DETENTION was a young
white trade union leader, who died in February 1982.) Gradually employers and the state were converted to the belief that
the best way to control African unionism was by recognizing it
and permitting the registration of African unions. This major
step, recommended by the WIEHAHN COMMISSION, was taken
in 1979. The new possibility of registration sparked off a
fierce debate within the labor movement, with some arguing that
because registration meant increased state control, it should
therefore be rejected. The Federation of South African Trade
Unions (FOSATU), formally constituted in 1979 but an outcome
of attempts to bring together unions formed during the strikes
of 1973 and after, sought to create a non-racial labor move-

ment, and encouraged the formation and affiliation of broadly
based industrial unions.   It was prepared to accept registration,
so long as its affiliated unions could be non-racial.   This was
conceded in 1981, during which year FOSATU made great gains,
such that it seemed that it might in time overtake TUCSA as
the largest trade union body in the country.   Of the unregistered unions, the most important in 1981 was probably the
South African Allied Workers' Union, which grew in size, especially in the eastern Cape and CISKEI, despite great police
harassment.

TRANSKEI (the land "across" the Kei River).   In the mid-19th century, "Transkei" usually meant immediately east of the Kei,
i.e., between that river and the Mbashe.   From the 1870s it
came to refer to the entire area from the Kei to the southern
border of Natal, and from the DRAKENSBERG to the Indian
ocean, 150 miles from southwest to northeast, 120 miles wide.
This area, annexed to the Cape in stages between 1879 and
1894, became a political entity through being incorporated within the Cape as a separate administrative unit.   The bulk, but
not all of it, became a BANTUSTAN in the 1950s, and was led
to "independence" in 1976.
    IRON AGE and probably BANTU-SPEAKING PEOPLE were
living on the Transkeian coast by the 7th century.   From the
16th century ship-wrecked European sailors told of mixed
farmers speaking NGUNI languages in the Transkeian area.   But
it is only from the 1820s that it begins to be possible to recreate a detailed history of the Transkei.   In that decade the small
northern chiefdoms were devastated by ZULU armies.   Disruption might have been greater had an intrusive group of NGWANE
under Matiwane (before 1800-1829) not been broken up at the
battle of Mbholompo in the central Transkei in 1828.   Large
numbers of refugees from the MFECANE--MFENGU, Bhaca and
others--settled in the Transkei at this time.   From the south,
MISSIONARY and trading networks began to spread across the
Kei.
    Though some XHOSA had moved well west of that river, the
senior branch remained east of it, where they were confronted
by British and colonial forces in the frontier wars of 1834-35,
1846-47 and 1850-53.   After the CATTLE KILLING (1856-57),
the Xhosa paramount Sarhili (c. 1814-1892) and his people were
ejected by the Cape colonial authorities from the land between
the Kei and the Mbashe.   They were subsequently allowed to return to a portion of it, but the remainder went to Mfengu and
other Africans from west of the Kei.   In the early 1860s, too,
a few thousand GRIQUA moved across the Drakensberg into what
was then called Nomansland, despite the fact that there were a
number of African groups there.   Establishing themselves as
overlords, the Griqua created a new Griqualand East.
    Once the Cape received responsible government (1872), it
began to throw an administration across the Kei, in the interests primarily of stability on its eastern border.   Hemmed in,
the eastern Xhosa under Sarhili took up arms against white

encroachment in a last desperate bid for continued independence
(Cape-Xhosa war, 1877-78). Colonial troops occupied their
country and a Cape administration was imposed. In 1880 a
large area of the Transkei which had come under Cape rule
peacefully in the 1870s went into rebellion. When the rebellion
had been put down, some of the land sequestered from the rebels fell into white hands. So did much of East Griqualand,
where after annexation most of the Griqua with individual titles
were persuaded to sell them. When the Transkei was given two
seats in the Cape parliament in 1887, there were enough whites
resident there to form a majority of voters in both constituencies. Otherwise, as the Transkeian territories were brought
under Cape rule, they were administered separately from the
rest of the colony, as an African RESERVE. Following the
GLEN GREY ACT (1894), twenty-six elected district councils
were set up. In 1931 these were integrated into a United
Transkeian General Council, commonly known as the Bunga,
which met annually in the Transkeian capital, Umtata. In its
early years the Bunga was a forum for the expression of views
of western educated Africans, but they became increasingly disillusioned with its powerlessness. By the 1950s it was overwhelmingly composed of government-paid chiefs and headmen,
and in November 1955 it voted itself out of existence.

Bantustan

Because the Transkei formed the largest single block of African-
held land in South Africa, and had a separate administrative and
council system, it formed the obvious pacesetter in VERWOERD's
Bantustan strategy. Its 1963 constitution, drafted in Pretoria,
provided that the majority of seats in the Transkeian legislature
were held by chiefs and not elected members. In the first general election (1963) most elected seats went to opponents of
Kaiser MATANZIMA, Pretoria's protégé, but with the help of
the chiefs he became First Minister. Emergency regulations,
renewed annually, provided for DETENTION WITHOUT TRIAL
and were frequently used by Matanzima against his opponents.
Gradually he consolidated his personal power and the dominant
position of his Transkei National Independence Party. In the
mid 1970s he accepted the offer of "independence," after the
South African government agreed to transfer the districts of
Glen Grey and Herschel from the Ciskei and also to cede Port
St. John's, which had not been included in the Bantustan. Separately annexed to the Cape in 1884, Port St. John's had then
become an integral part of the Transkeian territories, but was
by the 1950s a popular holiday resort for whites. Its natural
harbor, used by small commercial vessels in the 19th century,
had become so silted up that it could no longer be used.
   The Transkei became "independent" in 1976 with a per capita
income of R176 per annum and a per capita domestic product of
only R70 per annum. Over 80 percent of its budget was provided by Pretoria. Financial aid from Pretoria continued even

after the Transkei broke diplomatic ties with South Africa in
1978 over its claim to Griqualand East, which was at that time
being transferred from the Cape to Natal. Though Griqualand
East remained outside the Transkei, Matanzima restored diplomatic ties in 1980. Despite Transkeian protests, the South
African government insisted that all Xhosa not attached to another Bantustan automatically became Transkeian citizens and
lost their South African citizenship.

TRANSVAAL. (The land "across" (north of) the Vaal river). Much
of the land between the Vaal and the LIMPOPO rivers was disrupted during the MFECANE. In the southern portion Mzilikazi
(c. 1790-1868) incorporated large numbers of SOTHO-speakers
into his NDEBELE STATE. In the early 1830s, when its capital was near modern Pretoria, it had a population of perhaps
20, 000. Having moved across to the western Transvaal, Mzilikazi was attacked both by the ZULU and by VOORTREKKERS in
1836-1837, and as a result he led his people away to the north.
By then the revival of the PEDI kingdom was well underway,
and many THONGA refugees were establishing themselves in the
east of the region.
    The Voortrekkers settled in isolated communities scattered
over a vast area which had been thinly inhabited by BANTU-
SPEAKERS for perhaps a thousand years. Potchefstroom in
the west, founded in 1838, was for long the largest European
town. Separate Voortrekker republics were established at
Utrecht, Lydenburg and in the Zoutpansberg (Dutch: Saltpan
mountains) in the north. Though Britain recognized the independence of the whites north of the Vaal in 1852 (Sand River
Convention), it was only gradually that those scattered groups
were effectively brought under the central authority of the South
African Republic, as the Transvaal was known from 1858. It
took much longer still for white control to become effective
over all the African peoples living in the 110, 000 square miles
between the Vaal and the Limpopo. Whites were ousted from
the Zoutpansberg, and the trading center of Schoemansdal, in
the late 1860s, and it was not until just before the SOUTH
AFRICAN WAR that the last African resistance in the north was
crushed (see VENDA).
    In the mid 1870s the Transvaal state was weak, unstable,
poorly administered, and bankrupt. Its inability to defeat the
PEDI was used to justify the BRITISH annexation of 1877.
SHEPSTONE had been authorized by the Colonial Secretary to
see whether annexation was possible, in the interests of CON-
FEDERATION. After running up the Union Jack in Church
Square, Pretoria--named after the trekker leader Andries
Pretorius (1798-1853) and capital of the republic from 1860--
Shepstone became administrator of the new possession. The
British army, having defeated the ZULU, with whom the Trans-
vaal had been at odds over disputed territory, conquered the
PEDI. Once these African enemies had been dealt with, the
Transvalers rose to throw off the British yoke (see TRANS-
VAAL WAR OF INDEPENDENCE, 1880-1881). The Pretoria

Convention (August 1881) returned self-government to the republicans, but Britain made sure they could not ally with a foreign power or acquire direct access to the sea: expansion westward (see BECHUANALAND), northwards (see RHODES; ZIMBABWE) and eastward (see SWAZILAND) was blocked in turn. From the time of the 1880-1881 war, Britain feared that pan-Africaner sentiment, fuelled by the Transvaal, might unite sufficient white South Africans to pose a threat to continued imperial rule in the sub-continent.

The Transvaal's history was fundamentally transformed by the discovery of the main GOLD reef on the WITWATERSRAND in 1885. Britain feared the Transvaal would use the new wealth to forge a union of states outside the Empire. Both political and economic considerations led the British (see MILNER) to press matters until the point at which the Transvaal government, seeking initial military advantage, began the SOUTH AFRICAN WAR. In 1900 the Union Jack was again run up in Church Square. After the war Milner hoped both to outnumber the Transvaal Afrikaners by introducing thousands of immigrants of British descent, and to undermine Afrikaner culture through an English-medium educational system. But the devastation caused during the war, and the difficulties encountered getting the mines going again, helped foil such plans. Fundamental adjustments to white-black relations were not considered. The 1858 Grondwet (constitution) of the South African Republic had declared that there was to be no equality in church or state; only white males could vote or hold office. In the TREATY OF VEREENIGING (1902) the British promised not to extend the franchise to blacks before the Transvaal regained self-rule. So the racial tradition was maintained, and at the NATIONAL CONVENTION Transvaal delegates opposed any extension of the Cape's non-racial FRANCHISE.

After 1910 the Transvaal played an increasingly dominant role in the political and economic life of the country. Pretoria became the administrative capital in 1910; JOHANNESBURG was its commercial and financial heart. The Transvaal was in many ways the pacesetter for the rest of the country, where, for example, SHARPEVILLE and the SOWETO REVOLT occurred and where, in the early 1980s, most support was to be found for the extreme right in white politics (see CONSERVATIVE PARTY; HERSTIGTE NASIONALE PARTY; TREURNICHT).

TRANSVAAL WAR OF INDEPENDENCE (1880-81). Sometimes known as the first Boer or Anglo-Boer war or, in Afrikaans, the first freedom war, it was a short conflict in which the Transvaal Afrikaners sought to recover the independence they had lost with the BRITISH annexation of April 1877 (see TRANSVAAL). Over three years of peaceful protest and petition having failed, they took up arms in December 1880. Their strategy was to besiege the British garrisons in Potchefstroom, Pretoria, and other towns, and to prevent British troops entering the Transvaal from Natal. The fiercest fighting took place in Natal, and the Transvalers scored a series of victories,

culminating in that at the mountain of Majuba (February 1881).
By then the British had decided to give them back a large
measure of self-rule. KRUGER remembered the Transvaal's
success on the battlefields in 1881 when he decided to fight in
1899 (see SOUTH AFRICAN WAR).

Self-rule "subject to the suzerainty of Her Majesty" was restored by the Convention of Pretoria (1881). Foreign relations
remained under British control, and the Transvaal was forbidden to alter its boundaries without British consent. A British
veto over African legislation was removed by the Convention of
London (1884).

TREASON TRIAL (Regina v. F. Adams and Others). Following the
Congress of the People, which had adopted the FREEDOM CHAR-
TER, the police suddenly arrested 156 people in December 1956
and held them pending an arraignment for high treason. They
included AFRICAN NATIONAL CONGRESS leaders (see LUTHULI;
MANDELA) and prominent whites in the CONGRESS ALLIANCE.
The number of accused was gradually reduced as charges were
withdrawn. The remainder were acquitted in March 1961 at the
end of the marathon trial, when the judge found that there was
no evidence that the ANC had plotted the violent overthrow of
the state.

TREATY OF VEREENIGING. The British terms for ending the
SOUTH AFRICAN WAR were discussed by Boer representatives
at Vereeniging, on the north side of the Vaal river, in May
1902. When the delegates voted to accept the terms--by 54 to
6--the formal signing of the peace treaty took place at the British military headquarters in Pretoria on 31 May 1902. All
Boers were to lay down their arms and accept British rule.
Self-government was promised "as soon as circumstances permitted," and clause 8 of the treaty provided that "the question
of granting the franchise to natives would not be settled before
the introduction of representative government." This in effect
ensured the maintenance of white supremacy in the ex-republics.

TREKBOERS (Dutch: semi-nomadic [frontier] farmers). Term used
for the Dutch-speaking sheep and cattle farmers who moved out
of the southwestern Cape, with its Mediterranean climate, from
the end of the 17th century, into the drier interior where extensive pastoralism and hunting were the only possible modes
of production. By 1730 they were well beyond the area of winter rainfall. The main line of advance was then eastward,
parallel to the mountain ranges, to the Fish River, where they
met BANTU-SPEAKING people in the 1770s. Dispossessing the
KHOISAN people, who were killed, ejected, or allowed to remain as SQUATTERS or laborers, the trekboers took 6,000
acre farms for themselves. Some moved their herds and their
ox-wagons around or across the barren Great KARROO and beyond the colony's boundaries. This movement continued into
the GREAT TREK period. But the trekboers, unlike the VOOR-
TREKKERS, still regarded themselves as colonial subjects, and

did not deliberately break with the Cape.   (See also NEUMARK
THESIS.)

TREURNICHT, Dr Andries (1921-   ).   An arch-conservative, nick-
named "Dr NO, " for his rejection of any reform of apartheid.
A minister of the DUTCH REFORMED CHURCH, he helped persuade his church to reject the COTTESLOE declaration.   He
then edited Hoofstad, a Pretoria NATIONAL PARTY daily newspaper, before entering parliament in 1971.   Though his views
were not very different from those of the HERSTIGTE NASION-
ALE PARTY (HNP), he remained within the NP, insisting that
the NP was the vehicle of Afrikaner nationalism and the means
to protect Afrikaner identity through its policy of SEPARATE
DEVELOPMENT.   A man of personal charm and an outstanding
orator, he was made a Deputy Minister for BANTU EDUCATION
in 1976.   His decision to stand firm on the use of Afrikaans as
a teaching medium in African schools in the southern Transvaal
helped spark off the SOWETO REVOLT.   Elected leader of the
NP in the Transvaal in November 1978, he exercised a powerful right-wing influence in the party, resisting BOTHA's steps
to remove PETTY APARTHEID and co-opt "Coloureds" and Indians.   In February 1982, when Botha spoke of sharing power
with "Coloureds" and Indians, he led a revolt against the Prime
Minister and was forced out of the party.   In March he was
elected leader of the new CONSERVATIVE PARTY.

TSWANA (Bechuana).   SOTHO-speaking people.   Their name, first
recorded in the form "Moetjooaanas" in 1779, is of uncertain
origin.   In the early 19th century it was used for all those people today known as SOTHO, but as white settlers occupied the
central portions of the highveld, it was limited to those now
known as the western Sotho: the people of the northern Cape,
the western Transvaal, and the former BECHUANALAND.
Whites first made direct contract with the Tswana in 1801,
when a party from Cape Town visited the southernmost group,
the Tlhaping ("fish people") north of the ORANGE RIVER.
MISSIONARIES worked among the Tlhaping and the Rolong further north before the MFECANE; Kuruman was the most famous
Tswana mission.   The Tswana were probably saved massive
disruption when the marauding peoples driven from what is now
the eastern Free State into Tswana country were defeated at the
battle of Dithakong in 1823, a turning-point in the history of the
Mfecane (see also GRIQUA).   Recent work has suggested that
the increasing participation of the Tswana in grain production
for export in the decades after the Mfecane helped create a
semi-feudal society.   Some of those Tswana in the DIAMOND
area who had been brought under white rule in the early 1870s
participated in a rebellion against that rule in 1878.   Others
were given "British protection" when the ROAD TO THE NORTH
was annexed in 1885.   The annexation of Bechuanaland has-
tened the process which led the Tswana by the early 20th century into extensive involvement in MIGRANT LABOR.   The
Tswana north of the Molopo river were given their independence

by Britain in 1966; in the 1970s those within South Africa itself
found themselves citizens of BOPHUTHATSWANA, a BANTUSTAN
given its "independence" in 1977.

UITLANDERS (Afrikaans: "outlanders," "foreigners"). Term applied to non-Afrikaner whites in the Transvaal before the
SOUTH AFRICAN WAR. MILNER and other British officials
cited KRUGER's treatment of the Uitlanders as justification for
British actions against his state. After 1882 the Transvaal
franchise laws were progressively tightened, making it more
and more difficult for the new white immigrants, who poured in
after the discovery of GOLD, to obtain citizenship and the vote.
To the Afrikaners the new immigrants were brash, materialis-
tic, and their culture alien. No one knew how many of them
there were in the Transvaal in the late 1890s. Both Milner
and Kruger believed that if they were enfranchised Afrikaner
domination might be upset. In 1899 however Kruger was prepared to grant them the vote after seven years' residence.
This was not acceptable to MILNER, who called the Uitlanders
"political helots." After the war the franchise was extended to
them, but, despite massive Boer losses in the war and further
immigration from Britain, the Afrikaners remained a clear majority, and an Afrikaner party, HET VOLK, triumphed in the
elections of 1907.

UMKHONTO WE SIZWE (Xhosa: "Spear of the Nation"). Under-
ground military wing of the AFRICAN NATIONAL CONGRESS.
A group of leading CONGRESS ALLIANCE figures, including
Nelson MANDELA and members of the COMMUNIST PARTY,
decided in 1961 that, non-violent tactics having failed, SABO-
TAGE and guerilla war should be organized. Umkhonto was
responsible for numerous acts of sabotage carried out between
December 1961 and mid 1963, when its headquarters in the
Rivonia suburb of Johannesburg was raided and the Umkhonto
leadership arrested. Mandela was taken from jail to join the
other accused, and he admitted to having helped form Umkhonto.
Those tried--four of those arrested at Rivonia having escaped
from jail--were all sentenced to life imprisonment.
    After over ten years of inactivity within South Africa, Umk-
honto launched a major sabotage and guerilla campaign in the
late 1970s. It obtained thousands of highly-motivated recruits
from those who fled the police repression of 1976-77 (see
SOWETO REVOLT) and training camps were established in
ANGOLA, MOZAMBIQUE, and Tanzania. From 1978 armed
guerillas were regularly infiltrated into South Africa. The
ANC claimed that an Umkhonto unit clashed with the South
African Defence Force in the western Transvaal in August
1978. A number of the infiltrators were captured and tried.
The most spectacular sabotage operation was carried out
against the synthetic oil (SASOL) plant in 1980; in retaliation
the South African forces raided the ANC military headquarters

at Matola in Mozambique in January 1981. Though Umkhonto was said to have claimed responsibility for bomb blasts in shopping areas in Durban, East London, and Port Elizabeth in 1981, the main targets remained police stations, government offices or state-owned utilities.

UNION. For BRITISH attempts to unite South Africa in the 19th century see GREY; CONFEDERATION. After the SOUTH AFRICAN WAR, MILNER initiated a number of schemes to promote closer ties between the South African states: the railroad networks of the two ex-republics were amalgamated; an Inter-Colonial Council formed; a South African Native Affairs (LAGDEN) COMMISSION appointed (1903) and a South African Customs Union created (1903). While Lord Selborne (1859-1942), Milner's successor as HIGH COMMISSIONER, hoped that a federated South Africa would attract large-scale British immigration, BOTHA and SMUTS sought a united South Africa less subject to British interference. A discussion paper known as the Selborne Memorandum was issued to the colonial governments in 1907 and then published and widely debated. Written by Lionel Curtis (see KINDERGARTEN) at the High Commissioner's invitation, it urged that unity would bring political stability and promote economic progress. Unification seemed likely to pull the country out of the recession from which it had suffered from 1903 (see BUSINESS CYCLES) and eliminate the tensions that disagreements on customs and railway tariffs had produced. The confidence of Natal's whites in their ability to control their large African population had been shaken by the BAMBATHA REBELLION. A NATIONAL CONVENTION (1908-09) agreed that the four colonies should unite, and that South Africa should be a unitary state and not a federation. The proposals emanating from the National Convention were approved by the four colonies, then incorporated in a South Africa Bill, which went through the British parliament. The Union of South Africa was inaugurated on 31 May 1910, eight years to the day after the signing of the TREATY OF VEREENIGING.

A delegation of white liberals and blacks travelled to London to protest the color-bar in the Union constitution (see CONSTITUTIONAL CHANGE), but generally Union was hailed as a great achievement. It was clearly to Britain's advantage for South Africa to be one large state, able to defend itself, yet within the Empire, and in which there was hope of English-Afrikaner reconciliation and the prospect that the interests of finance and mining capital would be promoted. Nor were the Africans entirely overlooked. The Liberal government in Britain hoped that a strong Union would be in African interests and that the Cape's non-racial FRANCHISE--protected by the "entrenched clauses" of the constitution, which provided that it could be altered only by a vote of two-thirds of both houses of parliament sitting together--would in time be extended to the other provinces. It was made clear that the wish of the people of the HIGH COMMISSION TERRITORIES should be considered when the question of incorporating them came up. Liberal

historians have condemned the choice of a unitary rather than a
federal constitution for so heterogeneous a society, but it was
believed a unitary one would prove easier to work and would
provide the necessary strong government. Had South Africa
not been a close union, the white Southern Rhodesians might
have agreed to join it in the 1920s (see SOUTH AFRICAN EX-
PANSIONISM; ZIMBABWE).

UNIONIST PARTY. Name taken by the Cape PROGRESSIVE PARTY
shortly before union, to indicate its support for a federal union.
An English-speaking party, it became the main opposition in the
first Union parliament. After the formation of the NATIONAL
PARTY, Louis BOTHA became increasingly dependent on it, and
it was eventually absorbed by the SOUTH AFRICAN PARTY in
1920. Its lineal successor was the pro-British DOMINION PAR-
TY founded in 1934.

UNITED NATIONS. SMUTS was the author of the preamble to the
UN Charter, and South Africa a founder member of the world
body, but in that forum it soon became the most criticized
country of all. At the inaugural session in 1946, the Indian
delegation brought South Africa's treatment of its INDIAN minority before the General Assembly, which also rejected South
Africa's plea for the incorporation of South West Africa/
NAMIBIA. From 1952 the whole APARTHEID system came
under regular attack, despite South African objections that it
was a domestic matter and fell under article 2(7) of the UN
Charter, designed to protect a member from interference by
others in matters of domestic jurisdiction. After SHARPE-
VILLE, criticism was more strident, with a UN Special Committee Against Apartheid being appointed in 1962. That year
the General Assembly recommended that member states break
all ties with South Africa, including trade links. The following
year the Security Council imposed a non-mandatory arms embargo. Gradually South Africa left the various UN agencies--
Unesco in 1956, the ILO in 1961, the World Health Organisation in 1965.
     In 1966 the General Assembly voted to terminate South
Africa's mandate over South West Africa. After that, South
Africa's continued occupation of the territory, and its refusal
to acknowledge UN supervision of it, became a matter to which
the UN devoted much attention. In 1974 the General Assembly
rejected the credentials of the South African delegation, preventing its speaking, but South Africa remained a member of
the world body. Calls for mandatory economic sanctions
against South Africa came before the Security Council on a
number of occasions, but were vetoed by the Western members,
the United States, Britain and France. In 1977, however,
after BIKO's death and the clampdown on black organizations
(see BANNING), the Security Council did impose a mandatory
arms embargo against South Africa (see MILITARY). (See also
SANCTIONS.)

UNITED PARTY (UP) (1934-1977).   The United South African National Party emerged from the FUSION of HERTZOG'S NA-
TIONAL PARTY (NP) and SMUTS' SOUTH AFRICAN PARTY.
Its first major crisis came in September 1939, when Hertzog
and his supporters left it over South Africa's entry into WORLD
WAR II.   Then it lost power in 1948, despite winning a majority of votes, because of the urban concentration of its supporters, the weighting of rural constituencies, and the way delimi-
tation of the constituencies had been applied.   This shock defeat,
followed in short succession by the deaths of Jan Hofmeyr (1894-
1948), Smuts' deputy, and then of Smuts himself (1950), left the
party in great disarray.   It continued to outpoll the NP until the
1961 election but, as it lost seats in successive elections, it lost
confidence in its ability ever to return to power.   Committed to
white supremacy, it offered only the pre-1948 pattern of race
relations, the possibility of a few whites representing Africans
in parliament, and "white leadership with justice."   It became,
increasingly, a mainly English-speaking party.
    In an attempt to make itself more acceptable to the white
electorate, it moved closer to the NP, and even began to attack
that party from the right.   In response to VERWOERD'S SEPA-
RATE DEVELOPMENT vision in 1959, the right-wing in the UP
saw an opportunity to brand him a negrophile and urged the party congress to oppose the grant of more land for Africans if
such land was to be appended to potentially independent BANTU-
STANS.   The more liberally minded in the party, who included
many of its ablest debaters and intellectuals, could take its conservative drift no longer, and broke away (see PROGRESSIVE
PARTY).   The UP then enjoyed greater internal unanimity for a
time, but its mediocre leadership and ambivalent policies continued to alienate those on both its left and its right.   Another
break-away to the left took place in February 1975.   The following year six right-wing members of parliament split off to
form the South African Party, while six others formed a Committee for a United Opposition, which soon merged with the
Progressive Party.   The remaining UP members formed a New
Republic Party to the right of the Progressive Party, to which
Sir de Villiers Graaff, the long-time UP leader, gave his support.   That finally brought about the demise of the UP.

UNIVERSITIES.   The origins of the University of Cape Town lie in
the South African College, a private venture begun in 1829 to
provide education at a wide range of different levels.   In 1873
a non-teaching university was set up to offer examinations for
university degrees; by 1910 it administered eight constituent
colleges in the four colonies.   Cape Town and Stellenbosch were
the first of these to receive independent charters (1916, 1918).
The University of the Cape of Good Hope was transformed into
the University of South Africa, with headquarters in Pretoria.
As the colleges gained independence as universities, it became
a teaching university, but offered degrees through correspondence only.
    The older Afrikaans-medium universities emerged out of

what had been English-medium colleges: Stellenbosch, near
Cape Town; Pretoria, founded after the SOUTH AFRICAN WAR;
and Orange Free State, at Bloemfontein. The Potchefstroom
University for Christian Higher Education played an especially
important role in the development of AFRIKANER NATIONAL-
ISM after 1919. In the mid 1960s a dual medium English-
Afrikaans university was founded at Port Elizabeth and the Rand
Afrikaans University was established for Afrikaners in Johannes-
burg.

The four English-speaking universities--Cape Town, Witwatersrand (in Johannesburg), Rhodes (in Grahamstown), and
Natal, with its campuses in Durban and Pietermaritzburg--
suffered from an emigration of many of their leading staff for
political reasons after 1960, and, with South Africa's increasing isolation, their inability to attract people from other countries to South Africa. They remained, together with the
English-speaking churches, the main voice of white liberal opposition to the apartheid regime. (See also NATIONAL UNION
OF SOUTH AFRICAN STUDENTS.)

Prior to 1960 the universities of Cape Town and the Witwatersrand and the University of Natal Medical School admitted
black students on merit. The numbers were never large. In
1959 legislation, which the "open universities" strongly opposed,
provided that blacks could henceforth only attend such universities by permit. Four new ethnic universities were established:
the University of the North, for SOTHO, THONGA, and VENDA
speakers, the University College of Zululand for ZULU speakers, the University College of the Western Cape, for "COL-
OUREDS," and the University of Durban-Westville (as it became) for INDIANS. At the same time, FORT HARE was taken
over by the Government as a university for XHOSA speakers.
In the late 1970s it became somewhat easier for blacks to obtain permits to attend the Universities of Cape Town and the
Witwatersrand, and a few blacks were admitted for graduate
work at some of the Afrikaans-medium universities. The non-
residential University of South Africa admitted all races as
students, but examinations were given and degrees awarded on
a segregated basis. With the "independence" of TRANSKEI and
BOPHUTHATSWANA, new universities were established in those
territories; they were non-racial, but had very few non-African
students. In 1981 a new university, called Vista, was founded
for Africans in the metropolitan areas.

The black "tribal colleges," despite the repressive atmos-
phere on their campuses, became centers of dissidence in the
late 1960s and 1970s, with BLACK CONSCIOUSNESS finding
wide support among their students (see SOUTH AFRICAN STU-
DENTS ORGANISATION).

URBAN SEGREGATION. It was by custom rather than law that
Africans lived in LOCATIONS on the perimeter of Cape towns
in the 19th century. In the Transvaal INDIANS were the first
to have areas in towns set aside for their exclusive occupation
(1885). Both in CAPE TOWN and in PORT ELIZABETH the

advent of bubonic plague in the early years of the 20th century
was used as an excuse to move Africans out of the town. Some
capitalists opposed this because they wanted Africans to live
close to their work, but most saw considerable advantage in the
establishment of African locations: they served as labor pools;
the government took over the provision of housing; and locations
made possible tight control of the workforce. Besides fearing
the spread of disease (the "sanitation syndrome") many whites
saw towns as essentially the creations of the white man, in
which Africans had no permanent place--the philosophy embodied
in the STALLARD DOCTRINE (1922). Amenities for Africans
in the urban areas should therefore be minimal, to discourage
permanent settlement.

After UNION, governments planned to complement the NA-
TIVES LAND ACT with legislation for urban African administration, but this was not achieved until the 1923 Native Urban
Areas Act. The original Bill provided for freehold title to be
given in locations, as the LAGDEN COMMISSION had recommended in 1905. But under pressure from Stallard and HERT-
ZOG, SMUTS dropped that provision, ignoring African protest.
The Act empowered local authorities to establish locations, financed from separate revenue accounts, which could be funded
from the sale of "KAFFIR beer" (see DURBAN SYSTEM). No
restrictions were placed on Africans entering urban areas to
seek work, but in 1937 a 14-day limit was introduced, which in
1952 was reduced to 72 hours (see INFLUX CONTROL). The
1952 amendment created, in its important Section 10, statutory
rights for Africans to remain in urban areas if they were born
there or were qualified by long employment or long residence
there. After 1968 these rights were whittled away, by administrative fiat or new legislation relating to citizenship. In the
late 1970s 99-year leasehold was introduced for Africans in urban areas outside the western Cape (because of the "COLOURED"
LABOR PREFERENCE POLICY there).

INDIAN acquisition of property in DURBAN was restricted by
legislation in 1943 and 1946. In terms of the GROUP AREAS
ACT (1950), separate residential and sometimes commercial
ghettos were established for occupation by people of different
race classification. Most of those moved forcibly under this
legislation were "Coloureds" and Indians. A Natives Resettlement Act (1954) gave the government the powers it needed to
move Africans from JOHANNESBURG's western suburbs, where
many had acquired freehold title, to SOWETO (see MASS RE-
MOVALS).

URBANIZATION. In 1910 only a quarter of the total population
lived in towns; by 1980, 54 percent was urbanized, and the figure would have been greater had Africans been able to move
freely within the country (cf. INFLUX CONTROL). Before the
discovery of GOLD, AFRIKANER and AFRICAN urbanization
was negligible. The process of industrialization, the growth of
commercial AGRICULTURE, overcrowding and impoverishment
in the RESERVES, and the devastation left by the SOUTH

AFRICAN WAR, all impelled African SQUATTERS and white
BYWONERS to the towns.   By 1904, 53 percent of whites were
urban residents.   Between then and 1926 the proportion of the
total population living in urban areas rose by 55 percent.   The
great depression of the early 1930s (see BUSINESS CYCLES)
was probably more important in promoting Afrikaner than African urbanization.   During World War II jobs were available for
Africans in the towns (see, e. g. , MANUFACTURING INDUSTRY)
and influx controls were relaxed.   Between 1936 and 1946 the
African population in the urban areas increased by over half a
million or 47 percent, and by 1946 there were almost as many
Africans as whites in the cities.   Because of strict influx control provisions, the rate of African urban growth declined from
the late 1940s.   In 1980 there were 4. 9 million Africans in the
urban areas, 37 percent of the total African population, and
that 4. 9 million constituted roughly half the total urban population.   In that year 90 percent of Asians were urbanized (constituting 5. 5 percent of the total urban population); 77 percent of
"Coloureds" (15 percent of the urban population); 88 percent of
whites (30 percent of the urban population).

VELD.   DUTCH-AFRIKAANS term, now taken into English, for the
open grassland country that characterizes much of the interior
of South Africa.   The central portion of the interior plateau,
the highveld, became the chief pastoral and maize (corn)-
growing belt; the land east of the escarpment (see DRAKENS-
BERG) in the Transvaal and along the LIMPOPO RIVER--a hot,
humid region unsuited for mixed farming--the VOORTREKKERS
called the lowveld.

VENDA.   (1. people) BANTU-SPEAKERS, whose language is intermediate between Shona, the majority language in ZIMBABWE,
and SOTHO.   The royal lineage recognized today probably moved
south across the LIMPOPO RIVER in the 17th century.   Noted
as ironworkers and miners of copper, the Venda retained close
relations with people north of the Limpopo.   Those under Mak-
hado (d. 1895) and Mphephu (c. 1868-1924), put up lengthy resistance to white encroachment, especially after they had obtained large supplies of guns in exchange for ivory.   When the
TRANSVAAL finally ended this resistance in 1898, Mphephu
withdrew into Zimbabwe, returning when the British ruled the
Transvaal.
    (2. BANTUSTAN) Small state south of the Limpopo, separated
from Mozambique only by a strip of the Kruger National Park.
When given its "independence" in September 1979, its population
was said to be over 500,000.   President Patrick Mphephu had
himself installed as paramount (a traditional office) shortly before "independence."   The opposition Venda Independence Party
had won a majority of the elected seats in both the 1973 and
the 1978 elections, but Mphephu retained power thanks to support from the nominated members and by using emergency

powers to imprison opponents. In 1982 over 60 percent of Venda's economically active male population worked outside the Bantustan, mostly on the WITWATERSRAND.

VERKRAMPTES (Afrikaans: "narrow-minded ones"). Term coined by an Afrikaner journalist in 1966 to describe ultra conservative Afrikaner nationalists, as distinct from those he called "verligtes," "enlightened ones." Verkramptes opposed rapprochement with English-speakers, the entry of foreign sports teams if they included black members, large-scale immigration, especially of Roman Catholic southern Europeans, and the exchange of diplomats with black African states. Some verkramptes joined the HERSTIGTE NASIONALE PARTY in 1969, others remained within the NATIONAL PARTY and left to join the CONSERVATIVE PARTY in 1982. There was more support for verkrampte ideas in the Transvaal than in the Cape, and more among lower class whites than among Afrikaner business interests, who tended to be "verlig." But the "verligtes" sought only minor adjustments to policy, adjustments which they hoped would help ensure the continuation of white domination.

VERWOERD, Hendrik Frensch (1901-66). An immigrant from the Netherlands at the age of two, he obtained a brilliant academic record and then taught at the University of Stellenbosch before becoming editor of Die Transvaler, a new NATIONAL PARTY daily newspaper in Johannesburg (1937). He played a major role in rebuilding the NP in the Transvaal, and advocated republicanism in his newspaper. Though defeated in the 1948 election, he was appointed to the Senate and in the 1950s he was responsible for the BANTU EDUCATION ACT and other key APARTHEID laws.

On STRIJDOM's death in 1958, Verwoerd became Prime Minister even though he had only been in the Assembly a few months. The favorite son of the Transvaal, he was recognized as a man of formidable personality and as the architect of much of the great plan for the apartheid future. Though in 1951 he had rejected the idea of independence for African areas, he changed his mind and from 1959 spoke of independent "HOMELANDS" (see also BANTUSTANS) as the goal of SEPARATE DEVELOPMENT. Obsessive about color, and fanatical in his devotion to his grand design, he believed that any deviation from maximum racial separation in social and political life, however trivial, would endanger his whole system. One concession would lead to another, and so to black majority rule. Nationalists should therefore stand "like walls of granite" in defense of their policy. His quick recovery from an attempted assassination in 1960, when a white farmer with a record of mental instability fired two shots into his head, was seen by his followers as the hand of God. After bringing about the REPUBLIC in 1961 he was hero-worshipped. He hoped that the republic would provide a new framework for white unity, in which Afrikaners would be dominant, but English speakers would participate, for he believed that loyalty to the British

Crown had divided English-speakers from Afrikaners.
His apartheid vision was a fantasy, yet in trying to achieve
it he took South Africa a long way towards greater authoritarianism and isolation. In September 1966, while sitting in parliament, he was stabbed to death by a parliamentary messenger,
a recent immigrant of schizophrenic tendencies who had a year
earlier applied to be reclassified "Coloured" and who was about
to be served a deportation order as an undesirable.

VOORTREKKER (or trekker) (Dutch: "those who travel ahead";
"pioneers"). Those who went on the mass migration called the
GREAT TREK. Some had previously been TREKBOERS, but
unlike the trekboers the Voortrekkers were part of a mass
movement, and one that involved a deliberate rebellion against
British rule at the Cape, begun with the intention of establishing
new states in the interior.

VORSTER, Balthazar Johannes (John) (1915-). Having attended
Stellenbosch University, where VERWOERD was one of his lec-
turers, he became a lawyer in Port Elizabeth. During World
War II he was interned by the SMUTS government for his anti-
war activities as a member of the OSSEWABRANDWAG. Entering parliament after the 1953 election, he soon acquired a reputation as a formidable debater. As Minister of Justice from
August 1961, he claimed that strong-arm methods were necessary for the security of the state. The police acquired vast
new powers and a huge network of informers was created.
Many were DETAINED WITHOUT TRIAL and many of those detained alleged torture. Vorster not only smashed black opposition through such means; for him liberalism was virtually syn-
onymous with communism, and members of the LIBERAL PAR-
TY suffered BANNINGS and other harassment.
His fearsome reputation as a strongman secured him election
as Verwoerd's successor in 1966. As Prime Minister he proved
more pragmatic than Verwoerd in his efforts to maintain white
supremacy. The entry of black diplomats and moves away from
a rigid racist sports policy alienated rightwing Afrikaners, as
did his talk of a broad South African nationalism including all
whites. When the extreme right broke away and formed the
HERSTIGTE NASIONALE PARTY, he managed skilfully to keep
the damage to the NATIONAL PARTY to a minimum. His attempts to improve South Africa's international position through
his OUTWARD POLICY met some initial success and its most
dramatic moment came when he met President Kaunda of Zambia at the Victoria Falls, but the intervention of South African
forces into ANGOLA followed by the harsh suppression of the
SOWETO REVOLT ended all hope of further success. In 1977
Vorster's firm control of his party enabled him to secure its
acceptance for new constitutional proposals providing for the
political incorporation of "Coloureds" and Asians (see CON-
STITUTIONAL CHANGE). Though willing to negotiate with the
western powers about an election in NAMIBIA under United
Nations auspices, he announced plans for a South African-

organized election there as he left office in 1978.
He resigned as Prime Minister only a year after an overwhelming election victory because of the MULDERGATE scandal, but he accepted the office of State President. He had to
resign that office too in mid 1979 when his own involvement in
the scandal became public knowledge. In 1982 he gave some
support to TREURNICHT's right-wing revolt against BOTHA.

WALKER, Eric Anderson (1886-1976). Educated in London and at
Oxford, he became Professor of History at the University of
Cape Town in 1911. In 1936 he moved to Cambridge, England,
where he was Vere Harmsworth Professor of Imperial and
Naval History until his retirement. His detailed, one-volume
History of South Africa (1928; 3rd edition 1957) long remained
the basic work in English, and he produced the only substantial
Historical Atlas of South Africa (1922), as well as two major
biographies and a study of the GREAT TREK (1936). He edited
the South African volume of the Cambridge History of the British Empire (1936). A lecture he delivered at Oxford University
in 1930, entitled "The Frontier Tradition in South Africa," was
the main target of a powerful critique forty years later: see
FRONTIER TRADITION.

WALVIS BAY (Whale Bay). The only large harbor on the NAMIBI-
AN coast, it was visited by the PORTUGUESE explorer Dias in
1486, but not exploited for a long time because of the lack of
fresh water inland. From the late 17th century whales were
hunted off the coast of what became South West Africa, and
from the 1830s traders, missionaries and collectors of guano
(droppings of sea-birds) used Walvis Bay increasingly. There
was a rush for the guano on a number of off-shore islands in
the 1840s; in the 1860s British sovereignty was proclaimed over
twelve of the islands and they were annexed to the Cape Colony
in 1874. By that time traders and missionaries at Walvis Bay
had long asked for British protection, and in 1875 the Cape
parliament sent a commissioner north of the Orange River.
He recommended that the whole coast be annexed, but the British government would only authorize annexation of Walvis Bay
itself (1878), which was in turn incorporated in the Cape in
1884. Three weeks later Germany proclaimed a protectorate
over the remainder of the coast of South West Africa. The
boundary between Walvis Bay and the German territory was
much disputed, and not resolved until 1911. For reasons of
administrative convenience, Walvis Bay was administered as
part of South West Africa from 1922 to 1977, but when negotiations were conducted on a possible UNITED NATIONS-supervised
transfer of power in NAMIBIA, South Africa made it clear that
it insisted on its claim to sovereignty over Walvis Bay. As
the future began to look uncertain, however, get-rich-quick
South African fishing companies through over-fishing destroyed
the once considerable industry centered on the Bay.

WERNHER, BEIT--H. ECKSTEIN. In 1890 Julius Charles Wernher
(1850-1912) and Alfred Beit (1853-1906), mining magnates of
German origin, formed a private London-based partnership
which was represented in Johannesburg by a company formed
by Hermann Ludwig Eckstein (1847-1893). The group of companies was also known as the Corner House, from its Johannesburg building (but also a play on Eckstein's surname, meaning "corner-stone"). It in turn founded Rand Mines in 1893, a
holding company. Capital acquired from DIAMONDS (Beit was
one of the founder life-governors of DE BEERS) and through
continental connections enabled the group to control 10 outcrop
mines by 1895, which together produced 32 percent of Transvaal GOLD. It was the first to recognize the potential of deep
level mining, and from 1895 began exploiting the deep levels
south of the richest outcrop mines. By 1899 it was responsible
for about 50 percent of Transvaal gold production, and its combined budget was larger than that of either Natal or the Free
State.   The directors included Lionel Phillips (1855-1936) and
Percy Fitzpatrick (1862-1931), both actively involved in the
JAMESON RAID plot. As the confidant of Milner after the
SOUTH AFRICAN WAR, Fitzpatrick played an influential role
in Transvaal reconstruction, strongly advocating the introduction of CHINESE LABOR to get the mines going again, and he
was a key member of the Transvaal delegation to the NATION-
AL CONVENTION (1908-1909). Administrative control of the
group was taken over by the Central Mining and Investment
Corporation from 1911, with Wernher the first chairman. Phillips, who had been senior Johannesburg partner and President
of the Chamber of Mines before the Jameson Raid, was chairman of Central Mining from 1915 to 1924.   From 1958 Rand
Mines became autonomous of Central Mining and in 1971, having increased its general industrial investments considerably, it
was taken over in turn by the Barlow group, and a new conglomerate formed known as Barlow-Rand. (See also RANDLORDS.)

WHITE INTRUSION. White intrusion into the lands of the indigenous people occurred in four main phases. Between 1652 and
about 1700 whites from the settlement at Table Bay occupied
the arable land of the southwestern Cape. Then during the
18th and early 19th century the TREKBOERS took possession
of the more arid interior lands, east to the Fish River and
north to the ORANGE RIVER. The GREAT TREK began a
third phase, spreading white settlement into the far interior
north of the Vaal river and into Natal. This still left various
pockets--the TRANSKEI, the lands of the TSWANA, the ZULU,
the TSONGA, the PEDI and of a number of chiefdoms in the
north of the Transvaal--under African rule. During the last
quarter of the 19th century these territories were taken over
and their peoples subjected to white control. The extension of
such control did not always mean the ejection of the Africans
from their lands; see RESERVES.

WHITE RACISM.   Like those who settled in other parts of the

world, the Europeans who went to the Cape in the late 17th
century looked down upon the "heathen" and "barbarous" indigenous people as inferior. It has been suggested that because
the DUTCH, and the BRITISH settlers who followed them, came
from a Protestant, bourgeois, and northern European background,
they were more racially prejudiced than southern Europeans
would have been. At the Cape the Dutch found people--the
KHOIKHOI and SAN--whom they regarded as among the lowest
forms of human life anywhere and sometimes as not truly human at all. Though cohabitation with people of color was common in the Dutch period, there were few mixed marriages, and
the offspring of mixed unions joined the "non-white" group (see
MISCEGENATION). Racial prejudice imported from Europe was
reinforced by the system of racially based slavery at the Cape
and by the conflict between white and black on the frontier.
The weight once attached by some writers to the Calvinism of
the Afrikaners as a cause of racism can be discounted.
    Though racially prejudiced, the early white settlers did not
develop a systematic racial ideology. That emerged as the social order was challenged by the ideas of the British humanitarians (see MISSIONARIES) in the early 19th century. Racism was
then used to justify both dispossession of blacks, and their subordination and oppression. With the creation of an industrial
society, first at Kimberley and then on the Rand, a vast array
of discriminatory measures came into being to provide a cheap
African labor force, and these were buttressed by a racist ideology. In the 20th century racism was perhaps most blatantly
expressed by those whites who were threatened by African competition for jobs in the urban areas. In the late 1970s Afrikaner
leaders to some extent dropped their ideological commitment to
racial discrimination, because the co-optation of some blacks
(especially "Coloureds" and Indians) was seen as necessary for
the continued maintenance of white supremacy. Conservative
Afrikaners, however, led by Dr TREURNICHT, and perhaps a
majority of the white electorate, remained firmly committed to
racist beliefs.

WHITES. The more usual term for those not considered Asian,
    "Coloured," or African used to be "European," designating
    place of origin. "White" was used in place of "European" by
    the Mining Regulations Commission (1910) on the grounds that
    "Coloureds" might be "of European extraction." At the begin-
    ning of the APARTHEID regime, segregated amenities were
    labelled for "Europeans" and "Non-Europeans." From the
    1960s, however, as the Afrikaner leadership wished to assert
    its claim to belong to Africa, the term "white" replaced "Euro-
    pean."

WIEHAHN COMMISSION. A government commission under Profes-
    sor Nic Wiehahn was appointed in 1977 to investigate the coun-
    try's labor legislation. Its appointment was a response to the
    labor unrest since 1973 (see STRIKES) and to pressure for
    change from abroad, mediated in part through the multi-national

companies active in South Africa, in the wake of the SOWETO
REVOLT. Its first report (1979) recommended that the registration of African TRADE UNIONS be permitted, as a way of
controlling the new militant African labor movement. It also
recommended the abolition of the principle of statutory work
reservation (see JOB COLOR BAR), though it suggested that
existing work reservation determinations should remain in force
until they could be phased out in consultation with relevant white
unions. An amendment to the INDUSTRIAL CONCILIATION ACT
(1979) enacted these reforms.

WITWATERSRAND (Afrikaans: "ridge of white waters"). Also
known as "the reef" or "Goli" (from gold), this hilly ridge in
the southern Transvaal has produced more GOLD than anywhere
else on earth. The goldbearing rock extends for 62 miles, and
is in places some 23 miles wide. South Africa's largest city--
JOHANNESBURG--lies in the center of the WITWATERSRAND.

WORLD WAR I. On 4 August 1914 South Africa automatically found
itself, as part of the British empire, at war with Germany.
Louis BOTHA and Jan SMUTS both supported the war, and the
latter became a member of the Imperial War Cabinet. They
suppressed the AFRIKANER REBELLION, after Botha had agreed
to a British request that South African forces seize German
South West Africa (NAMIBIA). Over 20,000 South African
troops fought under SMUTS' command in German East Africa
(now Tanzania), and 4,648 South Africans lost their lives serving in Europe. Over 136,000 whites served in all, as well as
considerable numbers of "Coloureds" and Africans, the latter
allowed only non-combatant laboring duties. 12,452 South Africans died on active service during the war.

WORLD WAR II. When Britain declared war on Germany, the
South African cabinet divided 6 to 7 in favor of neutrality.
HERTZOG and the other former NATIONAL PARTY members
who had entered FUSION with him believed that South Africa
should assert its independence of Britain. As parliament was
sitting, the issue was put to the House of Assembly, which
voted 80 to 67 in favor of South Africa entering the war (4
September 1939). Hertzog then asked DUNCAN, the governor
general, to dissolve the Assembly and call a general election.
He refused and SMUTS became Prime Minister for the second
time, at once declaring war on Germany (6 September). To
many Afrikaner supporters of the UNITED PARTY this seemed
to run counter to the "South Africa First" principle of Fusion,
and they withdrew their support from Smuts, making virtually
inevitable his later defeat at the polls. In its first years,
however, the war brought enormous dissension to Afrikaner
ranks (see MALAN; OSSEWABRANDWAG). As late as 1944,
many Afrikaner nationalists expected the Germans to win the
war, and hoped that that would provide the opportunity for the
establishment of an Afrikaner republic.
   During the war 386,000 men and women volunteers served

in the armed forces. "Coloured" and African troops were supposed to participate only in non-combatant roles. South African
forces took part in the campaign against the Italians in Ethiopia
(1940-41). Of the three South African divisions that fought in
the campaigns against German and Italian forces in Egypt and
Libya, the second was captured by Rommel's Afrika Korps at
Tobruk (June 1942). A South African division landed with the
Americans in Sicily and fought its way up the Italian peninsula.
Almost 9,000 South Africans were killed in action during the
war.

XHOSA (probably from the KHOI "Kosa," meaning "angry men").
Cape NGUNI people who recognized the authority of the Tshawe
royal clan, members of which claimed descent from a mythical
ancestor named Xhosa. This clan established a chiefdom in the
northern Transkei sometime before 1600. Over two centuries
and more this polity expanded, by conquest and by incorporating
those willing to accept Tshawe authority, until it formed a barrier to white expansion eastwards from the Cape. By 1800 it
stretched from the Mbashe river in the Transkei south to the
Sundays river near present Port Elizabeth. The polity was divided into a number of sub-chiefdoms, each almost entirely independent of the other, and into two main sections, the senior
Gcaleka one in the east and the Rharabe one to the west. It
was the western Xhosa who clashed with the whites in the late
18th century, and 20,000 of them were expelled from the ZUUR-
VELD west of the Fish River in 1811-12. Settler pressure continued and wars were fought periodically over a century, until
in 1878 the Gcaleka living in the TRANSKEI were defeated and
brought under white rule.
    The Xhosa were the first African people among whom mis-
sionaries worked in the early 19th century. Because their dialect was the one reduced to writing by the missionaries, other
Cape NGUNI peoples--including the Thembu, Mpondo and
MFENGU--came to be classified as Xhosa-speaking. (See also
CATTLE KILLING; FRONTIER WARS; MFENGU.)

ZIMBABWE (formerly Southern Rhodesia; Shona: "place of stones").
Links between South Africa and the land to the north of the
LIMPOPO RIVER go back into the remote past; see BANTU-
SPEAKERS; IRON AGE; VENDA. In the late 1830s the
NDEBELE crossed from the Transvaal into south-western
Zimbabwe, where they settled. White hunters, traders, and
missionaries soon began to follow them north in increasing
numbers. In 1890 RHODES' British South Africa Company oc-
cupied part of "southern Zambesia," renamed Rhodesia. Many
of the early whites settlers there came from the Cape. As
late as 1970 more than a fifth of Rhodesian settlers were South
African-born. Yet when the British South Africa administration

came to an end, the settlers voted in a referendum (1922) not
to join the UNION of South Africa as a fifth province, despite
pressure from SMUTS and mining interests for Rhodesian incorporation.   After the collapse of the Central African Federation in 1963, Southern Rhodesia's government was driven into
closer ties with South Africa.   The Rhodesian Front government's race policies more closely approximated South African
ones than its predecessor.   Military cooperation grew.

South African financial support and the military equipment,
arms and ammunition, petroleum and fuel oil it supplied were
crucial to the survival of Rhodesia after the Unilateral Declaration of Independence (November 1965).   Britain refused to consider SANCTIONS against South Africa, despite its open flouting
of the sanctions imposed against the illegal regime, and instead
saw the VORSTER government as an ally in putting pressure on
Ian Smith.   From August 1967 South African paramilitary police
were deployed within Rhodesia, allegedly to help the Rhodesians
stop guerilla incursions aimed at South Africa.   After the coup
in Lisbon in 1974, and the impending independence of MOZAM-
BIQUE and ANGOLA, Vorster realized that the continued existence of the illegal regime was no longer in South Africa's
long-term interests, and he began to put pressure on Smith to
negotiate with the less radical African leaders.   The last of
the South African forces were withdrawn from Rhodesia in
August 1975, and in that month Vorster and Kaunda met to discuss the issue at the Victoria Falls on the Rhodesia-Zambia
border.   The following year Vorster agreed, under pressure
from American Secretary of State Henry Kissinger, to encourage
Smith to declare that white minority rule would end (September
1976).   The South African government supported the internal settlement which Smith then reached with Bishop Muzorewa and
others and hoped that it would bring the regime international
recognition.   It did not, the war continued, and the Lancaster
House talks in London provided for a British-run election.   The
South African government still hoped that Muzorewa would win,
and it supported his campaign financially.   Much white opinion
in South Africa was shocked by Robert Mugabe's electoral victory.   Most of the whites who left Zimbabwe at this time settled in South Africa.   South Africa cut off previously agreed
loans, withdrew locomotives in Zimbabwe on loan, and slowed
the transport of Zimbabwe's goods to South African ports (the
bulk of Zimbabwe's imports and exports were carried by South
African railways).   South Africa was believed to be responsible
for the assassination of a top AFRICAN NATIONAL CONGRESS
official in Salisbury (now Harare).   Though Mugabe allowed the
ANC to establish a diplomatic presence in his country, and
called for international sanctions against South Africa, he made
it clear that Zimbabwe could not afford to permit guerilla bases
to be established on its soil, or to participate in such sanctions
itself.

ZULU (old form: Zooloo).   In the late 18th century the Zulu were
one of many small groups among the northern NGUNI.   The

emergence of a powerful Zulu state was the culmination of a
process of political centralization that first saw the growth of
the Mthethwa confederacy and the Ndwandwe state (see MFE-
CANE).   The triumph of the Zulu was the work of Shaka (variants Chaka, Tshaka; c. 1787-1828), who was for a time a
tributary chief and military commander in the Mthethwa confederacy.   Giving his men a short stabbing spear and a large
shield, to make close fighting possible, he built up the Zulu
into a formidable fighting force.   When the Ndwandwe ruler
captured and put to death his Mthethwa rival, Shaka took up the
struggle against the Ndwandwe and at the battle of Gqokoli hill,
just south of the Mfolozi river (c. 1819) the Ndwandwe were put
to flight.   Shaka then continued on his path of conquest until he
had brought within the Zulu kingdom all the northern Nguni between the DRAKENSBERG and the sea, from the Pongola river
in the north to the Tugela in the south, while south of the Tugela
he kept a buffer zone of cleared land.   His armies raided as
far south as Mpondo country in what became the TRANSKEI.   To
the north, they fought the Swazi and enabled Shaka to control
much of the trade to DELAGOA BAY.

Shaka's was a militarized, highly centralized absolutist state.
It was surrounded by vassal communities in varying degrees of
subordination, who paid Shaka tribute.   Shaka did not initiate,
but he elaborated the regimental system that underpinned his
rule.   Age-groups (AMABUTHO) were quartered together and
forbidden to marry for a set period.   Besides its military function, the regimental system redistributed labor from the homesteads to the state and through it the king extracted surplus in
the form of cattle or crops.   Shaka himself, said to have been
terrified at the prospect of an heir, never married.   In 1828
two of his half-brothers stabbed him to death.   One of them,
Dingane (c. 1795-1840), then got rid of the other and took over
as the new ruler.   He seems to have intended to end the cease-
less military activitity and terror that characterized Shaka's
reign, but as soon as relaxation of control enabled a subordinate
group to break away, Dingane was quick to reimpose Shaka's
authoritarianism and militarism.

It was Dingane whom Piet Retief (1780-1838), the VOOR-
TREKKER leader, asked for land south of the Tugela.   Dingane,
seeing the trekkers as a threat, had Retief and his party mur-
dered.   The trekkers turned the tables at the battle of BLOOD
RIVER (1938).   Mpande (c. 1798-1872), another of Shaka's half-
brothers, in alliance with the trekkers, then drove out Dingane.
With the arrival of the BRITISH in 1843, Mpande switched sides
and won from the new regime recognition of the independence
of his kingdom north of the Tugela.   Mpande's bid to have his
favorite son named heir-apparent led to civil war in 1856, from
which his other son, Cetshwayo (c. 1832-1884) emerged victorious.   Cetshwayo consolidated his control over the country and
took full power on Mpande's death.   By then perhaps 150,000
people between the Tugela and Pongola rivers saw themselves
as Zulu, and Cetshwayo was able to put an army of 40,000 men
into the field.

The Anglo-Zulu war (1879) followed the presentation of an ultimatum by Bartle FRERE, the HIGH COMMISSIONER, demanding that Cetshwayo dismantle the Zulu military system, a demand which Frere knew it was impossible for Cetshwayo to accept. Frere had seen the war as a step towards the goal of
CONFEDERATION in South Africa. But the advance of the
British and colonial forces into Zululand from the west was
checked by the Zulu army at Isandhlwana (January 1979). The
British soon defeated the Zulu, and Cetshwayo was captured
and sent into exile at Cape Town. But the British were not
then prepared to spend more money on an administration for
Zululand. Garnet Wolseley (1833-1913), who had taken over
part of Frere's High Commission, imposed a "settlement"
which divided the Zulu country into thirteen units, each under
a ruler appointed by the British authorities, but the territory
was not annexed and the British resident was in theory merely to perform "diplomatic duties." The aim was a balance of
mutually antagonistic forces--many of the new rulers were
hostile to the Zulu royal establishment--but the result was
civil war (1883-1884).

Faced with growing anarchy in Zululand, the British let
Cetshwayo return to the central portion of a repartitioned Zululand. This intensified the warfare. Cetshwayo's capital was
sacked in July 1883. His successor Dinuzulu (c. 1869-1913)
sought aid from a group of Boers from the Transvaal against
his main rival Zibhebhu (c. 1841-1904). In return, they obtained land in the northwest, where they established their
"New Republic" in 1884. In 1887 Britain finally annexed what
was left of Zululand; the following year the New Republic was
incorporated into the Transvaal (it was transferred to Natal
after the SOUTH AFRICAN WAR).

Bitter at the British annexation, Dinuzulu went into rebellion (1888). When forced to surrender, he was tried for high
treason and exiled to the Atlantic ocean island of St. Helena.
After his return in 1898, he again sought to win recognition as
Zulu ruler. Whites interpreted his ambivalent role in the
BAMBATHA REBELLION as evidence of treason. This time
the outcome of a trial on that charge was a four-year sentence
for harboring rebels. From the mid 1920s white attitudes to
the Zulu royal family shifted, with even the Zululand sugar
planters seeing it as a bulwark against radical change. In the
1970s such land as was left in African occupation in Natal and
Zululand was constituted a "self-governing" BANTUSTAN known
as KWAZULU. In 1982 there were, by official estimate,
5, 867, 000 Zulu.

ZUURVELD (Suurveld) (Afrikaans: "Sour (grass) country"). The
land between the Fish and Bushman's rivers in what is now the
eastern Cape. It was where white TREKBOERS first came into
substantial contact with BANTU-SPEAKING Africans. The Zuurveld was ideal for summer grazing, and small African groups,
moving away to escape the domination of those further east, had
lived and farmed there for several generations before regular

relations with white settlers began in the 1770s. At the end of
that decade came the first armed clash, but neither then nor in
other wars in the late 18th century were the whites able to dislodge the XHOSA. The Fish river was easily crossed and both
sides ignored it as the boundary. So while the Zuurveld was
officially part of the Cape Colony from 1780, large numbers of
Africans remained within it until 1812, when Boer COMMANDOS,
aided by BRITISH troops, expelled 20,000 of them. A line of
forts was then built, the chief of which became Grahamstown.
In 1820, 5,000 British immigrants were settled in the Zuurveld,
renamed the Albany district of the colony (see BRITISH RULE;
ENGLISH-SPEAKING WHITES; FRONTIER WARS).

BIBLIOGRAPHY

Contents

BIBLIOGRAPHY: INTRODUCTION

More has been written on South Africa than on any other African country. The South African Bibliography to the Year 1925 alone lists over 50,000 works. The present bibliography, which follows the design of those in the other volumes in this series, aims to include the most useful works for the student of South African history. It does not include, however, any unpublished theses and it is essentially a list of secondary works by professional historians and other scholars. In general, priority has been given to books over articles or chapters in books; to recent publications over older ones; and to materials reasonably accessible to American and British students.

For those to whom the bibliography itself may appear daunting, the following notes may serve as a brief guide. In 1982 C.W. de Kiewiet's History of South Africa Social and Economic (1941) still remained probably the best and most readable one-volume history. T.R.H. Davenport's South Africa A Modern History (1978) contains a lot of detail, especially on the twentieth century. The two volume Oxford History of South Africa, co-edited by M. Wilson and L. Thompson (1969, 1971), was a landmark in South African historiography, presenting the first scholarly attempt at a liberal Africanist overview. The Shaping of South African Society (1979), edited by R. Elphick and H. Giliomee, and Economy and Society in Pre-Industrial South Africa (1980), edited by S. Marks and A. Atmere, are extremely useful collections of essays on the history of the country before the great change brought about by the discovery of diamonds and gold. The best introduction to the pre-history of the region is R. Inskeep's The Peopling of South Africa (1978).

Twentieth-century South African history is illuminated by a number of outstanding biographies and autobiographical accounts, which include W.K. Hancock, Smuts (1962, 1968), A. Paton, Hofmeyr (1964) and A. Luthuli, Let My People Go (1962). It is illuminated, too, by many striking works of literature, such as the novels of Alan Paton and Nadine Gordimer, the poetry of Breyten Breytenbach and the richly varied material to be found in the pages of Staffrider, a literary magazine published by Ravan Press in Johannesburg from 1978.

With increased international attention focussed on southern Africa in the late 1970s the number of analyses of the contemporary scene grew rapidly. R. Johnson's How Long Will South Africa

Survive? (1977) was followed by Why South Africa Will Survive by
L. Gann and P. Duignan (1980).   Among the best of this genre is
South Africa: Time Running Out (1981), the report of the Rocke-
feller Study Commission, a most readable introduction to the country's politics.   The best and most up-to-date survey of the economy
is J. Nattrass, The South African Economy (1981).

To help reduce the size of this bibliography, each item is
listed under one heading only.   In many cases it was not easy to
decide whether to place items in one category rather than another.
A useful book or article which does not appear under one subject
heading, may be elsewhere.   The guides listed in the first section
are an entrée to other sources.

ABBREVIATIONS

AYB	Archives Year Book for South African History
CSSA	Collected Seminar Papers, Societies of Southern Africa (Institute of Commonwealth Studies, University of London)
JAH	Journal of African History
JSAS	Journal of Southern African Studies
SAAB	South African Archaeological Bulletin
SAHJ	South African Historical Journal
SAJE	South African Journal of Economics

1. REFERENCE

Bibliographies and Guides

Boshoff, M. M. , ed. French Publications on South Africa to the Year 1935. Pretoria: State Library, 1978.

Eales, M. An Annotated Guide to the Pre-Union Government Publications of the Orange Free State 1854-1910. Boston: G. K. Hall, 1976.

Geyser, O. , et al. Bibliographies on South African Political History. 2 vols. Boston: G. K. Hall, 1979.

Index to South African Periodicals. Johannesburg: Public Library, 1940-

Index to the Manuscript Annexures and Printed Papers of the House of Assembly 1910-1961. Pretoria: Government Printer, 1961.

Kalley, J. A. The Transkei Region of Southern Africa 1877-1978. An Annotated Bibliography. Boston: G. K. Hall, 1979.

Long, U. Index to Authors of Unofficial, Privately Owned Manuscripts Relating to the History of South Africa, 1812-1920. London: Lund Humphries, 1947.

Mendelssohn, S. South African Bibliography. 2 vols. London: Kegan Paul, 1910.

Muller, C. , et al. , eds. South African History and Historians. A Bibliography. Pretoria: University of South Africa, 1979.

Musiker, R. South Africa. Oxford: Clio Press, 1979.

Musiker, R. South African Bibliography. 2nd ed. , Cape Town: David Philip, 1980.

Musiker, R. and N. Guide to Cape of Good Hope Official Publications 1854-1910. Boston: G. K. Hall, 1976.

Pollak, O. and K. Theses and Dissertations on Southern Africa: An International Bibliography. Boston: G. K. Hall, 1976.

Potgieter, P. J. Index to Literature on Race Relations in South Africa 1910-1975. Boston: G. K. Hall, 1979.

Robinson, A. M. , ed. Theses and Dissertations Accepted for Degrees at South African Universities 1918-1941. n. p. , 1943.

Schapera, I. Select Bibliography of South African Native Life and Problems. London: Oxford University Press, 1941. Supplements by M. A. Holden and others, University of Cape Town School of Librarianship, 1958-64.

Scholtz, P. L. , Bredekamp, H. C. , and Heese, H. F. Race Relations at the Cape of Good Hope, 1652-1795: A Select Bibliography. Boston: G. K. Hall, 1981.

A South African Bibliography to the Year 1925. 4 vols. London: Mansell, 1979.

Standard Encyclopaedia of Southern Africa.   12 vols.   Cape Town:
      Nasou, 1970-76.
Switzer, L. and D.   The Black Press in South Africa and Lesotho.
      Boston: G. K. Hall, 1979.
Theal, G. McC.   Catalogue of Books and Pamphlets Relating to
      Africa South of the Zambesi.   Cape Town: Cape Times, 1912.
Thompson, L. M., et al.   Southern African History Before 1900:   A
      Select Bibliography of Articles.   Stanford: Hoover Institution,
      1971.
Union Catalogue of Theses and Dissertations of South African Uni-
      versities.   Potchefstroom: University Library, 1942-
Union List of South African Newspapers.   Cape Town: South Afri-
      can Public Library, 1950.
Van Warmelo, N. J.   Anthropology of Southern Africa in Periodicals
      to 1950.   Johannesburg: Witwatersrand University Press, 1977.
Webb, C.   Guide to the Official Records of the Colony of Natal.
      Pietermaritzburg: University of Natal Press, 1965.

Serial Publications

Acta Diurna Historica, Bloemfontein, 1972-
Africa Perspective, Johannesburg, 1974-
Africa Seminar Collected Papers, Cape Town, 1978-
African Affairs, London.
Africana Notes and News, Johannesburg, 1943-
Archives Year Book for South African History, Cape Town and
      Pretoria, 1938-
Cabo, Cape Town, 1971-
Collected Papers, Centre for Southern African Studies, University
      of York, 1976-
Collected Seminar Papers, Societies of Southern Africa, University
      of London, 1970-
Communications Series, University of Cape Town, 1937-71 and 1979-
Contree, Pretoria, 1977-
The Critic, Cape Town, 1932-36.
Historia, Pretoria, 1952-
Historiese Studies, Pretoria, 1939-49.
International Journal of African Historical Studies, Boston, 1968-
Janus, Cape Town, 1974-
Journal for Contemporary History, Bloemfontein, 1975-
Journal of African History, London, 1960-
Journal of Natal and Zulu History, Durban, 1978-
Journal of Southern African Affairs, Maryland, 1976-
Journal of Southern African Studies, London, 1974-
Journal of the Methodist Historical Society of South Africa, Grahams-
      town, 1952-61.
Kleio, Pretoria, 1969-
Looking Back, Port Elizabeth, 1960-
Military History Journal, Johannesburg, 1967-
Mohlomi, Roma, 1976-
Natalia, Pietermaritzburg, 1971-
Occasional Papers, Centre for African Studies, University of Cape

Town, 1979-
Quarterly Bulletin of the South African Library, Cape Town, 1946-
Race Relations Journal, Johannesburg, 1933-50.
Review of African Political Economy, London, 1974-
Social Dynamics, Cape Town, 1975-
South African Archaeological Bulletin, Cape Town, 1945-
South African Historical Journal, Bloemfontein, 1969-
South African Journal of Economics, Johannesburg, 1933-
South African Journal of Science, Johannesburg, 1903-
South African Labour Bulletin. Durban, Institute of Industrial Edu-
    cation, 1974-
South African Outlook (Kafir Express, Christian Express), Lovedale,
    Cape Town, 1870-
South African Statistics. Pretoria, Government Printer.
The State, Johannesburg, 1908-12.
Survey of Race Relations, Johannesburg, 1951/2-
Transactions of the Royal Society of South Africa, Cape Town, 1908-
Ufahamu, Los Angeles, 1970-
Van Riebeeck Society Publications, Cape Town, 1st Series. 50 vols.,
    1918-69, 2nd Series, 1970-

Edited Source Material

Axelson, E. , ed. South African Explorers. London: Oxford Uni-
    versity Press, 1954.
Bird, J. , ed. The Annals of Natal 1495-1845. 2 vols. Cape
    Town: Maskew Miller, 1888.
Brookes, E. H. , ed. Apartheid: A Documentary Study of Modern
    South Africa. London: Routledge and Kegan Paul, 1968.
Chase, J. C. , ed. The Natal Papers, 1498-1843. 2 vols. Gra-
    hamstown: R. Godlonton, 1843.
Comoroff, J. L. , ed. The Boer War Diary of Sol T. Plaatje: An
    African at Mafeking. Johannesburg: Macmillan, 1973.
Davenport, T. R. H. and Hunt, K. , eds. The Right to the Land.
    Cape Town: David Philip, 1974.
Duminy, A. H. and Guest, W. R. , eds. Fitzpatrick. South African
    Politician. Selected Papers, 1886-1906. Johannesburg:
    McGraw-Hill, 1976.
Fouche, L. , ed. The Diary of Adam Tas. Cape Town: Van
    Riebeeck Society, 1970.
Fraser, M. and Jeeves, A. , eds. All that Glittered: Selected
    Correspondence of Lionel Phillips, 1890-1924. Cape Town:
    Oxford University Press, 1977.
Geyser, O. , ed. B. J. Vorster: Selected Speeches. Bloemfontein:
    Institute for Contemporary History, 1977.
Gordon, R. E. and Talbot, C. J. , eds. From Dias to Vorster.
    Source Material on South African History 1488-1975. Cape
    Town: Nasou Limited, 1977.
Hancock, W. K. and Van der Poel, J. , eds. Selections from the
    Smuts Papers. 7 vols. Cambridge: Cambridge University
    Press, 1966-73.
Hattersley, A. F. More Annals of Natal. London: Warne, 1936.

Headlam, C., ed. The Milner Papers. 2 vols. London: Cassell, 1931, 1933.

Houghton, D. H. and Dagut, J., eds. Source Material on the South African Economy. 3 vols. Cape Town: Oxford University Press, 1972-73.

Hugo, P., ed. Quislings or Realists? A Documentary Study of "Coloured" Politics in South Africa. Johannesburg: Ravan Press, 1978.

Kruger, D. W., ed. South African Parties and Policies, 1910-1960: A Select Source Book. Cape Town: Human and Rousseau, 1960.

La Guma, A., ed. Apartheid. New York: International Publishers, 1971.

Le Cordeur, B. A. and Saunders, C. C., eds. The Kitchingman Papers. Johannesburg: Brenthurst Press, 1976.

Le Cordeur, B. A. and Saunders, C. C., eds. The War of the Axe. Johannesburg: Brenthurst Press, 1981.

Lewsen, P., ed. Selections from the Correspondence of John X Merriman. 4 vols. Cape Town: Van Riebeeck Society, 1960-69.

Moodie, D., ed. The Record, or a Series of Official Papers Relative to the Condition and Treatment of the Native Tribes of South Africa. Reprint, Amsterdam: A. A. Balkema, 1960.

Pelzer, A. N., ed. Verwoerd Speaks: Speeches, 1948-1962. Johannesburg: APB Publishers, 1966.

Preston, A., ed. The South African Journal of Sir Garnet Wolseley, 1879-1880. Cape Town: Balkema, 1973.

Rees, W., ed. Colenso Letters from Natal. Pietermaritzburg: Shuter and Shooter, 1958.

Rose, B. and Tunmer, R., eds. Documents in South African Education. Johannesburg: Donker, 1973.

South African Archival Documents. Pretoria: Government Printer. Cape Series 1957- ; Natal Series 1958- ; Orange Free State Series 1952- ; Transvaal Series, 1949- .

South African Who's Who. Johannesburg: Ken Donaldson, 1908-

Theal, G. McC. Basutoland Records, 1833-1868. 4 vols. repr. Cape Town: Struik, 1964.

Theal, G. M. Records of the Cape Colony. 36 vols. London: Government of the Cape Colony, 1897-1905.

Theal, G. M. Records of South-Eastern Africa. 8 vols. Cape Town: 1898-1903.

Thom, H. B., ed. Journal of Jan van Riebeeck, 1651-62. 3 vols. Cape Town: Balkema, 1952-58.

Union Statistics for Fifty Years. Pretoria: Government Printer, 1960.

Van der Merwe, H. W., et al. African Perspectives on South Africa: Reports, Articles and Documents. Stanford: Hoover Institution, 1978.

Webb, C. and Wright, J. The James Stuart Archive. 3 vols. Pietermaritzburg: University of Natal Press, 1976-82.

Wilson, F. and Perrot, D., eds. Outlook on a Century: South Africa 1870-1970. Lovedale: Lovedale Press, 1973.

Wright, H. M., ed. Sir James Rose Innes Selected Correspondence, 1884-1902. Cape Town: Van Riebeeck Society, 1972.

2. BIOGRAPHY

Appelgryn, M. A. Thomas Francois Burgers: Staatspresident 1872-1877. Pretoria: HAUM, 1979.
Binns, C. T. Dinizulu: The Death of the House of Shaka. London: Longmans, 1968.
Cope, R. K. Comrade Bill. The Life and Times of W. H. Andrews, Workers' Leader. Cape Town: Stewart, 1944.
De Villiers, R. M. , ed. Better Than They Knew. 2 vols. Cape Town: Purnell, 1972, 1974.
Deane, D. S. Black South Africans. Cape Town: Oxford University Press, 1978.
Dictionary of South African Biography. 3 vols. Cape Town: Tafelberg, 1968-77; vol. 4, Durban: Butterworth, 1982.
Driver, J. Patrick Duncan. South African and Pan-African. London: Heinemann, 1980.
First, R. and Scott, A. Olive Schreiner. New York: Shocken, 1981.
Flint, J. Cecil Rhodes. Boston: Little, Brown, 1974.
Franken, J. L. M. Piet Retief se Lewe in die Kolonie. Cape Town: HAUM, 1949.
Gregory, T. Ernest Oppenheimer and the Economic Development of Southern Africa. Cape Town: Oxford University Press, 1962.
Hancock, W. K. Smuts. 2 vols. Cambridge: Cambridge University Press, 1962, 1968.
Harington, A. Sir Harry Smith Bungling Hero. Cape Town: Tafelberg, 1980.
Huttenback, R. A. Gandhi in South Africa. Ithaca: Cornell University Press, 1971.
Jabavu, D. D. T. The Life of J. T. Jabavu. Lovedale: Lovedale Press, n. d.
Kadalie, C. My Life and the I. C. U. London: Cass, 1970.
Kenney, H. Architect of Apartheid. H. F. Verwoerd--An Appraisal. Johannesburg: Jonathan Ball, 1980.
Kruger, D. W. Paul Kruger, 2 vols. Johannesburg: Dagbreek Boekhandel, 1961, 1963.
Lewsen, P. John X. Merriman. New Haven: Yale University Press, 1982.
Liebenberg, B. Andries Pretorius in Natal. Pretoria: Academica, 1977.
Lockhart, J. G. and Wodehouse, C. M. Rhodes. London: Hodder and Stoughton, 1963.
Luthuli, A. Let My People Go. New York: McGraw-Hill, 1962.
Macmillan, W. M. My South African Years, Cape Town: David Philip, 1975.
Mokgatle, M. M. N. The Autobiography of an Unknown South African, Berkeley: University of California Press, 1971.
Paton, A. S. Hofmeyr. London: Oxford University Press, 1964.
Paton, A. S. Apartheid and the Archbishop: The Life and Times of Geoffrey Clayton, Archbishop of Cape Town. Cape Town: David Philip, 1973.
Pirow, O. James Barry Munnik Hertzog. Cape Town: Howard Timmins, 1957.

Ritter, E. A. Shaka Zulu: The Rise of the Zulu Empire. London: Longmans, Green, 1955.
Rutherford, J. Sir George Grey, 1812-1898. London: Cassell, 1961.
Sanders, P. Moshoeshoe: Chief of the Sotho. London: Heinemann, 1975.
Saunders, C. , ed. Black Leaders in South African History. London: Heinemann Educational Books, 1979.
Skota, T. D. M. , ed. The African Yearly Register. Johannesburg: R. L. Esson & Co. , c. 1931.
Skota, T. D. M. , ed. The African Who's Who, 3rd ed. Johannesburg: Central News Agency, 1966.
Strangwayes-Booth, J. A Cricket in the Thorn Tree. Helen Suzman and the Progressive Party. Johannesburg: Hutchinson, 1976.
Tabler, E. C. Pioneers of Natal and South-Eastern Africa, 1552- 1878. Cape Town: Balkema, 1977.
Temkin, B. Gatsha Buthelezi: Zulu Statesman, Cape Town: Purnell, 1976.
Thompson, L. M. Survival in Two Worlds: Moshoeshoe of Lesotho, 1786-1870. Oxford: Clarendon Press, 1975.
Van der Heever, C. M. General J. B. M. Hertzog, Johannesburg: A. P. B. , 1946.
Walker, E. A. W. P. Schreiner: A South African. London: Oxford University Press, 1937.
Williams, D. When Races Meet. The Life and Times of William Ritchie Thomson. Johannesburg: A. P. B. , 1967.
Williams, D. Umfundisi A Biography of Tiyo Soga 1829-1871. Lovedale: Lovedale Press, 1978.
Woods, D. Biko. New York: Paddington Press, 1978.

3. CULTURE

Art, Music and Film

Bensusan, A. D. Silver Images: History of Photography in Africa. Cape Town: Howard Timmins, 1966.
Berman, E. The Story of South African Painting. Cape Town: Balkema, 1975.
Bradlow, F. Thomas Bowler. Cape Town: Balkema, 1967.
Bull, M. and Denfield, J. Secure the Shadow: The Story of Cape Photography. Cape Town: McNally, 1970.
Cooke, C. K. Rock Art of Southern Africa. Cape Town: Books of Africa, 1969.
De Bosdari, C. Cape Dutch Houses and Farms, 2nd ed. Cape Town: Balkema, 1964.
Gordon-Brown, A. Pictorial Africana. Cape Town: Balkema, 1975.
Greig, D. E. A Guide to Architecture in South Africa. Cape Town: Howard Timmins, 1970.
Greig, D. E. Herbert Baker in South Africa. Cape Town: Purnell, 1970.

Grut, M.   The History of Ballet in South Africa.   Cape Town: Human and Rousseau, 1981.

Gutsche, T.   The History and Social Significance of Motion Pictures
in South Africa, 1895-1940.   Cape Town: Howard Timmins,
1972.

Kirby, P. R.   The Musical Instruments of the Native Races of
South Africa, 2nd ed., Johannesburg: Witwatersrand University
Press, 1965.

Rudner, J. and I.   The Hunter and His Art: A Survey of Rock Art
in Southern Africa.   Cape Town: Struik, 1970.

Vinnicombe, P.   People of the Eland.   Pietermaritzburg: University
of Natal Press, 1976.

Willcox, A. R.   The Rock Art of South Africa.   Johannesburg: Nelson, 1963.

Crafts and Costume

Atmore, M. G.   Cape Furniture, 3rd ed.   Cape Town: Howard Timmins, 1976.

Davison, P. and Harries, P.   "Cotton Weaving in South-east Africa:
its History and Technology," Textile History, 11 (1980).

Schofield, J. F.   Primitive Pottery.   Cape Town: Rustica Press,
1948.

Smith, A. H.   Spread of Printing in South Africa.   Amsterdam:
Vangerdt, 1971.

Strutt, D. H.   Fashion in South Africa, 1652-1900.   Cape Town:
Balkema, 1975.

Telford, A. A.   Yesterday's Dress.   Cape Town: Purnell, 1972.

Welz, S.   Cape Silver and Silversmiths.   Cape Town: Balkema,
1976.

Woodward, C. S.   Oriental Ceramics at the Cape of Good Hope,
1652-1795.   Cape Town: Balkema, 1974.

Language, Literature, and the Press

Antonissen, R.   Die Afrikaanse Letterkunde van Aanvang tot Hede.
3rd ed.   Cape Town: Nasou, 1965.

Gordimer, N.   The Black Interpreters.   Johannesburg: Ravan
Press, 1973.

Gray, S.   Southern African Literature: An Introduction.   Cape
Town: David Philip, 1979.

Hepple, A.   Censorship and Press Control in South Africa.   Johannesburg: The Author, 1960.

Jordaan, K.   "The Origins of the Afrikaners and Their Language,
1652-1720:   A Study in Miscegenation and Creole," Race, 15
(1974).

Jordan, A.   Towards an African Literature.   Berkeley: University
of California Press, 1973.

Kannemeyer, J.   Geskiedenis van die Afrikaanse Literatuur, vol. 1.
Pretoria: Academica, 1978.

Pachai, N.   "The History of the 'Indian Opinion' 1903-1914," AYB,

24 (1962).
Potter, E. The Press as Opposition. London: Chatto and Windus, 1975.
Robinson, A. M. L. None Daring to Make Us Afraid: A Study of English Periodical Literature in the Cape Colony from its Beginnings in 1824 to 1835. Cape Town: Maskew Millar, 1962.
Scholtz, J. Die Afrikaner en sy Taal 1806-1875. 2nd ed. Cape Town: Nasou, n. d. [?1965].
Shaw, G. E. Some Beginnings. The Cape Times (1876-1910). Cape Town: Oxford University Press, 1975.
Snyman, J. P. L. The South African Novel in English (1880-1930). Potchefstroom: The University of Potchefstroom, 1952.
Valkhoff, M. F. New Light on Afrikaans and "Malayo-Portuguese." Louvain: Editions Peeters, 1972.
Valkhoff, M. F. Studies in Portuguese and Creole, with Special Reference to South Africa. Johannesburg: Witwatersrand University Press, 1966.
Varley, D. H. A Short History of the Newspaper Press in South Africa, 1652-1952. Cape Town: Nasionale Pers, 1952.
Westphal, E. O. J. "The Linguistic Prehistory of Southern Africa," Africa, 33 (1963).

Literature: Some Works in English

Abrahams, Peter. Mine Boy. London: Faber and Faber, 1946.
Breytenbach, Breyten. And Death White as Words. London: Rex Collings, 1978.
Breytenbach, Breyten. Season in Paradise. London: Jonathan Cape, 1980.
Brink, Andre. An Instant in the Wind. London: W. H. Allen and Co., 1976.
Brink, Andre. Rumours of Rain. London: W. H. Allen and Co., 1978.
Brink, Andre. Dry White Season. London: W. H. Allen and Co., 1979.
Campbell, Roy. Sons of the Mistral. London: Faber and Faber, 1941.
Coetzee, J. M. In the Heart of the Country. Johannesburg: Ravan Press, 1978.
Cope, J. and Krige, J., comp. The Penguin Book of South African Verse. Harmondsworth, England: Penguin, 1968.
Delius, Anthony. Border. Cape Town: David Philip, 1976.
Fugard, Athol. Three Port Elizabeth Plays. Cape Town: Oxford University Press, 1974.
Gordimer, Nadine. The Lying Days. London: Victor Gollancz Ltd., 1953.
Gordimer, Nadine. A World of Strangers. London: Victor Gollancz Ltd., 1958.
Gordimer, Nadine. The Late Bourgeois World. London: Jonathan Cape, 1966.
Gordimer, Nadine. The Conservationist. London: Jonathan Cape, 1974.

Gordimer, Nadine. Burger's Daughter. London: Jonathan Cape, 1979.

Gordimer, Nadine. July's People. Braamfontein: Ravan Press, 1981.

Jordan, A. C. The Wrath of the Ancestors. Lovedale: Lovedale Press, 1980.

Joubert, E. The Long Night of Poppie Nongena. Johannesburg: Jonathan Ball, 1980.

Mphahlele, Ezekiel. Down Second Avenue. London: Faber, 1965.

Mtshali, Oswald. Sounds of a Cowherd Drum. London: Oxford University Press, 1975.

Paton, Alan. Cry, the Beloved Country. New York: Scribners, 1948.

Paton, Alan. Too Late the Phalarope. Cape Town: Cannon, 1953.

Paton, Alan. Ah, But Your Land is Beautiful. Cape Town: David Philip, 1981.

Plaatje, Sol. T. Mhudi. Lovedale: Lovedale Press, 1930. New ed. London: Heinemann, 1977.

Plomer, W. Turbott Wolfe. London: Leonard and Virginia Woolf, 1925.

Schreiner, Olive [as "Ralph Iron"] The Story of an African Farm. London: Chapman and Hall, 1883.

Smith, Pauline. The Little Karoo. London: Jonathan Cape, 1925.

Smith, Pauline. The Beadle. London: Jonathan Cape, 1926.

4. THE ECONOMY

General

First, R., Steele, J., and Gurney, C. The South African Connection: Western Investment in Apartheid. London: Temple Smith, 1972.

Horwitz, R. The Political Economy of South Africa. London: Weidenfeld, 1967.

Houghton, D. H. The South African Economy. 4th Edition. Cape Town: Oxford University Press, 1976.

Hutt, W. The Economics of the Colour Bar. London: Macmillan, 1964.

Lombaard, J. A., ed. Economic Policy in South Africa. Cape Town: HAUM, 1973.

Macmillan, W. M. Complex South Africa. London: Faber and Faber, 1930.

Morris, M. "The Development of Capitalism in South Africa," Journal of Development Studies, 12 (1976).

Nattrass, J. The South African Economy. Cape Town: Oxford University Press, 1981.

Robertson, H. M. "150 Years of Economic Contact Between Black and White: A Preliminary Survey," SAJE, 2 and 3 (1934-1935).

Schlemmer, L. and Webster, E. Change, Reform and Economic Growth in South Africa. Johannesburg: Ravan Press, 1977.

Schumann, C. G. W. Structural Changes and Business Cycles in South Africa 1806-1936. London: Staples Press, 1938.

Agriculture and Rural Change

Bundy, C.   The Rise and Fall of the South African Peasantry.
    London: Heinemann Educational Books, 1979.
Cooper, F.   "Peasants, Capitalists, and Historians," JSAS, 7
    (1981).
Duly, L. C.   British Land Policy at the Cape, 1795-1844:   A Study
    of Administrative Procedures in the Empire.   Durham: Duke
    University Press, 1968.
Hurwitz, N.   Agriculture in Natal, 1860-1950.   Cape Town: Oxford
    University Press, 1957.
Keegan, T.   "The Restructuring of Agrarian Class Relations in a
    Colonial Economy: The Orange River Colony, 1902-1910,"
    JSAS, 5 (1979).
Knight, J. and Lenta, G.   "Has Capitalism Underdeveloped the
    Labour Reserves of South Africa?"   Oxford Bulletin of Eco-
    nomics and Statistics, 42 (1980).
Lees, R.   Fishing for Fortunes: The Story of the Fishing Industry
    in Southern Africa and the Men Who Made It.   Cape Town:
    Purnell, 1969.
Macmillan, W. M.   The South African Agrarian Problem and Its His-
    torical Development.   Johannesburg: Central News Agency,
    1919.
Morris, M.   "The Development of Capitalism in South African Ag-
    riculture: Class Struggle in the Countryside," Economy and
    Society, 5, 2 (1976).
Muller, C. F. J.   "Die Geskiedenis van die Vissery aan die Kaap tot
    aan die Middel van die Agtiende Eeu," AYB, 5, I (1942).
Palmer, R. and Parsons, N. , eds.   The Roots of Rural Poverty.
    London: Heinemann Educational Books, 1977.
Simkins, C.   "Agricultural Production in the African Reserves of
    South Africa, 1918-69," JSAS, 7 (1981).
Slater, H.   "Land, Labour and Capital in Natal: The Natal Land
    and Colonisation Company, 1860-1948," JAH, 16 (1975).
Thom, H. B.   Die Geskiedenis van die Skaapboerdery in Suid-Afrika.
    Amsterdam: Swets and Zeitlinger, 1936.
Van Rensburg, J.   "Die Geskiedenis van die Wingerdkultuur in Suid-
    Afrika Tydens die Eerste Eeu, 1652-1752," AYB, 17, 2 (1954).
Van Zyl, D. J.   "Die Geskiedenis van Graanbou aan die Kaap.   1795-
    1826," AYB, 31, I (1968).
Van Zyl, D. J.   Die Geskiedenis van Wynbou en Wynhandel in die
    Kaapkolonie, 1795-1860.   Cape Town: HAUM, 1975.
Wickens, P.   "The Natives Land Act of 1913," SAJE, 49 (1981).
Wilson, F. et al. , eds.   Farm Labour in South Africa.   Cape
    Town: David Philip, 1977.

Banking, Currency, and Finance

Arndt, E. H. D.   Banking and Currency Development in South Africa
    1652-1927.   Cape Town: Juta, 1928.
De Kock, G.   A History of the South African Reserve Bank (1920-
    1952).   Pretoria: Van Schaik, 1954.

Frankel, S. H.   Capital Investment in Africa; Its Course and Effects.
    London: Oxford University Press, 1938.
Henry, J. A.   The First Hundred Years of the Standard Bank.   Lon-
    don: Oxford University Press, 1963.
Kantor, B.   "The Evolution of Monetary Policy in South Africa,"
    SAJE, 39 (1971).
Shaw, E. M.   A History of Currency in South Africa.   Cape Town:
    South African Museum, 1956.

Commerce and Industry

Archer, S.   "The South African Industrialization Debate and the
    Tariff in the Inter-War Years," CSSA, 11 (1981).
Arkin, M.   Storm in a Teacup.   The Cape Colonists and the English
    East India Company.   Cape Town: Struik, 1973.
Bozzoli, B.   "Managerialism and the Mode of Production in South
    Africa," South African Labour Bulletin, 3, 8 (1977).
Bozzoli, B.   "The Origins, Development and Ideology of Local Man-
    ufacturing in South Africa," JSAS, 1, 2 (1975).
Bozzoli, B.   The Political Nature of a Ruling Class.   London:
    Routledge, 1981.
Cartwright, A. P.   Golden Age: The Story of the Industrialisation
    of South Africa and the Part Played in it by the Corner House
    Group of Companies, 1910-1967.   Cape Town: Purnell and
    Sons, 1968.
Kaplan, D.   "The Politics of Industrial Protection in South Africa,"
    JSAS, 3, 1976.
Myers, D., et al.   United States Business in South Africa.   Bloom-
    ington: Indiana University Press, 1980.
Seidman, A. and N.   South Africa and U. S. Multinational Corpora-
    tions.   Westport, Connecticut: Lawrence Hill, 1978.
Trapido, S.   "South Africa in a Comparative Study of Industrializa-
    tion," Journal of Development Studies, 7 (1971).
Van der Horst, S. T.   "The Economics of Decentralisation of Indus-
    try," SAJE, 33 (1965).
Van Eyk, H. J.   Some Aspects of the South African Industrial Revo-
    lution.   2nd ed.   Johannesburg: Institute of Race Relations,
    1953.

Labor, Strikes, and Trade Unions

Arkin, M.   "Strikes, Boycotts--and the History of Their Impact
    on South Africa," SAJE, 28 (1960).
Ballard, C. C.   "Migrant Labour in Natal 1860-1879:   With Special
    Reference to Zululand and the Delagoa Bay Hinterland," Journal
    of Natal and Zulu History, 1 (1978).
Beinart, W.   "Joyini Inkomo: Cattle Advances and the Origins of
    Migrancy from Pondoland," JSAS, 5 (1979).
Bonner, P. L.   "The Decline and Fall of the ICU--A Case of Self-
    destruction?"   South African Labour Bulletin, 1, 6 (1974).
Cock, J.   Maids and Madams.   Johannesburg: Ravan Press, 1980.

Dekker, L. D., et al. "Case Studies in African Labour Action in
  South Africa and Namibia" in R. Sandbrook and R. Cohen, eds.,
  The Development of an African Working Class. London: Long-
  mans, 1975.
Denoon, D. J. N. "The Transvaal Labour Crisis 1900-6," JAH, 7
  (1967).
Doxey, G. V. The Industrial Colour Bar in South Africa. Cape
  Town: Oxford University Press, 1961.
Du Toit, D. Capital and Labour in South Africa. Class Struggles
  in the 1970s. London: Kegan Paul International Ltd. 1981.
Etherington, N. "Labour Supply and the Genesis of South African
  Confederation," JAH, 20 (1979).
Hemson, D. "Dock Workers, Labour Circulation and Class Strug-
  gles in Durban, 1940-1959," JSAS, 4 (1977).
Horrell, M. South African Trade Unionism. Johannesburg: Insti-
  tute of Race Relations, 1961.
Jeeves, A. "The Control of Migratory Labour on the South African
  Gold Mines in the Era of Kruger and Milner," JSAS, 2, 1
  (1975).
Johns, S. "The Birth of Non-White Trade Unionism in South
  Africa," Race, 8 (1967).
Katz, E. N. A Trade Union Aristocracy: The Transvaal White
  Working Class and the General Strike of 1913. Johannesburg:
  University of the Witwatersrand, 1976.
Kirkwood, M. "The Mineworkers' Struggle," South African Labour
  Bulletin, 1, 8 (1975).
Myers, D. Labor Practices of U. S. Corporations in South Africa.
  New York: Praeger, 1977.
Nattrass, J. "Migrant Labour and South African Economic Develop-
  ments," SAJE, 44, I (1976).
O'Meara, D. "The 1946 African Mine Workers' Strike and the Po-
  litical Economy of South Africa," Journal of Commonwealth and
  Comparative Politics, 13, 2 (1975).
O'Meara, D. "White Trade Unions, Political Power and Afrikaner
  Nationalism," South African Labour Bulletin, 1, 10 (1975).
Roberts, M. Labour in the Farm Economy. Johannesburg: Insti-
  tute of Race Relations, 1959.
Tayal, M. "Indian Indentured Labour in Natal, 1890-1911," Indian
  Economic and Social History Review, 14 (1979).
Thomas, W. H., ed., Labour Perspectives on South Africa. Cape
  Town: David Philip, 1974.
Van der Horst, S. T. Native Labour in South Africa. Cape Town:
  Oxford University Press, 1942.
Walker, I. D. and Weinbren, B. 2000 Casualties: A History of the
  Trade Unions and the Labour Movement in the Union of South
  Africa. Johannesburg: South African Trade Union Council,
  1961.
Webster, E. Essays in Southern African Labour History. Johan-
  nesburg: Ravan Press, 1978.
Wickens, P. The Industrial and Commercial Workers' Union of
  Africa. Cape Town: Oxford University Press, 1978.
Wilson, F. Labour in the South African Gold Mines 1911-1969.
  Cambridge: Cambridge University Press, 1972.
Wilson, F. Migrant Labour. Johannesburg: Spro-cas, 1972.

Mining

Cartwright, A. P. The Corner House: The Early History of Johannesburg. Cape Town: Purnell and Sons, 1965.

Cartwright, A. P. The Gold Miners. Cape Town: Purnell and Sons, 1962.

Cartwright, A. P. Gold Paved the Way: The Story of the Gold Fields Group of Companies. London: Macmillan, 1967.

Chilvers, H. A. The Story of De Beers. London: Cassell, 1939.

Horner, D. and Kooy, A. Conflict on South African Mines 1972-1979. Cape Town: SALDRU, 1980.

Innes, D. "The Mining Industry in the Context of South Africa's Economic Development, 1910-1940," CSSA, 7 (1977).

Katzen, L. Gold and the South African Economy. Cape Town: Balkema, 1964.

Kubicek, R. V. Economic Imperialism in Theory and Practice: The Case of South African Gold Mining Finance, 1886-1914. Durham: Duke University Press, 1979.

Lanning, G. and Mueller, M. Africa Undermined. Harmondsworth, England: Penguin Books, 1979.

Mineral Resources of the Republic of South Africa. 5th ed. Pretoria: Government Printer, 1976.

Rosenthal, E. Gold! Gold! Gold! The Johannesburg Gold Rush. New York: Macmillan, 1970.

Smalberger, J. M. Aspects of the History of Copper Mining in Namaqualand, 1846-1931. Cape Town: Struik, 1975.

Turrell, R. "Rhodes, De Beers and Monopoly," Journal of Imperial and Commonwealth History, 10 (1982).

Transport and Communications

Frankel, S. H. The Railway Policy of South Africa. Johannesburg: Hortors, 1928.

McCormack, M. C. "Man with a Mission: Oswald Pirow and South African Airways, 1933-1939," JAH, 20 (1979).

Mossop, E. E. Old Cape Highways. Cape Town: Maskew Miller, 1928.

Murray, M. Union Castle Chronicle, 1853-1953. London: Longmans, Green, 1933.

Nock, O. S. Railways of Southern Africa. London: Black, 1971.

Van der Poel, J. Railway and Customs Policies in South Africa, 1885-1910. London: Longmans, Green, 1933.

Van Helten, J. J. "German Capital, The Netherlands Railway Company and the Political Economy of the Transvaal," JAH, 19 (1978).

5. HISTORY

General

Adler, T., ed. Perspectives on South Africa. Johannesburg:

University of the Witwatersrand, 1977.
Agar-Hamilton, J. A. I.   The Road to the North.   South Africa,
    1852-1886.   London: Longmans, 1937.
Atmore, A. and Marks, S.   "The Imperial Factor in South Africa:
    Towards a Reassessment," Journal of Imperial and Common-
    wealth History, 3 (1974).
Bonner, P. , ed.   Working Papers in Southern African Studies.
    Johannesburg: University of the Witwatersrand, 1977.
Bonner, P. , ed.   Working Papers in Southern African Studies, vol. 2.
    Johannesburg: Ravan Press, 1981.
Benyon, J. A.   Pro-Consul and Paramountcy in South Africa.   Pieter-
    maritzburg: University of Natal Press, 1980.
Cory, G. E.   The Rise of South Africa.   6 vols.   1910-39; repr. ,
    Cape Town: Struik, 1964.
Davenport, T. R. H.   South Africa: A Modern History.   London:
    Macmillan, 1978.
De Kiewiet, C. W.   A History of South Africa Social and Economic.
    London: Oxford University Press, 1941.
De Kiewiet, C. W.   The Imperial Factor in South Africa: A Study
    in Politics and Economics.   Cambridge: Cambridge University
    Press, 1937.
Denoon, D. with Nyeko, B.   Southern Africa Since 1800.   New
    York: Praeger, 1973.
Frederickson, G. M.   White Supremacy: A Comparative Study in
    American and South African History.   New York: Oxford Uni-
    versity Press, 1981.
Hattersley, A. F.   An Illustrated Social History of South Africa.
    Cape Town: Balkema, 1969.
Huttenback, R.   Gandhi in South Africa; British Imperialism and the
    Indian Question, 1860-1914.   Ithaca: Cornell University Press,
    1971.
Keppel-Jones, A.   South Africa A Short History, 5th ed. , London:
    Hutchinson, 1975.
Lamar, H. and Thompson, L. M. , eds.   The Frontier in History.
    North America and Southern Africa Compared.   New Haven:
    Yale University Press, 1981.
Lye, W. and Murray, C.   Transformations on the Highveld.   Cape
    Town: David Philip, 1980.
Marks, S. and Atmore, A. , eds.   Economy and Society in Pre-
    Industrial South Africa.   London: Longman, 1980.
Marks, S. and Rathbone, R. , eds.   Industrialisation and Social
    Change.   London: Longman, 1982.
Muller, C. F. J.   Die Britse Owerheid en die Groot Trek.   4th ed. ,
    Cape Town: H. and R. Academica, 1977.
Muller, C. F. J. , ed.   Five Hundred Years: A History of South
    Africa, 3rd ed. , Pretoria: Academica, 1981.
Oberholster, J. J.   The Historical Monuments of South Africa,
    Cape Town: National Monuments Council, 1972.
Oliver, R. and Fage, J. , general eds.   The Cambridge History of
    Africa, 8 vols.   Cambridge: Cambridge University Press,
    1975-
Omer-Cooper, J.   The Zulu Aftermath: A Nineteenth Century
    Revolution in Bantu Africa.   London: Longman, 1966.

Peires, J. B. , ed. Before and After Shaka. Studies in Nguni His-
tory. Grahamstown: Rhodes University, 1981.
Perspectives on the Southern African Past. Cape Town: University
of Cape Town, 1979.
Ross, R. Adam Kok's Griquas. Cambridge: Cambridge University
Press, 1976.
Schreuder, D. M. The Scramble for Southern Africa, Cambridge:
Cambridge University Press, 1980.
Simons, H. J. and R. E. Class and Colour in South Africa, 1850-
1950. Harmondsworth: Penguin, 1969.
Theal, G. M. History of South Africa, 11 vols. 1888-1919; repr.,
Cape Town: Struik, 1964.
Thompson, L. M. "The South African Dilemma," in L. Hartz, ed. ,
The Founding of New Societies, New York: Harcourt, Brace
and World, 1964.
Thompson, L. M. , ed. African Societies in Southern Africa, Lon-
don: Heinemann Educational Books, 1969.
Troup, F. South Africa: An Historical Introduction, London: Eyre
Methuen, 1972.
Walker, C. The Women's Suffrage Movement in South Africa.
Cape Town: University of Cape Town, 1979.
Walker, E. A. , ed. Cambridge History of the British Empire, VIII:
South Africa, 2nd ed. , Cambridge: Cambridge University Press,
1963.
Walker, E. A. The Great Trek, London: A and C Black: 1934.
Walker, E. A. Historical Atlas of South Africa, Cape Town: Ox-
ford University Press, 1922.
Walker, E. A. A History of Southern Africa, 3rd ed. London:
Longman, 1957.
Wilson, M. and Thompson, L. M. , eds. The Oxford History of
South Africa. 2 vols. Oxford: Clarendon Press, 1969, 1971.

Historiography

Atmore, A. and Westlake, N. "A Liberal Dilemma: A Critique of
The Oxford History of South Africa," Race, I4 (1972).
Auerbach, F. E. The Power of Prejudice in South African Educa-
tion. An Enquiry into History Textbooks. Cape Town: Bal-
kema, 1965.
Bosman, I. D. Dr George McCall Theal as die Geskiedskrywer van
Suid-Afrika. Amsterdam: Swets and Zeitlinger, 1932.
Cook, C. W. "The Writing of South African Church History," SAHJ,
2 (1970).
Cornevin, M. Apartheid: Power and Historical Falsification.
Paris: Unesco, 1980.
Gann, L. H. "Liberal Interpretations of South African History,"
Rhodes-Livingstone Journal, 25 (1959).
Johnstone, F. "'Most Painful to Our Hearts': South Africa Through
the Eyes of the New School," Canadian Journal of African Stud-
ies, 16 (1982).
Jones, S. "On Economic History in General and the Economic His-
tory of South Africa in Particular," Perspectives in Economic

History, 1 (1982).
Legassick, M. C.   "The Dynamics of Modernisation in South Africa,"
    JAH, 13 (1972).
Marks, S.   "African and Afrikaner History," JAH, 11 (1970).
Marks, S.   "Liberalism, Social Realities and South African History,"
    Journal of Commonwealth Political Studies, 10 (1972).
Marks, S.   "Southern African Studies Since World War Two," in
    C. Fyfe, ed., African Studies Since 1945.   London: Longman,
    1976.
Marks, S.   "Towards a People's History of South Africa?   Recent
    Developments in the Historiography of South Africa," in R.
    Samuel, ed., People's History and Socialist Theory.   London:
    Routledge, 1981.
Thompson, L. M.   "Afrikaner Nationalist Historiography and the
    Policy of Apartheid," JAH, 3 (1962).
Thompson, L. M.   "South Africa," in R. Winks, ed., The Historiog-
    raphy of the British Empire-Commonwealth.   Durham: Duke
    University Press, 1966.
Trapido, S.   "South Africa and the Historians," African Affairs,
    71 (1972).
Van Jaarsveld, F. A.   The Afrikaner's Interpretation of South Afri-
    can History.   Cape Town: Simondium Publishers, 1964.
Wright, H. M.   The Burden of the Present: Liberal-Radical Contro-
    versy over Southern African History.   Cape Town: David Philip,
    1977.
Wright, H. M.   "The Burden of the Present and its Critics," Social
    Dynamics, 6 (1980).

Before White Settlement

Axelson, E. V.   South-East Africa 1488-1530.   London: Longmans,
    Green, 1940.
Deacon, H. J.   Where Hunters Gathered.   Cape Town: South Afri-
    can Archaeological Society, 1976.
Derricourt, R. M.   Prehistoric Man in the Ciskei and Transkei.
    Cape Town: Struik, 1977.
Ehret, C.   "Patterns of Bantu and Central Sudanic Settlement in
    Central and Southern Africa (ca. 1000 B. C. -A. D. 500)," Trans-
    african Journal of History, 3 (1973).
Ehret, C.   "Agricultural History in Central and South Africa ca.
    1000 B. C. to A. D. 500," Transafrican Journal of History, 4
    (1974).
Fagan, B. M.   Southern Africa During the Stone Age.   London:
    Thames and Hudson, 1965.
Huffman, T. N.   "The Early Iron Age and Spread of the Bantu,"
    SAAB, 25 (1970).
Inskeep, R. R.   The Peopling of Southern Africa.   Cape Town:
    David Philip, 1978.
Maggs, T. M. O'C.   Iron Age Communities of the Southern Highveld.
    Pietermaritzburg: Natal Museum, 1976.
Mason, R. J.   Prehistory of the Transvaal.   Johannesburg: Wit-
    watersrand University Press, 1962.

Parkington, J. "Southern Africa: Hunters and Gatherers," in G.
Mokhtar, ed. General History of Africa, vol. 2 Paris:
Unesco, 1981.
Phillipson, D. W. The Later Prehistory of Eastern and Southern
Africa. London: Heinemann Educational Books, 1977.
Raven-Hart, R. Before Van Riebeeck: Callers at South Africa
from 1488 to 1652. Cape Town: Struik, 1967.
Sampson, C. G. The Stone Age Archaeology of Southern Africa.
New York: Academic Press, 1974.
Schweitzer, F. R. "Archaeological Evidence for Sheep at the Cape,"
SAAB, 29 (1974).
Tobias, P. V., ed. The Bushmen. Cape Town: Human and Rous-
seau, 1978.
Willcox, A. R. Southern Land: The Prehistory and History of
Southern Africa. Cape Town: Purnell, 1976.
Wilson, M. "The Early History of the Transkei and Ciskei,"
African Studies, 18 (1959).
Wilson, M. The Thousand Years Before Van Riebeeck. Johannes-
burg: Institute for the Study of Man, 1970.
Wright, J. B. "Hunters, Herders and Early Farmers in Southern
Africa," Theoria 8 (1977).

The Cape

Beinart, W. "European Traders and the Mpondo Paramountcy,
1878-86," JAH, 20 (1979).
Beyers, C. Die Kaapse Patriotte. 2nd ed. Pretoria: Van
Schaik, 1967.
Böeseken, A. J. Slaves and Free Blacks at the Cape, 1658-1700.
Cape Town: Tafelberg, 1977.
Bradlow, E. "The Cape Government Rule of Basutoland, 1871-
1883," AYB, 31, 2 (1968).
Burman, S. B. Chiefdom Politics and Alien Law. London: Mac-
millan, 1981.
Butler, G. The 1820 Settlers: An Illustrated Commentary. Cape
Town: Human and Rousseau, 1974.
Davenport, T. R. H. The Afrikaner Bond: The History of a South
African Political Party, 1880-1911. Cape Town: Oxford Uni-
versity Press, 1966.
Davis, R. H. "Elijah Makiwane and the Cape School Community,"
African Affairs, 78 (1979).
Duly, L. "A Revisit with the Cape's Hottentot Ordinance of 1828,"
in Kooy, M., ed. Studies in Economics and Economic History.
London: Macmillan, 1972.
Duminy, A. H. "The Role of Sir Andries Stockenstrom in Cape
Politics," AYB, 23, 11, 1960.
Du Toit, A. E. "The Cape Frontier: A Study of Native Policy with
Special Reference to the Years 1847-1866," AYB, 17, 1 (1954).
Edgecombe, D. R. "The Non-Racial Franchise in Cape Politics,
1853-1910," Kleio, 10 (June 1978).
Edwards, I. E. Towards Emancipation: A Study in South African
Slavery. Cardiff: University of Wales Press, 1942.

Elphick, R. Kraal and Castle. Khoikhoi and the Founding of White
    South Africa. New Haven: Yale University Press, 1977.
Elphick, R. and Giliomee, H. , eds. The Shaping of South African
    Society. Cape Town: Longman, 1979.
Forbes, V. S. Pioneer Travellers of South Africa. Cape Town:
    Balkema, 1965.
Freund, W. "The Eastern Frontier of the Cape Colony During the
    Batavian Period, " JAH, 13 (1972).
Freund, W. M. "Race in the Social Structure of South Africa, 1652-
    1836, " Race and Class, 17 (1976).
Galbraith, J. S. Reluctant Empire: British Policy on the South Af-
    rican Frontier, 1834-1854. Berkeley: University of California
    Press, 1963.
Giliomee, H. B. Die Kaap Tydens die Eerste Britse Bewind 1795-
    1803. Cape Town: HAUM, 1975.
Greenstein, L. J. "Slave and Citizen: The South African Case, "
    Race, 15 (1973).
Guelke, L. "Frontier Settlement in Early Dutch South Africa, "
    Association of American Geographers, Annals, 66 (1976).
Hancock, W. "Trek, " Economic History Review. 2nd Series, 10 .
    (1957-58).
Idenburg, P. J. The Cape of Good Hope at the Turn of the Eighteenth
    Century. Leiden: Leiden University Press, 1963.
Kallaway, P. "Tribesman, Trader, Peasant and Proletarian, "
    Africa Perspective, 10 (1979).
Kirk, T. E. "Progress and Decline in the Kat River Settlement,
    1829-1854, " JAH, 14 (1973).
Le Cordeur, B. A. The Politics of Eastern Cape Separatism. Cape
    Town: Oxford University Press, 1981.
Lewsen, P. "The Cape Liberal Tradition: Myth or Reality?"
    Race, 13 (July 1971).
McCracken, J. L. The Cape Parliament, 1854-1910. Oxford:
    Clarendon Press, 1967.
MacCrone, I. D. Race Attitudes in South Africa. London: Oxford
    University Press, 1937.
Macmillan, W. M. Bantu, Boer, and Briton: The Making of the
    South African Native Problem. rev. ed. , Oxford: Clarendon
    Press, 1963.
Macmillan, W. M. The Cape Colour Question: A Historical Survey.
    London: Faber and Gwyer, 1927.
Marais, J. S. The Cape Coloured People, 1652-1937. 2nd ed. ,
    Johannesburg: Witwatersrand University Press, 1957.
Marais, J. S. Maynier and the First Boer Republic. repr. , Cape
    Town: Maskew Miller, 1962.
Marks, S. M. "Khoisan Resistance to the Dutch in the Seventeenth
    and Eighteenth Centuries, " JAH, 13 (1972).
Muller, C. F. M. Die Oorsprong van die Groot Trek. Cape Town:
    Tafelberg, 1974.
Neumark, S. D. Economic Influences on the South African Frontier,
    1652-1836. Stanford: Hoover Institution, 1957.
Newton-King, S. and Malherbe, C. The Khoikhoi Rebellion in the
    Eastern Cape (1799-1803). Cape Town: University of Cape
    Town, 1981.

Peires, J. B.   The House of Phalo.   The Xhosa in the Days of
    Their Independence.   Johannesburg: Ravan Press, 1981.
Ross, R.   "Oppression, Sexuality and Slavery in the Cape of Good
    Hope," Historical Reflections, 6 (1975).
Ross, R.   "The 'White' Population of the Cape in the Eighteenth
    Century," Population Studies, 29 (1975).
Saunders, C. and Derricourt, R., eds.   Beyond the Cape Frontier.
    London: Longman, 1974.
Strauss, T.   War Along the Orange.   The Korana and the Northern
    Border Wars of 1868-9 and 1878-9.   Cape Town: University of
    Cape Town, 1979.
Trapido, S.   "African Divisional Politics in the Cape Colony, 1854-
    1910," JAH, 9 (1968).
Van der Merwe, P. J.   Die Noordwaartse Beweging van die Boere
    voor die Groot Trek.   Den Haag: Van Stockum, 1937.
Van der Merwe, P. J.   Die Trekboer in die Geskiedenis van die
    Kaap Kolonie.   Cape Town: Nasionale Pers, 1938.
Worden, N.   "The Distribution of Slaves in the Western Cape Dur-
    ing the Eighteenth Century," African Seminar: Collected Pa-
    pers, 2 (1981).

Natal and Zululand

Ballard, Charles.   "John Dunn and Cetshwayo: The Material
    Foundations of Political Power in the Zulu Kingdom, 1857-
    1878," JAH, 21 (1980).
Brookes, E. H. and Webb, C. de B., A History of Natal.   Pieter-
    maritzburg: Natal University Press, 1965.
Daniel, J. B. M.   "A Geographical Study of pre-Shakan Zululand,"
    South African Geographical Journal, 55, 1 (1973).
Duminy, A. and Ballard, C., eds.   The Anglo-Zulu War.   New
    Perspectives.   Pietermaritzburg: University of Natal Press,
    1981.
Etherington, N.   Preachers, Peasants and Politics in Southeast
    Africa 1835-1880.   London: Royal Historical Society, 1978.
Guy, J. J.   "Production and Exchange in the Zulu Kingdom,"
    Mohlomi, 2 (1978).
Guy, J. J.   The Destruction of the Zulu Kingdom: The Civil War
    in Zululand 1879-1884.   London: Longman, 1979.
Hattersley, A. F., The British Settlement of Natal.   Cambridge:
    Cambridge University Press, 1950.
Herd, N.   The Bent Pine: The Trial of Langalibalele.   Johannes-
    burg: Ravan Press, 1976.
Le Cordeur, B. A.   "The Relations Between the Cape and Natal
    1846-1879," AYB, 28, 2 (1965).
Marks, S.   "The Ambiguities of Dependence: John L. Dube of
    Natal," JSAS, I (1975).
Morris, D. R.   The Washing of the Spears: A History of the Rise
    of the Zulu Nation....   New York: Simon and Schuster, 1965.
Wright, J. B.   Bushman Raiders of the Drakensberg, 1840-1870.
    Pietermaritzburg: University of Natal Press, 1971.
Wright, J. B.   "Pre-Shakan Age-Group Formation Among the
    Northern Nguni," Natalia, 8 (1978).

The Orange Free State and Transvaal

Blainey, G. "Lost Causes of the Jameson Raid," Economic History
     Review, 2nd series, 18 (1965).
Bonner, B. "Factions and Fissions: Transvaal/Swazi Relations in
     the Mid Nineteenth Century," JAH, 19 (1978).
Butler, J. "The German Factor in Anglo-Transvaal Relations," in
     P. Gifford and W.R. Louis, ed., Britain and Germany in Africa.
     New Haven: Yale University Press, 1967.
Butler, J. The Liberal Party and the Jameson Raid. London:
     Oxford University Press, 1968.
Cope, R.L. "Shepstone, the Zulus and the Annexation of the Trans-
     vaal," SAHJ, 4 (1972).
De Kiewiet, C.W. British Colonial Policy and the South African
     Republic, 1848-1872. London: Longmans, Green, 1929.
Garson, N.G., "The Swaziland Question and a Road to the Sea,
     1887-1895," AYB, 20, 2 (1957).
Gordon, C.T. The Growth of Boer Opposition to Kruger, 1890-
     1895. Cape Town: Oxford University Press, 1970.
Kubicek, R.V. "The Randlords in 1895: A Reassessment," Jour-
     nal of British Studies, 11 (1972).
Lehmann, J.H. The First Boer War. London: Jonathan Cape,
     1972.
Lye, W. "The Ndebele Kingdom South of the Limpopo River," JAH,
     10 (1969).
Marais, J.S. The Fall of Kruger's Republic. Oxford: Clarendon
     Press, 1961.
Mendelsohn, R. "Blainey and the Jameson Raid: The Debate Re-
     viewed," JSAS, 6 (1980).
Midgley, J.F. "The Orange River Sovereignty, 1848-1854," AYB,
     12 (1949).
Pakenham, E. Jameson's Raid. London: Weidenfeld and Nicolson,
     1960.
Phimister, I.R. "Rhodes, Rhodesia and the Rand," JSAS, 1, 1
     (1974).
Pillay, B. British Indians in the Transvaal: Trade, Race Rela-
     tions and Imperial Policy in Republican and Colonial Transvaal,
     1885-1906. London: Longman, 1976.
Rasmussen, R.K. Migrant Kingdom: Mzilikazi's Ndebele in South
     Africa. London: Rex Collings, 1978.
Schreuder, D.M. Gladstone and Kruger. London: Routledge,
     1969.
Trapido, S. "Landlord and Tenant in a Colonial Economy: The
     Transvaal 1880-1910," JSAS, 5, 1 (1978).
Van der Poel, J. The Jameson Raid. London: Oxford University
     Press, 1951.
Van Zyl, M.C. Die Protesbeweging van die Transvaalse Afrikan-
     ers, 1877-1880. Cape Town: Academica, 1979.

South Africa 1899-1910

Callinicos, L. Gold and Workers. Johannesburg: Ravan Press,
     1980.

Davey, A. M.   The British Pro-Boers, 1877-1902.   Cape Town: Tafelberg, 1978.

Denoon, D.   "'Capitalist Influence' and the Transvaal Crown Colony Government," Historical Journal, 12 (1969).

Denoon, D.   A Grand Illusion: The Failure of Imperial Policy in the Transvaal Colony During the Period of Reconstruction. London: Longman, 1973.

Duminy, A. H.   The Capitalists and the Outbreak of the Anglo-Boer War.   Durban: University of Natal, 1977.

Garson, N. G.   "'Het Volk': The Botha-Smuts Party in the Transvaal, 1904-11," Historical Journal, 9 (1966).

Grundlingh, A.   Die Hensoppers en Joiners.   Cape Town: HAUM, 1979.

Hyam, R.   "African Interests and the South Africa Act, 1908-1910," Historical Journal, 13 (1970).

Le May, G. H. L.   British Supremacy in South Africa, 1899-1907. Oxford: Clarendon Press, 1965.

Marks, S.   Reluctant Rebellion: The 1906-1908 Disturbances in Natal.   Oxford: Clarendon Press, 1970.

Marks, S. and Trapido, S.   "Lord Milner and the South African State," History Workshop, 8 (1979).

Mawby, A. A.   "Capital, Government and Politics in the Transvaal, 1900-1907," Historical Journal, 17 (1974).

Ngcongco, L. D.   "Jabavu and the Boer War," Kleio, 2 (1970).

Pakenham, T.   The Boer War.   London: Weidenfeld and Nicolson, 1979.

Spies, S. B.   Methods of Barbarism?   Roberts and Kitchener and Civilians in The Boer Republics, January 1900-May 1902. Cape Town: Human and Rousseau, 1977.

Thompson, L. M.   The Unification of South Africa.   Oxford: Clarendon Press, 1960.

Van Onselen, C.   "The Randlords and Rotgut, 1886-1903," History Workshop, 2 (1976).

Van Onselen, C.   "'The Regiment of the Hills': South Africa's Lumpenproletarian Army, 1890-1920," Past and Present, 80 (1978).

Van Onselen, C.   "The World the Mine Owners Made," Review, 3 (1979).

Van Onselen, C.   Studies in the Social and Economic History of the Witwatersrand 1886-1914.   2 vols.   London: Longman, 1982.

Warwick, P., ed.   The South African War.   Harlow, Essex: Longman, 1980.

South Africa 1910-1970

Ballinger, M.   From Union to Apartheid: A Trek to Isolation. Cape Town: Juta, 1969.

Beinart, L. and Bundy, C.   "State Intervention and Rural Resistance: The Transkei, 1900-1965," in Klein, M., ed., Peasants in Africa.   Beverly Hills: Sage, 1980.

Bozzoli, B.   "Capital and the State in South Africa," Review of

African Political Economy, 11 (1978).
Bozzoli, B.   The Political Nature of a Ruling Class: Capital and
    Ideology in South Africa, 1890-1933.   London: Routledge, 1981.
Clarke, S.   "Capital, 'Fractions' of Capital and the State: 'Neo-
    Marxist' Analyses of the South African State," Capital and Class,
    5 (1978).
Davenport, T. R. H.   "The South African Rebellion, 1914," English
    Historical Review, 78 (1963).
Davies, R., Kaplan, D., Morris, M. and O'Meara, D.   "Class
    Struggle and the Periodisation of the State in South Africa,"
    Review of African Political Economy, 7 (1976).
Davies, R.   Capital, State and White Labour in South Africa 1900-
    1960.   Brighton: Harvester, 1979.
Davies, R.   "Mining Capital, the State and Unskilled White Workers
    in South Africa, 1901-1913;" JSAS, 3 (1976).
Edgar, E.   "Garveyism in Africa: Dr Wellington and the American
    Movement in the Transkei," Ufahamu, 6 (1976).
Geyser, O. and Marais, A. H.   Die Nasionale Party.   Vol. I.
    Bloemfontein: Instituut vir Eietydse Geskiedenis, 1975.
Grundy, K. W.   Confrontation and Accommodation in Southern Africa,
    the Limits of Independence.   Berkeley: University of California
    Press, 1973.
Horton, J. W.   "South Africa's Joint Councils," SAHJ, 4 (1972).
Johnstone, Frederick, A.   Class, Race and Gold.   London:
    Routledge, 1976.
Kallaway, P.   "F. S. Malan, the Cape Liberal Tradition and South
    African Politics," JAH, 15 (1974).
Kuper, L.   Passive Resistance in South Africa.   New Haven: Yale
    University Press, 1967.
Lacey, M.   Working for Boroko.   The Origins of a Coercive Labour
    System in South Africa.   Johannesburg: Ravan Press, 1981.
Leftwich, A., ed.   South Africa: Economic Growth and Political
    Change.   London: Allison and Busby, 1974.
Legassick, M.   Class and Nationalism in South African Protest:
    The South African Communist Party and the "Native Republic"
    1928-34.   Syracuse: Syracuse University Press, 1973.
Legassick, M.   "Legislation, Ideology and Economy in Post-1948
    South Africa," JSAS, 1 (1974).
Legassick, M,   "South Africa: Capital Accumulation and Violence,"
    Economy and Society, 3 (1974).
Legassick, M.   "South Africa: Forced Labour, Industrialisation and
    Racial Discrimination," in The Political Economy of Africa, ed.
    Harris, R.   Boston: Schenkman, 1974.
Legassick, M.   "Race, Industrialisation and Social Change in South
    Africa: The Case of R. F. A. Hoernle," African Affairs, 75
    (1976).
Marks, S.   "Natal, the Zulu Royal Family and the Ideology of Seg-
    regation," JSAS, 4, 2 (1978).
Mbeki, G.   South Africa: The Peasants' Revolt.   Baltimore: Pen-
    guin, 1964.
Michelman, C.   The Black Sash of South Africa: A Case Study in
    Liberalism.   Oxford: Oxford University Press, 1975.
Rich, P.   "Liberalism and Ethnicity in South African Politics,

1921-1948," African Studies, 35 (1976).

Roberts, M. and Trollip, A. The South African Opposition, 1939-1945. London: Longmans, Green, 1947.

Robertson, J. Liberalism in South Africa, 1948-1963. London: Oxford University Press, 1971.

Saker, H. The South African Flag Controversy. Cape Town: Oxford University Press, 1980.

Sampson, A. The Treason Cage: The Opposition on Trial in South Africa. London: Heinemann, 1958.

Simson, H. The Social Origins of Afrikaner Fascism and Its Apartheid Policy. Stockholm: Almqvist and Wiksell, 1980.

Stadler, A. W. "The Afrikaner in Opposition, 1910-1948," Journal of Commonwealth Political Studies, 7, 3 (1969).

Stultz, N. M. Afrikaner Politics in South Africa, 1934-1948. Berkeley: University of California Press, 1974.

Ticktin, D. "The War Issue and the Collapse of the South African Labour Party 1914-15," SAHJ, I (1969).

Wolpe, H. "Capitalism and Cheap Labour Power in South Africa: From Segregation to Apartheid," Economy and Society, 1, 4 (1972).

Wolpe, H. "The 'White Working Class' in South Africa," Economy and Society, 5, 2 (1976).

6.   POLITICS

General

Adam, H. Modernizing Racial Domination: South Africa's Political Dynamics. Berkeley, University of California Press, 1971.

Adam, H. "Minority Monopoly in Transition: Recent Policy Shifts of the South African State," Journal of Modern African Studies, 18 (1980).

Bissell, R. E. and Crocker, C., eds. South Africa Into the 1980's. Boulder: Westview Press, 1979.

Brotz, H. M. The Politics of South Africa: Democracy and Racial Diversity. London: Oxford University Press, 1977.

Carter, G. M. The Politics of Inequality: South Africa Since 1948. 2nd ed. New York: Praeger, 1962.

Carter, G. M. and O'Meara, P., eds. Southern Africa: The Continuing Crisis. Bloomington: Indiana University Press, 1979.

Carter, G. Which Way Is South Africa Going? Bloomington: Indiana University Press, 1980.

Cervenka, Z. and Rogers, B. The Nuclear Axis. Secret Collaboration Between West Germany and South Africa. London: Julian Friedman, 1978.

De St. Jorre, J. A House Divided: South Africa's Uncertain Future. New York: Carnegie Endowment for International Peace, 1977.

Gann, L. and Duignan, P. Why South Africa Will Survive. London: Croom Helm, 1981.

Hanf, T., et al. South Africa: The Prospects of Peaceful Change. London: Rex Collings, 1981.

Heard, K. A. General Elections in South Africa, 1943-1970. New

York: Oxford University Press, 1974.
Hellman, E. and Lever, H., eds. Conflict and Progress. Fifty
    Years of Race Relations in South Africa. Johannesburg: Mac-
    millan, 1979.
Hodder-Williams R. "Well, Will South Africa Survive?" African
    Affairs, 80 (1981).
Horrell, M. Laws Affecting Race Relations in South Africa.
    Johannesburg: Institute of Race Relations, 1978.
Johnson, R. W. How Long Will South Africa Survive? London:
    Macmillan, 1977.
Johnstone, F. A. "White Prosperity and White Supremacy in South
    Africa Today," African Affairs, 69 (1970).
Kane-Berman, J. South Africa: The Method in the Madness. Lon-
    don: Pluto Press, 1979.
Lapchick, R. E. The Politics of Race and International Sport: The
    Case of South Africa. Westport, Conn.: Greenwood Press,
    1975.
Lawrence, J. C. Race, Propaganda and South Africa. London:
    Gollancz, 1979.
Lerumo, A. Fifty Fighting Years: The Communist Party of South
    Africa, 1921-1971. London: Inkululeko Publishers, 1971.
Magubane, B. The Political Economy of Race and Class in South
    Africa. New York: Monthly Review Press, 1980.
Molteno, F. "The Coloured Persons' Representative Council,"
    Africa Perspective, 10 (1979).
Price, R. M. and Rosberg, C. G., eds. The Apartheid Regime.
    Berkeley: University of California, 1980.
Rees, M. and Day, C. Muldergate. Johannesburg: Macmillan,
    1981.
Robertson, I. and Whitten, P., eds. Race and Politics in South
    Africa. New Brunswick, N. J.: Transaction Books, 1978.
Rotberg, R. Suffer the Future. Policy Choices in Southern Africa.
    Cambridge, Mass.: Harvard University Press, 1980.
Schrire, R., ed. South Africa. Public Policy Perspectives. Cape
    Town: Juta, 1982.
Study Commission on U. S. Policy Toward Southern Africa. South
    Africa: Time Running Out. Berkeley: University of California
    Press, 1981.
Thompson, L. M. and Butler, J., eds. Change in Contemporary
    South Africa. Berkeley: University of California Press, 1975.
Thompson, L. M. and Prior, A. South African Politics. New
    Haven: Yale University Press, 1982.
Van den Berghe, P., ed. The Liberal Dilemma in South Africa.
    London: Croom Helm, 1979.

African Resistance

Adam, H. "The Rise of Black Consciousness in South Africa,"
    Race, 15, 2 (1973).
Arnold, M., ed. Steve Biko: Black Consciousness in South Africa.
    New York: Random House, 1978.
Benson, M. South Africa: The Struggle for a Birthright. New

York: Funk and Wagnalls, 1969.

Feit, E. African Opposition in South Africa: The Failure of Passive Resistance. Stanford: Hoover Institution, 1967.

Feit, E. South Africa. The Dynamics of the African National Congress. London: Oxford University Press, 1962.

Feit, E. Urban Revolt in South Africa, 1960-1964; a Case Study. Evanston: Northwestern University Press, 1971.

Gerhart, G. M. Black Power in South Africa. Berkeley: University of California Press, 1978.

Hirson, B. Year of Fire, Year of Ash--The Soweto Revolt. London: Zed Press, 1979.

Kadalie, C. My Life and the I. C. U. London: Frank Cass, 1970.

Mafeje, A. "Soweto and Its Aftermath," Review of African Political Economy, 11 (1978).

Rathbone, R. "The People and Soweto," JSAS, 6 (1979).

Roux, E. Time Longer Than Rope: A History of the Black Man's Struggle for Freedom in South Africa. 2nd ed. Madison: University of Wisconsin Press, 1964.

Walshe, A. P. The Rise of African Nationalism in South Africa: The African National Congress, 1912-1952. Berkeley: University of California Press, 1971.

Williams, D. "African Nationalism in South Africa. Origins and Problems," JAH, 11 (1970).

Afrikaner Politics

Adam, H. and Giliomee, H. Ethnic Power Mobilized: Can South Africa Change? New Haven: Yale University Press, 1979.

Archibald, D. "The Afrikaners as an Emergent Minority," British Journal of Sociology, 20 (1969).

De Klerk, W. A. The Puritans in Africa: A Story of Afrikanerdom. London: Rex Collings, 1975.

Loubser, J. "Calvinism, Equality and Inclusion: The Case of Afrikaner Nationalism," in Eisenstadt, S. N. , ed. The Protestant Ethic and Modernization: A Comparative View. New York: Basic Books, 1968.

Moodie, T. D. The Rise of Afrikanerdom: Power, Apartheid, and the Afrikaner Civil Religion. Berkeley: University of California Press, 1975.

O'Meara, D. "The Afrikaner Broederbond 1927-1948: Class Vanguard of Afrikaner Nationalism," JSAS, 3, 2 (1977).

O'Meara, D. "Analysing Afrikaner Nationalism: The 'Christian National' Assault on White Trade Unionism in South Africa 1934-1948," African Affairs, 77 (1978).

Serfontein, J. H. P. Brotherhood of Power. London: Rex Collings, 1978.

Stultz, N. M. Afrikaner Politics in South Africa 1934-1948. Berkeley: University of California Press, 1974.

Trapido, S. "Political Institutions and Afrikaner Social Structure in the Republic of South Africa," American Political Science Review, 57 (1963).

Van Jaarsveld, F. A. The Awakening of Afrikaner Nationalism.

Cape Town: Human and Rousseau, 1961.
Welsh, D. "Urbanisation and the Solidarity of Afrikaner National-
    ism, " Journal of Modern African Studies, 7 (1969).
Wilkins, I. and Strijdom, H. The Super-Afrikaners: Inside the
    Afrikaner Broederbond. Johannesburg: Jonathan Ball, 1978.

Bantustans

Buthelezi, M. G. White and Black Nationalism. Ethnicity and the
    Future of the Homelands. Johannesburg: Institute of Race Re-
    lations, 1974.
Butler, J. , Rotberg, R. , and Adams, J. The Black Homelands of
    South Africa: The Political and Economic Development of
    Bophuthatswana and Kwazulu. Berkeley: University of Cali-
    fornia Press, 1977.
Carter, G. M. , Karis, T. and Stultz, N. M. South Africa's Trans-
    kei: The Politics of Domestic Colonialism. Evanston: North-
    western University Press, 1967.
Kotzé, D. A. African Politics in South Africa, 1964-1974: Parties
    and Issues. London: Hurst, 1975.
Lawrence, P. The Transkei: South Africa's Politics of Partition.
    Johannesburg: Ravan Press, 1976.
Legassick, M. and Wolpe, H. "The Bantustans and Capital Accu-
    mulation in South Africa, " Review of African Political Economy,
    7 (1976).
Molteno, F. "The Historical Significance of the Bantustan Strategy,"
    Social Dynamics, 3 (1977).
Southall, R. "The Beneficiaries of Transkeian 'Independence,' "
    Journal of Modern African Studies, 15 (1977).
Southall, R. "Buthelezi, Inkatha and the Politics of Compromise, "
    African Affairs, 80 (1981).
Streek, B. and Wicksteed, R. Render unto Kaiser. A Transkei
    Dossier. Johannesburg: Ravan Press, 1981.
Stultz, N. M. Transkei's Half Loaf: Race Separatism in South
    Africa. Cape Town: David Philip, 1980.

Constitutional, Legal, and Administrative

Benyon, J. , ed. Constitutional Change in South Africa. Pieter-
    maritzburg: University of Natal Press, 1978.
De Crespigny, A. , and Schrire, R. , eds. The Government and
    Politics of South Africa. Cape Town: Juta, 1978.
Dugard, C. J. R. Human Rights and the South African Legal Order.
    Princeton: Princeton University Press, 1978.
Fryer, A. K. "The Government of the Cape of Good Hope, 1825-
    54, " AYB, 27, 1 (1964).
Hahlo, H. R. and Kahn, E. The South African Legal System and Its
    Background. Cape Town: Juta, 1968.
Hahlo, H. R. and Kahn, E. South Africa: The Development of Its
    Laws and Constitution. Cape Town: Juta, 1960.
Matthews, A. S. Law, Order and Liberty in South Africa. Berkeley:

University of California Press, 1972.

Matthews, A. S.   The Darker Reaches of Government.   Cape Town:
Juta, 1978.

Maud, J. P. R.   City Government: The Johannesburg Experiment.
Oxford: Clarendon Press, 1938.

May, H. J.   The South African Constitution.   3rd ed. , Cape Town:
Juta, 1955.

McCracken, J. L.   The Cape Parliament, 1854-1910.   Oxford:
Clarendon Press, 1967.

Ross, R.   "The Rule of Law at the Cape of Good Hope in the
Eighteenth Century," Journal of Imperial and Commonwealth
History, 9 (1980).

Sachs, A.   Justice in South Africa.   Berkeley: University of California Press, 1973.

Seymour, S. M.   Native Law in South Africa.   2nd ed. , Cape Town:
Juta, 1960.

Simons, H. J.   African Women: Their Legal Status in South Africa.
London: Hurst, 1968.

Thompson, L. M.   "Constitutionalism in the South African Republics," Butterworths South African Law Review, (1954).

Thompson, L. M.   The Government and Politics of South Africa.
Boston: Little Brown, 1966.

Worrall, D. , ed.   South Africa: Government and Politics.   Pretoria: Van Schaik, 1971.

Police and Military

Brinton, W.   History of the British Regiments in South Africa 1795-
1895.   Cape Town: University of Cape Town Extra-Mural Studies, 1977.

Bouch, R. J. , ed.   Infantry in South Africa 1652-1976.   Pretoria:
South African Defence Force, 1977.

De Villiers, J.   "Hottentot-Regimente aan die Kaap, 1781-1806,"
AYB, 33, 2 (1970).

De Villiers, J.   "Die Militere Tradiesie van die Kleurling,"
Historia, 13 (1968).

Hattersley, A. F.   The First South African Detectives.   Cape Town:
Timmins, 1960.

Johns, S.   "Obstacles to Guerilla Warfare: A South African Case
Study," Journal of Modern African Studies, 11 (1973).

Marks, S. and Atmore, A.   "Firearms in Southern Africa: A Survey," JAH, 12 (1971).

Orpen, N. , et al.   South African Forces in World War II.   7 vols.
Cape Town: Purnell, 1968-79.

Tylden, G.   The Armed Forces of South Africa.   Johannesburg:
Africana Museum, 1954.

Tylden, G.   "The Development of the Commando System in South
Africa 1715-1922," Africana Notes and News, 13, 8 (1959).

Willan, B.   "The South African Native Labour Contingent, 1916-
1918," JAH, 19 (1978).

Young, P. J.   Boot and Saddle: A Narrative Record of the Cape
Regiment, the British Cape Mounted Riflemen, the Frontier

Armed and Mounted Police and the Colonial Cape Mounted Riflemen. Cape Town: Maskew Millar, 1955.

South Africa and the Wider World

Austin, D. Britain and South Africa. London: Oxford University Press, 1966.
Barber, J. South Africa's Foreign Policy, 1945-1970. London: Oxford University Press, 1973.
Chanock, M. Unconsummated Union: Britain, Rhodesia and South Africa 1900-45. Manchester: Manchester University Press, 1977.
Clifford-Vaughan, F. M. , ed. International Pressure and Political Change in South Africa. Cape Town: Oxford University Press, 1978.
Hailey, Lord. The Republic of South Africa and the High Commission Territories. London: Oxford University Press, 1963.
Hallett, R. "South Africa's Involvement in Angola, 1975-76, " African Affairs, 77 (1978).
Hyam, R. The Failure of South African Expansion, 1908-1948. London: Macmillan, 1972.
Lemarchand, R. , ed. American Policy in Southern Africa: The Stakes and the Stance. Washington, D. C. : University Press of America, 1978.
Nolutshungu, S. South Africa: A Study of Ideology and Foreign Policy. New York: Africana Pub. Co. , 1975.
Pachai, B. The International Aspects of the South African Indian Question, 1860-1971. Cape Town: Struik, 1971.
Potholm, C. and Dale, R. , ed. Southern African in Perspective. New York: Free Press, 1972.
Spence, J. E. Republic Under Pressure. London: Oxford University Press, 1965.
Vandenbosch, A. South Africa and the World. Lexington: University Press of Kentucky, 1970.

White Rule of Africans

Baldwin, A. "Mass Removals and Separate Development, " JSAS, 1 (1975).
Brookes, E. H. White Rule in South Africa, 1830-1910. Pietermaritzburg: University of Natal Press, 1974.
Desmond, C. The Discarded People. Baltimore: Penguin, 1970.
Edgecombe, D. R. "The Glen Grey Act, " in Benyon, J. , et al. , eds. , Studies in Local History. Cape Town: Oxford University Press, 1976.
Etherington, N. A. "The Origin of 'Indirect Rule' in Nineteenth Century Natal, " Theoria, 47 (1976).
Hammond-Tooke, W. D. Command or Consensus: The Development of Transkeian Local Government. Cape Town: David Philip, 1975.
Maré, G. African Population Relocation in South Africa. Johannes-

burg: Institute of Race Relations, 1980.

Smalberger, J. M. "The Role of the Diamond Mining Industry in the Development of the Pass Law System in South Africa," International Journal of African Historical Studies, 9 (1976).

Tatz, C. M. Shadow and Substance in South Africa: A Study in Land and Franchise Policies Affecting Africans, 1910-1960. Pietermaritzburg: University of Natal Press, 1962.

Welsh, D. The Roots of Segregation. Native Policy in Colonial Natal, 1845-1910. Cape Town: Oxford University Press, 1971.

7. RELIGION

Batts, H. J. The Story of a Hundred Years, 1820-1920: Being the History of the Baptist Church in South Africa. Cape Town: Maskew Miller, n. d.

Boas, J. "The Activities of the London Missionary Society in South Africa, 1806-1836: An Assessment," African Studies Review, 16 (1973).

Briggs, D. N. and Wing, J. The Harvest and the Hope: The Story of Congregationalism in Southern Africa. Johannesburg: United Congregational Church of South Africa, 1970.

Brown, W. E. The Catholic Church in South Africa. London: Burns and Oates, 1960.

Davids, A. The Mosques of Bo-Kaap. A Social History of Islam at the Cape. Athlone, Cape: Arabic and Islamic Research, 1980.

De Gruchy, J. The Church Struggle in South Africa. Grand Rapids: Eerdmans, 1979.

Dubb, A. Community of the Saved: An African Revivalist Church in the Eastern Cape. Johannesburg: Witwatersrand University Press, 1976.

Dubb, A. A. and Schutte, A. G. , eds. Black Religion in South Africa. Johannesburg: African Studies, 33, 2 (1974).

Du Plessis, J. A History of Christian Missions in South Africa. London: Longman, 1911.

Gerdener, G. B. A. Studies in the Evangelisation of South Africa. London: Longmans, 1911.

Hanekom, T. N. Ons Nederduitse Gereformeerde Kerk. Cape Town: N. G. Kerk Uitgewers, 1952.

Hinchliff, P. B. The Anglican Church in South Africa. London: Darton, Longman and Todd, 1963.

Hinchliff, P. B. John William Colenso, Bishop of Natal. London: Nelson, 1964.

Hinchliff, P. B. The Church in South Africa. London: Society for Promoting Christian Knowledge, 1968.

Hodgson, J. Ntsikana's Great Hymn. Cape Town: University of Cape Town, 1980.

Holt, B. Joseph Williams and the Pioneer Mission to the South-Eastern Bantu. Lovedale: Lovedale Press, 1954.

Jooste, J. P. Die Geskiedenis van die Gereformeerde Kerk in Suid-Afrika, 1859-1959. Potchefstroom: Potchefstroom Herald, 1959.

Kruger, B. The Pear Tree Blossoms: A History of Moravian Mission Stations in South Africa, 1737-1869. Genadendal: Moravian Church, 1966.

Lewis, C. and Edwards, G. B. Historical Records of the Church of the Province of South Africa. London: Society for Promoting Christian Knowledge, 1934.

Moore, B., ed. Black Theology: The South African Voice. London: Hurst, 1973.

Norman, E. R. Christianity in the Southern Hemisphere: The Churches in Latin America and South Africa. Oxford: Clarendon Press, 1981.

Pauw, B. A. Christianity and Xhosa Tradition. Cape Town: Oxford University Press, 1975.

Pont, A. D. 'n Oorsig van die Algemene Kerkgeskiedenis en die Geskiedenis van die Nederduitsch Hervormde Kerk van Afrika. 3rd ed., Pretoria: HAUM, 1978.

Prior, A., ed. Catholics in Apartheid Society. Cape Town: David Philip, 1982.

Sales, J. M. Mission Stations and the Coloured Communities of the Eastern Cape, 1800-1852. Cape Town: Balkema, 1975.

Sales, J. M. The Planting of the Churches in South Africa. Grand Rapids: Eerdmans, 1971.

Shimoni, G. Jews and Zionism: The South African Experience 1910-1967. Cape Town: Oxford University Press, 1980.

Strassberger, B. The Rhenish Mission Society in South Africa, 1830-1950. Cape Town: Struik, 1969.

Sundermeier, T., ed. Church and Nationalism in South Africa. Johannesburg: Ravan Press, 1975.

Sundkler, B. G. M. Bantu Prophets in South Africa, London: Oxford University Press, 1948.

Sundkler, B. G. M. Zulu Zion. Oxford: Clarendon Press, 1976.

West, M. Bishops and Prophets in a Black City. Cape Town: David Philip, 1975.

Whiteside, J. History of the Wesleyan Methodist Church of South Africa. London: Stock, 1906.

8. SCIENCES

Geography and General

Brown, A. C., ed. A History of Scientific Endeavour in South Africa. Cape Town: Royal Society of South Africa, 1977.

Christopher, A. J. Southern Africa. Folkestone, Kent: Dawson, 1976.

Cole, M. M. South Africa. 2nd ed. New York: E. P. Dutton, 1966.

Gunn, M. and Codd, L. E. Botanical Exploration of Southern Africa. Cape Town: Balkema, 1981.

Pollock, N. V. and Agnew, S. An Historical Geography of South Africa. London: Longman, 1963.

Raper, P. E. Source Guide for Toponymy and Topology. Pretoria: Human Sciences Research Council, 1975.

Summers, R., comp. A History of the South African Museum, 1825-1975. Cape Town: Balkema, 1975.

Talbot, A. M. and W. J. Atlas of the Union of South Africa. Pretoria: Government Printer, 1960.

Truswell, J. F. Geological Evolution of South Africa. Cape Town: Purnell, 1977.

Warner, B. Astronomers at the Royal Observatory, Cape of Good Hope: A History with Emphasis on the Nineteenth Century. Cape Town: Balkema, 1979.

Wellington, J. H. Southern Africa: A Geographical Study. 2 vols. Cambridge: Cambridge University Press, 1955.

Health, Disease, and Medicine

Burrows, E. H. A History of Medicine in South Africa Up to the End of the Nineteenth Century. Cape Town: Balkema, 1958.

Cluver, E. H. Public Health in South Africa. 4th ed. Johannesburg: Central News Agency, 1944.

Grobler, V. History of Dentistry in South Africa, 1652-1900. Cape Town: HAUM, 1977.

Laidler, P. W. and Gelfand, N. South Africa: Its Medical History 1652-1808. Cape Town: Struik, 1971.

Searle, C. History of the Development of Nursing in South Africa, 1652-1960. Cape Town: Struik, 1965.

Van Onselen, C. "Reactions to Rinderpest in Southern Africa, 1896-1897," JAH, 13 (1972).

Westcott, G. and Wilson, F., eds. Economics of Health in South Africa. 2 vols. Johannesburg: Ravan Press, 1979.

9. SOCIETY

General

Adam, H., ed., South Africa: Sociological Perspectives. London: Oxford University Press, 1976.

De Villiers, A., ed. English-Speaking South Africa Today. Cape Town: Oxford University Press, 1976.

Desmond, C. The Discarded People: An Account of African Resettlement in South Africa. Baltimore: Penguin Books, 1971.

Greenberg, S. Race and State in Capitalist Development. New Haven: Yale University Press, 1980.

Hammond-Tooke, W. D., ed. The Bantu-Speaking Peoples of South Africa. London: Routledge and Kegan Paul, 1974.

Hare, A. P., et al., eds. South Africa: Sociological Analyses. Cape Town: Oxford University Press, 1979.

Kuper, L. An African Bourgeoisie: Race, Class and Politics in South Africa. New Haven: Yale University Press, 1965.

Lever, H. South African Society. Johannesburg: Jonathan Ball, 1978.

Mayer, P., ed. Black Villagers in an Industrial Society. Cape Town: Oxford University Press, 1980.

Murray, C. Divided Families. Cambridge: Cambridge University
    Press, 1981.
Orpen, C. and Morse, S. J. , eds. Contemporary South Africa:
    Social and Psychological Perspectives. Cape Town: Juta,
    1975.
Rex, J. "The Compound, The Reserve and the Urban Location:
    The Essential Institutions of Southern African Labour Exploita-
    tion, " South African Labour Bulletin, 1, 4 (1974).
Saron, G. and Hotz, L. , eds. The Jews in South Africa: A His-
    tory. Cape Town: Oxford University Press, 1955.
Stone, J. Colonist or /Uitlander ? A Study of the British Immigrant
    in South Africa. Oxford: Clarendon Press, 1973.
Van der Merwe, N. J. and West, M. , eds. Perspectives on South
    Africa's Future. Cape Town: University of Cape Town, 1979.

Education

Behr, A. L. and Macmillan, R. G. Education in South Africa, 2nd
    ed. , Pretoria: Van Schaik, 1971.
Behr, A. L. New Perspectives in South African Education. Dur-
    ban: Butterworths, 1978.
Boucher, M. Spes in Arduis: A History of the University of South
    Africa. Pretoria: University of South Africa, 1973.
Boucher, M. "The University of the Cape of Good Hope and the
    University of South Africa, 1873-1946, " AYB, 35, 1 (1972).
Brookes, E. H. A History of the University of Natal. Pietermaritz-
    burg: University of Natal Press, 1966.
Burchell, D. E. "African Higher Education and the Establishment of
    the South African Native College, Fort Hare, " SAHJ, 8 (1976).
Davis, R. H. "Charles T. Loram and an American Model for Afri-
    can Education in South Africa, " African Studies Review, 19
    (1976).
Horrell, M. Bantu Education to 1968. Johannesburg: Institute of
    Race Relations, 1968.
Horrell, M. The Education of the Coloured Community in South
    Africa. Johannesburg: Institute of Race Relations, 1970.
Horton, J. W. The First Seventy Years, 1895-1965: Being an Ac-
    count of the Growth of the Council of Education, Witwatersrand.
    Johannesburg: Witwatersrand University Press, 1968.
Kerr, A. Fort Hare, 1915-1948: The Evolution of an African Col-
    lege. Pietermaritzburg: Shuter and Shooter, 1968.
Malherbe, E. G. Education in South Africa. 2 vols. Cape Town:
    Juta, 1925, 1977.
Mugomba, A. and Nyaggah, M. , eds. Independence Without Free-
    dom. The Political Economy of Colonial Education in Southern
    Africa. Santa Barbara: ABC-Clio, 1980.
Ritchie, W. The History of the South African College, 1829-1918.
    2 vols. Cape Town: Maskew Miller, 1918.
Rose, B. , ed. Education in Southern Africa. Johannesburg:
    Collier-Macmillan, 1970.
Shepherd, R. H. W. Lovedale, South Africa: The Story of a Century,
    1841-1941. Lovedale: Lovedale Press, n. d.

Spro-cas. Education Beyond Apartheid. Johannesburg: Spro-cas, 1971.
Van der Merwe, H. W. and Welsh, D., eds. Student Perspectives in South Africa. Cape Town: David Philip, 1972.
Van der Merwe, H. W. and Welsh, D., eds. The Future of the University in Southern Africa. Cape Town: David Philip, 1977.

Urbanization

Bozzoli, B., ed. Labour, Townships and Protest. Johannesburg: Ravan Press, 1979.
Davenport, T. R. H. "African Tribesmen? South African Natives (Urban Areas) Legislation Through the Years," African Affairs, 68 (1969).
Davenport, T. R. H. "The Triumph of Colonel Stallard: The Transformation of the Natives (Urban Areas) Act Between 1923 and 1937," SAHJ, 2 (1970).
Davenport, T. R. H. The Beginnings of Urban Segregation in South Africa. Grahamstown: Rhodes University, 1971.
Ellis, G., et al. The Squatter Problem in the Western Cape. Johannesburg: Institute of Race Relations, 1977.
Gluckman, M. "Tribalism, Ruralism and Urbanism in South and Central Africa," in Colonialism in Africa, 3, ed. V. Turner. Cambridge: Cambridge University Press, 1971.
Saunders, C. C., et al., eds. Studies in the History of Cape Town. 4 vols. Cape Town: University of Cape Town, 1978-81.
Smit, P. and Booysen, J. J. Swart Verstedeliking. Cape Town: Tafelberg, 1981.
Swanson, M. W. "The Urban Origins of Separate Development," Race, 10 (1969).
Swanson, M. W. "The Durban System: Roots of Urban Apartheid in Colonial Natal," African Studies, 35 (1976).
Swanson, M. W. "The Sanitation Syndrome," JAH, 17 (1977).
Van Jaarsveld, F. Stedelike Geskiedenis as Navorsingsveld vir die Suid-Afrikaanse Historikus. Johannesburg: Rand Afrikaanse Universiteit, 1973.
West, M. Divided Community. Cape Town: Balkema, 1971.
Western, J. Outcast Cape Town. Minneapolis: University of Minnesota Press, 1981.

INDEX OF ORGANISATIONS AND INSTITUTIONS

(Where there is a main entry, the page numbers are underlined.)

INDEX OF PERSONAL NAMES

(Where there is a main entry, the page numbers are underlined.)